Assassinations and Executions

Assassinations and Executions

AN ENCYCLOPEDIA OF POLITICAL VIOLENCE, 1865–1986

by

Harris M. Lentz, III

McFarland & Company, Inc., Publishers
Jefferson, North Carolina, and London

Library of Congress Cataloguing-in-Publication Data

Lentz, Harris M.
Assassinations and executions.

Bibliography: p. 239.
Includes index.
1. Assassination — History — Chronology.
2. Executions and executioners — History — Chronology.
I. Title.
HV6278.L45   1988   909.8   87-46383

ISBN 0-89950-312-8 (50# acid-free natural paper)

Manufactured in the United States of America.

McFarland   Box 611   Jefferson NC 28640

This book is dedicated to
Helene Lentz and Mary Zollo
without whom I would not have been possible

and

Dina Stinnett
with gratitude and affection

and

to all of my friends
at Spike & Rail, Hastings and Shucks

Acknowledgments

I would like to take this opportunity to thank the many people whose assistance and support have made the book possible. I would like to give special thanks to my mother, Helene Z. Lentz; my grandmother, Mary V. Zollo; and Kent Nelson, Anne Taylor, Dina Stinnett, David Hyde, Brian Artz, S. Newton Anderson, Fred Gibson, Tracy Cianciola, Dawn Perry, Jennifer Habecker, Cindy Young, and Nina Heffington.

I would also like to thank the following people whose encouragement, interest and help greatly aided my completion of this project. Many thanks to Andy and Missy Branham, Jack and Kathy Hildebrand, Eddie and Edith McNeil, Darlene Brady, Missy Wallace, Joy Martin, Louis 'Stretch' Hansen, Cindy Saunier, David Christopher, Susan Kendall, Janet Roach, Edgar and Hollye Mattox, Mark Heffington, Ronalyn Presley, Robert and Beverly Stinnett, Monte Taylor, Bill and Cheryl Dabbs, F. Scott Graves, Doy L. Daniels, Jr., Paul Geary, Wade DeHart, Terry and Eva Murphy, Bobby and Diane Sawyers, Cathy Kelly, Susie Miller, Kelly Gillespie, Charles and Coleen Griffin, Brenda Davis, Paige Reed, Lori Shelton, David Scott, Kent Stoneking, Willie Trigg, Bettye Dawson, Jim Daves, Tedra Lind, Vicki Mason, Bill Rokas, Rob Lee, Athenee Alderson, Lisa Stafford, Lisa Kirby, Laurie Churchill, Wendy Jones, John Van Hannigan, Lisa Clemons, Scott Hubbard, Dan Kohr, Wyatt Morgan, John Commings, Chris Dunlap, Vanwayne Landfair, Travelor Crawford, Kim Rodgers, Brian Brasher, Kevin Henson, Evelyn Thomas, Kay Gaines, Chip Scott, Rob Hudson, Brian Rittenauer, Evelyn Hurt, Connie Arata, Amy Harvill, Debbie Davis, Debbie Malito, Michael Mackey, Bobby Conway, Brenda Calhoun, William Jones, Bobbie McKinley, Mike Hardin, Steve Boysen, Bert Maclin, Teresa Van Eaton, Belinda Stafford, Michelle Adkins, Greg and Shawna Stanton, Dewayne Breckenridge, Mike Smith, Jim Weaver, Aretha Greer, Joanne Trussell, Lynn Moore, Mary Moore, Sidney Shields, Charlotte Mayfield, Christi Messer, Jackie Ciulla, Darryl Mayfield, Nick Coundourides, Jimmy Robinson, Steve Collier, David Bond, Allison Dennen, Jim and Margaret Dennen, Becky McAdams, Kathy Hassenmuller, Gosta Goff, Kelley Greene, George 'Sonny' Flynn, Troy Upchurch, Donna and Larry Purvis, Dana Nauer, Joe Watson, Bobby K. Flaherty, Ron Bishop, Bing Bingham, Kellye Franks, Lou and Carol Phillips, Jackie Gibbons, Debbie Ballard, Kris Berg, Sandy Berg, Todd Wilson, Mike Mosteller, Chris

Macaffee, Tim Pritchard, Alex McBryant, Melissa Grubbs, Mark Eaton, Ralph Smith, Russ Benge, Bob Voss, Frank Tusa, Gene Kelly, Steve White, Terry and Peggy Nickens, Charles Trub, Betty Grumbles, Louis Berretta III, Mr. and Mrs. Louis Berretta, Jr., Letsie Axmaker, Phil Spaulding, Phil Hugel, Allison Fortune, Preston Bridgewater, Michael Williams, Smoochie Smith, Harry Veltman, Kurt Kobes, Keith Roberts, Mike King, Tricia Orsak, Nikki and Jimmy Walker, Joe and Jean Garbarini, Cliff Willis, Diane Meucci, Teresa Gstohl, Don Akey, Ellen Wanamaker, Sid Cromwell, Vicky Holmes, Marge Vann, Sally Nguyen, Polly McCabe, Pam Bingham, Kathy Terry, Joelle Pippin, Janette Campbell, Desiree Box, Nanci Gallagher, John Kelly, Ann Shanaghan, Michelle Patton, Dale Carpenter, Steve Morrow, David Brooks, Clay Foster, Johnnie Williams, Mike Miller, Bo and Gail Hurt, Anna Cromwell, Mattie Coleman, Aileen Orians, Leon Levy, Vickie Prince, Debbie Malito, Kirsten Burger, Dominic Cara and others.

Contents

Introduction

The purpose of this book is to present to the reader a concise and thorough look at the many world leaders who have met their end in a violent manner. This book primarily deals with those leaders who have perished as victims of political assassination, though others who have been merely "executed" are also included. This was done because often an execution is merely an assassination given legal justification. (A leader is deemed "assassinated" if he perishes during a coup, but "executed" if his killing is subsequent to his fall from power.) The inclusion of such executions broadens the scope to include the many victims of the purges of Stalin and Hitler, as well as those Nazi leaders whose crimes against humanity resulted in their justified execution.

The time scope of this book is a little over 120 years, with the assassination of President Abraham Lincoln in 1865 being the first entry in the book proper. I have noted in the Prologue a brief summary of those major leaders whose assassinations fell before this period. I have also included in the body of the book unsuccessful assassination attempts against major world figures. (Names of victims of unsuccessful attempts are given in Roman type, while names of persons actually killed are given in **boldface**.)

Selecting the individuals to be included who actually met death in a politically violent manner has been difficult. Naturally I have attempted to include all heads of state and government who so perished. I have also endeavored to include the other major world figures who so died. I have made an attempt to record the deaths of ambassadors, leading national figures, and military officers. A major problem develops in research regarding various third world nations in Africa, South America and Asia, where political violence seems to be a way of political ife. It would be virtually impossible to name every victim of political violence in El Salvador or Guatemala, record the victims of Pol Pot's massacre in Cambodia, or list those who perished under Macias Nguema in Equatorial Guinea or the Duvaliers in Haiti. In these cases I have attempted to give an overview of these violent political situations and record the major victims.

The entries in this book are generally listed in chronological order. It has not always been possible to determine the exact date of some of the assassinations recorded, particularly the earlier ones, so using available information I have endeavored to list them as closely as possible in their proper order. I have also varied from the strict chronological format in several other special cases. When the assassinations or executions of several individuals occurring in a particular year were directly related to one another, such as victims of the purges of Stalin, Hitler, and Amin, or the violent political upheavals in Ethiopia or Iran, I have grouped these incidents together in the yearly entry, even though the actual deaths may have been several months apart. I felt that this would better clarify the impact and ramifications of the initial and succeeding deaths.

In writing this book I have attempted to give the facts regarding the assassination, including the manner, the motive, and the assailant, when known. I have included brief biographical information on some of the major victims. I have also attempted to record the immediate effects of the assassination on the political climate of the day. In some cases I have also recorded the final fate of the assassins, who, on occasion, have themselves become victims of the same violence they unleash, thus deserving their own passages in this book.

Prologue

The term assassin, originally *hashshashin*, or taker of hashish, was derived from the eleventh century Isma'ili sect of the Shi'ite Moslims. It was used to describe the followers of Hasan ibn al-Sabah, the "Old Man of the Mountain," who, for several centuries, gained great power in the Middle East by violence and threats of violence against the area's rulers. European crusaders brought the word and legend back from Syria, and it soon became a common term used to describe someone "who undertakes to murder in a sudden, premeditated assault," quoting *American College Dictionary*.

Though episodes of political murders date back through biblical times, and likely before recorded history, the murder of Julius Caesar, the legendary Roman general and dictator, is perhaps the best-known historical assassination. He was stabbed to death in 44 B.C. in the Roman Senate by a band of political opponents.

Caesar was but the first in a long line of leaders of the Roman Empire to so perish. Gaius Caesar, known as Caligula, was murdered along with his family by members of the Praetorian Guard in A.D. 41, and his uncle and successor, the Emperor Claudius I, was poisoned by his wife, Agrippina the Younger, in A.D. 54. She was, in turn, executed by the order of her son, the Emperor Nero, in A.D. 59. Nero was also responsible for the executions of his wife, Octavia, and the daughter of the late Claudius, Claudia Antonia, before he took his own life during an army rebellion in A.D. 68.

Other slain emperors included Servius Sulpicius Galba and Aulus Vitellius in 69, Domitian in 96, Lucius Aelius Aurelius Commodus in 192, Decimus Clodius Septimus Albinus in 197, Publius Septimus Geta in 212, Caracalla in 217, Elagabalus in 222, Marcus Aurelius Alexander Severus in 235, Marcus Julius Philippus in 249, Aurelian in 275, Marcus Claudius Tacitus in 276, Carinus in 285, Flavius Julius Constans in 350, Valentinian II in 392, Maximus Tyrannus in 422, Valentinian III in 455, and Anthemius in 472.

Many emperors of the Eastern Roman Empire in Constantinople were also recorded as victims of political violence. Valens was killed by the Goths in 378. Flavius Tiberius Mauricius was murdered in 602 by Phocas, who succeeded him. Phocas was, in turn, overthrown and executed eight years later. Others included Constantine III in 641, Constans II in 668, Justinian II in 711, Anastasius II in 721, Constantine VI, who was murdered by order of his mother in 797, Romanus IV Diogenes in 1072, Alexius II Comnenus in 1183, and Alexius IV Angelius, who was murdered by Alexius V in 1204. Alexius V, who served shortly as emperor himself, was thrown from a column in Constantinople by crusaders later in the year.

Other early assassinations included those of Visigoth kings Theodoric II in 466 and Alaric II in 507. Gundimar II, the king of Burgundy, was murdered in 532, and the Ostrogoth king Theodat was slain in 536. Totila, another king of the Ostrogoths, was killed in battle in 552. Alboin, the king of the Lombards, was poisoned by his wife in 572. Two kings of the Franks, Sigebert I in 575, and Chilperic I in 584, were also assassinated. Brunhilde, the Queen of Austrasia, was executed by being dragged behind a wild horse in 613. King Oswald of the Northumbrians died in battle in 642, and Newt, son of Ander, a Northumbrian prince, was defeated in battle and beheaded in 676.

In Persia, several rulers also perished. King Ormizd IV was deposed and murdered in 590, and Khosrau II was killed in battle in 628. His nine-year-old successor, Ardashir III, was murdered by his general in 630.

In 644 Omar I, the second caliph, or deputy to the Prophet Mohammed, was assassinated by a Persian slave. The third and fourth Moslem caliphs were also murdered, Othman in 656, and Ali in 661.

Abd-er-Rahman, the Arabian emir of Spain, died in battle in 732, and Marwan II, the caliph of Ommiad, was overthrown and murdered in 750. Ethelbert, the king of the East Angles, was beheaded in 794, and Al-Amin, the caliph of Baghdad, was murdered by his brother in 813. Leo V, the Byzantine emperor, was assassinated on Christmas Day in 820.

Several Roman Catholic popes also perished as victims of political violence. John VIII was murdered in 882, and Stephen VI was strangled in prison in 897. Benedict VI was also strangled in 974, and Christophorus, an antipope, was murdered in prison in 904.

William I, the duke of Normandy, was assassinated by the count of Flanders in 943 and, on May 26, 946, Edmund I, the king of England, was stabbed to death. Edward the Martyr, who ruled as England's king for three years, was murdered by an agent of his stepmother on March 18, 978.

In Norway, King Haakon the Great was murdered by his soldiers in a pigsty in 995. In Scotland, King Duncan I was defeated in battle and murdered in 1040. His successor, Macbeth, was killed in battle by Malcolm III in March of 1057. Sancho II, the king of Spain, died in battle in 1072, and Sancho IV, the king of Navarre, was murdered by his brother in 1076. Denmark's King Canute IV was murdered by a mob on July 10, 1086.

King William II of England was assassinated while on a hunting trip on August 2, 1100. Charles the Good, Count of Flanders, was murdered at Bruges in 1127, and Randulf de Gernons, Earl of Chester, an Anglo-Norman leader, was poisoned in 1153. In 1157 King Canute V of Denmark was assassinated by Sweyn III. Sweyn was killed in battle later in the year. Two kings of Norway were assassinated, Eystein II in 1157, and Haakon II in 1162. Charles VII, king of the Swedes and Goths, was assassinated in 1167.

On December 25, 1170, Thomas à Becket, the archbishop of Canterbury, was murdered in his cathedral by knights from the court of King Henry II of England.

Conrad, Marquis of Montferrat, the Italian leader of the Third Crusade who become king of Jerusalem, was murdered by an assassin in 1192. Baldwin I, the leader of the Fourth Crusade and emperor of Constantinople, was murdered following his defeat in battle in 1205. Engelbert I, the French Roman Catholic archbishop of Cologne, was slain in 1225.

In 1240, Raziya, the queen of Delhi, was murdered, and, on August 9, 1250, Eric IV, the king of Denmark, was murdered by his brother. Conradin, the king of Jerusalem and Sicily, was defeated in battle and beheaded on October 29, 1268, and Przemsyl II, the king of Poland, was assassinated in 1296. In 1306, Vaclav II, another Polish king, was assassinated. Adolf of Nassau, the king of Germany, was killed in battle in 1298, and King Albert I of Germany was murdered in 1308.

King Edward II of England was deposed and executed in September of 1327. Pedro the Cruel, the king of Castile and Leon, was murdered by his brother in 1369. In 1381, Wat Tyler, an English peasant leader, was executed for treason. Charles of Durazzo, the king of Naples and Hungary, was assassinated in Hungary on February 27, 1386, and King Richard II of England was presumed murdered in prison on February of 1400.

On May 30, 1431, Joan of Arc, a heroine of France, was burned at the stake. King Henry VI of England was murdered in the Tower of London on February 18, 1478. Edward V, the fourteen-year-old king of England, was smothered with his brother, Richard Plantagenet, the Duke of York, by the order of King Richard III on June 26, 1483. Richard III himself died in battle on August 22, 1485. James III, the king of Scotland, was murdered during a revolt on June 11, 1488.

Mohammed X, the Moslem king of Granada, was deposed and assassinated in 1500, and Cesare Borgia, an Italian nobleman and Roman Catholic cardinal, was killed during the siege of Vienna on March 12, 1507. On September 9, 1513, James IV, the king of Scotland, was defeated and killed by the army of England's King Henry VIII.

Vasco Nuñez De Balboa, the Spanish explorer who discovered the Pacific Ocean, was condemned for treason and beheaded in Panama in 1519. Ferdinand Magellan, the Portuguese explorer who led the first expedition to circumnavigate the globe, was killed by natives on the Pacific island of Mactan on April 27, 1521.

Guatemotzin, the last Aztec emperor of Mexico, was executed by Cortes in 1525, and Atahualpa, the last king of the Incan Empire of Peru, was strangled by order of Francisco Pizarro on August 29, 1533. His son, Prince Huascar, was also murdered. Pizarro was himself assassinated by followers of Diego de Almargo on June 26, 1541. De Almargo, the Spanish governor of Peru, was, in turn, deposed and executed in 1542.

In 1535 Sir Thomas More, a leading British statesman, and Saint John Fischer, the English Roman Catholic bishop of Rochester, were beheaded by the order of King Henry VIII. Anne Boleyn, King Henry's second queen, was beheaded on May 19, 1536, and Catherine Howard, Henry's fifth queen, was beheaded for adultery in 1542. Thomas Cromwell, Earl of Essex, an advisor to King Henry and a leader of the Reformation, was executed for treason on July 28, 1540.

Ibraham Pasha, the grand vizier of Turkey, was strangled by order of the Sultan in 1536, and David Beaton, a Scottish Roman Catholic cardinal in France, was murdered by Reformationists in 1546.

Lady Jane Grey, who served as England's queen for less than a month in 1553, was beheaded on February 12, 1554. Her father, Henry Grey, Duke of Suffolk, was executed for treason later in the year.

In 1555 Hugh Latimer and Nicholas Ridley, English Reformationist leaders, were burned at the stake for heresy. Thomas Cranmer, the first archbishop of Canterbury of the Church of England, was also burned at the stake on March 21, 1556.

Henry Stewart, Lord Darnley, the second husband of Mary, Queen of Scots, was killed in Edinburgh when his house was blown up on February 9, 1567. Queen Mary was herself beheaded by the order of Queen Elizabeth I of England on February 8, 1587.

William the Silent, the king of Holland, was assassinated on July 10, 1584. Louis II De Lorraine, the French Roman Catholic archbishop of Reimes, was assassinated in 1588, and Henry III, the king of France, was murdered by a monk on August 2, 1589. In 1591 Dimitri Ivanovich, the Czarevitch of Russia and the son of Ivan the Terrible, was murdered. Czar Feodor II of Russia was killed by the Boyars on June 1, 1605, and Czar Dimitri I was murdered on May 17, 1606.

On January 31, 1606, Guy Fawkes, Henry Garnett, Thomas Winter, Robert Winter, Robert Keyes, and Ambrose Rokewood were hanged for conspiracy to blow up the English Parliament in the Gunpowder Plot.

King Henry IV of France was murdered by a religious fanatic on May 14, 1610, and British nobleman George Villiers, the first Duke of Buckingham, was assassinated in August of 1628. Ibrahim, the sultan of the Ottoman Empire, was overthrown and murdered in 1648, and King Charles I of Great Britain was deposed and executed on January 30, 1649.

In 1681 Oliver Plunket, an Irish Roman Catholic prelate, was hanged for treason, and Donald Cargill, the Scottish leader of the Covenanters, was beheaded as a traitor.

Govind Singh, the guru of the Sikhs of India, was murdered in 1709, and Nadir, the shah of Persia, was assassinated in 1747. On July 17, 1762, Czar Peter III of Russia was deposed by his wife, Catherine the Great, and assassinated. Emelyan I. Pugachev, a Russian cossack rebel leader, was executed by order of Catherine on January 11, 1775.

American patriot Nathan Hale was hanged by the British for treason on September 22, 1776, and Major John Andre, a British army officer, was hanged as a spy on October 2, 1780. Button Gwinnett, a signer of America's Declaration of Independence, was slain in a duel in 1777.

Jose Gabriel Condorcanqui, known as Tupac Amaru, a Peruvian rebel leader, was captured and executed in 1781. Nicolae Horea, a rebel leader in Romania, was put to death in 1785, and Jacques Vincent Oje, a Haitian rebel, was executed in 1791.

On March 16, 1792, Gustavus III, the king of Sweden, was shot to death during an aristocratic plot.

Following the French Revolution, King Louis XVI of France was executed on January 21, 1793. His wife, Marie Antoinette, was put to death on October 16, 1793. Many other prominent French royalists and revolutionaries were also guillotined during this period, including Armand de Coetnempren, Count of Kersaint, Jacques Pierre Brissot, Armand Gensonne, Louis Philippe Joseph, Duc d'Orleans, Jean Bailly, the mayor of Paris, Countess Marie DuBarry, Anacharsis Cloots, Georges Jacques Danton, Camille Desmoulins, Jean Baptiste Gobel, the Roman Catholic archbishop of Paris, Marguerite Elie Guadet, Louis Saint-Just, and Maximilien Robespierre. Jean Paul Marat, a leading figure in the Revolution, was stabbed to death in his bath on July 13, 1793.

Luft Ali Akhan, the shah of Persia, was assassinated in 1795. His successor, Agha Mohammed Khan, was murdered in 1797. On March 23, 1801, Czar Paul I of Russia was assassinated by soldiers. Alexander Hamilton, a leading figure in the American Revolution and the United States' first secretary of the treasury, was mortally wounded in a duel with Aaron Burr on July 11, 1804.

Jean Jacques Dessalines, the emperor of Haiti, was assassinated on October 17, 1806, and Mustafa IV, the sultan of Turkey, was deposed and murdered in 1808. In 1812 Spencer Perceval, the prime minister of England, was assassinated. Jose Miguel de Carrera, a former head of state of Chile, was captured and executed in 1821, and Ali, the Turkish pasha of Janina, was deposed and shot in 1822. On July 19, 1824, Agustin de Iturbide, the deposed emperor of Mexico, was executed, and Manuel Dorrego, the provisional president of Argentina, was executed by rebels in 1828.

Chaka, the chief of the Zulu tribe in Africa, was assassinated in 1828, and Antonio Jose de Sucre, a former president of Bolivia, was assassinated on June 4, 1830. Vicente Guerrero, an ex-president of Mexico, was shot by rebels on February 14, 1831, and Felipe Santiago Salaverry, the president of Peru, was executed in 1836.

The king of Afghanistan, Shah Shuja, was murdered in 1842, and Francisco Morazan, the former president of the Central American Federation, was captured and shot on September 15, 1842. Braulio Carrillo, the exiled president of Costa Rica, was executed in 1845.

Denis Affre, the Roman Catholic archbishop of Paris, was killed during a revolt on June 27, 1848, and Archbishop Marie-Dominique-Auguste Sibour, his successor, was stabbed to death by a mad priest in 1857.

Abbas I, the pasha of Egypt, was murdered by slaves in 1854, and Tantia Topi, an Indian Hindu rebel leader, was hanged for insurrection in 1859. John Brown, the American abolitionist who led the raid on Harper's Ferry, was hanged for treason on December 2, 1859, and William Walker, an American adventurer who served as president of Nicaragua from 1856 to 1857, was court-martialed and shot in Honduras on September 12, 1860.

Danilo I, the Prince of Montenegro, was assassinated in 1860, and Santo Guardiola, the president of Honduras, was murdered in 1861. In 1863 Radama II, the king of Madagascar, was assassinated. Ignacio Comonfort, a former president of Mexico, was ambushed and slain in 1863, and Omar El-Hadj, a Sudanese leader, was killed by opponents in 1864.

These pages mark some of the more prominent victims of political violence prior to the assassination of United States president Abraham Lincoln in 1865.

Assassinations
and
Executions

1865

Abraham Lincoln, the sixteenth president of the United States, was assassinated on April 14, 1865, while attending a play at Washington, D.C.'s, Ford's Theatre. Lincoln was born near Hodgenville, Kentucky, on February 12, 1809. His family was poor and lived off the land. Lincoln moved with his family to Illinois in 1830. He was self-educated and, after studying the law at home, passed the bar in 1836. He was also elected to the Illinois state assembly in the 1830s. His law practice was successful and in 1842, he married Mary Todd. In 1846 Lincoln was elected to the U.S. Congress as a member of the Whig party, serving only one term. He was an opponent of slavery, but had little sympathy with the radical abolitionists.

Lincoln was active in the campaign of Zachary Taylor against incumbent president James K. Polk in 1848, and was disappointed at not receiving a federal appointment after Taylor's election. Lincoln joined the Republican Party in 1856. Two years later he challenged Stephen Douglas for a seat in the U.S. Senate. While defeated in that election, a series of debates he engaged in with Douglas gave Lincoln national recognition.

In 1860 Lincoln gained the Republican nomination for the presidency on the third ballot at the Chicago convention. He was elected to the presidency in November of that year, defeating three other candidates. His election was met with dismay by pro-slavery forces in the South, with South Carolina announcing its withdrawal from the Union shortly before Lincoln's inauguration. His administration's policies to contain the spread of slavery in the western territories resulted in six other states seceding from the Union and forming the Confederate States of America. On April 12, 1861, shortly after Lincoln's inaugural address, the first shots of the American Civil War were fired at Fort Sumter, South Carolina. Confederate troops attacked the Union garrison there after being notified that government forces were being sent to relieve the state of siege the garrison had been placed under. Shortly thereafter four other Southern states joined the Confederacy, and the Civil War was begun in earnest.

Lincoln's first term of office was primarily concerned with the waging of the war. On January 1, 1863, Lincoln issued his Emancipation Proclamation, which decreed the freeing of the slaves in the Confederate states. After a succession of generals placed in charge of the Union armies, Lincoln decided in March of 1864 on Ulysses S. Grant as commander of the federal forces. Lincoln was handily reelected as president later in the year. The Union forces emerged victorious in battle, and the troops of the Confederacy under Gen. Robert E. Lee surrendered on April 19, 1865.

Lincoln was in the process of planning for the reconciliation of the Union when he was assassinated. The president was shot and killed by John Wilkes Booth, who fired a bullet from a single-shot derringer into the back of Lincoln's head. At the time of the shooting, the president was sitting in the presidential box while attending a performance of *Our American Cousin*. He died the following morning without regaining consciousness. Andrew Johnson, the vice president, succeeded him to the presidency.

Lincoln's assailant, Booth, leaped to the stage after firing the fatal shot, and fractured his ankle, though he was still able to escape on horseback. Booth, a Confederate sympathizer, had been planning either the kidnapping or murder of the president for months prior to Lincoln's death. Booth had gathered together a group of conspirators to assist him in his plot. On the evening of Lincoln's assassination an attempt was made also to kill William H. Seward, the secretary of state, when Lewis Payne attacked him with a knife at Seward's home. The secretary, who was then in bed, was recovering from injuries suffered in a carriage accident, received a stab wound, but survived. Another co-conspirator, George A. Atzerodt, was assigned to murder the vice president, Andrew Johnson, but failed to carry through with the attempt. Booth, the brother of famed actor Edwin Booth, and a well-known stage actor himself, was easily identified following Lincoln's shooting. The assassin was pursued by federal troops and ultimately cornered in a barn near Fort Royal, Virginia. The barn was set afire, and Booth died within from a pistol shot, presumably by his own hand. Other members of the conspiracy were subsequently arrested and tried for complicity. Payne, Atzerodt, David Herrold (who had accompanied Booth during his flight and had been captured at the time of Booth's death), and Mary Surratt (who had run the boarding house where the conspirators had held their meetings and was the mother of an alleged conspirator who had disappeared), were convicted and sentenced to be executed. They were hanged on July 7, 1865. Mrs. Surratt's son, John Surratt, was apprehended several years later. He was tried and acquitted in 1867.

1867

On June 19, 1867, **Emperor Maximilian** of Mexico, **Gen. Miguel Miramon**, and **Gen. Tomas Mejia** were executed by firing squad following their capture and trial by the Republican Army of Benito Juarez.

Ferdinand Maximilian Joseph was born on July 6, 1832, in Vienna, Austria. He was the younger brother of Austria's Emperor Francis Joseph. In 1857 he was appointed governor of Lombardy-Venetia, and married Carlota, the daughter of King Leopold I of Belgium, the same year. In 1864, following an invitation by a group of leading exiled Mexican conservatives to serve as Mexico's emperor, Maximilian departed to claim his throne there. The French army was in control of most of the country on his arrival, and was able to keep his crown secure for a time. Maximilian initiated many populist reforms during his reign, which alienated many of the conservative leaders and the Catholic church. In 1865 the United States government, citing the Monroe Doctrine, demanded the withdrawal of the French troops. The French ultimately abandoned Maximilian in March of 1867. The emperor remained in Mexico as leader of the imperial army. He was captured at Queretaro on May 15, 1867, when his small army was surrounded by the forces of Benito Juarez. Despite the efforts of his wife, Carlota, and pleas by many world figures for clemency, Maximilian was court-martialed and executed on the Hill of Bells on June 19, 1867.

Miguel Miramon was born in Mexico City on September 29, 1832. He joined the Mexican army and was active in the Mexican War against the United States in 1847. In 1856 he was active on the side of the conservatives in the Puebla revolt, and became Mexico's president from 1859 until 1860. He remained an important leader in the conservative army, scoring many successes against the liberal forces of Benito Juarez. Following the eventual liberal victory, Miramon went into exile in Europe, where he was instrumental in arranging for Maximilian to be named emperor of Mexico. Miramon returned to Mexico in 1863 and, following the departure of the French troops in 1867, served as a general in the imperial army. He was wounded and captured with Maximilian during the siege of Queretaro, and was subsequently tried and executed.

1868

Venancio Flores, the president of Uruguay, was killed during a rebellion on February 19, 1868. Flores was born in Trinidad, Uruguay, in 1808. He served in the military and was active in the successful revolt by former president Fructuoso Rivera against Manuel Oribe. He was active in Uruguay's war against Argentina in the 1840s, and, in 1851, was named political chief in Montevideo. In 1853 Flores was instrumental in the ouster of President Juan Francisco Giro, and served as a member of the junta that succeeded him. Soon after, Flores became head of state of Uruguay, though he was forced to resign in September of 1855. He left Uruguay for Argentina, where he was active in that country's War of Federation. He returned to Uruguay in 1863, and, with the assistance of Brazil, began a revolt against the government of Bernardo Prudencio Bero. Flores was ultimately the victor, and, in January of 1865, became Uruguay's dictator. He remained in power throughout the Paraguayan War. In February of 1868 Flores resigned from office and called for elections to be held. Four days later he was murdered during a revolt. The leader of the rebellion, **Bernardo Bero**, had served as Uruguay's president from 1860 until 1864. The revolt proved unsuccessful, and Bero was killed the same day as Flores.

Thomas D. McGee, an Irish-Canadian journalist and politician, was shot to death in Ottawa on April 7, 1868. McGee was born in Ireland on April 13, 1825. He was a strong advocate of Irish nationalism, and was forced to flee to the United States following the Irish rebellion of 1848. He remained in New York, where he had founded two newspapers, until 1857, when he moved to Canada. Once there, he became active in political circles, being elected to the legislative assembly in 1858. McGee served as minister of agriculture in the Canadian government from 1865 until 1867, and was a leading proponent of Canadian federation. He was slain, after his denunciation of the Finians, by P.J. Whelan, who was tried and executed for the crime.

Michael, the prince of Serbia, was assassinated on June 10, 1868, in Kosutnjak, near Belgrade. Michael was born on September 16, 1823, the son of Prince Milosh Obrenovich I. He succeeded to his father's throne on July 8, 1839, following the death of his older brother, Milan. Michael served as Serbia's ruler until he was deposed by a revolt in September of 1842. He lived in exile until 1858, when he returned to Serbia as commander and chief of the army under his father, who had reclaimed the throne. Michael again became ruler on Milosh's death on September 26, 1860. He was a popular and enlightened monarch and instituted many reforms and advancements before his murder.

1869

In 1869 Japanese defense minister Musajiro was murdered by radical nationalists.

1870

Justo Jose de Urquiza, who served as president of Argentina from 1854 until 1860, was murdered with his two sons on April 11, 1870. Urquiza was born in 1801 in Entre Rios province, Argentina. Urquiza was a prosperous landowner in the area, and, in 1841, became governor of Entre Rios. In 1852, he defeated Juan Manuel de Rosas, the governor of Buenos Aires and dictator of Argentina, at the battle of Caseros. Urquiza became the first president of the Argentine Confederation on March 5, 1854. He was unsuccessful in his attempt to bring the province of Buenos Aires into the confederation, and left office on March 5, 1860. He remained active in national politics and was again serving as Entre Rios' governor when he was assassinated by allies of his rival, Ricardo Lopez Jordan.

Francisco Solano Lopez, the dictator of Paraguay, was killed in battle by Brazilian soldiers on March 1, 1870. Lopez was born in Asuncion in 1826. His father, Carlos Antonio Lopez, served as president of Paraguay from 1844. He served with distinction in the Paraguayan army, and later as his father's personal diplomatic representative. As vice president, Lopez succeeded to the presidency on the death of his father in 1862. In 1864 Lopez invaded Uruguay in an attempt to diminish the power of Brazil in that country. He soon involved his country in the Paraguayan War, which included Uruguay, Brazil, and Argentina as enemies. Against hopeless odds Lopez led Paraguay's army until his death on the battlefield at Cerro Cora six years later.

Juan Prim y Prats, a leading Spanish statesman and soldier, was assassinated in Madrid on December 18, 1870. Prim was born in the Catalonia province of Spain on December 6, 1814. He served in the Spanish army during the First Carlist War from 1833 until 1839, and, in 1841, became involved in politics. He was elected to the Chamber of Deputies that year, and, in 1843, led a revolt which resulted in the deposing of Baldomero Espartero as regent. Soon after, Prim was named military governor of Madrid. He was later involved in a conspiracy against Prime Minister Ramon Narvaez, and went into exile following the coup's failure. He returned to Spain in 1847, and was appointed governor of Puerto Rico. In 1853 he was again active in the Spanish military, serving in Granada, Morocco, and, in 1861, Mexico, where he commanded the European expeditionary forces. Prim was again exiled for conspiracy in 1864, returning to Spain four years later, after the deposing of Queen Isabella II. Prim served as minister of war in the government of Francisco Serrano, and succeeded him as prime minister in 1869. He was slain by assassins in Madrid shortly after arranging the selection of Amadeo as king of Spain.

1871

Cirilo Antonio Rivarola, who served as the first president of the Republic of Paraguay, was killed shortly after leaving office in 1871. Rivarola, who had fought in Argentina during the Paraguayan War, was selected as president on September 1, 1870, following the death of Francisco Solano Lopez (q.v.) in battle. Rivarola left office on December 18, 1871, and was murdered later in the month.

Georges Darboy (1813–71), the archbishop of Paris from 1863, was held as a hostage and killed by French revolutionaries during the Paris Commune revolt. Darboy, who had previously served as bishop of Nancy from 1859 until 1863, was ordered shot by Charles-Theophile Ferre (q.v.) when the French government of Adolphe Thiers refused to negotiate the release of captured revolutionary leaders.

Charles-Theophile Ferre (1845–71), a French Socialist politician and revolutionary leader, was court-martialed and shot on November 28, 1871. Ferre was involved in the Paris Commune revolt of 1870, serving as a member of the Committee for Public Safety. He was captured while in hiding in Paris by French troops in August of 1871, and tried for rebellion at Versailles.

1872

Richard Southwell Bourke, Lord Mayo (1822–72), the British viceroy of India, was stabbed to death by Shere Ali, a Moslem convict, at Port Blair prison in the Andaman Islands. Lord Mayo had served in the British government as chief secretary for Ireland in 1852, 1858–59, and 1866–68. He had been appointed viceroy to India in 1869. He was an advocate of limited self-government of the Indian provinces. The assassin was tried and hanged for the murder.

President **Jose Balta** (1816–72) of Peru was killed during an army uprising in 1872. Balta had aided Mariano Prado in his successful coup in 1865. Two years later he assisted in the overthrow of Prado, and, in 1868, Balta himself became Peru's president. His administration was noted for its attempt to restore constitutional rule in Peru. He was also successful in modernizing Peru's transportation system, constructing improved railroad and harbor facilities. Balta's free-spending policies led the Peruvian economy deep into debt. Balta was fatally shot during a military rebellion led by the Gutierrez brothers. He was succeeded as president by Manuel Pardo (q.v.).

President **Augustin Morales** (1810–72) of Bolivia was assassinated on November 24, 1872. Morales, a Bolivian general, had served as his country's head of state from January of 1871.

1874

Carlos Manuel de Cespedes (1819–74), a Cuban revolutionary leader, was killed by Spanish soldiers in 1874. Cespedes had begun an armed revolt against the Spanish rule of Cuba in 1868. He served as president of the revolutionary government from 1869 until he was deposed in 1873.

1875

President Gabriel Garcia Moreno of Ecuador was slain by an assassin on August 6, 1875. Garcia was born in Guayaquila on December 24, 1821. He entered into a career in law and was a strong supporter of the Jesuit order. He was forced into exile with the Jesuits under the administration of President Jose Maria Urbina. Garcia was elected to the Ecuadorian senate while in exile, but was unable to claim his seat. He returned to Eduador in 1856 and was elected mayor of Quito the following year. He remained an opponent of the government of Gen. Urbina, and soon became the leader of the revolutionary forces seeking to take control of the country. He was initially unsuccessful in this regard, and was forced to flee to Peru for a period. Events in Ecuador succeeded in destabilizing the Urbina regime further, and, in September of 1860, Garcia returned to his homeland as its leader. Garcia's first term of office was primarily concerned with repelling several attempts by Gen. Urbina to regain power and leading two unsuccessful military adventures against Colombia. Garcia relinquished his office in 1865 to Jeronimo Carrion, his hand-picked successor. He served as a diplomatic representative of the Carrion government the following year. In 1867, after Carrion tried to establish his independence from Garcia, Garcia forced the president's resignation. Javier Espinosa, the new president, was an ally of Garcia, but he too was removed from office in January of 1869. Garcia again became Ecuador's president and initiated policies designed to modernize Ecuador's education and transportation systems. Shortly before his inauguration for another term of office, the president was murdered by a Colombian, who hacked him to death with a machete. The assassination was believed to have been encouraged by liberal opponents of the Garcia administration.

Charles Caldwell, a black state senator from Mississippi, was killed by a gang of Ku Klux Klan members on December 25, 1875. Caldwell, an ex-slave, was a leader of the Mississippi black community.

1876

Abdul-Aziz, the sultan of Turkey, was deposed and possibly murdered on June 2, 1876. Abdul-Aziz was born in Istanbul on February 9, 1830. He succeeded his brother to the throne on June 25, 1861. His foreign policies were originally marked by an improved relationship with Western Europe, but domestically he drained the Turkish treasury for his personal use. Following the Franco-German War, the sultan began to rule by decree, and initiated an alliance with Russia. This move proved unpopular with the majority of his Moslem subjects, and resulted in his overthrow on May 29,

1876, by rebels led by Midhat Pasha (q.v.) and Hussein Avni Pasha (q.v.). Abdul-Aziz's death in Istanbul four days later was officially announced as a suicide, but he was likely slain by political enemies.

Hussein Avni Pasha (1819–76), a Turkish army leader and statesman, was shot and killed in 1876. Hussein was killed by a Turkish soldier while participating in a cabinet meeting. Several other Turkish politicians were also killed in the assault. Hussein had served as Turkey's minister of war from 1869 until 1871. He was appointed grand vizier in 1874, and again served as minister of war in 1875. He was a leader in the coup that overthrew Sultan Abdul-Aziz (q.v.).

George Armstrong Custer, a United States Cavalry officer, was killed in battle by Indians at the Little Bighorn River in Montana on June 24, 1876. Custer was born in Ohio on December 5, 1839. He graduated from West Point in 1861 and served as an officer during the latter part of the Civil War. He was assigned to duty in the Midwest and saw action against the Plains Indians in Kansas. In 1868 Custer led a successful attack on the Cheyenne village of Chief Black Kettle. Custer was assigned to the Dakota Territory in 1874, and was in charge of the expedition that verified the existence of gold deposits in the Black Hills of South Dakota. The advent of the gold rush in an area that was held sacred by the Sioux and Cheyenne Indians led to increased hostility. The Sioux Indians flocked to the banner of Chief Sitting Bull (q.v.) and had set up camp at the Little Bighorn River. Custer attacked the encampment with a column of over 250 on the morning of June 24, 1876. Custer was defeated in battle and all of his men were killed.

1877

Juan Bautista Gil (1840–77), the president of Paraguay, was assassinated on April 12, 1877. Gil had succeeded President Salvador Jovellanos as Paraguay's head of state on November 25, 1874.

Crazy Horse (1848–77), a Sioux Indian chief, was killed by United States soldiers while he was attempting to escape from Ft. Robinson on September 5, 1877. Crazy Horse was a member of the Oglala tribe and an early leader of Indians in Montana who were hostile to the United States. He participated in several battles with the United States Cavalry in the mid-1860s. In 1876 Crazy Horse was a leader of an army of Sioux and Cheyenne Indians who successfully defended themselves against an attack by Gen. George Crook, who had been assigned to remove the Indians from an area in the Black Hills of South Dakota where gold had been discovered. Soon after, Crazy Horse joined his forces with those of Chief Sitting Bull (q.v.) at the Little Bighorn River and participated in the battle there, which resulted in the defeat and death of troops led by Lt. Col. George Armstrong Custer (q.v.). Crazy Horse tried to continue his war against the government, but was forced to surrender on May 6, 1877, when his braves were faced with starvation. He was killed several months later when he attempted to escape from confinement.

On September 14, 1877, **Saigo Takamori** (1822–77), a Japanese general and statesman, was killed while leading the unsuccessful Satsuma Rebellion. Saigo had been instrumental in defeating the shogun's troops in 1868 and restoring the power of the emperor. He was a proponent of war against Korea in 1873, and retired from the government when his positions were rejected. Saigo died following the defeat of his army of samurai warriors. On September 14, 1877, he ordered one of his men to stab him with a sword.

1878

Toshimichi Okubo (1830–78), a leading Japanese statesman, was assassinated in 1878. Okubo, a Satsuma samurai, was an influential leader in the overthrow of the shogunate and the restoration of the emperor. He served as a leading advisor to the Japanese government and was a proponent of the modernization of Japan. He rejected plans for the invasion of Korea in 1873. Okubo was serving as Japan's home minister at the time of the Satsuma Rebellion, led by Saigo Takamori (q.v.), a member of Okubo's own clan. Okubo was successful in putting down the rebellion, but was assassinated the following year by six fellow clansmen who wished to avenge Saigo.

Manuel Pardo, who served as president of Peru from 1872 until 1876, was assassinated in Lima in 1878. Pardo, a wealthy businessman, served as mayor of Lima during the 1860s. In 1871 he founded the Civilista Party, and, the following year, was elected the first civilian president of Peru under its banner. He enacted many reforms during his term of office and was instrumental in diminishing the power of the army. Pardo was serving as president of the Peruvian Senate when he was slain by an army sergeant who resented his military policies.

On August 16, 1878, **Gen. N.V. Mesentsov**, the Russian prefect of police for Moscow, was stabbed to death by two assailants in the streets of Moscow.

Mehemet Ali Pasha (1827–78), a Turkish army leader, was killed by a mob of rebels in Albania on September 7, 1878. Mehemet had been the commander of the Turkish army during the Russo-Turkish War prior to his death.

1879

Gen. Kropotkin, a Russian military advisor to the Czar, was slain by revolutionaries in Kharkov in 1879.

Francis Cadell (1822–79), a Scottish explorer who had mapped the Murray River in Australia in the 1850s, was murdered by his crew in 1879.

1881

Alexander II, emperor of Russia, was slain by assassins in 1881. Alexander was born on April 29, 1818, in Moscow. He succeeded to the throne of his father, Nicholas I, on March 2, 1855. During the first year of his reign Alexander signed a treaty in Paris ending the Crimean War. Alexander's reign was marked by a number of political reforms, including the emancipation of the serfs. He also introduced local self-government and a revised judicial system in 1864, and introduced mandatory military service in 1874. He tried to tread the middle ground between the conservatives, who wished to maintain the status quo, and the liberals, who desired more reforms than he was willing to provide. Alexander attempted to keep Russia out of foreign involvements, but, in 1877, following an anti–Turkish uprising in Bosnia, Russia again entered war against Turkey in the last of the Russo-Turkish Wars. The conflict was settled the following year with the Treaty of San Stefano, which restored much territory to Russia.

Toward the end of Alexander's reign Russia became increasingly beset by revolutionary activities. The emperor himself fell victim to the terrorists on March 1, 1881, after having survived at least three earlier assassination attempts. While driving through the streets of St. Petersburg, he was fatally injured by two small bombs thrown at his carriage, dying several hours after the attack. He was succeeded by his son, Alexander III. The assassins were members of a terrorist organization known as Narodnaya Volya ("People's Will"). A number of the plotters were captured and tried by a military court. On April 15, 1881, Andrei Zhelyabov, Sophia Perovskaya, and three other conspirators were executed for planning the assassination.

James A. Garfield in 1881 became the second president of the United States to be assassinated. Garfield was born on November 19, 1831, in Cuyahoga County, Ohio. He joined the Republican party after graduating from college and, in 1859, was elected to the Ohio state legislature. He served in the Union army during the Civil War, and in 1863 he was elected to the United States House of Representatives as a Republican congressman from Ohio. In 1880 Garfield was campaign manager for John Sherman, but, following the failure to select a candidate after 36 ballots, the Republican convention turned to Garfield as a compromise presidential candidate. He defeated W.S. Hancock in the general election and was sworn in as the twentieth president of the United States on March 4, 1881. On July 2, 1881, Garfield was shot twice in his back at a Washington train station by Charles J. Guiteau (1841–82). The president died of his wounds eleven weeks later, on September 19, 1881, and was succeeded by his vice president, Chester A. Arthur. Guiteau was a self-styled evangelist who supported Garfield in the presidential election. Following Garfield's victory, Guiteau had petitioned the president for political favors and had been ignored. Guiteau, whose sanity was doubtful, was tried and found guilty of the assassination. He was hanged in June of 1882.

1882

Lord Frederick Charles Cavendish was born on November 30, 1836, in Eastbourne, Sussex, England, the second son of the seventh duke of Devonshire. He became a member of Parliament for the West Riding of Yorkshire in 1865 and became private secretary for William Gladstone in 1872, also serving as his financial adviser. In 1882, at Gladstone's request, Cavendish assumed the office of chief secretary for Ireland. He arrived in Dublin, Ireland, on May 5, 1882, and on the following day was stabbed to death in Phoenix Park by members of an Irish secret society known as "The Invincibles." Thomas H. Burke, the permanent undersecretary in Ireland, was also killed during the attack. James Carey (1845–83), the leading conspirator in the assassination, betrayed his accomplices, resulting in the trial and execution of five of the assassins the following year. Carey, who subsequently fled Ireland, was shot to death at sea by Patrick O'Donnell as a traitor to the Sinn Fein cause.

Edward Henry Palmer, an English Orientalist and explorer, was murdered by Arab brigands on August 11, 1882. Palmer, who was born in Cambridge on August 7, 1840, was a renowned linguist and traveler in the Middle East. He was killed in Egypt while on a mission for the British government to gain the support of the sheikhs of the Sinai for the British occupation of the area.

1883

Midhat Pasha, the former Turkish grand vizier, was murdered in prison on May 8, 1883. Midhat was born in Constantinople in 1822. He entered the Turkish civil service as a young man, and served in the government of Sultan Abdul-Aziz (q.v.). In August of 1872 he succeeded Mahmud Nedim as grand vizier, but remained in power for only three months. Midhat remained a powerful leader of the moderate Turkish elements, and was instrumental in deposing the Sultan in 1876. Midhat again served as grand vizier in the government of Sultan Abdul-Hamid II, and assisted in drafting a new Turkish constitution. In February of 1877 Midhat was accused of conspiracy against the Sultan, and exiled. He returned to Turkey the following year, and was named governor of Syria. He was again arrested in May of 1881, and accused of conspiracy and the murder of Sultan Abdul-Aziz five years earlier. Midhat was tried and sentenced to death, but the sentence was later reduced to banishment to At Ta'if, Arabia. It was there that Midhat was murdered by political enemies.

Col. William Hicks (1830–83), known as Hicks Pasha, was killed by forces of the Mahdi on November 4, 1883. Hicks, a British soldier, was the leader of the army of the khedive of Egypt. He was sent to put down an uprising of Moslem fanatics under the leadership of the Mahdi in the Egyptian Sudan, and was killed with most of his forces on November 4, 1883.

1885

Charles George Gordon was born at Woolwich, England, on January 28, 1833, the son of Gen. H.W. Gordon. He became an officer-cadet there in 1848, and in June 1852 became a second lieutenant in the royal engineers. He saw active duty in the Crimean War and for the next several years he remained as a member of the international commission establishing the new boundary lines between Turkey and Russia. The following year he become a captain and again saw active duty in China, participating in the occupation of Peking. Following a bout with smallpox and now a brevet major, Gordon became commander of the "Ever-Victorious Army," a collection of Shanghai peasants and brigands, founded to protect European interests in Shanghai. The next year and a half saw his army emerge victorious over a more numerous foe. It was after this tour of duty that he acquired the nickname of "Chinese Gordon."

He was appointed a member of the Danubian commission in Romania in September 1871 by Gladstone, and in 1873 accepted the position of governor of Equatoria, a province of North Africa stretching south down the Nile from the Egyptian Sudan. For the next two years Gordon was active in mapping the uncharted areas along the Nile and in stamping out the slave trade in that region. Following a return to England in 1876, Gordon again accepted a position in Egypt, becoming governor general of the Sudan and the Equatorial provinces. He was instrumental in putting down a rebellion against King John IV (q.v.) of Ethiopia by Walad-el-Michael and crushed a rebellion by slave traders.

In 1880 Gordon resigned his position in Egypt. Following a brief stay in India as private secretary to the Marquess of Ripon, the viceroy delegate, Gordon again traveled to China. There he succeeded in preventing a war between China and Russia. Between 1881 and 1882 Gordon commanded the Royal Engineers in Mauritius, then spent a year of contemplation in Palestine. During this period the British situation in Egypt had deteriorated due to the appearance of the Mahdi, or "expected one," who led an army of Moslem fanatics in the Egyptian Sudan. The Mahdi had begun a holy war, or "jihad," and had crushed an army of the khedive of Egypt led by Col. William Hicks (q.v.). Gordon was sent in 1884 to rescue the Egyptian garrisons in the Sudan and evacuate the capital of Khartoum before the Mahdi's forces conquered it. Once in Khartoum, Gordon held off the Mahdi's forces for over 10 months, despite English refusals of reinforcements. A relief force under Lord Wolseley was only three days distant when the Khartoum garrison was overrun by the Mahdi on January 26, 1885. Gordon was butchered by the triumphant invaders.

Justo Rufino Barrios (1835–85), who served as Guatemala's president from 1873, was killed in battle in El Salvador. Barrios had become the leader of the Guatemalan army in 1871 and became president two years later. He initiated many reforms during his rule, improving transportation, education and communication systems. He attempted to expand his power throughout Central America and was killed on April 2, 1885, while leading Guatemalan troops in an invasion of El Salvador.

Japanese education minister **Arinori** was assassinated in 1885 by Japanese nationalist fanatics.

Louis Riel was born on October 22, 1844, in St. Boniface, Red River Settlement, Canada. Riel succeeded his father as leader of the French half-breeds, known as the metis, who inhabited the Red River area. The metis feared the loss of their lands due to the incorporation of the Northwest Territories into the Canadian Dominion and began a rebellion in 1869, culminating in the seizure of Ft. Garry, in Winnipeg. Riel established a provisional government and became president. In 1870 a delegation of metis was sent to Ottawa, where the Canadian Parliament passed the Manitoba Act, allowing the Red River area to become part of the province of

Manitoba. The Canadian government then reneged on the amnesty promised to the rebellion leaders, and Riel left the area. He was elected to the Canadian parliament on several occasions, though he never held his seat. Riel moved to Montana and became an American citizen in 1883. In June of 1884 Riel returned to Canada and led the Second Riel Rebellion from the Saskatchewan Valley, forming a provisional government in March of 1885. He was defeated at Batoche by Canadian troops and tried for treason. He was executed at Regina on November 16, 1885.

1889

John IV, the king of Ethiopia, was killed in battle at Metamma in March of 1889. John, then known as Kassa, was the chief of Tigre in 1872 when he defeated several rival claimants and assumed the throne of Ethiopia. His reign was marked by internal and external disputes. He was faced with several insurrections as well as armed disputes with the Egyptians and the Moslem fanatics led by the Mahdi. John was also beset by European incursions into Ethiopian territory once the Suez Canal was constructed. Menelik II, the heir to the Solomid dynasty, was preparing to engage John in a battle for the throne when the king was killed in battle against Mahdist forces. Menelik claimed the throne on John's death.

1890

Maj. Konstantin Panitsa, a Bulgarian army officer, was shot and killed in 1890 following an unsuccessful conspiracy against Prime Minister Stefan Stambulov (q.v.).

Gen. Seliverstov, the chief of the Russian secret police for overseas affairs, was assassinated in 1890 by Padlewski, a Pole, while he was staying at the Hotel de Bade in Paris.

Francisco Menendez, the sixty-year-old president of El Salvador, died in office on June 22, 1890. Menendez had launched the revolt that ousted Rafael Zaldivar and had served as his country's president from June 22, 1885, until his ouster by Carlos Ezeta on the day of his death.

On Secember 15, 1890, **Sitting Bull** was killed while under arrest by American soldiers. Sitting Bull, American Indian chief of the Teton Dakota Prairie Sioux tribe, was born in 1831 in Grand River, South Dakota. He was known as a fearless warrior and, in the 1850s, became leader of the Strong Heart Warrior Society. The Sioux nation became involved in a serious conflict with the United States Army in 1863, and shortly after, Sitting Bull first entered battle against American soldiers. For five years he often battled the army which had virtually ruined the Indian economy by stamping out the Sioux's buffalo hunting grounds. In 1866 he became chief of the northern Sioux, and two years later signed a treaty with the United States. The treaty was broken following the discovery of gold in 1874 in part of the guaranteed reservation area in the Black Hills. In 1876 Sitting Bull called a great war council of the Sioux, Cheyenne, and other tribes and, in June, defeated Gen. George Crook at the Rosebud River. On June 25, 1876, Sitting Bull led the Indian army at the Little Bighorn River to defeat and kill Lt. Col. George Armstrong Custer (q.v.). Following a period of military reversals and the near starvation of his followers, Sitting Bull led the remainder of his tribe into Canada in May of 1877. Four years later Sitting Bull was forced to surrender due to continued famine. In 1883 Sitting Bull was sent to live at the Standing Rock agency until 1890, when unrest among the Sioux began again. Sitting Bull was arrested by the army at Grand River to prevent him again leading the Sioux nation to war. He was killed on December 15, 1890, during a rescue attempt by some of his Indian followers.

1891

Khristo Belchev, Bulgarian minister of finance under Prime Minister Stefan Stambulov (q.v.), was assassinated by Macedonians in 1891. Belchev was slain during an attempt on the life of Stambulov. Four men were tried and convicted of the crime, and were executed by hanging.

James Wallace Quinton, the British Commissioner in Assam, India, was stabbed to death with four associates while attending a conference in Manipur Province in 1891. The commissioner's assailants were rebels with whom he had come to negotiate a peace settlement. The British army put down the rebellion and executed the leaders of the band of assassins who killed Quinton.

1892

Dr. Georgi Vulkovich, the Bulgarian diplomatic minister to Turkey, was stabbed to death in Constantinople by a Macedonian terrorist by the name of Christo in 1892.

German explorer **Mehmed Emin Pasha** was killed in Africa in 1892. Born Eduard Schnitzer on March 28, 1840, in Silesia, he entered into the service of the Turkish government in his youth and adopted a Moslem name. He served as medical officer to Gen. Charles Gordon (q.v.) at Khartoum from 1875 until 1878, when he was named the governor of the Equatoria Province in the Sudan. He remained in that position during the Mahdist uprising until 1888, when he was rescued by H.M. Stanley. Following an unsuccessful attempt to regain his position, he accepted to undertake an expedition to Central Africa for the German East Africa Company in 1890. He was brutally murdered on October 23, 1892, by agents of Chief Kibonge, a leading African slave trader.

1893

Abdullah Nadim, an Egyptian nationalist and publisher of the newspaper *al Ustadh*, was murdered in 1893.

Jules Ferry, a former premier of France, was shot and killed by a religious fanatic on March 17, 1893. Ferry was born on April 5, 1832, in Vosges, France. As a lawyer and a journalist, Ferry was an influential critic of the French government in the 1860s. He became mayor of Paris in 1870, but his inability to alleviate a famine there forced his removal from office the following year. He remained active as a member of the opposition to the conservative government during the 1870s. In 1879, Ferry was appointed minister of public instruction in a Republican cabinet. Ferry became France's premier for the first time in 1880, serving until the following year. He was again premier from 1883 until 1885. Under his administration, France established its modern school system, mandating free and compulsory primary education. Anti-clerical measures accompanied Ferry's education policies, and Jesuits and members of other religious orders were forbidden to teach under the new system. Ferry's administration was also responsible for the expansion of the French colonial empire. France occupied Tunis, Tonkin, and Madagasar, and entered the Niger and Congo regions in Africa during Ferry's term of office. His Indo-China expansion policy met with public disapproval following the temporary defeat of the French army there. Ferry was forced from office in March of 1885 by Georges Clemenceau. Ferry remained active in politics and had been elected president of the French senate shortly before his assassination in 1893.

Gen. Margallo, the Spanish commander-in-chief of Morocco, was shot and killed for selling rifles to belligerent tribesmen. He was killed by Miguel Primo de Rivera, who was later to become the dictator of Spain.

1894

Hilarion Daza was a general in the Bolivian army when he helped engineer the overthrow of President Mariano Melgarejo in 1871. Five years later Daza himself seized the office of the president on May 4, 1876. He led an administration known for its corruption and cruelty. In 1879 he joined Peru in a war against Chile known as the War of the Pacific. Following his failure as a general to win a victory, he was deposed and exiled in December of 1879. He returned from exile in 1894 and was killed by an angry mob.

Marie François Sadi Carnot was born at Limoges, France, on August 11, 1837. He entered public life in 1871 as a prefect of the Department of Seine–Inferieure and then served as a Republican member of the National Assembly for the Cote d'Or. He served as minister of public works from 1880 to 1881 and again in 1885, until his appointment as minister of finance, a position he held until 1886. Carnot became president of France on December 2, 1887, following the resignation of Jules Grevy. During his presidency the Boulangist crisis was launched by Gen. Georges Boulanger. Carnot's popularity did much to diminish this potential threat to the republic, which ended in Boulanger's exile in 1889. Carnot was stabbed to death on June 24, 1894, while giving a speech in Lyons; he died three hours later. His assailant was Sante Caserio, an Italian anarchist who was tried and, on August 11, executed.

1895

The year 1895 saw the murder of **Queen Min** of Korea. Queen Min was born in 1851 and began her reign in Korea in 1866 as the consort of King Kojong. She was instrumental in gaining China's recognition of her son, Sunjong, as the crown prince of Korea. In 1894 Japan's defeat of China led to an increased domination of Korean affairs by the Japanese, culminating in the brutal murder of Queen Min on April 8, 1895. The murder was arranged by the Japanese consul, Gen. Goro Miura, and carried out by an armed band of Koreans and Japanese. The immediate result of this assassination was a backlash against the Japanese, resulting in a greater Russian influence in Korea. Gen. Miura was ordered to return to Japan, where he was tried for conspiring to murder the queen. He was convicted but served no time in prison.

Jose Julian Marti was born in Havana, Cuba, on January 28, 1853. He became involved in the fight for Cuban independence and was arrested in 1870 and deported to Spain the following year. Four years later he went to

France and in 1875 settled briefly in Mexico City. In 1877 he went to teach literature in Guatemala, but returned to Cuba in December of 1878. His political activities again resulted in his deportation to Spain in the following year. After brief stays in France and Venezuela, Marti settled in New York City in 1881; there he wrote and published Latin-American newspapers. In 1892 Marti was elected as leader of the Partido Revolucionario Cubano, which was actively involved in the fight for Cuban independence. Marti returned to Cuba on April 11, 1895, following the start of the revolution. On May 19, 1895, Marti was killed in battle on the plains of Dos Rios, Oriente Province. Marti's name is a symbol of liberty throughout South and Central America, and he is revered as one of his country's greatest patriots.

Stefan Stambulov was born on January 31, 1854, at Turnovo, Bulgaria. He became involved with revolutionaries while in Romania, and returned to Bulgaria to lead an anti–Turkish uprising at Nova Zagora in 1875. He again fought against the Turks in 1876 and during the war of 1877–78. Stambulov was elected president of the National Assembly, or Sobranye, in 1884, resulting in the Serbo-Bulgarian War. In 1886 Stambulov became head of government following the abduction of Prince Alexander by pro–Russian officers, and served as head of the Council of Regency following the prince's abdication. In 1887 Stambulov was instrumental in gaining the Bulgarian throne for Prince Ferdinand of Saxe-Coburg-Gotha, becoming his prime minister and minister of the interior. Stambulov's major policy was to eliminate Russian interference in the affairs of Bulgaria and to build a strong military for his country. There were many threats to Stambulov's rule, particularly from Macedonian nationalists. Stambulov was forced to resign by Prince Ferdinand in May of 1894 due to growing unrest throughout the country. On July 15, 1895, he was attacked by a group of four Macedonians in the streets of Sofia, and died three days later, on July 18, 1895.

1896

Nasir Ad-Din, the shah of Persia, was assassinated on May 1, 1896. Nasir Ad-Din was born on July 17, 1831, the son of Mohammed Shah of Persia. He succeeded his father to the throne on September 13, 1848. Nasir Ad-Din began a number of reformist measures in the early years of his reign, assisted by his grand vizier, Mirza Taqi Khan, who was subsequently murdered. In 1856, Nasir Ad-Din did much to modernize Persia during his reign, instituting postal and telegraph services, and improving roads to accommodate wheeled traffic. As Nasir Ad-Din grew older, his desire for reforms diminished, causing much unrest. On May 1, 1896, he was assassinated in Teheran by Mullah Reza Kermani, a servant and follower of Sayyed Jamal ad-Din "al-Afghani." Al-Afghani, a leading Moslim reformer and pan–Islamist, was a political enemy of the shah. The assassin was hanged along with **Mirza Aqa Khan Kermani**, a writer and the editor of the newspaper *Akhtar*, and **Shaikh Ahmad Ruhi**, a writer and scholar. Kermani and Ruhi were allies of al-Afghani, but do not appear to have been involved in the conspiracy against Nasir Ad-din. Al-Afghani died in exile the following year.

Cuban patriots **Antonio Maceo y Granajles** (1848–96) and his brother, **Jose Maceo y Granajles** (1846–96), were killed on December 7, 1896, in a skirmish with Spanish forces during the Cuban War for Independence. The brothers had joined the rebellion the previous year and had been active in the victories against the Spanish at Jobito and Sal del Indio.

Jose Rizal y Mercado was born on the island of Luzon in 1861. He spent most of his early years in Europe, studying at the University of Madrid. While in Europe he authored several books concerning the Spanish rule in the Philippines, *Noli Me Tangere* (1896) and *El Filibusterismo* (1891). He returned to the Philippines in 1892 and founded Liga Filipina, a nationalist organization, resulting in his exile for four years to Mindanao. He did not take an active role in the Philippine Revolution of 1896, but was arrested on charges of insurrection. He was found guilty by a military court and shot on December 30, 1896.

1897

On January 4, 1897, **J.R. Phillips**, the acting British consul general of the Niger Coast protectorate, was killed by tribesmen of King Overami of Benin. Phillips was on route to visit the king with intentions of abolishing the slave trade and ending human sacrifice. Nearly all of the more than 200 members of Phillips' traveling party were massacred. The British government responded by attacking and capturing Benin and deporting King Overami.

On August 8, 1897, **Antonio Canovas del Castillo** was assassinated. Canovas was born on February 8, 1828, in Malaga, Spain. He worked as a journalist while a legal student at Madrid University. He was elected to the Cortes as a deputy in 1852 and served as charge d'affaires in Rome in 1854. A member of the Liberal party, Canovas was a cabinet minister in several governments, serving as minister of interior in 1864, and minister of colonies in 1865. He was instrumental in returning the Bourbon monarchy to the throne of Spain following the abdication of King Amadeo in 1873, and he helped secure the throne for King Alfonso XII. He was also a principal author of the Spanish constitution of 1876 and a founder of the Conservative party. He served as premier of Spain on four occasions (1874–81, 1884–85, 1890–92, 1895–97), alternating as head of government with Praxades M. Sagasta, the leader of the Liberal party. During the midst of the Cuban insurrection, which began in 1895, Canovas was assassinated by an anarchist at Santa Agueda, in the Basque province.

President Juan Idiarte Borda of Uruguay was assassinated on August 5, 1897. Idiarte Borda had come to power on March 1, 1894, but had seriously abused his constitutional powers. He was abandoned by his supporters and was killed in Montevideo following a populist revolt.

1898

On February 8, 1898, President **Jose Maria Reina Barrio** (1856–98) was assassinated by a rebel in Guatemala. Reina Barrio, who had served as Guatemala's president since March 14, 1892, was the nephew of former president Justo Rufino Barrios (q.v.).

On September 10, 1898, **Elizabeth**, Empress of Austria and consort of Emperor Francis Joseph I, was slain in an attack by Luigi Luccheni, an Italian anarchist, on a boat dock in Geneva. Elizabeth was born on December 24, 1837, in Munich. She was the daughter of Maximilian Joseph, Duke of Bavaria. She married Francis Joseph, emperor of Austria, in Vienna on April 24, 1854. In 1867 she was crowned queen of Hungary following the Austro-Hungarian Ausgleich. She was popular with her people due to her charity, charm and beauty. After the death by suicide of her only son, Crown Prince Rudolf, in 1889, the empress became increasingly reclusive. She was vacationing in Geneva for her health at the time of her murder.

1899

Ulises Heureaux was born in 1845 near Puerto Plata in the Dominican Republic. He fought actively and well against the Spanish in his country's war of independence and in subsequent civil wars. Heureaux, as a leader of the army, seized power in the Dominican Republic on September 1, 1882, and served as president until 1884. He was again president from January 6, 1887, until his death, and had remained a virtual dictator during the period between his terms of office. Though his reign was characterized as often cruel, he succeeded in bringing about numerous reforms, particularly in the areas of agriculture and transportation. These reforms unfortunately nearly bankrupted his already impoverished country. On July 26, 1899, Heureaux was assassinated by a group of political enemies led by Ramon Caceres (q.v.), who himself became president in 1906 and was subsequently assassinated.

'Abdullahi Ibn Mohammed was born in the Southern Darfur region of the Sudan in 1846. He joined Mohammed Ahmed, later known as "the Mahdi," as a disciple in 1850 and soon became a leading adviser. In 1881 he was named "the Khalifa" by the Mahdi, and went on to lead Mahdist forces to numerous victories against the Egyptians, including the defeat of Khartoum in 1885, which resulted in the death of Charles Gordon (q.v.). In June 1885 'Abdullahi became the leader of the Mahdist forces upon the death of the Mahdi. He continued to lead the movement to a number of military successes, including the attacks on Gordar and Metemma, the latter resulting in the death of King John IV (q.v.) of Ethiopia in 1889. During the 1890s the movement suffered a number of military reversals due to an increased European presence in the area. The Italians and Belgians inflicted defeat on the Mahdist armies at Kassala in 1894 and Rejaf in 1897 respectively. An Anglo-Egyptian army led by Gen. Horatio H. Kitchener finally succeeded in driving the remaining Mahdists from the Sudan in 1898. 'Abdullahi was killed on November 24, 1899, at Umm Diwaikarat, with the last of his followers, by an Egyptian force led by Sir F.R. Wingate.

1900

William Goebel (1856–1900) was Kentucky's Democratic gubernatorial nominee in the election of 1899. Goebel was narrowly defeated by the Republican nominee, Taylor, but he contested the election, charging fraud. The matter was sent to be settled by the Kentucky legislature, but Goebel was shot by an unknown assailant on January 30, 1900. The legislature decided in Goebel's favor, and he was sworn in as governor as he lay dying from his wounds. He died four days later, on February 3, and was succeeded by Lt. Gov. J.C.W. Beckham. Many Republican leaders and office holders were implicated in the assassination and several were convicted, though most convictions were overturned on appeal. Caleb Powers (1869–1932), the Republican secretary of state for Kentucky, was sentenced to eight years in prison for complicity in the crime. After serving his prison term, he was elected to Congress for the first of four terms in 1911. A man named Yountsey was convicted of the actual shooting and did not appeal, receiving a life sentence.

Baron Klemens von Ketteler (1853–1900), who had served as the German minister to Peking from 1899, was murdered on June 19, 1900, by Chinese Nationalists. Von Ketteler had previously served as Germany's minister to Mexico from 1896 to 1899. The murder of von Ketteler co-incided with attacks on foreign legations throughout Peking by young members of a nationalist secret society known as "The Society of Harmonious Fists." The outbreak of anti–Western violence, which had the tacit support of Empress Tzu Hsi, became known as the Boxer Rebellion. The rising was suppressed by a six-nation expeditionary force, and a later German expedition took punitive action against the supporters of the Boxers in retaliation for von Ketteler's murder.

Humbert I was born on March 14, 1844, in Turin. He was the son of King Victor Emmanuel II of Italy and a member of the Savoy-Carignan line. Humbert, as prince of Piedmont, played an active role in the army during Italy's wars of unification between 1858 and 1870. In 1868 he married Margherita Teresa Giovanni, a cousin, who gave birth the following year to the future King Victor Emmanuel III. Humbert became king of Italy on January 9, 1879, following the death of his father. Humbert proved a relatively popular monarch and was instrumental in establishing the Triple Alliance between Italy, Germany and Austria in 1882. In the later years of his reign Humbert became increasingly tyrannical, often resorting to rule by decree. On July 29, 1900, Humbert was shot and killed at Monza, while traveling to his villa. His assassin was anarchist Gaetano Bresci, a former silk weaver from Paterson, New Jersey. Bresci confessed that the killing had been planned with other anarchists in the United States. He was convicted of the murder and, on August 29, was sentenced to life imprisonment.

1901

The year 1901 saw the third assassination of an American president when **President William McKinley** was shot and killed. McKinley was born on January 29, 1843, in Niles, Ohio. He served during the Civil War and later practiced law in Canton, Ohio. He was elected as a Republican member of the United States House of Representatives in 1876 and served till 1883. He again served in Congress from 1885 till 1891. In 1890, as chairman of the House Ways and Means Committee, he was instrumental in passing the McKinley Tariff. From 1892 till 1896 he served as governor of Ohio and, in 1896, he was elected president of the United States.

On February 15, 1898, during McKinley's first term of office, the United States battleship *Maine*, while on an official visit to Cuba, was sunk by a mine while in the Havana harbor. The United States subsequently became involved in Cuba's fight for independence from Spain, resulting in the Spanish-American War. Following the United States victory, a peace treaty was signed in December of 1898, which resulted in Spain's granting independence to Cuba and relinquishing Puerto Rico, Guam and the

Philippines to United States control. Philippine independence fighters, under the leadership of Emilio Aquinaldo, then transferred their hostilities from their Spanish rulers to the new United States occupation forces. The guerrilla forces continued their battle for independence until Aquinaldo's capture the following year.

McKinley was reelected president in 1900 and was at the start of his second term of office when he was shot by Leon Czolgosz, an anarchist, at the Temple of Music at the Pan-American exposition in Buffalo, New York, on September 6, 1901. Czolgosz, who had been inspired to commit the assassination after having read accounts of the murder of Italy's King Humbert (q.v.) the previous year, approached the president following the completion of his speech. The assassin had a gun in his hand with a handkerchief wrapped around it. As he drew near McKinley, as if to shake his hand, Czolgosz fired two shots into the president before being wrestled to the ground.

McKinley's wounds were not immediately considered serious, but his condition worsened, and he died on September 14. Czolgosz was tried and convicted of murder and executed in the electric chair on October 29, 1901.

Nikolai Pavlovich Bogolepov, the Russian minister of education, was killed in 1901 by an expelled student.

1902

In 1902 **Dimitri S. Sipiagin,** the Russian minister of the interior, was murdered by S.V. Balmashov, a revolutionary student, in St. Petersburg; and **M. Kanzchev,** a Bulgarian cabinet minister, was assassinated in Sofia.

1903

Alexander Obrenovich was born on August 14, 1876, the only son of King Milan of Serbia. he was proclaimed King of Serbia under a regency on March 6, 1889, upon the abdication of his father. On April 13, 1893, he assumed full authority as king and dismissed the regency council. The following year he abolished the constitution of 1888 and restored the earlier conservative constitution of 1869. In 1900 Alexander married **Madame Draga Mashin** (1867–1903), a former lady-in-waiting to his mother. This act proved to be very unpopular with his government and his people. He attempted to restore confidence in his reign by instituting a new constitution in 1901, but he suspended it arbitrarily when he felt the need. On July 11,

1903, a group of officers conspired to remove the king. Alexander's palace was surrounded by mutinous officers, and the royal couple was ultimately found hiding in a secret room behind their private bath. Alexander and Draga were then repeatedly shot and butchered with sabers before their bodies were thrown from a window into the courtyard beneath.

In 1903, Social Revolutionaries assassinated **N.M. Bogdanovich**, the Russian governor of Ufa, in Kiev.

1904

Bogoslovski, the Russian governor of the Caucasus, was killed by local separatists in 1904, following Russia's persecution of the Armenian church in that region.

On June 16, 1904, **Nikolai Bobrikov**, the sixty-five-year-old Russian governor general of Finland from 1899, was shot and killed by a nationalist student after he incurred Finnish displeasure by his extreme effort of Russification and his suspension of the constitution guaranteeing Finnish autonomy. His assassin was the son of a Finnish senator, who committed suicide following the attack.

Vyacheslav K. Plehve, the Russian minister of the interior, was assassinated on July 28, 1904. Plehve was born in the Kaluga province of Russia on April 20, 1846. A member of the Department of Justice from 1867, Plehve was named to the Ministry of the Interior as police director in 1881. His success in abating terrorist activities resulted in his appointment as deputy minister of the interior in 1884 and head of the Imperial Chancellery in 1894. In 1902 Plehve became minister of the interior. His ruthless suppression of dissent earned him the enmity of various organizations and resulted in his assassination by Social Revolutionary member E.S. Sazonov in the streets of St. Petersburg on July 28, 1904. The assassination occurred while Plehve was driving to a railway station in St. Petersburg and a bomb was tossed under his carriage. Sazonov was apprehended and sentenced to life imprisonment.

1905

In 1905 the Russian prefect of police in Moscow, **Count Pavel Andreevich Shuvalov**, was killed by a Social Revolutionary agent.

In February of 1905 **M. Johnson**, the procurator of the Finnish senate and a leading supporter of Russification for Finland, was assassinated.

On February 17, 1905, **Grand Duke Sergius** (1857–1905), a son of Czar Alexander II (q.v.) and commander in chief of the military district of Moscow, was killed by a bomb tossed at his carriage by Social Revolutionaries. Sergius was a leader of the conservative faction in the court of his nephew, Czar Nicholas II (q.v.).

Theodoros Deliyannis (1820–1905), who had served as the premier of Greece 1885–86, 1890–92, 1902–03, and from December 28, 1904, until his death, was assassinated on June 22, 1905. His murderer was a disgruntled gambler who resented the government's closing of the Greek gambling houses.

Frank Steunenberg (1861–1905), who had served as governor of Idaho from 1897 to 1901, was killed by a bomb planted at the front gate of his home on December 30, 1905. Steunenberg, a Democrat, had served two terms of office as Idaho's governor. It was during his administration that the Western Federation of Miners rioted and Steunenberg called in federal assistance in maintaining order. Harry Orchard (1866–1954) admitted planting the bomb which killed Steunenberg at the order of officials of the Western Federation of Miners, but no convictions of union leaders resulted from the subsequent trial. Orchard was sentenced to life imprisonment for his role in the murder of Steunenberg and other union foes.

1906

Prof. Mikhail Yakovlevich Gerstenstein, a member of the Russian Duma, was shot to death in Terioki in 1906 by a fanatical anti–Semite after Gerstenstein had accused members of the Russian nobility of corruption. **Gen. Mann**, who was responsible for putting down the riots in Moscow, was shot to death at the Peterhof railway station, and **Count Ignatieff**, a member of the czar's court and the founder of the League of True Russians, was also murdered.

Georgii Apollonovich Gapon (1870–1906), a Russian priest and the founder of the Russian Factory Workers in St. Petersburg in 1903, was lynched by Social Revolutionaries, who believed him to be a spy of the Czarist police. **Gen. Liarpiarski**, the military governor of Warsaw, Poland, was also killed in 1906.

1907

Amin As-Soltan (Ali Asghar Khan), the premier of Persia, was stabbed to death by radicals on August 31, 1907. Amin as-Soltan had been Persia's most powerful political figure since the 1880s. He had served as prime minister under Nasir ad-Din Shah and instituted Iran's pro–Russian policies in 1892. He was dismissed as prime minister following the assassination of Nasir ad-Din Shah (q.v.) in 1896, but returned as premier in 1898. Amin as-Soltan, having taken the title of Atabak, was unpopular with the progressives, who believed he was leading Iran to Russian control. He was again dismissed in 1903. In January of 1907 he was reappointed as premier by Mohammad Ali Shah, who had succeeded to the throne. Shortly after his appointment, Amin as-Soltan was assassinated by members of a radical group. The Shah attempted to use the killing as an excuse to crush the radicals, but the action instead encouraged them and increased their strength.

Dimiter Petkov, a Bulgarian cabinet minister, was shot to death in Sofia later in 1907.

1908

King Carlos I and **Crown Prince Luis Philippe** of Portugal were assassinated on February 1, 1908. Carlos I was born on September 28, 1863, in Lisbon, the son of Luis I. He became king of Portugal in 1889 on the death of his father. Carlos' reign was marked by opposition at home, rebellions in Portugal's overseas possessions, and a straining of relations with Great Britain. His appointment of Joao Franco as dictator and his suspension of the constitution resulted in an anti–Royalist revolt in January of 1908. On February 1, upon the royal family's return to Lisbon, Carlos I and his eldest son, Crown Prince Luis Philippe, were ambushed and assassinated by revolutionaries.

Count Andrzej Potocki (1861–1908), the Hapsburg governor of Polish Galicia from 1903, was murdered by a Ukrainian nationalist.

In June 1908, following a coup d'etat against the constitutional assembly of Persia by Mohammad Ali Shah, several prominent progressive leaders were arrested and executed. **Jamal Ad-Din Esfahani** and **Malek Al-Motakallemin**, both radical preachers from Isfahar, and **Mirza Jahangir Khan**, the editor of the newspaper *Sur-e Esrafil*, were executed on the orders of the shah.

Edward Ward Carmack, a prominent Tennessee newspaper editor and political figure, was shot to death by political rivals on the streets of Nashville on November 9, 1908. Carmack was born in Sumner County, Tennessee, on November 5, 1858. He was elected to the Tennessee state legislature in 1884 and, soon after, served as editor of the *Columbia Herald*. In 1888 he became editor of the *Nashville American*, and, four years later, the *Memphis Commercial Appeal*. He used these forums to advance his position as a proponent of prohibition. In 1897 Carmack was elected to the United States Congress, and, in 1901, he was elected to the Senate. Rather than run for reelection in 1906, he chose to challenge Malcolm Patterson for governor of Tennessee, and was defeated. He continued his fight to eliminate liquor sales in the state as, again, editor of the *Nashville American*. He was slain by Duncan B. Cooper and his son, Robin, while campaigning to enact his prohibition policies before the Tennessee state legislature. The Coopers were political allies of Governor Patterson and were subsequently pardoned by the governor for the murder of Carmack.

1909

In July of 1909 **Sir Curzon Wyllie**, the British political aide-de-camp of the India office, was assassinated by an Indian while at the Imperial Institute in London.

On October 26, 1909, **Prince Hirobumi Ito**, a Japanese statesman and former premier, was killed while in Manchuria. Ito was born in southeast Japan on September 2, 1841, and, in his youth, was an extreme nationalist. In 1863 Ito made a clandestine visit to England and there first realized that the removal of foreigners from Japan was a hopeless mission. In 1868 Ito joined the Japanese government following the overthrow of the shogunate, and after several trips abroad, was named to the position of minister of the interior in 1878, serving until 1882. In 1885 Ito became Japan's first prime minister and oversaw the writing of the Japanese Constitution of 1889. Following his first term of office as his country's prime minister, which ended in 1888, he served on three other occasions: 1892–96, 1898 and 1900–01. Following the Russo-Japanese War in 1905, Ito became the first resident general of Korea. On October 26, 1909, Ito was assassinated by a Korean nationalist in Harbin, Manchuria.

Francisco Ferrer Guardia (1859–1909), a Spanish educator and Socialist politician, was court-martialed and executed in October of 1909 for having taken part in anarchist riots in Barcelona.

In December 1909, **Arthur Jackson**, the British district magistrate of Naski, India, was shot to death at his farewell party in India.

1910

Butrus Pasha Ghali, the premier of Egypt since 1908, was shot to death on February 10, 1910, on the steps of the Ministry of Justice, two days after he had introduced a bill for an extension of the Suez Canal company's concession. Ghali, who had previously served as foreign minister and minister of finance, had signed the 1899 Condominium Convention on the Sudan. The assassination of Ghali, a Copt, alienated the Coptic community from the Nationalist government. Ghali's assassin was Ibrahim Wardani, a young pharmacist, who claimed that he had shot the premier because Ghali had presided over the Denshaway Tribunal, which had, in 1906, sentenced four peasants to death for the killing of a British officer. Wardini's other motives included the revival of the Press Law and Ghali's Suez Canal policy. Wardani was tried and executed on June 30, 1910.

Sayyed Abdollah Behbehani, a prominent Persian politician and leader of the Moderate party, was assassinated by left-wing extremists in 1910.

On August 3, 1910, William J. Gaynor (1849–1913), the mayor of New York City from 1909 to 1913, was shot and seriously wounded by a discharged city employee. Mayor Gaynor survived his wounds and remained in office until his death three years later.

Miguel Bombarda, a Portuguese physician and Republican leader, was murdered on October 3, 1910. Bombarda's assassination led to an uprising that deposed King Manuel II.

1911

In June of 1911 **Robert Ashe**, the British district magistrate of Tinevelly, was killed in Madras, India.

Petr Arkadevich Stolypin, the Russian prime minister, was shot by an assassin on September 14, 1911. Stolypin was born on April 14, 1862, at Dresden, in Saxony. Stolypin was appointed governor of Grodno in 1902 and governor of Sarotov in 1903. In May of 1906 he became the Russian minister of the interior and, two months later, he was appointed premier. Stolypin sought to institute a number of reformist measures designed to slow the increasing popular displeasure against the rule of Czar Nicholas II (q.v.). As a centrist, Stolypin gained enemies on both the left and the right, and incurred the resentment of members of the royal family. On September 14 he was shot by Dmitri Bogrov, at a Kiev theatre, while in the company of the czar. Stolypin died of his wounds four days later. Bogrov was hanged for his crime.

Ramon Caceres, the president of the Dominican Republic, was slain on November 19, 1911. Caceres, who was born in 1866 of a wealthy family, first came to prominence in the Dominican Republic when he assassinated Ulises Heureaux (q.v.), then president, in 1899. Five years later, following a period of political instability, Caceres became vice president of the Dominican Republic. He succeeded to the presidency in 1906. Caceres brought a number of major improvements to the economy and way of life of his country, reforming the constitution and instituting a public works system. Despite his accomplishments and popularity, he was beset by numerous plots against his reign, culminating in his fatal shooting. His death led to direct United States military intervention in the Dominican Republic from 1916 to 1924.

1912

Ecuadorian revolutionary leader **Gen. Pedro Montero**, who had been proclaimed president by his troops in Guayaquil, Ecuador, following the death of President Emilio Estrada, was killed by a mob on January 24, 1912. Montero had been court-martialed for his participation in the revolt and was sentenced to sixteen years' imprisonment. A mob, angered by what they considered too light a sentence, dragged Montero from the courtroom, riddled his body with bullets, cut off his head, and burned his remains in a bonfire. Montero, an ally of Eloy Alfaro (q.v.), had been the chief of the military in the Guayaquil district. He had formed a provisional ministry and awaited the return of Alfaro from exile. On January 23, 1912, government troops, led by Gen. Leonidas Plaza, defeated the rebels and captured the leaders.

Former Ecuadorian president **Eloy Alfaro** was killed on January 28, 1912. Alfaro and other revolutionary leaders, including his brothers, **Gen. Flavio Alfaro**, ex-minister of war and commander in chief of the revolutionary forces and **Gen. Medardo Alfaro**, and **Gen. Ulpiano Paez** and **Gen. Manuel Serrano**, were dragged from their jail cells and lynched by an angry mob. Eloy Alfaro was born in Monteristi, Ecuador, in 1864. He served as the leader of the liberals and was exiled in 1875. He led the uprising against the conservative regime of President Cordero in 1893, resulting in Cordero's overthrow in 1895. Alfaro became dictator of Ecuador in 1895 and became president in 1897, serving until 1901. In 1906 he led the revolt against President Lisardo Garcia and became president after his defeat of the government troops in 1907. His terms in office were marked by an attempt to reduce the power of the Roman Catholic church in Ecuador. Alfaro's candidate for the presidency, Emilio Estrada, was elected in 1911, but died soon afterward. Alfaro himself then again attempted to return to power in January, 1912, but he was arrested in Guayaquil with other rebel leaders and imprisoned. He was killed by a mob while awaiting trial.

On October 14, 1912, Theodore Roosevelt (1858–1919), the president of the United States from 1901 to 1909, was shot and wounded by John N. Schrank (1876–1943) before addressing a crowd in Milwaukee, Wisconsin. Roosevelt was in the midst of a campaign for the presidency on the Progressive (or Bull Moose) party ticket. Following his shooting in front of the Gilpatrick Hotel, Roosevelt proceeded to the Milwaukee Auditorium and gave his speech to the crowd before seeking medical attention. Roosevelt recovered from his wounds and went on to place second, ahead of Republican incumbent William Howard Taft, in the November election. Schrank was judged insane and sentenced to the Central State Hospital in Wisconsin, where he remained until his death over thirty years later.

Jose Canalejas y Mendez, the premier of Spain, was slain on November 12, 1912. Canalejas y Mendez was born in El Ferrol, Spain, on July 31, 1854. He became a member of the Cortes in 1881. He subsequently held several cabinet positions, including minister of public works and justice in 1888 and minister of finance in 1894. He served as president of the Cortes in 1906, and was appointed premier on February 8, 1910. Canalejas y Mendez was a leftist member of the Spanish Liberal party, and he was active in enacting social reforms during his term of office. His administration was also marked by civil and military unrest and worker's strikes. His attempts to deal with these problems resulted in the alienation of many of his followers. Canelejas y Mendez was shot and killed by Pardinas, an anarchist, while he was entering the Ministry of the Interior for a conference. The assassin fired two shots at the premier and then killed himself.

Haitian president **Michael Cincinnatus Leconte**, who had held office from August 14, 1911, was killed in an explosion which destroyed the Palais National on August 8, 1912. The explosion occurred when a large stockpile of arms and ammunition stored in the basement of the presidential palace was ignited. It remains a mystery whether the explosion was an accident or an assassination, though there is some evidence to suggest that Leconte had been murdered before the detonation, and the explosion was used to cover the evidence of the crime.

1913

On January 23, 1913, **Nazim Pasha**, the Turkish minister of war, and two other Turkish officials were assassinated during a cabinet meeting by a group of young revolutionaries led by Envery Bey.

Manuel Enrique Araujo, the president of El Salvador, was assassinated on February 8, 1913. Araujo had succeeded President Fernando Figueroa on February 28, 1911, and served until his death.

Francisco I. Madero, the president of Mexico, and **Jose Pino Suarez**, his vice president, were slain on February 23, 1913, after having been overthrown and arrested by Gen. Victoriano Huerta. Madero was born in Parras, Coahuila, Mexico, on October 30, 1873, the son of a wealthy landowner. Following completion of his studies in Europe, Madero returned to Mexico in 1893. A liberal and an idealist, Madero entered politics. He actively supported democratic measures and, in 1910, challenged Porfirio Diaz, the Mexican dictator, in the presidential election of that year. The election was not an honest one, and Madero was arrested the day before the balloting. He subsequently escaped to the United States, where he authored a manifesto demanding effective suffrage and no presidential reelection. The rebellion continued in his absence and Diaz was forced to resign. Following new elections, Madero was sworn in as president on November 6, 1911. Madero's term of office was a difficult one as he was besieged both by opponents from the old regime and by former allies who felt his reform measures were not sweeping enough. In February of 1913 Gen. Huerta led a military revolt against the government and Madero was overthrown. Both Madero and Suarez were shot and killed while being transferred from the presidential palace to prison, allegedly while trying to escape.

On March 18, 1913, **George I**, the king of Greece, was assassinated in Salonika by Schinas, a Greek. George I was born Prince William of Denmark on December 24, 1845, in Copenhagen. He was the second son of Christian IX, the Danish king. In 1862 he was selected by the European powers to succeed the deposed king of Greece, Otho I. He was accepted as king of the Hellenes by the Greek national assembly on March 30, 1863, and acceded to the throne. During his reign as constitutional monarch, Greece grew greatly in size, incorporating most of Thessal and part of Epirus in 1881. The unsuccessful Cretan insurrection of 1896 and Greece's involvement in the First Balkan War in 1912–13 also took place during his fifty-year reign. Upon his assassination he was succeeded by his son, Constantine I.

Mahmud Shevket, the Turkish grand vizier, was assassinated on June 11, 1913, in Istanbul. Mahmud Shevket was born in 1858, in Baghdad, and served in the Turkish army. He supported the Young Turk Revolution in 1908 and, as commander of the Third Army, suppressed a counterrevolution the following year. Following the abdication of Sultan Abdul-Hamid II, Mahmud Shevket became minister of war. Following an insurrection by members of the Committee of Union and Progress and the subsequent resignation of Kiamil Pash, the grand vizier, Mahmud Shevket assumed that office on January 23, 1913. He was serving in this capacity at the time of his assassination six months later.

On September 5, 1913, **Abe**, the director of the Japanese foreign office's political affairs bureaus, was murdered in Tokyo by militant Japanese nationalists.

1914

On March 16, 1914, **Gaston Calmette** (1858–1914), a French journalist, was shot and killed. Calmette was the editor of *Le Figaro* from 1913, and had tried to expose the financial corruption of the French government, particularly the policies of Joseph Caillaux, the minister of finance. Calmette was murdered by Mme. Caillaux in his office while he was preparing further incriminating evidence against her husband. Mme. Caillaux was acquitted in the subsequent trial, but the scandal resulted in the resignation of her husband.

On June 28, 1914, **Archduke Francis Ferdinand** of Austria and his wife, **Countess Sophie Chotek**, Duchess of Hohenberg, were assassinated by Gavrilo Princip, a Serbian nationalist student, while on a visit to Sarajevo, Bosnia. Francis Ferdinand was born in Graz on December 18, 1863, the son of Archduke Charles Louis. He became the heir apparent to the crown of Emperor Francis Joseph of Austria, his uncle, following the suicide of the emperor's only son, Archduke Rudolf, on January 30, 1899. On July 1, 1900, Francis Ferdinand married Countess Sophie Chotek, following a bitter confrontation with his uncle, and only after renouncing the future rights of succession for their children. Francis Ferdinand used his prestige and office to attempt a reconciliation with the Russians and to effect a solution to the internal problems of Hungary. His assassination was considered to be the immediate cause of World War I. Twenty-five people were tried and convicted in connection with the assassinations, including Danilo Ilic, who was sentenced to be hanged for his part in organizing the conspiracy. Gavrilo Princip, who had fired the fatal shots, was sentenced to twenty years in prison. He died of tuberculosis in April of 1918.

French Socialist leader **Jean Leon Jaures** was assassinated on July 31, 1914, while dining in a Paris cafe. His assailant was Raoul Villain, a right-wing fanatic. Jaures was born on September 3, 1859, in Tarn. He was a teacher and writer when he was elected a deputy from Tarn in 1885. Four years later he was defeated for reelection and returned to teaching. During this period he also authored several important essays on philosophy. He returned to the Chamber of Deputies in 1893 and served until 1899. He was again elected in 1902, serving until his death. He was the leader of the French Socialist party in the chamber during much of his tenure. In 1904 he was a founder and editor of *L'Humanite*, the Socialist newspaper. Jaures was active in seeking a Franco-German reconciliation, and opposed militarist legislation prior to World War I. His assassination removed the most prominent and respected Socialist leader from the French scene. Villain, his assassin, was himself murdered in Spain in 1936, by leftists avenging the murder of Jaures.

Jacobus Hercules De la Rey was shot and killed by a police patrol in Johannesburg on September 15, 1914. De la Rey was born in 1847 in the Orange Free State and was raised in Transvaal. He entered the South African parliament in 1893, and on the advent of the South African War in 1899, he became a general. He conducted many successful guerrilla campaigns against the British, and was considered a worthy and honorable foe. Following the conclusion of the war, De la Rey became a leading supporter of Louis Botha, and was active in his political party, Het Volk ("The People"). He was a representative in the legislative assembly 1907–10, and from 1910 to 1914 he was a member of the Union of South Africa's first senate. He sided with the rebels seeking to restore republican independence at the start of World War I, but was shot to death before he could lead the rebellion. His killing was instrumental in the revolt which began the month following his death.

1915

Joao Chagas (1863–1925), the premier designate of Portugal, was shot and seriously wounded in 1915 by **Joao de Freitas**, a member of the Portuguese Senate, who was slain by Chagas' bodyguards. Chagas, a supporter of the Allies against Germany, was prevented from assuming office because of the seriousness of his wounds.

On July 28, 1915, **Jean Vilbrun Guillaume Sam**, the president of Haiti from March 4, 1915, was overthrown and murdered by a mob. Sam, who had led the revolution of January 1915, had previously executed more than 167 of his political opponents. Following a revolution against his oppressive rule, he took refuge in the French Legation in Port-au-Prince. An angry mob stormed the legation, dragging Sam into the streets. He was then impaled on the iron fence surrounding the legation and torn to pieces. His regime and the subsequent civil disorders led to American military intervention in August of 1915.

1916

On Easter Monday, April 24, 1916, the Easter Rising in Dublin took place, with the leaders of the rebellion proclaiming Ireland as an independent republic. The rebellion was quickly put down by the British, and many Republican leaders who took part were executed or imprisoned. The more prominent leaders killed included **Patrick Henry Pearse, James Connolly, Sir Roger David Casement**, and **Thomas MacDonagh** (1878–1916), a poet. Other insurgent leaders who were executed by firing squad within twelve days of the rising were **Tom Clarke, Joseph Plunkett, Edward Daly, Michael O'Hanrahan, Willie Pearse, John MacBride, Eamonn Ceannt, Michael Mallin, Sean Heuston, Cornelius Colbert**, and **Sean MacDermott**.

Patrick Pearse was born on November 10, 1879, in Dublin. He was a writer and poet of some renown when he became active in the movement for Irish independence. He was a proponent of a teaching system incorporating Irish traditions and culture, and, in 1906, founded St. Enda's College in Dublin based on these attributes. He also authored several essays on education. He was active in the Irish Republican Brotherhood, becoming a member of its ruling council in 1914. Later in the year, when the Republican movement splintered, Pearse became director of organization of the more extreme Nationalist faction. During World War I he opposed assistance to Great Britain. At the time of the Easter Rising, Pearse was commander-in-chief of the Nationalist forces, which announced independence. On the steps of the general post office in Dublin, Pearse proclaimed himself president of the Irish provisional government. On April 29, 1916, he surrendered to the British forces and, following a court-martial, was executed by firing squad on May 3, 1916, at Kilmainham Prison.

James Connolly was born on June 5, 1870, in County Monaghan, Ireland. As an early Irish Socialist leader, Connolly became active in the formation of trade unions, working with James Larkin. At the start of World War I, Connolly took charge of the Irish labor movement in Larkin's absence. He called for non-participation in the Allied war effort and the overthrow of all capitalistic states. He accompanied Pearse during the Easter Rising in Dublin. He was captured by the British and, on May 12, 1916, was executed at Kilmainham Prison.

Sir Roger David Casement was born in County Dublin on September 1, 1864. He became associated with the British consular service, serving as consul to various African colonies from 1892 to 1903. He also served in diplomatic posts in South America, notably Brazil, from 1906 to 1911. Casement gained an international reputation for his expose of the slave trade in areas in which he had served, particularly the Congo and Peru. His investigation in these matters led to changes in the colonial administration and earned Casement a knighthood in 1911. The following year he retired and returned to Ireland. He became active in Nationalist activities and opposed Irish assistance to Britain in World War I. During the war he undertook a mission to Germany to seek aid in achieving Irish independence. Casement, upon hearing of the proposed Easter Rising, returned to Ireland aboard a German submarine, bringing arms to the Irish rebels. The ship was captured, and Casement was arrested on April 24, 1916. He was tried and convicted of treason and, on August 3, 1916, was hanged in London at Pentonville Prison.

On October 21, 1916, **Count Karl Von Strukh**, who had served as Austria's prime minister from November 3, 1911, was shot and killed by Friedrich Adler (1879–1960) while eating lunch at a hotel dining room in Vienna. Adler, a Socialist and a scholar, claimed that he had killed the fifty-seven-old prime minister as a protest against World War I. He was convicted of the crime and sentenced to death. This sentence was subsequently commuted and, two years later, Adler was released from prison.

Sultan 'Ali Dinar of Darfur renounced his allegiance to the government of the Sudan in 1916, resulting in a battle with troops commanded by Lt. Col. P.J. Kelly near El Fasher in May of 1916. Dinar's army was routed, and the Sultan fled to Jabal Marrah, where he was killed on November 6, 1916.

Charles Foucauld, a French soldier and adventurer, was assassinated in North Africa on December 1, 1916. Foucauld was born on September 15, 1858, in Strasbourg. He served in the French army in Algeria before embarking on a personal exploration of North Africa and the Middle East. During this period he became interested in religion, and, in 1890, he became a Trappist monk. In 1897 he left the order and, in 1901, he was ordained into the priesthood. He then returned to North Africa, settling with the Tauregs in the Hoggar Mountains. He was largely responsible for retaining the area's loyalty to France, and it was for this reason that his assassination was accomplished by the rebellious Senusi in Tripoli.

On December 31, 1916, **Grigori E. Rasputin**, the Russian mystic and advisor to the court of Czar Nicholas II (q.v.), was murdered by a group of Russian noblemen who perceived him to be a baneful influence on the emperor. Rasputin was born in 1872 at Pokrovskoe, near Tyumen. At an early age he devoted himself to a life of religion, though of an unorthodox sort. Having a magnetic personality, and likely possessed of hypnotic powers, Rasputin gained a large following among the peasantry. In 1903 he began a pilgrimage to St. Petersburg, where he became a part of aristocratic circles. In 1905 he gained the attention of the court of the Romanovs. His efforts to comfort and cure the heir apparent, Alexis (q.v.), who suffered from hemophilia, won him the lasting gratitude of the Czarina Alexandra (q.v.). She considered him a great holy man who had been sent by God to ensure the czar's continued rule. Rasputin exercised his newly won powers by advocating strong, autocratic measures against the czar's opponents.

Following the outbreak of World War I and Nicholas' absence from the capital as field commander, Rasputin gained near absolute control of Russia through the empress. IIis debauchery and reputation for moral corruption brought him the hatred and contempt of many leading Russian politicians, and his position of power brought him the jealousy of many others. The major opposition to his influence was espoused by the rightists in the court, who eventually effected his execution. A group of conspirators, headed by Prince Felix F. Yousupov (1887–1967), took it upon themselves to dispose of Rasputin, feeling they were ridding the empire of a malevolent individual who threatened the entire dynasty. On the evening of December 30, 1916, Rasputin was lured to what he presumed to be a party at the home of Prince Yousupov. After an attempt to poison him had seemingly no effect, the conspirators shot and stabbed him. He was then bound and thrown, still alive, into the icy waters of a river, where he finally perished.

1917

Ivan Longinovich Goremykin (1839–1917), the Russian prime minister in 1906, and again during World War I (January 3, 1914–January 20, 1916), was executed by the Bolsheviks in the Caucasus in 1917. Goremykin, a supporter of the czar, had been arrested following the Revolution in March. Goremykin had also served as Russia's minister of the interior from 1895 to 1899.

Other leading Russian politicians were murdered during the year. **A.I. Shingarev** (1869–1917), a deputy of the fourth Duma and the minister of agriculture in the first cabinet of the Russian provisional government in 1917, was murdered. **F.F. Kokoshkin** (1871–1917), a deputy of the fourth Duma and member of the provisional government, was assassinated. **Admiral Nepenin** (1871–1917), the commander of the Russian Baltic Fleet, was also murdered in March.

Dragutin Dimitrijevic, a Serbian army officer and nationalist leader, was executed on June 27, 1917, along with two of his associates, **Ljobomir Vulovic** and **Rade Malobatic**. Dimitrijevic, who was also known as Colonel Apis, was born in August of 1876 in Belgrade. As a member of the army, he was active in the conspiracy that resulted in the assassination of King Alexander (q.v.) in 1903. He became a leading member of the cadre of officers that ruled the army under the new king. In 1911 he was the founder of the secret society known as "Union or Death," which sought the unification of all the Serbs. The society, commonly known as the Black Hand, was instrumental in the assassination of Archduke Francis Ferdinand (q.v.) in 1914. In December of 1916 Dimitrijevic was arrested on charges of attempting the assassination of the regent Alexander (q.v.). Though his guilt was not fully proved, it granted his political opponents the opportunity to remove a leading obstacle in the way of their control of the army, and Dimitrijevic's subsequent court-martial resulted in a sentence of death.

Mata Hari, the Dutch dancer who became a spy during World War I, died by firing squad on October 15, 1917. She was born Gertrude Zelle on August 7, 1876, in the Netherlands. She learned oriental dances while in Java with her husband, Capt. Campbell MacLeod. Following their divorce she returned to Europe and, taking the name of Mata Hari, began a career as a dancer. After settling in Paris in 1908, she soon became an agent of the German government, using her connections in French society and government circles to learn French military information. The French eventually learned of her intrigues and, in July of 1917, she was tried by a French court-martial and sentenced to death by firing squad.

1918

On July 16, 1918, **Gen. Count Wilhelm Von Mirbach-Harff**, the German ambassador to Moscow, was assassinated by two members of the Social Revolutionary party. Mirbach-Harff had become his nation's ambassador to Russia following the signing of the Brest Litovsk Treaty earlier in the year. His killing was intended to force resumption of hostilities with Germany and was followed by an attempted coup. The rising was suppressed, and peace was maintained by the two countries.

In mid–July much of the Russian royal family was executed by the Bolsheviks, who had held them in captivity since the Revolution of 1917.

Grand Duke Michael, the czar's younger brother, who had declined succession to the throne after Nicholas' abdication on March 15, 1917, was exiled to Perm in the Ural region in February of 1918. On July 13, 1918, the grand duke and his English secretary were murdered by Cheka agents under the leadership of Miasnikov. Their bodies were presumably burned, as they were never located.

On July 18, 1918, the Russian royal family was executed. **Czar Nicholas II**, his wife, the **Czarina Alexandra**, and their five children, the **Czarevitch Alexis** (1904–18) and the **Grand Duchesses Olga** (1895–1918), **Tatiana** (1897–1918), **Marie** (1899–1918), and **Anastasia** (1901–18), were all slain. Several members of their household were also executed with them in Ekaterinburg by a Bolshevik firing squad, led by Jakov Yurosky. The royal family had been held under arrest at various locations in Russia following the abdication of Nicholas on March 15, 1917.

Nicholas II was born on May 18, 1868, in Tsarkoe Selo, the eldest son of Czar Alexander III. Nicholas succeeded his father to the throne on November 1, 1894. On November 26 of that year, he married Alexandra. Nicholas' reign was marked by a growing discontent among the Russian people against the excesses of the crown. Nicholas' rule became increasingly autocratic in the face of these threats to his reign. In 1904 he involved his country in the Russo-Japanese War. His failure in that campaign the following year stymied his goal of making Russia a great Eurasian power. In 1905 he was forced to create a national legislative assembly, the Duma, in answer to increasing pressure by liberals. Nicholas, through his prime ministers, particularly Pytr Stolypin (q.v.), continued granting liberal reforms, but also continued to maintain a firm control of the Russian government.

He joined the Allied cause against Germany at the start of World War I in 1914. He replaced his uncle, the Grand Duke Nicholas, as commander-in-chief of the Russian army and, on September 5, 1915, assumed personal command. Popular discontent against both his foreign and domestic policies increased and, in March of 1917, following rioting in Petrograd, the government resigned and the Duma, backed by the army, called for Nicholas' abdication. On March 15, 1917, he relinquished his crown in favor of his brother Michael (q.v.), who refused to accept. The former czar and his family were detained at Tsarkoe Selo, then taken to Tobolsk, in western Siberia, and finally to Ekaterinburg (now Sverdlovk), where they were killed.

Alexandra, the wife of Nicholas II, was born on June 6, 1872, in Darmstadt, Germany. She was the daughter of Grand Duke Louis IV of Hesse-Darmstadt. She changed her name from Alix Victoria Helene Luise Beatrix to Alexandra Feodorovna on her marriage to the czar on November 26, 1894. In 1904, after having given birth to four daughters, she gave Nicholas a male heir to the throne, the Czarevitch Alexis. The czarevitch was a sickly child, suffering from hemophilia. His condition kept Alexandra in a constant state of nervous anxiety, and led her to place her faith in Grigori Rasputin (q.v.), a disreputable holy man who seemed to bring comfort to her son. Through Alexandra, Rasputin attained great influence in the court, which added to the discontent of the populace and the displeasure of Russian society.

Following the start of World War I and the czar's absence from the capital while serving as commander-in-chief of the army, Alexandra and Rasputin were left in virtual control of the government. Her German heritage nurtured the distrust of many prominent Russians, some even suspecting her as being an agent of the Germans. Rasputin's assassination in 1916 served only to make her more extreme in her belief of Nicholas' God-given right to rule. Her influence and unpopular nature were thus largely responsible for the Revolution of March 1917, following which she accompanied her husband and family to their exile and eventual death.

On July 17, 1918, the Russian **Grand Dukes Sergius Mikhailovich, Ivan Constantinovich, Constantine Constantinovich, and Igor Constantinovich,** the **Grand Duchess Elisabeth,** widow of Grand Duke Sergius Alexandrovich (q.v.), and **Prince Vladimir Paley,** the son of Grand Duke Paul, who were being held at Alapayevsk following the ouster of the monarchy, were brutally murdered by the Bolsheviks.

Herman Von Eichhorn (1848–1918), the German field marshal who led the Tenth Army against the Russians during World War I, was assassinated in the Ukraine on July 31, 1918. Eichhorn had also commanded the Eichhorn military group in Kurland from 1916 to 1918.

On August 13, 1918, **Moses S. Uritsky,** the local head of the Russian Bolshevik security police, or Cheka, was shot and killed by a Social Revolutionary student.

Vladimir Ilyich Lenin (1870–1924), who led the Bolshevik Revolution in Russia and served as premier of the Soviet Union from 1917, was seriously injured in an assassination attempt on August 30, 1918. Lenin was shot twice by Fanya Kaplan, a revolutionary. Kaplan was seized by guards and summarily executed. Lenin recovered from his injuries and returned to his duties as premier until his death in 1924.

Aleksandr D. Protopopov (1866–1918), the Russian czar's last minister of the interior, was executed in September of 1918. Protopopov had served as a member of the Octoberist party in the third and fourth Duma. An ally of Grigori Rasputin (q.v.), Protopopov was named as Russia's minister of the interior on October 1, 1916. His reactionary policies further inflamed the population against the government and the royal family. Following the Revolution of March 1917, Protopopov was arrested and imprisoned in the Peter and Paul Fortress. He was held there until his execution by the order of the Communist Cheka.

Many other leading Russian politicians were executed during the year by the Bolshevik regime. Those killed include **A.N. Khvostov** (1872–1918), the Russian minister of the interior from 1915 to 1916; **I.G. Shcheglovitov** (1861–1918), minister of justice from 1906 to 1915 and president of the state council in 1917; **N.A. Maklakov** (1871–1918), a member of the state council and minister of the interior from 1912 to 1915; **S.P. Beletsky** (1873–1918), deputy minister of the interior from 1916 to 1917; **N.A. Dobrovolsky** (1854–1918), minister of justice from October 1916 to February 1917; **Roman V. Malinovsky** (1878–1918), a Social Democratic deputy in the fourth Duma who worked as an agent for the interior ministry; **I.F. Manasevich-Maanuilov** (1869–1918), an agent of the Russian police; and **G.S.**

Khrustalev-Nosar (1877–1918), who served as chairman of the Petersburg Soviet in 1905. **Gen. Nikolai V. Russky** (1854–1918), the commander-in-chief of the Northern Front, was captured and shot by Bolshevik sailors in Kislovodsk. Russky's predecessor as Northern Front commander, **Pavel K. Rennenkampf** (1854–1918), was also executed by the Bolsheviks.

On October 31, 1918, **Count Istvan Tisza**, the former prime minister of Hungary, was murdered by a group of discharged soldiers who charged him with responsibility for involving Hungary in World War I. Tisza was born on April 22, 1861, in Pest. He was elected to Parliament in 1886 and, on November 3, 1903, he was named premier of Hungary. He served until June 18, 1905, when following free elections, he was soundly defeated due to his unpopular measures aimed at maintaining the Austro-Hungarian compromise of 1867. On June 10, 1913, following his establishment of the National Party of Work, Tisza was again named as prime minister. During this second term of office, Hungary entered World War I. Tisza resigned his office on June 5, 1917, but was still held largely responsible for Hungary's actions during the war.

Sidonio Bernardino Cardosa da Silva Paes (1872–1918), the Portuguese president, was shot and killed at a railway station in Lisbon on December 14, 1918. His assassin was immediately slain by a mob. Paes had been active in the republican movement and a member of the cabinet in 1911. He had served as Portugal's minister to Germany from 1913 to 1916 and was a leader in the 1917 revolt. He became provisional president of Portugal in December of 1917, and was confirmed in office through an election in June of 1918.

1919

On January 15, 1919, German Socialist leaders **Rosa Luxemburg** and **Karl Liebknecht** were arrested and murdered by right-wing Freikorps troops while being transferred to a West Berlin prison.

Rosa Luxemburg was born on March 5, 1870, in Russian Poland. She became involved in the Polish Socialist movement and was forced to flee to Switzerland to escape imprisonment for her political activities. In 1893 she became the leader of the Social Democratic Party of Poland with the non-nationalistic aim of spreading Socialism throughout Poland and the Soviet Union. In 1898 she settled in Germany, joining the German Social Democratic Party. She and Karl Liebknecht became leaders of the extreme left wing of the German Socialist movement. At the start of World War I in 1914, she and Liebknecht founded the Spartacus League to promote their view of establishing Communism through proletarian democracy. She was imprisoned during much of the war, but her writings still greatly influenced the socialist movement. Following her release from prison in November of 1918, Luxemburg was instrumental in transforming the Spartacus League into the German Communist party. Early the next year she was arrested and murdered.

Karl Liebknecht was born in Leipzig on August 13, 1871. He became involved with the extreme left wing of the Social Democratic party and became internationally known for his promotion of Socialism. He was elected to the German Reichstag in 1912. He opposed the German war effort in 1914, breaking with the leadership of the Social Democratic party in doing so. He was subsequently expelled from the party in early 1916 and arrested later in the year for his anti-war activities. On November 9, 1918, following his release from prison, Liebknecht declared Berlin a German Socialist Republic and, with Rosa Luxemburg, transformed their Spartacus League into the German Communist party. Shortly thereafter the Communist rising against the central government of Friedrich Ebert was crushed and Liebknecht, with Rosenburg, was arrested and murdered.

Grand Duke Nikolai Mikhailovich (1859–1919) of Russia, the grandson of Czar Nicholas I and a leading Russian historian, and **Grand Duke Paul Aleksandrovich** (1860–1919), the son of Czar Alexander II (q.v.), were executed in Petrograd on January 28, 1919. **Grand Duke George Michaelovich** and **Prince Dmitri Constantinovich** were also slain by the Bolsheviks at this time.

Habibullah Khan, the amir of Afghanistan from 1901, was shot to death on February 20, 1919, in the Laghman Valley by one of his subjects. Habibullah Khan was born in 1872 in Tashkent, the eldest son of Abd-er-Rahman Khan. He succeeded his father as amir in October of 1901. During his reign Habibullah did much to improve the conditions of his people, establishing the Habibia school and founding a weekly Persian paper, *Sairj-ul-Akhbar*. In international affairs he encouraged a friendly relationship with the British in India. He also maintained strict Afghan neutrality during World War I. He was assassinated at his hunting camp shortly after petitioning the British at the Paris Peace Conference to recognize the "absolute liberty, freedom of action and perpetual independence" of Afghanistan.

Kurt Eisner, a leading German Socialist politician, was assassinated in Munich by a German student on February 21, 1919. Eisner was born on May 14, 1867, in Berlin. He was a journalist on several German newspapers, including the *Frankefurter Zeitung* and the Berlin *Vorwarts*. In 1907 he became editor of the Nuremburg Socialist newspaper, *Socialist Frankische Tagespost*, serving until 1910, when he became a citizen of Bavaria. He joined the Independent Social Democratic party (USPD) in 1917, in opposition to the German war effort. He was instrumental in the Munich revolution of 1918 that resulted in the overthrow of the monarchy and, on November 7, 1918, he proclaimed the establishment of the Bavarian Republic, becoming its first prime minister and minister of foreign affairs. Three months later he was assassinated in Munich by Count A. von Arco-Valley, a right-wing student.

Emiliano Zapata, the Mexican revolutionary leader, was ambushed and killed on April 10, 1919. Zapata was born in Anenecuilco, Morelos, Mexico in 1877. He was active in Francisco Madero's (q.v.) revolution against President Porfirio Diaz in 1910. Zapata continued the revolution after the fall of Diaz and into the administrations of Maderos, Victoriano Huerta and Venustiano Carranza (q.v.). Zapata was a proponent of agrarian reform and continued to pressure the government to accede to his demands for a fair distribution of land to the poor. He allied himself with Pancho Villa (q.v.) from 1914 and 1915 and maintained control of the province of Morelos during much of his rebel activities. He was ambushed and killed by Jesus Guajardo, acting under the orders of a Carranza ally, Gen. Pablo Gonzalez.

On April 12, 1919, **Otto Neuring**, the German Socialist war minister of Saxony, was assassinated in Dresden by soldiers protesting a pay cut.

Radko Dmitriev (1859–1919), a Bulgarian-born Russian army general, was captured and murdered by the Bolsheviks in 1919.

Hugo Haase (1863–1919), a German Socialist leader and president of the German Social Democratic party, was assassinated in Berlin by right-wing gunmen on October 8, 1919. Haase had served as a member of the German Reichstag in 1897 and organized the independent Socialist party in 1917, in disagreement with the government's war policy. He served as a member of a coalition cabinet from November till December of 1918.

1920

On February 7, 1920, **Aleksandr V. Kolchak**, the Russian naval officer who led the "White" Russian forces from 1918 to 1920, was executed by the Bolsheviks. Kolchak was born in 1873 and had served in World War I as a rear admiral, commanding the Black Sea fleet. Following the Revolution of June of 1917, he went to the United States for a period, then returned to Omsk, in Russia, where he became absolute ruler of the White Russian forces there. Though his armies were initially successful in battling the Bolshevik forces, later military reversals and the loss of support from the

Allies resulted in the fall of Omsk on November 14, 1919. Moving his command post to Irkutsk, Kolchak was forced to resign his position on January 4, 1920, following an insurrection there. He was captured by the Bolsheviks soon after and executed. His body was thrown into the Angara River.

Venustiano Carranza, a Mexican revolutionist and president, was murdered on May 21, 1920. Carranza was born on December 29, 1859, in Cuatro Cienegas, Coahula, Mexico. He became active in local politics, taking part in the revolt in Coahula in 1893. He served in numerous state offices, including municipal president, state senator, national deputy, and national senator. He was governor at the time of the 1911 Revolution in which he supported Francisco Madero (q.v.). He led the "Constitutionalist" army following the overthrow of Madero in 1913, and, with the assistance of Alvaro Obregon (q.v.) and Pancho Villa (q.v.), he forced the ouster of Gen. Victoriano Huerta in July of 1914. Civil war continued with battles among the former allies. The defeat of Villa in 1915 solidified Carranza's claim to power as provisional president. On May 1, 1917, Carranza became the constitutional president of Mexico. Near the end of his term of office, in December of 1920, Carranza attempted to pass the presidency on to a hand-picked candidate. This resulted in a split with Obregon, who started a revolt in April 1920. Carranza's forces were defeated and forced to retreat from Mexico City. On May 21, 1920, he was ambushed and murdered by forces of Rodolfo Herrera at Tlaxcalaltongo, Puebla.

Albanian politician **Essad Pasha** was assassinated on June 13, 1920, by Avni Rustem, an Albanian, at the Hotel Continental in Paris. Essad Pasha was born in 1864 in Tirana, Albania. He became active in politics and served as an Albanian deputy in the Turkish parliament under the Young Turks in 1908. He betrayed his country in 1913 by turning over his military command at Shkoder to Montenegro. He then served as minister of interior and war at Durres, but was forced to flee after having attempted to betray them to the Italians. He was recognized as leader of the Albanian government in exile by the French during World War I, but his further political ambitions were cut short by his assassination.

1921

Nikolai S. Gumilev (1886–1921), a leading Russian poet and a founder of the Acmeiest school of poetry in 1912, was executed by the Bolsheviks in 1921 for allegedly conspiring against the government. Gumilev's poems include those found in the collection *The Pillar of Fire* (1912).

Premier **Eduardo Dato Iradier** of Spain was assassinated by anarchists in Madrid on March 8, 1921. Dato was born on August 12, 1856, in Corunna.

He served as minister of interior from 1899 to 1900, minister of justice from 1902 to 1903, and mayor of Madrid in 1907. On October 27, 1913, he formed a Conservative government and served as premier until December 6, 1915. His first term in office was marked by his success in keeping Spain neutral during World War I. He again served as premier from June 9 till October 27, 1917, and was minister of foreign affairs in 1918. On May 5, 1920, he once again became premier. His attempts to mediate a solution to the political crisis in Catalonia and heal the rifts in the Conservative party were cut short by his assassination.

On March 15, 1921, Turkish political leader **Mehmed Talat Pasha** was shot and killed while in exile in Berlin. Mehmed Talat Pasha was born in 1874 in Edirne, Turkey, and became a leader of the Young Turk movement during the Revolution. In 1909 he became minister of the interior and later president of the Society of Union and Progress, the Young Turks' political party. He again served as minister of the interior at the start of World War I, and became grand vizier in 1917. Talat was considered responsible for the Turkish policy of genocide against Armenians, in which more than 500,000 were reported massacred. He went into exile following Turkey's defeat in 1918. His assassin, Saro Melikian (1897–1960), was an Armenian who claimed to have acted in revenge for his people. He confessed to the crime, but was acquitted of the murder by a German court.

Karl Gareis, a Socialist deputy in the Bavarian Landtag, was shot to death in front of his Munich home by a member of the right-wing paramilitary Einwohnerwehr on June 10, 1921.

Milorad Draskovic (1873–1921), minister of the interior for the provisional Yugoslavian government from 1920, was shot and killed by a Bosnian Communist on July 21, 1921. Draskovic had retired earlier in the year following a previous unsuccessful attempt on his life.

V.D. Nabokov (1870–1921), a Russian law professor who served as head of the chancellery of the provisional government in 1917, was assassinated by right-wing extremists in 1921.

German statesman **Matthias Erzberger** was shot and killed by nationalists on August 26, 1921. Erzberger was born in Wurttemberg on September 20, 1875. He became a member of the German Reichstag in 1903, establishing himself as the leader of the left wing of the Center party. He opposed the German war policy and was a proponent of a negotiated peace. In 1918 he became secretary of state without portfolio and chaired the armistice commission later in the year. He resigned his office in 1920, following charges of questionable financial practices while in office. He was assassinated while vacationing in the Black Forest. His assassins were not brought to trial until the conclusion of World War II in the late 1940s.

Baron Roman Nikolaus von Ungern-Sternberg (1885–1921), a Russian Czarist army general who fought against the Bolsheviks in Eastern Siberia, was captured and shot on September 18, 1921.

On October 19, 1921, **Dr. Antonio Granjo** (1881–1921), who had served as Portugal's premier from August 28, 1921, and, earlier, from July 17 to November 16, 1920, was assassinated with **Antonio Machado Dos Santos**, a founder of the Portuguese Republic and member of the ruling triumvirate in 1917. **Jose Carlos De Maia**, former government minister of marine and of the colonies, and **Carlos Silva** were also killed during rioting in Lisbon by a band of men in sailors' uniforms.

Prime Minister **Takashi Hara** of Japan was stabbed to death by a young assassin on November 4, 1921, near the Tokyo train station. Hara was born on February 9, 1856, in Morioka. He became minister of communications in 1900, and served in the House of Representatives from 1902. He twice served as home minister, in 1905 and 1911, and became leader of the Seiyukai party in 1914. On September 29, 1918, Hara became premier of Japan, serving until his death.

Former Turkish grand vizier **Said Halim Pasha** was slain by an Armenian in Rome on December 6, 1921. Said Halim Pasha was born in Cairo in 1863, and became a member of the state judicial council in 1888, becoming its president in 1911. Later in the year he became foreign minister, serving in that position until the assassination of Mahmud Shevket (q.v.), the grand vizier. Said Halim succeeded Shevket and, during his term, opposed Turkey's entry into World War I. He resigned his position in 1916, becoming a member of the Senate. He was sent into exile following the signing of the armistice in 1918.

1922

Heikki Ritavuori, the Finnish interior minister, was assassinated by right-wing extremists in 1922.

Ahmet Jemal Pasha, a Turkish army officer and political leader, was killed in 1922 by Armenian nationalists while traveling to Tbilisi. Jemal was born in Istanbul in 1872. He served in the army and became a member of the military administration in Istanbul following the revolution of 1908. During World War I Jemal was recognized as one of the three most powerful figures in the Turkish government. He was unsuccessful in his attempt to invade Egypt in 1914 and was later made governor of Syria. Following the armistice of 1918, Jemal went into exile in Germany, and later accepted a position to train the Afghan army. He death was the result of his barbarous treatment of Armenians during his term of office in Syria.

On January 22, 1922, British army officer **Sir Henry Hughes Wilson** was slain by two Irish Nationalists in front of his London home. Wilson was born in County Longford, Ireland, on May 5, 1854. Joining the army, he served in Burma from 1885 to 1887 and fought in the South African war from 1899 to 1902. He became commandant of the Camberley Staff College in 1907 and, in 1910, served as director of military operations. In this position he was a proponent of military cooperation with France in the event of war in Europe. In 1914 and 1915 he served as the British liaison officer with the French army headquarters and became a member of the Allied Supreme War Council in 1917. He became chief of the British general staff in February, 1918, and was promoted to field marshal in 1919. In 1922 he left his position in the army and was elected to Parliament from Northern Ireland, where his position on Ireland earned him the enmity of the Sinn Fein and cost him his life. Two members of the Irish Republican Army, Reginald Dunne and Joseph O'Sullivan, were tried and convicted of Wilson's assassination. They were hanged in Wandsworth Prison.

On January 24, 1922, German statesman and industrialist **Walther Rathenau** was killed in Germany by right-wing nationalists while going to his office. Rathenau was born in Berlin on September 29, 1867. He became a director of the family-owned Allgemeine Elektrizitats-Gesellschaft, a leading German power industry, in 1899. He became the company's president in 1915. During World War I Rathenau was instrumental in managing the disposition of raw materials needed for the war effort. He was active in preparing the German delegation to the Versailles Peace Conference in 1919 and the London Conference of 1921. He served as minister of reconstruction in 1921 and was the German representative to the Cannes Conference of 1922. As Germany's foreign minister, he signed the Rapallo Treaty with Russia. His career earned him the admiration of many, but the hatred of the fanatical nationalist elements. Soon after Rathenau's murder his two assailants were killed during a shoot-out with the police while trying to flee the country.

Irish Republic leader **Michael Collins** was ambushed and murdered on August 22, 1922, near Brandon in County Cork, Ireland. Collins was born on October 16, 1890, in County Cork. He joined the Irish Republican Brotherhood in 1909, and particiapted in the Easter Rising in 1916. Following a short time in prison for his part in the revolt, Collins quickly became a leader of the Sinn Fein movement. As minister of home affairs in the Sinn Fein government, he planned and conducted the escape of Eamon de Valera, the leader of the Sinn Feiners, from Lincoln Jail in 1919. From 1919 to 1922 he served as Sinn Fein minister of finance, and remained in this position following the peace treaty with Great Britain. With Ireland in a state of civil war, Collins, as commander-in-chief of the army, became head of state of the Irish Free State following the death of President Arthur Griffith on August 12, 1922. It was during the course of the Civil War that Collins was ambushed and killed by rebellious forces.

Lama Bodo, the head of the Mongolian government from March 13, 1921, was arrested by the Soviet political police in April of 1922. He and fifteen other Mongolian political leaders were executed as alleged Chinese spies.

On November 24, 1922, **Robert Erskine Childers**, the Irish writer and Republican leader, was tried and executed during the Irish Civil War. Childers, who was born in London on June 25, 1870, had been active in the struggle for Ireland's independence. He was well known as a novelist and authored *The Riddle of the Sands* in 1903. He fought with British forces during World War I, and served in the 1917 convention to determine home rule for Ireland. As a Sinn Fein deputy, he was active in the negotiations concerning the Anglo-Irish treaty, but did not support the final agreement. He joined the Republican dissenters in the subsequent Civil War, and was tried and executed after being arrested for possessing an unauthorized pistol.

Dimitrios Gounaris, who had served as prime minister of Greece in 1915 and again from 1921 to 1922, was executed by order of Gen. Nikolaos Plastiras after an anti–Royalist revolution. Gounaris was court-martialed and killed on November 28, 1922, along with **Petros Protopapadakis** (1860–1922) and **Nikolaos Stratos** (1872–1922), both prime ministers of Greece during 1922. Also executed were **Theotokis**, the former Greek war minister, **Baltassiz**, a former cabinet minister, and **Gen. Hadjanestis**, the former commander of the Greek armed forces. The Greek leaders were tried in connection with the Greek military disaster in Asia Minor.

Gabriel Narutowicz was killed by a madman on December 16, 1922, two days after assuming office as the first president of the Polish Republic. Narutowicz was born in 1865 at Teleze, Samogitia. He first became active in politics in June of 1920, serving as minister of public works and, later, minister of foreign affairs. On December 9, 1922, Narutowicz was elected to the presidency after a bitter campaign against the nationalists. he was shot three times in the back by Niewadomski, a deranged artist, while attending an exhibition of paintings at the Palace of Fine Arts. His assassin was tried, sentenced to death, and executed.

1923

Nicolai Genadiev, a member of the Bulgarian cabinet, was assassinated in 1923.

Suhe Baato, a leader of the Mongolian People's party's armed forces, was poisoned on February 22, 1923.

Vaslov V. Vorovsky (1871–1923), a Bolshevik politician and diplomat who had served as the Soviet minister in Rome, was assassinated on May 10, 1923, in Switzerland.

Cardinal Soldevilla y Romero, the Roman Catholic archbishop of Saragossa, Spain, since 1901, was shot and killed by two young assassins on June 4, 1923. As the Vatican's spokesman in Spain and a leading reactionary, the cardinal had gained many enemies among Republicans and Socialists. Soldevilla y Romero was seated in his car at a monastery near Saragossa at the time of his murder. His assassins were two anarchists, Francisco Ascaso and Buenaventura Durruti (q.v.), both of whom were killed in the early days of the Spanish Civil War.

Aleksandr Stamboliski, a Bulgarian stateman and former prime minister, was slain by his opponents on June 14, 1923. Stamboliski was born on March 1, 1879, in Slavovitsa, and was an early member of the Agrarian League, serving as editor of its newspaper. He was elected to the Narodno Sobranye (National Assembly) in 1908 as leader of the Agrarian party. His political activities often brought him into conflict with King Ferdinand, resulting in his imprisonment prior to Bulgaria's entry in World War I. In September of 1918 he was released from prison and led rebel troops to the capital, forcing the king's abdication. Stamboliski joined the cabinet of King Boris III (q.v.) in January of 1919, and became prime minister on October 19 of that year. After nearly four years of exercising nearly absolute power in Bulgaria, Stamboliski was ousted in a military coup on June 9, 1923. While attempting to flee the country, he was captured and shot.

Gen. Juan Cristonomo Gomez, who had been named vice president of Venezuela the previous year by President Juan Vicente Gomez, was assassinated in his sleep in Caracas on June 29, 1923.

On July 20, 1923, **Francisco "Pancho" Villa**, the Mexican bandit and revolutionary leader, was shot and killed in Parral, Chihuahua. Pancho Villa was born Doroteo Arango on June 5, 1878, in Durango, Mexico. He spent his early life as the leader of a group of bandits. In 1910 he joined Francisco Madero's (q.v.) revolution against the regime of Gen. Porfirio Diaz. In 1912 Villa was sentenced to death while serving in the army under Gen. Victoriano Huerta. His sentence was commuted, and Villa escaped from prison and went to the United States. He returned to Mexico following the death of Madero and joined forces with Venustiano Carranza (q.v.) in battle against Huerta. Following Huerta's defeat in 1914, Villa and Carranza began battling among themselves. Carranza defeated Villa's forces in 1915. Villa continued to harass both the Mexican and United States governments with a series of raids across the United States border. Brig. Gen. John J. Pershing was sent to Mexico to capture Villa for his activities north of the border, but failed in his mission. Following the overthrow of Carranza in 1920, Villa retired from his revolutionary activities and received a ranch in Durango from the government. It was during his period of retirement that he was ambushed and killed by a group of gunmen led by Mexican congressman Jesus Salas Barrazas (d. 1957). Barrazas was convicted of the murder, but served virtually no time in prison for the crime.

1924

Heinz Orbis, the German pro–French separatist leader in the Rhenish Palatinate, was shot to death in 1924 in Speyer by four right-wing nationalists while dining in a hotel restaurant. Four of his colleagues were also killed during the attack.

Petko Petkov, who had succeeded the slain Aleksandr Stamboliski (q.v.) as head of the Bulgarian party, was shot and killed by political opponents in the streets of Sofia in 1924.

On June 10, 1924, Italian Socialist leader **Giacomo Matteotti** was kidnapped by Fascists in Rome. He was taken outside of the city and brutally murdered. His body was not discovered until August 16. Matteotti was born on May 22, 1885, in Rovigo, Italy. He was first elected to the Chamber of Deputies as a member of the Italian Socialist party in May of 1919. Shortly before his death he also became the secretary general of the Socialist party. Matteotti was a leading critic of the Fascists and of Benito Mussolini (q.v.). His murder provoked numerous anti–Fascist demonstrations, but with little result. The six Fascists who perpetrated the crime were identified as Amerigo Dumini, Augusto Malacria, Filippo Panzeri, Amleto Poveromo, Giuseppe Viola, and Albino Volpi. They were alleged to have been hired by Fascist leaders Cesare Rossi, Francisco Giunta, Giovanni Marinelli (q.v.), and Filippo Filippelli. Following a trial in 1926, light sentences were handed down to those assassins tried and not acquitted. Another trial in 1947, after World War II, resulted in a sentence of 30 years imprisonment for Dumini, Poveromo, and Viola.

In August 1914, **Danzan Khorlo**, a leader of the Mongolian People's party and commander-in-chief of the Mongolian army, was executed as a "Japanese spy" following an "anti–Russian" speech made at the Mongolian People's party's third congress in Urya.

On August 31, 1924, **Todor Aleksandrov**, a Macedonian nationalist and leader of the Internal Macedonian Revolutionary Organization (IMRO), was assassinated. Aleksandrov had been instrumental in aligning the IMRO with other nationalist organizations and had signed an agreement with Bulgarian Communists to attempt to form a Balkan federation, with Macedonia as an integral part. He was murdered en route to an IMRO meeting, where he hoped to explain his position. His assassination caused an increase of violence within Macedonia.

Sir Lee Stack, the British governor-general of the Sudan and the sirdar (commander-in-chief) of the English-trained Egyptian army, was shot to death on November 19, 1924, in Cairo.

1925

Gen. Kosta Georgiev, a high-ranking Bulgarian army officer, was shot and killed on April 15, 1925, while outside the war ministry. Georgiev's assassination followed an unsuccessful attempt on the life of King Boris III (q.v.). At Georgiev's funeral at the cathedral of Sveta Nedelya, in Sofia, a bomb exploded, killing nearly 125 people. The government proclaimed martial law and executed five persons for the crime.

In May of 1925 **Boris V. Savinkov** (1879–1925), a leading Russian revolutionary, died in prison. His death was officially announced as a suicide. Savinkov had joined the Socialist-Revolutionary party in 1903. He had been active in the assassination of Interior Minister Plehve (q.v.) in 1904. Savinkov served in the army during World War I and, in 1917, as deputy minister of war, became one of the most powerful figures in the provisional government. Following the Bolshevik revolution, Savinkov went into exile in Paris, seeking Allied help in toppling the Bolshevik regime. He returned to Russia on August 18, 1924, and was promptly arrested, tried, and sentenced to death. His sentence was commuted to life imprisonment at Lubyanka Prison. A year later he was dead.

1926

Giovanni Amendola, an Italian journalist, died in Cannes, France, on April 6, 1926, as a result of injuries inflicted on him by Fascists who had attacked him at Montecatini, an Italian spa. Amendola, who was born in Rome on April 15, 1882, was a leading opponent of Fascism. He was elected to Parliament in 1919, and, in 1922, served as the Italian minister for colonies. Following the assumption of power by Benito Mussolini (q.v.), Amendola frequently attacked the dictator in a series of columns in his newspaper, *Il Mondo*. He withdrew from Parliament following the murder of Giacomo Matteotti (q.v.) in 1924, and continued to oppose Mussolini and Fascism until his death.

Simon Petlyura, the Ukranian nationalist leader, was shot to death in Paris on May 25, 1926. Petlyura was born on May 17, 1879, in Poltava. He became active in Ukrainian political affairs and was the publisher of several nationalist newspapers. During World War I, Petlyura served as an officer in the Russian army. He joined the Ukrainian Central Council following the Russian Revolution of 1917, serving as minister of defense. As leader of the Ukranian army following the German occupation, Petlyura enlisted the aid of Poland in the hopes of securing an independent Ukraine. Polish assistance was not sufficient, and Petlyura was forced to establish a government in exile in Paris. There he was assassinated by Shalom Schwarzbard, who was seeking vengeance for the persecution of Ukrainian Jews.

On August 26, 1926, Javid Bey (1875–1926), a leading Turkish politician, was executed in Turkey for plotting against the regime of Mustafa Kemal. Javid was a member of the Committee of Union and Progress and had served as minister of finance and public works in several Turkish cabinets. Dr. Nazim Kemal, another early Committee of Union and Progress member, was also put to death at this time.

1927

Kevin Christopher O'Higgins was shot to death near Dublin on July 10, 1927. O'Higgins was born in Queen's County, Ireland, on June 7, 1882. He joined the Sinn Fein movement in 1916. Following the Easter Rising, he was arrested. While imprisoned he was first elected to Parliament. As a member of the revolutionary Dail, O'Higgins supported the creation of the Irish Free State in 1921. He served as minister of economic affairs in the first provisional government in 1922, and became vice president of the Executive Council in 1923. He was the founder and leader of the Civil Guard, established to restore order during the insurrection by the republicans. A proponent of Ireland's continued membership in the British Commonwealth, O'Higgins also served on the committee which created the Irish Constitution. He was murdered amidst the continuing controversy surrounding Ireland's relationship to Great Britain.

On August 23, 1927, **Nicola Sacco** (1891–1927) and **Bartolomeo Vanzetti** (1888–1927), were executed in the electric chair after having been convicted of robbery and murder in a 1921 trial. The two Italian immigrants had been accused of robbing a Massachusetts shoe company paymaster and killing him and his guard on April 15, 1920. The defendants were anarchists, and it was believed that their radical political beliefs were instrumental in their conviction. The trial was widely denounced by Socialists and others who believed Sacco and Vanzetti did not recieve a fair trial. The Massachusetts Supreme Court denied a new trial on appeal in 1927. A three-man special panel appointed by Massachusetts governor Alvan T. Fuller ruled that proper judicial procedures had been followed in the original trial and that the two men should be executed as sentenced.

In October of 1927, Mexican army officers and politicians who opposed the anti–Catholic policies of the regime of President Plutarco Elias Calles and the presumed election of his hand-picked candidate, Gen. Alvaro Obregon (q.v.), in the presidential campaign, broke out in open revolt against the government. The revolution was quickly put down and many of the leaders were captured and executed. **Gen. Francisco Serrano** and **Gen. Arnulfo R. Gomez**, the zone commandant of the Mexican State of Vera Cruz, both of whom were considered leading opposition candidates against Gen. Obregon for the election scheduled in 1928, were among those executed. **Gen. Alfredo Rueda Quijano**, **Gen. Adalberto Palacios**, **Col. Salvado Costanos**, **Maj. Francisco Meza Perez** and several dozen other generals and legislators were also executed during October and November.

Jesuit priest **Miguel Pro** was executed on November 23, 1927, after being accused of conspiracy against Mexican president Alvaro Obregon (q.v.). Pro was born in Concepcion del Oro, Zacatecas, Mexico, on January 13, 1891. In 1911 he joined the Jesuit order, but was forced to flee Mexico under the anti-clerical measures of President Carranza (q.v.) in 1914. He did not return to his homeland until 1926 and was then still required to stay in hiding and conduct worship services in secret. After three years of clandestine operations, he was located by the Mexican authorities and condemned with little evidence of his guilt.

1928

Gen. Luis Mena, who had served as acting president of Nicaragua in 1910, was assassinated in Ponelova on May 20, 1928. Mena, who led the revolt against President Jose Santos Zelaya in 1909, became acting president of Nicaragua in early 1910 after Zelaya fled the country. He relinquished the presidency shortly afterward to Juan M. Estrada, and served in the new administration as minister of war. Following United States intervention, Estrada was forced to leave office, and Adolfo Diaz became president. In November of 1911 Gen. Mena was selected as president by the Nicaraguan Congress, but the election was nullified, and Diaz resumed the office. Mena began an insurrection against Diaz, but was forced to flee to Panama, where he remained until 1913. At the time of his death he was actively supporting the candidacy of Gen. Maria Jose Moncada, the Liberal party nominee, for the presidency.

On June 20, 1928, **Stefan Radic** (1871–1928), the founder and leader of the Croatian Peasant party, was assassinated in Parliament with his nephew, **Paul Radic**, and **Dr. George Basaritchik**. Radic had served as a member of the legislature of Yugoslavia and was minister of education from 1925 to 1926.

Alvaro Obregon, the former president of Mexico, was shot to death on July 17, 1928, shortly before taking office to serve another term. Obregon was born in Sonora on February 19, 1890. In 1912 he supported the presidency of Francisco Madero (q.v.) against revolutionists. Following Madero's overthrow, Obregon joined with Gen. Venustiano Carranza (q.v.) and led the forces which defeated the usurper, Gen. Victoriano Huerta. He remained allied with Carranza against the later rebellions of Villa, Zapata, and Leon after Huerta's overthrow, defeating them in a series of battles. He remained in command of the army during most of Carranza's presidency from 1915. When Carranza attempted to handpick a successor in the elections of 1920, Obregon was instrumental in leading the revolt which overthrew him. On December 1, 1920, Obregon was himself elected president. During his administration he instituted a number of reforms that threatened Mexico's relationship with the United States, which did not recognize his government until 1913. In the same year Mexico was again faced with a rebellion, led by Adolfo de la Huerta. Obregon quickly reestablished order and left office peacefully at the end of his term in 1924. In 1928 Obregon again ran for the presidency, being elected after his major opponents had been executed following an abortive military uprising. At a victory party in his honor held in Sonora, he was slain by Jose de Leon Toral, who claimed Obregon was responsible for the persecution of Roman Catholics in Mexico.

On October 10, 1928, **Chang Tso-Lin**, the Chinese warlord of Manchuria, was killed by a bomb planted by Japanese extremists. Chang was born in Fengtien Province in 1873. He joined the Chinese army in 1905 and, in 1911, became the military governor of Fengtien. In 1918, with the assistance of the Japanese, Chang gained control of three major provinces in Manchuria. He led his forces in an attempt to capture the capital of Peking, but was driven back to Manchuria by Wu P'ei-fu. In 1924 he again challenged the armies of Gen. Wu, this time meeting with success. Shortly after this victory, Gen. Wu joined with Chang to put down a rebellion led by Feng Yu-hsiang, a former ally of Wu who had abandoned him in his previous encounter with Chang. This victory established Chang as the military ruler of northern China. In 1927 his armies were challenged by Chiang Kai-shek, leading the armies of the Kuomintang Nationalists. After a series of military setbacks, Chang was forced to abandon Peking and again retreat to Manchuria. Shortly thereafter he was killed by Japanese extremists while traveling by rail. The assassins felt his elimination would result in the Japanese occupation of Manchuria. His position was assumed by his son, Chang Hsueh-liang.

1929

In 1929 **Habibullah Ghazi**, a brigand chief formerly known as Bacha Sakao, or "The Water Carrier," deposed King Amanullah Khan of Afghanistan in January of the year. During his brief reign Habibullah executed many prominent Afghanistani politicians including two of the deposed emperor's brothers and **Mohammed Osman**, the former governor of Kandahar and a leading advisor to the former emperor. Habibullah was in turn ousted by an army led by the ex-king's cousin, Mohammed Nadir Shah (q.v.). Nadir Shah defeated the forces of Habibullah in Kabul on October 13, and subsequently executed the usurper and many of his followers.

1930

During 1930 the first Stalin purge trials in the Ukraine took place. Thirteen Ukrainian leaders, including **Serhiy Efremov**, were tried and executed.

In February of 1930, **Nguyen Thai Hoc**, the leader of the pro-independence Viet Nam Quoc Dan Dang, or Vietnam Nationalist party, was guillotined with twelve of his followers by the French colonial authorities. Nguyen Thai Hoc was executed shortly after a rebellion by Vietnamese soldiers at the French garrison at Yen Bay.

On June 7, 1930, **Dr. Albert von Baligand**, the German minister to Portugal, was assassinated in Lisbon.

Prince Yuko Hamaguchi (1870–1931), the prime minister of Japan, was shot and seriously wounded by a right-wing assassin on November 14, 1930. Hamaguchi died six months later of the wounds. He had served as vice minister of finance from 1914 to 1916 and finance minister from 1924 to 1925. Hamaguchi was also minister of home affairs from 1927 to 1929. He had become prime minister on July 2, 1929, and served till his death on March 10, 1931.

1931

The Stalin purge trials continued in the Ukraine during 1931. During the trial of the "National Centre" many politicians, including **Vsevolod Holubovych**, were sentenced to death.

On March 23, 1931, **Sardar Bhagat Singh** (1907–31), an Indian revolutionary, was executed. Singh was the founder and first secretary of the Naujawan Bharat Sabha, or Indian Youth Association, in 1925. In 1928 Singh was active in the formation of Hindustan Socialist Republican Association, and took part in the murder of J.P. Saunders, a Lahore police officer, on December 17, 1928. In April of 1929 Singh and another revolutionary bombed the Indian Legislative Assembly. Singh was arrested following this incident and sentenced to life imprisonment. He was later tried for the murder of the police official and received a death sentence. He was executed with two other revolutionaries.

1932

Junnosuke Inouye (1869–1932), the Japanese minister of finance, was slain on February 9, 1932, by a young member of the ultra-nationalist "League of Blood" as he was entering a meeting hall in Tokyo to give a speech. Inouye had also served as governor of the Bank of Japan in 1924 and from 1927 until 1928.

On March 5, 1932, **Dan Takuma**, a leading Japanese businessman, was assassinated at his office by nationalists who resented the powerful role of high finance in the Japanese government. Takuma was born in 1858 and studied mining engineering in the United States. From 1888 Takuma worked with the House of Mitsui and joined the Mitsui Trading Company following its founding in 1909. His success brought increased wealth and power to the Mitsui family, and, during the 1920s, Takuma was considered one of the most powerful figures in Japan.

Paul Doumer, the president of the French Republic, was assassinated on May 6, 1932. Doumer was born at Aurillac on March 22, 1857. He served in the Chamber of Deputies from 1888 to 1895 as a member of the Radical party. He was France's minister of finance from 1895 to 1896. He was appointed the governor general of French Indo-China in January of 1897, serving until 1902, when he was again elected to the chamber of deputies. He became president of the chamber in 1905, and was defeated for the presidency of the republic in 1906. He served in the French cabinet in 1917, and was again minister of finance 1921–22 and 1925–26. He served as president of the senate 1927–31 and, in May of 1931, was elected the thirteenth president of the French Third Republic. The following year he was assassinated by Paul Gorgoulov, a Russian exile in Paris.

Japanese prime minister **Ki Tsuyoshi Inukai** was assassinated on May 16, 1932, when nine young officers broke into his home and shot him in the neck and stomach. Inukai, who was born in 1855, had an early career as a journalist. In 1890 he became a Conservative party member of the first House of Representatives in the Imperial Diet. On December 13, 1931, Inukai became Japan's prime minister. His killing was intended to give more power to the armed forces. His assailants, including Lt. Yamagishi, their leader, were all tried and convicted of his death, but served no time in prison.

In 1932 **Sidi 'Umar Al-Mukhtar**, a Bedouin Sanusiya sheikh, was captured by Italian troops under the command of Marshal Rodolfo Graziani (q.v.), and executed. Mukhtar had led a decade-long war against the Italian colonization of Libya.

1933

During 1933 the Stalin purge trials continued in the Ukraine. **Yury Kotsiubinsky**, the deputy premier of the Ukrainian Communist government, and other prominent Ukrainian leaders, were tried and executed on orders of the Soviet secret police.

Prof. Theodor Lessin, a German writer and teacher, was murdered in 1933 in the Czechoslovakian spa of Marianske Lazne by agents of Adolf Hitler. Lessin, a champion of pacifism and humanitarianism, had become a prominent target of German nationalists.

On February 15, 1933, an assassination attempt was made against United States president-elect Franklin D. Roosevelt (1882–1945), following a speech made from a motorcade at Miami Bayfront Park in Florida. Guiseppe Zangara (1901–33), an Italian immigrant and anti-capitalist, missed his target, instead shooting **Anton J. Cermak** (1873–1933), the mayor of Chicago, who was one of the dignitaries greeting Roosevelt. Cermak, who had served as Chicago's mayor from 1931, died of his wounds on March 6. Zangara was tried and, on March 20, electrocuted.

Luis M. Sanchez Cerro, the president of Peru, was shot and killed on April 30, 1933. Sanchez Cerro was born in 1889 in Piura. He spent most of his youth engaged in plots against the government, culminating in 1930, when he led a military-civilian coup against President Augusto Leguia y Salcedo. He served as provisional president of Peru from August 1930 until March 1931, when a naval junta forced him from office. In a presidential election held later in the year he defeated Victor Haya De la Torre, the leader of the Alianza Popular Revolucionaria American (APRA). Sanchez Cerro took office in December of 1931 and waged a campaign to destroy APRA, which he considered the greatest threat to his regime. A violent struggle ensued between his administration and his political enemies, ending with Sanchez Cerro's assassination by Abelardo Hurtado de Mendoza, an APRA member, who was subsequently slain by presidential guards.

On June 6, 1933, **Assis Khan**, the fifty-six-year-old elder brother of King Nadir (q.v.) of Afghanistan, was shot and killed by an Afghanistani student in Berlin.

Sardar Mohammed Nadir Khan, the king of Afghanistan, was himself the victim of an assassination on November 8, 1933. Nadir Khan was born in 1880 and served as the Afghan minister in Paris from 1924 to 1926. He returned from France in 1929 after his cousin, King Amanullah, was deposed by the brigand chief Habibullah (q.v.). Nadir Khan organized an army and defeated the usurper in October of 1929. Following this victory, he was elected king of Afghanistan. One of the first acts of his reign was to track down Habibullah and his leading followers, who were quickly captured and executed. Nadir Khan ruled as a popular monarch and used his powers to bring about many beneficial reforms for his people. In 1930 he introduced a new constitution which provided for a bicameral legislature. The constitution was enacted in 1932. His popular reign was cut short when he was assassinated in Kabul while distributing prizes at an Afghan school.

Romanian premier **Ion G. Duca** (1879–1933) was shot and killed by Radu Constantinescu, an Iron Guardist, while standing in a Carpathian railway station in Sinaia on December 30, 1933. Duca was first elected a deputy in 1907. He was appointed to the Romanian cabinet in 1916, and subsequently held the posts of minister of the interior, minister of foreign affairs, and minister of public instruction. He became the leader of the Liberal party in 1930, and was selected as premier on November 14, 1933, six weeks before his assassination. Duca was a firm opponent of Fascism, and one of his first acts as premier was to order the Iron Guard and other similar anti–Semitic groups disbanded.

1934

On January 10, 1934, **Marinus van der Lubbe**, an unemployed Dutch bricklayer, was executed at Leipzig Prison on charges of burning the German Reichstag on February 27, 1933. Van der Lubbe had been discovered inside the burning building by police and confessed to the charges. The Nazis used the fire as an excuse to arrest political opponents and dissolve civil liberties. It has been speculated that the fire was planned by Hermann Goering and carried out by Nazi agents, with van der Lubbe serving as a convenient scapegoat. He was tried by the Leipzig Supreme Court near the end of 1933 and condemned to death.

Cesar Augusto Sandino, a Nicaraguan rebel leader, was assassinated in the Nicaraguan capital of Managua on February 21, 1934, by members of the National Guard. Sandino was born in 1893, the son of a farmer. In 1926 he fought with Nicaraguan vice president Juan Bautista Sacasa in support of Sacasa's claim to the presidency. Following the intervention of the United States Marines, Sandino refused to abandon his fight. The United States forces, along with the Nicaraguan National Guard, under the command of Gen. Anastasio Somoza Garcia (q.v.), attempted to destroy Sandino and his followers. He was forced to retreat to the mountains of northern Nicaragua and adopt guerrilla tactics. The failure of the superior forces of the United States and Nicaraguan governments to suppress the revolt led to President Franklin Roosevelt's decision to withdraw the Marines in 1933. Following the removal of the American troops, Sandino expressed his willingness to negotiate with the administration of Juan Bautista Sacasa, who had become president following the 1932 elections. He petitioned the government for the right to establish a semi-autonomous agricultural colony at his stronghold in Nueva Segovia. While the administration was willing to accept his terms, Gen. Somoza and the National Guard opposed any negotiations, still hoping to gain an outright victory in battle. On February 21, 1934, following a dinner with the president, Sandino and several of his aides were seized by members of the National Guard and murdered. Gen. Somoza soon seized the Nicaraguan presidency himself. Sandino's assassination led to his establishment as a martyr and a symbol of nationalism throughout Latin America. Years later, those who were inspired by his activities and operated under the name of Sandinistas seized power in Nicaragua by deposing the son of the man who ordered Sandino murdered.

On June 30, 1934, Adolf Hitler conducted a purge of members of the German Nazi party, liquidating numerous members of his own paramilitary force of Brown-shirts, or Sturmabteilungen (SA), including their leader, **Ernst Roehm**. Other German leaders who were viewed as possible threats to Hitler's rule also perished during the so-called "Night of the Long Knives." Among those killed were former German Chancellor **Kurt von Schleicher**, early Nazi party member **Gregor Strasser**, and former Bavarian State Commissioner **Gustav von Kahr**. **Edmund Heines** (1897–1934), a close associate of Roehm and the group leader of the SA in the Breslau district, also perished. Others killed during the purge included **Gen. Kurt von Bredow**, an associate of Gen. Schleicher; **Obergruppenfuehrer Schneidhuber**, the chief of police of Munich; **Father Bernhard Stempfle** of the Hieronmymite Order, who had assisted Hitler in the editing of *Mein Kampf*; and **Erich Klausener**, a leader of Catholic Action, who was slain in his office at the Ministry of Communications. Chancellor Franz von Papen managed to escape with his life, but his principal secretary, **Herbert von Bose**, and **Edgar Jung**, a Munich lawyer and writer who served as von Papen's advisor, were both killed.

Ernst Roehm was born on November 28, 1887, in Munich. He joined the army in 1906 and served during World War I. He was a founder of the Nazi party and formed his own Brown-shirt paramilitary group, known as the Sturmabteilungen, or SA. He was an early supporter of Adolf Hitler, and participated in the Munich "Beer Hall Putsch" on November 8, 1923, for which he was briefly imprisoned. In 1931 Roehm reorganized the SA and, in 1933, led a national revolution in Bavaria, becoming the Reich secretary of state there. He was in disagreement with Hitler over what he perceived as Hitler's unwillingness to continue the revolution after the Nazi leader's selection as chancellor. Hitler was still not ready to challenge the power of the German army, and realized the Wehrmacht was strongly opposed to Roehm and the SA. In order to appease the army while consolidating his power, Hitler ordered a purge of the SA on charges of conspiracy, with Roehm being one of the first victims.

Gen. Kurt von Schleicher was born on April 7, 1882, in Brandenburg. He joined the German army in 1900 and, in 1917, was named the personal assistant in the political division of general headquarters under Wilhelm Groener, the quartermaster general. In 1923 he was promoted to aide-de-camp to the chief of army command and, in 1926, he became head of the armed forces division. His influence increased when Gen. Groener was named minister of defense in 1928, and von Schleicher was named as head of the newly created Reichswehr ministry. In 1932 he succeeded Groener as defense minister and, on December 2, 1932, he became chancellor, following the resignation of Franz von Papen. As chancellor, von Schleicher recognized the danger to Germany the Nazi party represented, but also attempted to exploit the political influence of Adolf Hitler to promote his own goals. Schleicher's negotiations with Hitler proved unsuccessful, and Hitler attained the chancellorship for himself, with the aide of von Papen, on January 28, 1933. Hitler continued to view von Schleicher as one of his primary political foes and, on June 30, 1934, von Schleicher and his wife were murdered in their home in Berlin by the S.S.

Gregor Strasser was born in Lower Bavaria on May 31, 1892. He served in the German army during World War I, and later joined the rightist Freikorps in Bavaria. In 1923 he participated in Hitler's Munich "Beer Hall Putsch," and was briefly imprisoned following its failure. In 1924 Strasser was elected as a member of the Bavarian legislature and was subsequently released from prison. While Hitler was still serving a prison term, Strasser became the co-chairman of the Nationalist Socialist party, and used his organizational skills to greatly expand the party. He, with his brother Otto Strasser, founded the *Berliner Arbeiterzeitung*, a weekly Nazi newspaper. Strasser remained one of Hitler's greatest rivals for power in the Nazi organization. Strasser was an advocate of more Socialistic ideals than Hitler was willing to commit to, and Strasser opposed the many compromises Hitler made with the military and the wealthy industrialists. Strasser was propaganda minister for the party from 1926 to 1932, when he resigned his party posts after Hitler opposed his acceptance of a cabinet position in the government of Gen. Kurt von Schleicher. Strasser remained inactive in politics, but was still viewed by Hitler as a potential rival. Due to the possible threat he presented to Hitler's power in the Nazi party, Strasser was murdered during Hitler's purge.

Gustav von Kahr (1862–1934) was general commissioner of state in Bavaria at the time of Hitler's "Beer Hall Putsch" in Munich. He participated in the revolt under duress, and abandoned Hitler as soon as opportunity allowed. The putsch failed, and von Kahr was apparently never forgiven for his betrayal. He later served as the president of the Administrative Court of Justice from 1924 to 1930. During the Nazi purge of 1934, von Kahr, a nearly forgotten figure from Germany's past, was murdered while in retirement.

German anarchist **Erich Muhsam** died in prison on July 10, 1934. Muhsam, who was born in Berlin on April 6, 1878, was a leading German Jewish playwright and was active in the Bavarian Socialist Revolution of 1918. After serving a term in prison for his activities, he became an outspoken critic of the Nazis. He was arrested by the Nazis shortly after the Reichstag fire in February of 1933, and was imprisoned in several concentration camps, where he was subjected to brutal treatment. His badly beaten body was found hanged in the latrine at Oramenberg shortly after Hitler's "Night of the Long Knives."

On July 25, 1934, Austrian Chancellor **Engelbert Dollfuss** was assassinated in the chancellery in Vienna by Austrian Nazi rebels. Dollfuss was born on October 4, 1892, in Lower Austria. He served in the Peasant Federation of Lower Austria, serving as minister of agriculture from 1927. On March of 1931 he was appointed minister for agriculture and forests in the federal government. On May 20, 1932, Dollfuss was named prime minister in a coalition government. He was vehemently opposed to Nazi Germany's plan to annex Austria and, in March of 1933, he declared himself dictator of Austria. Several months later he formed the Patriotic Front, which he planned to institute as Austria's only political party. During the early part of 1934, Dollfuss dissolved the Parliament and abolished freedom of speech and assembly. He was also successful in obtaining the assistance of Mussolini's Italy in maintaining Austria's independence. He also attempted to crush the Nazi party in Austria, which had increased domestic tension. The violence culminated with the murder of Dollfuss during an attempt by local Nazis to seize the chancellery. Otto Planetta, the leader of the rebels, was captured and subsequently hanged.

On October 9, 1934, **King Alexander I** of Yugoslavia and **Jean Louis Barthou**, the foreign minister of France, were assassinated by Vlada Cherzozensky, a Croatian terrorist, in Marseille.

Alexander I was born on December 16, 1888, at Cetinje, the son of Peter I and grandson of Alexander Karageorgevich. In 1909 Alexander became heir to his father's throne as king of Serbia, following his elder brother's renunciation of his rights of succession. He served actively and well in the Serbian army during the First and Second Balkan Wars in 1912 and 1913 respectively. He was appointed regent of Serbia on June 24, 1914, due to the ill health of his father. During World War I Alexander also served as commander-in-chief of the Serbian army and, at the conclusion of the war, was named regent of the new Kingdom of the Serbs, Croats, and Slovenes on December 1, 1918. He succeeded his father as king in name as well as in power on August 16, 1921, when Peter I died. Alexander ruled as a constitutional monarch until the murder of Croatian leader Stefan Radic (q.v.) by a Serb in 1928. Fearing that tension between the Serbs and Croats would result in disaster for the new country, Alexander abolished the constitution and dismissed the parliament in 1929 and changed the name of the country to Yugoslavia. In 1931 he proclaimed a new constitution and attempted to establish friendly relations with the countries bordering Yugoslavia. He was assassinated while on a state visit to France by a member of a Croatian terrorist group who had been trained in Hungary and Italy. He was succeeded by his son, Peter II.

Jean Louis Barthou was born in Obron-Sante-Marie on August 25, 1862. He began practicing law in 1884 and, in 1889, was elected to the Chamber of Deputies. In 1894 he first became minister of public works and, in 1896, was named minister of the interior. He again served as minister of public works in 1906 and from 1909 to 1910. In March of 1913 Barthou became premier, serving until December of that year. During his term of office he managed to secure passage of a bill which extended compulsory service in the French army from two to three years. Between 1917 and 1921 he again served in the French cabinet as minister of state and minister of war and, in 1922, was named minister of justice by Premier Raymond Poincare. He served as the French representative to the Genoa Conference later in the year and, upon his election to the Senate, was named president of the Reparation Commission. He returned to head the Justice Ministry in 1926 and, in 1934, was named minister of foreign affairs. In this position he arranged the visit to France by Yugoslavia's King Alexander I. During that visit Barthou was killed while unsuccessfully attempting to thwart the assassination of the king.

In December of 1934, **Gendung**, the prime minister of Mongolia, was executed as a "Japanese spy" following the signing of an agreement with the Soviet Union regarding a military alliance with Mongolia.

On December 1, 1934, **Sergei M. Kirov**, a leading Soviet politician, was assassinated in Leningrad. Kirov was born in Russia on March 27, 1886. He joined the Bolsheviks in 1905 and was active in the Revolution of that year. He served several terms in prison during the reign of the czar, and was active in the Revolution of 1917. Following the success of the Revolution, he took part in the wars against the counter-revolutionaries in northern Caucasia. In 1921 Kirov was named the first secretary of the Azerbaijan Communist party and, in 1926, he became secretary of the party's organization in Leningrad. In 1930 he became a member of the ruling Politburo and was a close aide to Joseph Stalin. In 1934 Kirov became involved with Stalin's opponents on the central committee. He was shot to death in Leningrad by Leonid Nikolayev, presumably on the orders of Stalin. Nikolayev and others were executed shortly after, and Kirov's murder was used as a pretext by Stalin to initiate the purge trials to eliminate his rivals.

1935

Ch'u Ch'iu-Pai (1899–1935), an early Chinese Communist leader, was arrested and executed as a leftist extremist in 1935. Ch'u became the chairman of the Communist party in China in 1927. His administration was marked by a policy of insurrection, which caused his removal in 1928, and his eventual execution.

On August 12, 1935, **Maj. Gen. Tetsuzan Nagata**, the chief of the Military Affairs Bureau in the Tokyo War Office, was assassinated. Nagata, considered a moderate, was killed by three strokes of a sword wielded by Lt. Col. Sabura Aizawa, following Nagata's dismissal of some of the more militant war office personnel. Aizawa was tried for the murder and executed on July 3, 1936.

Louisiana politician and United States Senator **Huey P. Long** was shot and fatally injured near his office in Baton Rouge by Dr. Carl Austin Weiss (1906–35) on September 8, 1935. Weiss was in turn slain by Long's bodyguards, who fired over 60 bullets into the senator's assailant. Huey Long was born in Winnfield, Louisiana, in 1893 and began his political career practicing law. His oratorical skills and political demagoguery resulted in Long's election as Louisiana's governor in 1928. He served in that position as a virtual dictator and became known as "the Kingfish." He retained a firm control on the Louisiana legislature after his election to the United States Senate in 1930 and initiated a series of welfare measures as part of his "Share the Wealth" campaign. Long attained national prominence as a leading opponent of President Franklin Roosevelt and was considered a likely challenger for the Democratic presidential nomination of 1936. Long's assailant was the son-in-law of a prominent Louisiana jurist who was a political opponent of Huey Long. It is believed that Weiss shot Long because of the senator's attacks on the reputation of his wife's family. There is still doubt if the bullet that killed Huey Long was fired by his alleged assassin or was a ricochet fired by a bodyguard. Long lived for two days after the shooting, succumbing to his injuries on September 10, 1935.

1936

On February 4, 1936, **Wilhelm Gusloff**, a German Nazi agent operating in Switzerland, was assassinated at Davos by David Frankfurter, a Jewish student.

Michael Stelescu, the founder and leader of the Romanian Fascist organization "The Brothers of the Cross," was murdered on July 16, 1936, while in a hospital. Stelescu's group had merged with a similar organization led by Corneliu Codreanu (q.v.) to become the Iron Guard. Stelescu was presumably killed by Iron Guardists following his disagreement with Codreanu over the issue of closer ties with Nazi Germany.

On February 26, 1936, Japanese right-wing militarists conducted a purge of moderate Japanese statesmen and politicians. **Viscount Makota Saito** (1858–1936), a Japanese admiral and close advisor to the emperor, was shot and killed while returning from a dinner at the American embassy. Saito, who was born in 1858, had served as minister for the navy from 1913 to 1914 and was governor general of Chosen 1919–27 and again 1929–31. He had served as Japan's prime minister from May 26, 1932, until July 4, 1934, and was the keeper of the privy seal at the time of his murder.

Viscount Korekiyo Takahashi (1854–1936), who had been Japan's premier from November 13, 1921, until June 12, 1922, was shot and hacked to death with a sword. Takahashi served as governor of the Bank of Japan in 1911 and was Japan's minister of finance on five occasions: 1913–14, 1918, 1927, 1931–34, and again in 1934 until his death.

Gen. Jotaro Watanabe, the fifty-eight-year-old inspector general of military training, was murdered in his home.

Several of the rebels' targets survived the attempts on their lives. Prime Minister Keisuke Okada (1868–1952) hid in the toilet of his house upon hearing the arrival of the mutineers. His brother-in-law was killed by the armed band by mistake. The emperor's grand chamberlain, Admiral Suzuki (1867–1948), was injured by assailants, but recovered from his wounds. Other prominent Japanese had also been marked for assassination, including Prince Saionji (1849–1940) and Count Nobuaki Makino (1861–1949), but they were not found by the assassins. The rebellion was quickly put down by government troops and most of those involved were arrested and court-martialed in secret. Thirteen of the rebels, as well as **Kita Ikki**, a leading right-wing writer and agitator, were executed on July 3, 1936.

On July 12, 1936, **Jose Calvo Sotelo**, a Spanish Monarchist political leader and minister of finance in Miguel Primo De Rivera's government, was shot and killed by left-wing Asaltus gunmen. He was murdered immediately after the killing of **Lt. Jose Castillo** by Falangists. Castillo's comrades blamed Calvo Sotelo's speeches in the Cortes for Castillo's slaying. Captain Condes of the Civil Guard and his aides took Calvo Sotelo from his home and shot him to death. His body was dumped beside a cemetery outside of Madrid. Condes went into hiding following the murder, and died during the early days of the Civil War.

On July 17, 1936, Spanish Republican **Gen. Quintero Romerales**, having discovered plans of the Nationalist uprising in the Moroccan town of Melilla, was arrested by Col. Segui. He was subsequently shot with the Mayor of Melilla. Later in the month **Gen. Julio Mena Fuenco** and **Gen. Domingo Batet Mestres** (1872–1936), both Loyalists, were shot and killed following the military rising in Burgos. Loyalist **Gen. Miguel Nuñez De Prado** was killed by Gen. Miguel Cabanellas after he was sent to confirm Cabanellas' loyalty. Cabanellas joined the military rising and shot Nuñez. Other Republican generals executed by the Nationalists in the early days of the Civil War included **Gen. Molero Lobero** (1870–1936) of Valladolid, **Gen. Enrique Salcedo Molinvero** (1871–1936) of Corunna, **Gen. Caridad Pita**, the military governor of Corunna, **Gen. Campins** of Granada, **Gen. Lopez De Ochoa y Portuondo** (1877–1936), and **Adm. Manuel Azarola Grusillon**, the commander of the arsenal at El Ferrol.

On August 23, 1936, Spanish Republican forces executed a number of leading rightist leaders who had been imprisoned in Model Prison in Madrid. They included **Melquiades Alvarez y Gonzalez** (1864–1936) and **Jose Martinez De Velasco** (1875–1936), two prominent rightists; **Fernando Primo De Rivera**, the brother of Jose Antonio Primo De Rivera (q.v.); **Julio Ruiz De Alda y Miqueleiz** (1897–1936); a leading Falangist; **Dr. Jose Maria Albinana y Sanz** (1833–1936), leader of the Nationalist party; and **Gen. Rafael Villegas Montesinos**.

In August of 1936, Spanish military leader **Manuel Goded Llopis** (1882–1936) was tried and executed for treason following his participation in the Nationalist rising. Goded Llopis served in the Spanish army, and assisted Primo De Rivera in seizing power in Spain in 1923. He later broke with the dictator due to Primo's treatment of the army and, in 1929, was involved in the unsuccessful Andalusian rising. When the Spanish Republic was formed, Goded Llopis was named inspector general of the army. Following his support of the unsuccessful Sanjurjo coup in August of 1932, Goded Llopis was dismissed from his posts and arrested. He was later released and made joint chief of staff with Gen. Francisco Franco in October of 1934. He was subsequently named the director of the air force. In early 1936 Goded Llopis became a major figure in the Nationalist rising. He was captured by Loyalist forces on July 19, while leading an assault on Barcelona. He was court-martialed and executed in early August.

Joaquin Fanjul Goni (1880–1936), a right-wing Spanish soldier and politician, was also executed for treason in 1936. Fanjul Goni was a leading conservative figure in the Spanish army. He served with distinction in Morocco and, following the establishment of the republic, became actively involved in conservative politics. He served in the Cortes and, in May of 1935, was named undersecretary of war by Gil Robles. He became involved in the Nationalist rising early in 1936 and, on July 18, was captured by the Nationalists during his unsuccessful attempt to capture Madrid. He was subsequently court-martialed and shot for treason.

Federico Garcia Lorca, the thirty-seven-year-old Spanish poet and playwright, was arrested in his home town of Granada for harboring left-wing sympathies. He was condemned to death by the commander of the Falangist militia and executed on August 19, 1936.

Republican forces murdered numerous members of the Roman Catholic clergy in Spain, including a number of bishops. Killed during the early days of the Civil War were **Manuel Basulto Jimenez**, bishop of Jaen; **Salvio Huix Miralpeix** (1877–1936), bishop of Lerida; **Miguel Serra Sucarrats** (1867–1936), bishop of Segorbe; **Cruz Laplana Laguna** (1876–1936), bishop of Cuenca; **Manuel Irurita Almandoz** (1876–1936), bishop of Barcelona; **Diego Ventaja Milan** (1882–1936), bishop of Almeria; **Juan Medina Olmos** (1869–1936), bishop of Guadix, **Narcisco De Estenaga y Echevarria** (1882–1936), bishop of Ciudad Real; **Manuel Borras Ferrer**, suffragan bishop of Tarragona; **Juan De Ponce**, apostolic administrator of Orihuela; and **Florencio Asensio Barroso** (1876–1936), apostolic administrator of Barbastro and the titular bishop of Epirus.

The first of the major Soviet purge trials of the Stalin regime concluded on August 26, 1936. This trial, known as the "Trial of the Trotsky-Zinoviev Terrorist Center," ended with the shooting of Lenin's close associate **Grigori E. Zinoviev**, a Politburo member since 1921; **Lev B. Kamenev**, a Politburo member since 1919; and **G.E. Evdokimov**, a former member of the Secretariat. Thirteen other defendants were also convicted, including the Trotskyites **Ivan M. Smirnov**, an ex–Central Committee member; **Sergei V. Mrachkovsky**, a fighter; **V.A. Ter-Vaganian**, an intellectual Armenian; and **E.A. Dreitzer**, head of Trotsky's bodyguards. Other defendants included **Ivan P. Bakayev**, **Valentin Olbert**, **K.B. Berman-Yurin**, **Fritz David**, **Moissei Lurye**, **Nathan Lurye**, **Isak Reingold**, **E.S. Holtzman**, and **Richard Pickel**. All were convicted of treason and most were executed. Another Politburo member, Mikhail P. Tomsky, committed suicide on August 22, 1936, after having been incriminated.

Grigori E. Zinoviev was born in September of 1883 in the Ukraine. He joined with the Bolsheviks in 1901 and was active in the 1905 Revolution. He served as a close aide to Lenin during his period of exile from 1909 to 1917, and returned with him to Russia following the March Revolution. Zinoviev, along with Kamenev, were leaders of the right-wing bloc of the Bolsheviks who opposed Lenin's seizure of power, urging a Socialist coalition government. As leader of the Communist party in Petrograd, Zinoviev was named a candidate member of the ruling Politburo and full member two years later. He was chairman of the Communist International's Executive Committee from 1919 to 1926, and was a leading candidate to succeed Lenin at the time of Lenin's death in 1924. Zinoviev initially aided Stalin in his struggle against Trotsky, but later broke with him. This move led to his expulsion from the Communist party and his subsequent trial and execution.

Lev B. Kamenev was born on July 22, 1883, in Moscow. He became a member of the Social Revolutionary party in 1901 and was active in the Bolshevik movement. He served as a close aide to Lenin, having joined him in exile in 1908. In 1914 Kamenev returned to Russia and, the following year, was arrested and banished to Siberia for revolutionary activities. He returned to Petrograd following the start of the Revolution in March of 1917. Kamenev differed with Lenin over the issue of the Bolsheviks sharing power with other revolutionary groups, with Kamenev taking a consistently conciliatory position. He became a member of the first Soviet Politburo in October of 1917 and was a supporter of Stalin in his opposition to Trotsky in 1923. Kamenev subsequently opposed Stalin's policies, resulting in Kamenev's loss of power. He served as the Soviet Ambassador to Italy from 1926 to 1927, when he was expelled from the Communist party. In 1935 he was tried for treason and sentenced to prison, but was retried the following year and executed.

On October 29, 1936, **Ramiro De Maeztu y Whitney**, a Spanish political journalist, was shot and killed by Republicans in Madrid. Maeztu y Whitney was born on May 4, 1874, in Victoria, Spain. He served as a political correspondent for various Spanish newspapers in London from 1905 to 1916, and later supported the dictatorship of Primo De Rivera. Following the establishment of the Spanish Republic, he opposed the government through a series of political articles and books. He was murdered shortly after the outbreak of the Spanish Civil War.

Former Iraqi prime minister **Ja'Far Al-'Askari** was assassinated on October 30, 1936. Askari was born in Baghdad in 1887, and served in the Turkish army from 1909. He was captured by the British during World War I and subsequently joined the Arab Nationalist movement with his brother-in-law, Nuri as-Sa'id (q.v.). Askari served as a leading advisor to the amir, Faisal, in the Hejaz and Syria. He was named minister of defense in Iraq's first cabinet in 1921, and was instrumental in the formation of the Iraqi army. He served as Iraq's prime minister from November 22, 1923, to August 3, 1924, and again from November 21, 1926, to December 31, 1927. He continued to be a major figure in Iraqi politics and was serving as minister of defense when he was murdered by insurgent troops under the orders of Gen. Bakr Sidqi al-'Askari (q.v.).

Jose Antonio Primo De Rivera, the son of the former Spanish dictator Gen. Miguel Primo De Rivera, was executed on November 20, 1936. Jose Antonio was born in Madrid on April 24, 1903. He became active in politics at an early age, and was a leading conservative spokesman at the time of his election as a deputy in the Cortes in 1933. The same year he founded the right-wing Falange party, which he led until his death. Jose Antonio lost his seat in the Cortes in 1936 and was arrested soon afterward. He was again elected to the Cortes while imprisoned, but his election was nullified by the Republican government. Jose Antonio remained imprisoned through the start of the Spanish Civil War, and was eventually tried and convicted of treason on November 18. He was executed in Alicante prison two days later.

Spanish anarchist **Buenaventura Durruti** was shot and killed in front of Model Prison in Madrid on November 21, 1936. Durruti was born in 1896, and first became involved in the anarchist movement in 1917, by sabotaging railway lines in Leon. In 1923 he, along with Francisco Ascaso, assassinated Cardinal De Soldeville (q.v.), the archbishop of Saragossa, and the following year the two made an unsuccessful attempt on the life of King Alfonso XIII of Spain. Following a brief period of imprisonment, Durruti became active in the Federation Anarchista Iberica (FAI), and orchestrated many acts of political violence prior to the start of the Spanish Civil War. When the Nationalist rising began, Durruti served on the Anti-Fascist Militia Committee, which ruled Catalonia. He led an anarchist army against the Nationalist forces in Saragosa, and later led his column in defense of Madrid. Speculation exists that Durruti was shot in the back by his own men, but there is also evidence to suggest that his shooting was an accident that occurred when his aide's machine pistol caught on a car door, firing a bullet into Durruti's chest.

1937

In January of 1937 the Soviet purge trials continued with the trial known as the "Trial of the Anti-Soviet Trotskyite Center." The defendants included Politburo member **Grigori Sokolnikov**, journalist **Karl Radek**, **Grigori L. Pyatakov**, **Leonid P. Serebryako**, **A.A Shestov**, **M.S. Stroilov**, **B.O. Norkin**, **N.I. Muralov**, **Valentin Arnold**, **Yakov Livshits**, **I.A. Knayev**, **A.S. Rataichak**, and five others. Most of the defendants were convicted, and the sentences ranged from execution to imprisonment.

Grigori Yakovlevich Sokolnikov was born in 1888 and became a member of the Bolshevik faction in 1905. He lived in exile until the Revolution of 1917, and served as a member of the Russian delegation which negotiated the Brest Litovsk peace treaty with Germany in 1918. Sokolnikov served as the assistant people's commissar of finance in 1922, and was the Soviet ambassador to Great Britain from 1929 to 1932. At the time of his arrest he was the assistant commissar for the timber industry. He was sentenced to ten years' imprisonment following the trial, but reportedly died in a prison camp in 1939.

Karl Bernardovich Radek was born in Lwow, Gallicia, in 1885. He became a member of the Social Democrat party of Poland and Lithuania in 1901, and served as a journalist on numerous left-wing publications in Poland and Germany. He accompanied Lenin across Germany following the Russian Revolution of 1917. Returning to Germany he was instrumental in the establishment of the German Communist party. Following his arrest he returned to the Soviet Union in 1920. He was charged with being a follower of Leon Trotsky (q.v.), and was dismissed from the Communist party in 1925, but was later readmitted. Following his trial for treasonable activities he was sentenced to ten years' imprisonment, but was reportedly murdered in a prison camp in 1939

Grigori L. Pyatakov, who was born in 1890, served as the assistant commissar for heavy industries from 1931 to 1937. He was tried for treason as a follower of Leon Trotsky (q.v.), and was executed on January 31, 1937.

On February 18, 1937, Soviet politician **Grigori Konstantinovich Ordzhonikidze** was forced to commit suicide on Stalin's orders. Ordzhonikidze was born in Georgia, Russia, on October 27, 1886. He joined the Bolsheviks in 1903. Following a period of exile in Germany, he returned to Russia in 1907 and was arrested on several occasions. After the 1917 Revolution Ordzhonikidze became a member of the Bolshevik Communist Party Committee. In January of 1918 he was appointed commissar extraordinary for the Ukraine. In 1926 he became a candidate member of the Politburo and served in several important positions. In 1930 he became the chairman of the Council of National Economy and a member of the Politburo. He became people's commissar for heavy industry in 1932. Ordzhonikidze, a supporter of Stalin, became a victim of Stalin's distrust of potential rivals.

In February of 1937 an attempt was made on the life of Marshal Rodolfo Graziani (1882–1955), the Italian viceroy of Ethiopia. Graziani was uninjured in the attack, but the Italian army retaliated cruelly against the Ethiopian people.

On June 12, 1937, executions were carried out against a number of leading Soviet military leaders during the Soviet army purge trials. It has been estimated that over 35,000 Russian army officers, representing over half of the officers corps, were executed during the year. Among those tried and executed were **Marshal Mikhail Tukhachevski**; **Gen. Yakir**, commander of the Kiev Military District and a Central Committee member; **Gen. Uborevich**, commander of the Byelorussian Military District; **Gen. R.P. Eideman**, head of the civil defense organization "Osoaviakhim"; **Gen. Kork**, head of the Military Academy; **Corps Cmdr. Vitovt Putna**, military attache in London; **Corps Cmdr. Feldman**, head of the Red Army administration; and **Corps Cmdr. Primakov**, deputy commander of the Leningrad Military District. **Yan Gamarnik**, head of the political administration of the Red Army and first deputy commissar of defense, committed suicide on June 1, 1937, after having been implicated in the trials.

Mikhail Nikolaevich Tukhachevski was born in Smolensk province in 1893. He served in the Russian army during World War I and joined the Communist party and the Red Army in 1918. He led a successful campaign against the White Army during the Civil War. From 1921 to 1922 he was commander of the War Academy, before returning to command the Western Army Group. Tukhachevski became chief of the general staff of the Red Army in 1925 for three years. In 1934 he was elected as a candidate member of the Communist party's Central Committee and was made a marshal of the army in 1935. He was executed following Stalin's purge of the army.

Purge trials and executions against Communist party members continued throughout the year, claiming victims from the Soviet Union and many other countries. Ten of the twelve arrested leaders of the Hungarian Revolution were killed, including **Deszo Bokanyi**, theorist **Lajos Magyar**, and **Jozsef Pogany**, who, as John Pepper, was the Comintern's representative to the American Communist party.

Romanian Communist leaders **Marcel Pauker** and **Alexandru Dobrogeanu** were shot during the year, as was Italian Communist party member **Edmondo Peluso**.

Beginning in 1937, all twelve members of the Polish Communist party's Central Committee present in Russia, and several hundred others, were executed. These included Polish Communist leaders **Adolf S. Warski**, **Wera Kostrzewa**, and **Budzynski**, who were shot on August 20, 1937. **Jeezy Ring** and **Henryk Henrykowski**, Polish Politburo members, and **Henry Walecki**, the Polish Communist party representative to the Executive Committee and Control Commission of the Comintern, were also purged by Stalin.

Panas Lyubchenko, the premier of the Ukraine, was ordered to Moscow and executed.

Much of the entire Yugoslav Central Committee perished in 1937, including **Milan Gorkic** (1890–1937), the general secretary of the Yugoslav Communist party, and **Vlada Copic**, the Yugoslav party's organization secretary. Gorkic had become active in the Communist party in 1918, and was a founding member of the Yugoslav Communist party. From 1922 to 1937 he lived in Moscow, becoming the leader of the Yugoslav party. Following his execution, Josip Broz Tito succeeded him in that position.

On June 16, 1937, **Andres Nin**, the Spanish political secretary of POUM (Marxist Party of Catalonia), was arrested in Spain. He was tortured and killed by agents of Stalin. **Jose Diaz**, the secretary general of the Spanish Communist party, jumped, or was pushed, from a window in Moscow.

During the summer of 1937, **Nikolai Smernov**, the Soviet NKVD resident in France, was recalled to Moscow and executed.

On September 4, 1937, **Ignace Reis**, a former Communist party functionary and NKVD resident in Switzerland, was shot to death in Lausanne, Switzerland.

In August of 1937, **Gen. Demid**, the commander-in-chief of the Mongolian army, was poisoned while traveling to Moscow by train.

On June 3, 1937, Spanish **Gen. Emilio Mola Vidal** was killed when his plane crashed under suspicious circumstances. Mola, who was born in 1887, was the last director general of security under the Spanish monarchy. He supported the right-wing coup in 1936, which resulted in the Spanish Civil War, and he served in the junta which governed Nationalist Spain. Mola's power diminished after Gen. Francisco Franco was selected to lead the combined forces of Falangists and Carlists.

Gen. Bakr Sidqi Al-'Askari, the leader of the Iraqi army, was assassinated on August 11, 1937. Sidqi, who was born in 1890 in Kurdistan, served in the Turkish army from 1908 to 1918. In 1919 he joined the Iraqi army under King Faisal. As acting chief of the Iraqi General Staff in 1936, he led the army coup d'etat which forced the resignation of Yasin al-Hashimi, the prime minister, and replaced him with Hikmat Sulayman. During the army uprising, Sidqi gave the order to assassinate Ja'far al-'Askari (q.v.), the minister of defense and a former prime minister. During the following year, Sidqi remained as head of the Iraqi army. The indulgences and corruption of Sidqi and his followers increased the hatred and distrust of the populace. Amid rumors of Sidqi's intended assumption of dictatorial powers, he was sent as head of a military mission to Mosul. Following his arrival, Sidqi and **Major Muhammad 'Ali Jawad**, the commander of the Iraqi Royal Air Force, were shot and killed by Muhammad 'Ali Tallafari, an Iraqi soldier.

1938

In March of 1938 the third major Soviet purge trial began. This trial was known as the "Trial of the Anti-Soviet Bloc Rightists and Trotskyites." The defendants in this trial included **Nikolai I. Bukharin**, a Politburo member since 1924; **Alexei Rykov**, a Politburo member since 1922 and Lenin's successor as prime minister; **Nikolai Krestinsky**, a Politburo member since 1919; and **Genrikh G. Yagoda**, who as head of the NKVD inaugurated the Soviet system of forced labor. Other defendants included **Christian Rakovsky**, the former Soviet ambassador to France; **Fayzullah Khodhayev**, the prime minister of the Uzbek Soviet Socialist Republic; **Akmal Ikramov**, the Uzbek Communist party leader; and **Arkady**

Rosenglots, V.I. Ivanov, M.A. Chernov, G.F. Grinko, Izaak Zelensky, V.F. Sharangovich, Sergei Bessonov, P.T. Zubarev, Prof. D. Pletnev, Dr. L. Levin, Dr. I.N. Kazako, Boris Kamkov, Vladimir Karelin, P.P. Kryuchkov, P.P. Bulano, and V.A. Maximov-Dikovsky. As in earlier show trials, most of the defendants were executed or imprisoned. Of those that received prison sentences, most did not survive their incarceration.

Nikolai Ivanovich Bukharin was born in Moscow on October 9, 1888. He was an early supporter of the Bolsheviks and was imprisoned in 1911. He went into exile throughout Europe, meeting Lenin in Vienna in 1913. In 1916 he settled briefly in New York City and edited *Novy mir*, the Communist newspaper. Bukharin returned to Russia at the start of the Russian Revolution in 1917. He was elected to the Central Committee of the Soviet Communist party and became the editor of *Pravda*. In 1924 Bukharin was selected as a member of the ruling Politburo. He supported Stalin in his struggle against Leon Trotsky (q.v.), but in 1928 he broke with Stalin over economic and political matters. In November of 1929 he was expelled from the Politburo, and his political power was seriously diminished. In March of 1938 he was arrested and tried as an alleged member of a counterrevolutionary organization. He was sentence to death and shot.

Aleksei Ivanovich Rykov was born on February 25, 1881, in Saratov. He joined the Social Democratic party in 1899, and was a close associate of Lenin during the period of their shared exile prior to the Revolution of 1917. He served as commissar of the interior in the first Bolshevik government and, from Lenin's death in 1924 until 1930, was president of the Soviet of People's Commissars. He was associated with the right wing of the Communist party and resisted Stalin's policies. He was subsequently dismissed from his offices, expelled from the Communist party, and later tried for treason and executed.

Khristian Georgievich Rakovski was born in Bulgaria on August 13, 1873. His home was annexed by Romania in 1878, and he subsequently served in the Romanian army. During the early years of World War I Rakovski was arrested as a subversive. He was freed by the Russians following the 1917 Revolution, and became a member of the Communist party's Central Committee in 1919. Later in the year he was named president of the Soviet of People's Commissars of the Ukraine. He was also named as the Soviet charge d'affaires in London in 1924, and was the Soviet ambassador to France from 1926 to 1927. His support for Leon Trotsky (q.v.) resulted in his expulsion from the Communist party in 1927. He was tried in March of 1939 and sentenced to twenty years' imprisonment. He is presumed to have died in the early 1940s while serving his term in a concentration camp.

Genrikh Grigoryevich Yagoda was born in 1891 and, as commissar of internal affairs, was instrumental in carrying out the early stages of the Stalin purges. He became head of the NKVD in 1934, serving until

September of 1936, when he was demoted to the position of commissar of posts and telegraphs. Soon after, he was arrested and himself tried during the purges. He was convicted of treason and executed.

Earlier in the year, **A.A. Slutsky**, the head of the Soviet NKVD foreign department, died in Moscow. His death was officially announced as a heart attack, but poisoning by cyanide seems the more likely cause.

Throughout the year Stalin's agents purged the Communist ranks both inside and outside the Soviet Union. Many members of the German Communist party were killed during the year. **Heinz Neumann**, former member of the German Communist party's Politburo and a member of the Comintern living in the Hotel Lux, was arrested on April 28, 1937. German politburo members **Herman Remmele**, **Fritz Schulte**, and **Herman Schubert**; **Hans Kippenberger**, head of the party's military apparatus; **Leo Flieg**, organizational secretary of the German Central Committee; **Heinrich Suskind** and **Werner Hirsch**, editors-in-chief of the German Communist newspaper *Rote Fahne*, and four assistant editors; and **Hugo Eberlein**, German Comintern delegate, all vanished and were presumed killed.

G.A. Agabekov, the former Soviet OGPU resident in Turkey, was murdered in Belgium in 1938.

Lev Sedov, the son of exiled Soviet Communist leader Leon Trotsky (q.v.), died in a Paris hospital in 1938. He was admitted suffering from a minor ailment, but later was found wandering the halls in a disoriented state. He died shortly thereafter, presumably poisoned by a Soviet agent.

Han Fu-Chu, a leading Chinese general from the Shantung province, was shot for treason in Hankow by troops of Chiang Kai-shek. Gen. Han sided with the Nationalist government against his former ally, Fen Yuhsiang, in 1929. In 1930 he became governor of Shantung province and still held that post when war broke out with Japan in 1937. He was ordered shot in 1938 by Chiang for suspected treasonous activities with the Japanese.

In 1938, **Sayyed Hasan Modarres**, a clerical opponent to Iran's Reza Shah, was killed while in prison. He had been imprisoned since 1929.

Walter Gempp (1878–1938), the chief of the Berlin Fire Department, was strangled and killed on May 2, 1938, while imprisoned by the Nazis. Gempp had gained the animosity of leading Nazis following the Reichstag fire in February of 1933. He claimed that his department had been prevented from performing its duty adequately by high-ranking Nazi officials. His testimony at the trial of those accused of setting the fire was damaging to the case of the prosecution. In September of 1937 Gempp was arrested and convicted of malpractice. His death occurred while he was awaiting an appeal.

On May 23, 1938, **Col. Evhen Konovalets**, the forty-seven-year-old leader of the underground Ukranian Military Organization (UVO) and the Organization of Ukrainian Nationalists (OUN) in Poland, was killed by a Soviet agent in Rotterdam, Netherlands.

Lothar Erdman, a German Socialist and journalist, died after a brutal beating in the Sachsenhausen concentration camp on September 18, 1938. Erdman, who was born on October 12, 1888, in Halle, joined the Fabian Socialists while attending a London university. He later worked as a journalist and served as a trade union leader. He was arrested at the start of World War II by the Nazis, and imprisoned as a subversive. He died as a result of injuries inflicted upon him by the concentration camp guards.

Ernest von Rath, a German embassy official in Paris, was shot and killed by a young Polish Jew, Herschel Grynszpan, on November 7, 1938. Von Rath, the embassy's councillor and an anti–Nazi, was killed when Grynszpan went to the German embassy intending to shoot the ambassador in revenge for the expulsion of Jews from Poland, including his family. The killing of von Rath was used as an excuse by the German Nazis to further persecution of German Jews, and led directly to the so-called "Crystal Night," in which angry mobs smashed the store windows of Jewish shopkeepers.

On November 30, 1938, **Corneliu Zelea Codreanu**, the founder and leader of the Romanian Fascist group the Iron Guard, was shot and killed, while reportedly trying to escape from prison. Codreanu was born on September 13, 1899, in Iasi. He became involved with anti–Semitic groups while in college and, in 1923, founded the National Christian League. He was tried and acquitted in 1925 on charges of murdering a police official and subsequently left the country. He returned to Romania in 1927, and the following year he merged his organization, now called the Legion of the Archangel Michael, with Michael Stelescu's (q.v.) Brothers of the Cross. The new organization, led by Codreanu, became known as the Iron Guard. The Guard became the leading voice of Romanian Fascism, becoming closely associated with Adolf Hitler's Nazi Germany. Iron Guardists were responsible for many anti–Semitic terrorist activities and were implicated in the 1933 assassination of Romanian prime minister Ion Duca (q.v.). In 1938 the Guard was ordered disbanded, and Codreanu and many of his followers were ordered arrested by Armand Calinescu (q.v.), the minister of the interior. Codreanu and thirteen of his followers were shot and killed while in transit between two prisons.

1939

In February of 1939 **Vlas Chubar**, the premier of the Ukraine in 1923, and a Soviet politburo member from 1935, was shot during the Stalin purges. **S.V. Kossior**, the first secretary of the Ukrainian Communist Party from 1928 to 1938 was also executed at this time.

During the year **Nikolai Ivanovich Yezhov**, the Communist politician who, as commissar for internal affairs and leader of the NKVD from September 1936, had orchestrated the Stalinist purges during their bloodiest period, himself fell victim to them. Yezhov, who was born in 1895, had joined the Communist party in 1917 and became a member of its Central Committee in 1927. As an ally of Stalin, his powers increased, until he replaced Genrikh Yagoda (q.v.) as director of the purges. He organized the major show trials of 1936–38 and the purge of the army. He also was responsible for the elimination of dissident elements in the NKVD. The era of the purges became known as the "Yezhovshchina" due to his activities. As Stalin's interest in the purges decreased in 1938, Yezhov fell out of power and was subsequently arrested and shot.

On February 5, 1939, several Spanish Nationalist leaders who had been held by the Republican forces in prison at Gerona were murdered when Gerona fell to the Nationalists. They included **Anselmo Polanco y Fontecha** (1883–1939), the bishop of Teruel, and **Col. Rey D'Harcourt**.

Ralph Cairns, a British police official in Palestine, was assassinated in 1939 by the Irgun zwei Leumi, a Jewish underground group.

Armand Calinescu, the Romanian prime minister who had attempted to destroy the Fascist Iron Guard, was assassinated by members of the group on September 21, 1939. Calinescu was born on May 22, 1893, in Pitesti. After studying law he became a leader in the National Peasant party. He served as undersecretary of the interior from 1928 to 1931. In December of 1937 he became the minister of the interior, and actively pursued a policy designed to eliminate the Iron Guard. In November of 1938, a number of their leaders, including Corneliu Codreanu (q.v.), were arrested and killed. Calinescu subsequently became vice premier and, on the death of Premier Miron Cristea on March 7, 1939, assumed the office of premier. He continued his opposition to the Iron Guard, and was, in turn, killed by members of the organization while driving to his home at Cotroceni.

Hungarian Communist leader **Bela Kun** was executed on November 30, 1939, a victim of the Stalin purges. Kun was born in 1886 in Transylvania. He became active in politics, and was a leader of the Transylvanian Social Democratic party. As a member of the Austro-Hungarian army during WW I, he was taken prisoner by the Russians. Following the Russian Revolution of 1917, Kun became involved with the Communist party and, in 1918, returned to Hungary to found the Communist newspaper *Voros Ujsag* and the Hungarian Communist party. Following a brief imprisonment, Kun became the premier of Hungary at the head of a Communist–Social Democratic administration on March 20, 1919. During his period of power he served as a pawn of Lenin and the Soviet Union. He was ousted by popular will, which resented his extreme policies. He fled first to Vienna and then to the Soviet Union. With the exception of a brief attempt to again promote revolution in Hungary in 1928, Kun remained in the Soviet Union for the rest of his life. During the Stalin purges Kun fell out of favor, was arrested on May 30, 1937, and was executed two years later.

1940

Sir Michael Francis O'Dwyer, a British colonial officer who had served in India, was murdered in 1940. O'Dwyer, who was born in 1864, was revenue commissioner in the Punjab from 1901 to 1908. He became lieutenant governor of the region in 1913. He incurred much hostility because of his autocratic rule, and he was held responsible for the massacre of Indians at Amritsar. Following his retirement and the publication of his autobiography, he remained a leading symbol of the excesses of the British colonial empire. This hostility resulted in his assassination by an Indian.

Willi Munzenberg, a leading German Communist propaganda expert, was murdered and hung from a tree in a forest near Grenoble in 1940. He had refused to return to the Soviet Union during the purges.

On January 18, 1940, **Rustum Haydar**, the Iraqi finance minister, was assassinated. He had served as minister of finance in the first government of Prime Minister Nuri as-Sa'id (q.v.) in 1931. When Nuri returned to power in 1938, Haydar again became finance minister. He was the subject of much criticism by Arab nationalists for his support of Nuri's pro–British policies. On January 18, Haydar was shot by Husayn Rawzi Tawfiq, a former government employee. Haydar died of his wounds four days later. Tawfiq was tried and convicted and hanged on March 27.

In June of 1940, following the German occupation of Poland, many prominent political leaders were shot, including **Macief Rataj** (1884–1940), the former speaker of the Sejm, who had assumed the presidency of Poland for several months in 1926, and **Mieczyslaw Niedzialkowski** (1893–1940), the Socialist leader. Also executed during this period was **Stefan Starzynski** (1893–1940), who had served as mayor of Warsaw from 1937 until 1938, and had led the defense of Warsaw against the German occupation army.

Italo Balbo, the marshal of the Italian air force, was killed when his plane was shot down at Tobruk, Libya. Balbo was born on June 6, 1896, in Ferrara. He become involved in the Italian Fascist movement and led

Mussolini's March on Rome as the head of the black-shirt militia in 1922. Balbo was instrumental in creating the Italian air force, serving as undersecretary of air from 1926 and air minister from 1929. In 1933 he was appointed air marshal. Balbo also became a popular rival of Mussolini, and disagreed with Mussolini's policies of cooperation with Nazi Germany. In 1933 he was appointed governor general of Libya. He was killed in Libya on June 19, 1940, when his plane was shot down by Italian troops when it failed to give the correct recognition signals.

On August 20, 1940, **Leon Trotsky** was the victim of an assassination attempt by a Stalinist agent, dying the following day. Trotsky was born Lev Bronstein on October 26, 1879, in the Ukraine. He became involved in revolutionary activities in 1897, and was arrested soon after. He was exiled to Siberia, but managed a successful escape, joining Lenin in exile. Trotsky broke with Lenin soon after, fearing that Lenin's policies were designed to install a dictatorship. He became a leader of the Menshevik faction, advocating the theory of "constant revolution." He was active in the 1905 Revolution in St. Petersburg, and was again arrested and exiled to Siberia. In 1907 he once more escaped, settling in Vienna. During this period he attempted to serve as a conciliator and unite the various Socialist factions. He served as the first editor of *Pravda*, the revolutionists' newspaper. He was a strong opponent of World War I and was expelled from Germany. He left for France in 1916 and briefly settled in the United States, before returning to Russia following the Revolution of 1917. He again joined with Lenin's Bolsheviks and was active in the seizure of power in the capital. He served as commissar for foreign affairs in Lenin's first Communist government, and was the leader of the committee whose actions resulted in the Brest-Litovsk peace treaty with Germany. In 1918 he served as leader of the commissariat of war and successfully established a viable Red Army to repel the counter-revolutionaries during the subsequent period of civil war. Following the death of Lenin in 1924, Trotsky was a leading candidate to replace him as leader of the Soviet Communist party, but he was defeated by Stalin, with the assistance of Zinoviev (q.v.) and Kamenev (q.v.). He remained a member of the ruling Politburo, but was removed from most positions of power. In 1926 he again challenged Stalin's power, with the support of both Zinoviev and Kamenev. He again suffered defeat as Bukharin (q.v.) and Rykov (q.v.), leader of the Soviet Communist's right wing, rallied with Stalin to undermine Trotsky. He was subsequently removed from his positions and expelled from the Communist party. The following year he was forced into exile, finally settling in Mexico in 1937. He remained a consistent enemy of Stalin and constituted Stalin's only real opponent for the leadership of the Communist movement. Trotsky was denounced and reviled throughout the major purge trials during the late 1930s, and many of his supporters were executed by Stalin's regime. In 1940 Ramon Mercader

(1924–78), using the name of Frank Jackson, gained Trotsky's trust and breached his stronghold outside of Mexico City. While reviewing a political paper "Jackson" had authored, Trotsky was attacked by his assailant wielding an alpine axe. Trotsky was mortally wounded and died the following day. Mercader served twenty years in a Mexican prison for his crime, being released in March of 1960. He was later declared a hero of the Soviet Union before his death in Havana, Cuba, on October 18, 1978.

During 1940 a number of leading Spanish Republican leaders were captured in France by the Vichy government. They included **Luis Companys y Jover** (1883–1940), the Catalan Nationalist leader and president of Catalonia in 1936, and **Jurgen Zugazagoitia**, a former Socialist minister of the interior. They were returned to Spain and executed in October on the orders of Gen. Francisco Franco.

On November 28, 1940, the Iron Guard of Romania assassinated sixty-four prominent members of the old Romanian regime, including **Nikolae Iorga** (1871–1940), the prime minister 1931–32, and **Virgil Madgearu**, a peasant leader.

1941

Modesto Maidique (1890–1941), a former Liberal party member of the Cuban senate, was shot and killed in Havana on January 13, 1941.

On February 10, 1941, **Gen. Walter G. Krivitsky**, the forty-one-year-old former Red Army chief of intelligence for Western Europe until 1937, was found shot to death at the Bellevue Hotel in Washington, D.C. Though Krivitsky's death was ruled a suicide, it was suspected that he had been murdered by the Soviet secret police on orders of Stalin.

On February 17, 1941, **Juvenal Viegas Silva**, the leader of the Brazilian Communist party, was slain by police while resisting arrest.

Rudolf Hilferding, a leading German Social Democratic politician, died in a French prison on February 11, 1941, after having been brutally beaten by the Gestapo. Hilferding was born on August 10, 1877, in Vienna. He became active in the Social Democratic party, serving as a teacher at the party's training center in Berlin. He was the political editor of the Socialist newspaper *Vorwarts* from 1907 to 1915, and authored several books on political theory. He was elected as a deputy in the Reichstag in 1924, serving until 1933. In 1923 and from 1928 to 1929 he served as minister of finance in the German cabinet. In 1933 he was forced to flee

Germany as the Nazis came to power, going first to Denmark, then settling in France. He was arrested by Vichy French police in unoccupied France and turned over to the Gestapo.

1942

On March 5, 1942, **Alfredo Zarate Albarran**, the governor of the State of Mexico, was shot and seriously injured while attending a party at Toluca, the state capital. Fernando Ortiz Rubio, the son of a former Mexican president, was charged in the shooting. Zarate Albarran died on March 8, 1942.

Juan Peiro (1887–1942), the anarchist minister of industry in Spain's last Republican government during the Spanish Civil War, was captured in France by the Vichy government and returned to Spain. He was executed on the orders of Gen. Francisco Franco in 1942.

Gen. Vladimir Zaimov, the former Bulgarian minister of the interior, was executed on June 1, 1942, following his court-martial in Sofia. He was convicted of espionage for the Russians.

On June 2, 1942, **Albert Clement**, the editor of the pro–Nazi newspaper *Le Cri du Peuple*, was shot to death in Paris by members of the French Resistance.

Gen. Alois Elias, the premier of the Protectorate of Bohemia-Moravia from April 1939 until October 1941, was executed by the Nazis on June 19, 1942.

In 1942 the German Abwehr uncovered many Germans in strategic locations who were supplying the Soviet Union with extensive espionage information. The spy group was known as the "Rote Kapelle," or "Red Orchestra." The leader was **Harold Schulze-Boysen**, who worked in the Luftwaffe espionage bureau. Other associates who were positioned in ministries and military offices included **Arvid Harnack**, an economist in the Ministry of Economics; his wife, **Mildred Fish Harnack**; **Franz Scheliha** in the Foreign Office; **Countess Erika von Brockdorff** in the Ministry of Labor; and **Horst Heilmann** in the Propaganda Ministry. Seventy-five members of this organization were tried for treason and fifty were sentenced to death. The condemned were strangled by a rope, which was attached to a meathook, and slowly hanged.

Reinhard Heydrich, the German Reich protector of Czechoslovakia, was critically injured by a bomb tossed at his car by two Czech Resistance agents on May 27, 1942. He died in Prague on June 4, 1942. Heydrich was born in Prussian Saxony on March 7, 1904. He served in the right-wing Freikorps after the end of World War II, and later served in the German navy. In the early 1930s he joined the Nazi movement, becoming a protege of Heinrich Himmler, the head of the S.S. Heydrich served as Himmler's field agent and, in this position, was privy to the many files the S.S. maintained on prominent and powerful Germans. He was instrumental in supplying evidence used as a pretext for Hitler's purge of the S.A. in 1934 during the "Night of the Long Knives." Heydrich soon rose in power to become Himmler's deputy as head of the S.S. and the Gestapo. Following the Anschluss with Austria, in 1938, he was placed in charge of police affairs there. The following year he was involved in fabricating a border incident with Poland to justify the German invasion of that country. During the early years of World War II Heydrich was in charge of the mass deportation of Jews and others from German occupied areas in Poland and the Soviet Union, earning the nickname "the Hangman" for his efforts. Soon after, he was placed in direct charge of the establishment and operation of the extermination centers used by the Nazis to liquidate Jews and other "undesirables," with Adolf Eichmann (q.v.) as his second-in-command. Heydrich's main ambition was to supplant Himmler as one of Hitler's most trusted advisors. In September of 1941, he was named the Reich protector for Bohemia and Moravia. While serving in this capacity he also retained control of the extermination centers. In May of 1941 Jan Kublis and Joseph Gablitz, two Czechoslovakians who had been trained in England to kill Heydrich, parachuted into Czechoslovakia to perform the assassination. Following their attempt on Heydrich's life, Kublis and Gablitz went into hiding in the Karl Borromaeus Church in Prague. They were betrayed to the Germans by Karel Curda and were killed along with 120 other members of the Czech Resistance in fighting with the S.S. Curda was later killed by members of the Czech underground. Heydrich died of his wounds eight days after the attack. The S.S. conducted a vigorous retaliation for the killing, including the complete destruction of the Czech village of Lidice.

On November 28, 1942, **Marceli Nowotko**, the leader of the Polish Communist party, was murdered by Boleslaw Molojec. Nowotko had been accused of collaborating with the Germans during the occupation of Poland. Molojec was subsequently tried by a Communist party court and executed.

Admiral Jean Francois Darlan, who was in charge of the French armed forces under the Vichy regime, was assassinated on December 24, 1942, in Algiers. Darlan was born in Aquitaine, France, on August 7, 1881. He entered the French navy in 1902, serving as a commander during World War I. He was appointed rear admiral in 1929 and vice admiral three years later. In 1935 he was named as chief of staff of the navy and, in 1939, he became the commander-in-chief of French naval forces. Following the fall of France, in 1940, Darlan served the Vichy regime as vice premier and, from August 1941, as minister of defense. After the invasion of North Africa by British and American troops, and the subsequent occupation of all of France by the German army, Darlan surrendered the French troops in North Africa to the Allies. He then announced his intention to collaborate with them in their fight against Germany. He was granted authority as chief of state for French Africa, and was to be placed in charge of all French Resistance forces. On Christmas Eve of 1942 he was shot and killed by Fernand Bonnier De la Chappille (1922–42), a French anti–Fascist, who viewed Darlan as a traitor to France for his earlier collaboration with the Germans. The assassin, who had been trained by the British as a secret agent, was quickly tried and executed for his act.

1943

Carlo Tresca (1877–1945), an Italian-American labor leader and anti–Fascist spokesman, was murdered in New York City on January 11, 1943. Tresca was a Socialist party organizer in Italy in the late 1800s, until he was forced into exile in Switzerland. He settled in the United States in 1904, where he became involved in the labor movement. He was also an active opponent of Benito Mussolini's (q.v.) government in Italy. Tresca served as editor of *Martello*, a publication he used to vehemently denounce Fascism. He escaped several assassination attempts before his fatal shooting on a New York street. His assailant, who was never apprehended, was believed to have been an agent of Mussolini.

In February of 1943 **Sotir Yanev**, a leading Bulgarian politician and a minister in the National Assembly, was murdered.

Hendrik Alexander Seyffardt, the chief of staff of the Dutch army from 1929 to 1934, was assassinated in the Hague on February 5, 1943. Seyffardt had come out of retirement during the German occupation of the Netherlands and formed a volunteer military unit called the Vrijkorps, which fought with German troops in Russia. He was killed by Dutch Resistance members as a collaborationist.

On February 22, 1943, **Hans Scholl** and his sister, **Sophie Scholl,** were executed by hanging following a trial by the Nazi People's Court. They were active in the "White Rose" resistance group which operated out of Munich University. The Scholls were born in Forchtenberg, Wurttemberg, Hans in 1918, and Sophie in 1921. After meeting Kurt Huber (q.v.), a professor of philosophy, while attending the University of Munich, they joined the resistance to Adolf Hitler's regime. They printed and distributed leaflets denouncing the Nazis, taking the name of their group from the emblem of a white rose which was printed on the leaflets. On February 18 they distributed fliers from the main building at the university, calling on the youth of Germany to rise up against the Nazis. They were subsequently arrested by the Gestapo and executed after a summary trial.

Pierre Brossolette, a leader of the French Resistance, died in prison of injuries received after being tortured by the Gestapo, on March 22, 1943. Brossolette was born on June 15, 1902, at Angouleme. He was a Socialist and served as editor of the party newspaer *Le Populaire* in the late thirties. Following the German occupation of France, Brossolette went to London in 1942, to join General Charles de Gaulle. He subsequently returned to France to serve as a leader of the resistance movement, where he was captured by the Germans.

Isoruku Yamamoto (1884–1943), the commander-in-chief of the Japanese navy during World War II, was killed on April 18, 1943, when his plane was shot down by U.S. forces over the Solomon Islands. Yamamoto was instrumental in planning the Japanese attack on Pearl Harbor. His use of Japanese naval air power scored him early victories against the Allies in the Java Sea, but United States forces were able to defeat Yamamoto's Imperial Navy at the Battle of Midway in June of 1942. Yamamoto was targeted for death when United States intelligence agents decoded a Japanese message giving details of a planned inspection tour by Yamamoto.

On May 2, 1943, **Col. Atanas Pantev**, the Bulgarian chief of police from 1939 to 1941, was shot and killed in Sofia.

Wladyslaw Sikorski, the leader of the Polish government in exile during World War II, died in an airplane crash near Gibraltar on July 4, 1943. Sikorski's difficulties in establishing and maintaining an effective relationship with Joseph Stalin's Soviet government led to speculation that the crash which claimed his life may not have been an accident. Sikorski was born in Galicia on May 20, 1881. He served under Jozef Pilsudski during World War I, leading the Polish troops which fought against Russia. Following the Russo-Polish War, Sikorski was named chief of the Polish general staff. In December of 1922 Sikorski became prime minister of Poland, serving until May of 1923. He remained active in political and military affairs and was instrumental in the modernization of the Polish army. Sikorski was dismissed from public service in 1928, but remained a leader of the opposition to the Pilsudski government. Sikorski became Poland's prime minister in exile and commander-in-chief of the Free Polish Army after the fall of

Poland to Germany in 1939. He located his government in London after the fall of France in 1940, and was serving in this capacity at the time of his death.

Jean Moulin, another leader of the French Resistance, died on July 8, 1943, in a German prison following brutal beatings. Moulin was born on June 20, 1899, in Beziers. He served in the French civil service as a prefect in the Eure-et-Loir Department. He was removed from his position after his refusal to cooperate with the Germans following the occupation of France. Moulin joined the French Resistance and escaped to London. He returned to France to help organize the maquis, French Resistance guerrilla fighters, as delegate general for Gen. de Gaulle for unoccupied France. He took the code name "Max" and served as the first chairman of the National Council of the Resistance. In June of 1943 he was captured by the Gestapo and imprisoned. He was taken to Germany and subjected to torture and beatings, resulting in his death.

Prof. Karl Huber, a professor of philosophy at the University of Munich, was beheaded on July 13, 1943. Huber, who was born on October 24, 1893, in Switzerland, was a leading member of the German resistance to the Nazis in Munich, and had inspired Hans and Sophie Scholl (q.v.) in the formation of the "White Rose" movement. He was arrested in February, along with the Scholls, and sentenced to death.

Boris III, the king of Bulgaria, died mysteriously on August 28, 1943, following a meeting with Adolf Hitler. The cause of the king's death was variously reported as a heart attack, poison, or a gunshot, but it seems likely that he was the victim of an assassination. Boris III was born in Sofia, Bulgaria, on January 30, 1894. His father, Ferdinand I, abdicated the Bulgarian throne in favor of Boris on October 4, 1918. During the early years of his reign, Boris was faced with hostility from the Agrarian Peasant's party. Following the overthrow and murder of Aleksandr Stamboliski (q.v.) during a military coup in 1923, the left wing of the Agrarians, in conjunction with the Communists, staged a number of bloody, though ultimately unsuccessful, risings against the government. Boris succeeded in regaining the loyalty of the peasants following the ouster of the right-wing prime minister, Aleksandr Tsankov, in 1926 and the subsequent restoration of a constitutional government. Boris' rule suffered another blow in 1934 following a coup by the republican Military League. His throne was saved primarily through the diplomatic intervention of Great Britain. Thereafter Boris became more directly involved in affairs of state, and attempted to maintain

Bulgarian neutrality prior to the start of World War II. Under increasing pressure from the Germans, Boris signed a pact with the Axis powers in March of 1941 and declared war on Great Britain later in the year. Boris was a reluctant ally of Hitler; therefore his sudden death following a meeting with the German leader appears to have been the result of some form of foul play by the Nazis. Boris was succeeded by his six-year-old son, Simeon II.

On September 22, 1943, **Wilhelm Kube**, the German commissioner general for White Russia, was killed in Minsk by a bomb planted at his headquarters by Russian agents.

Bernhard Lichtenberg, a leading Catholic member of the resistance to the Nazis, died on November 3, 1943, while en route to Dachau concentration camp. Lichtenberg was born in Silesia on December 3, 1875. He became a Catholic priest in 1899 and served during World War I as a military chaplain. Following the war he joined the Catholic Centre party and served as a city councillor in Berlin. As provost of St. Hedwig's Cathedral in Berlin, Lichtenberg attacked the Nazi program of euthanasia, and publicly prayed for the Jews during church services. He was arrested on October 23, 1941, by the Gestapo, serving two years in Tegel Prison in Berlin. His death occurred while he was being transferred to a concentration camp.

1944

On January 6, 1944, **Kaj Munk** (1898–1944), a Danish playwright and clergyman, was murdered near Silkeborg, Denmark. Munk, an outspoken critic of the Nazis, was the author of *An Idealist* (1928), *The Word* (1932), and the anti–Nazi play *He Sits by the Melting Pot* (1938). Local police were forbidden by the Gestapo from investigating the murder.

On January 11, 1944, five Italian Fascist leaders were found guilty of treason by a Fascist tribunal at Verona. **Count Galeazzo Ciano**, Mussolini's foreign minister from 1936 to 1943, **Emilio De Bono**, former commander-in-chief of Italy's armed forces, **Luciano Gottardi**, **Giovanni Marinelli**, and **Carlo Pareschi** had all voted against Mussolini at the Fascist Grand Council of July 24, 1943. They were all tried and convicted at the insistence of Germany.

Count Galeazzo Ciano was born on March 18, 1903, in Leghorn, Italy. In the 1920s Ciano entered the Italian diplomatic corps, following a brief career in journalism. In April of 1930 he married Edda, the eldest daughter of Benito Mussolini (q.v.), and soon after was appointed Italy's envoy to China. He served in that position for two years and, in 1934, was named minister of propaganda. In January of 1936 he was appointed by his father-in-law to the position of foreign minister.

Ciano was an early advocate of Italy's alliance with Germany and was instrumental in Mussolini's decision to enter Italy into World War II on the side of the Axis powers, following the fall of France in 1940. Ciano's enthusiasm for the German cause soon decreased due to the increasing number of Axis military defeats and the treatment of the Italians by their German allies. In 1942 he began advocating a separate peace with the Allies and, in February of 1943, was removed from his position as foreign minister. He was given the post of ambassador to the Vatican, over the objection of the Germans, who felt he might enter into negotiations with the Allies from that diplomatic position. On July 25, 1943, Ciano voted with the majority of the Fascist Grand Council in forcing Mussolini's resignation. He fled to northern Italy soon after, as the new government began investigating charges that he had used his positions of influence for his personal financial gain. While in hiding, Ciano was lured to Munich by agents of Joachim von Ribbentrop (q.v.), the German foreign minister. He was arrested there by the Gestapo and tried and executed for treason at the insistence of Hitler, who held him personally responsible for Mussolini's ouster.

Gen. Emilio De Bono was born on March 19, 1866, in Cassano d'Adda. He joined the Italian army at an early age, and served on the general staff during Italy's war with Turkey. During World War I he rose from the rank of regimental commander to that of general. He later became active in Mussolini's Fascist movement and took part in the March on Rome in 1922. He served in the subsequent Fascist government and, following the Italian invasion of Ethiopia in 1935, was named commander-in-chief of the Italian forces.

De Bono became decreasingly removed from Mussolini's policies during World War II, and supported his ouster at the Fascist Grand Council in July of 1943. Soon after, he was seized by supporters of the deposed dictator and was among the foes of Mussolini who were tried and executed for treason.

Chang Yao-Tsu, the fifty-one-year-old Japanese puppet governor of Kwangtun Province, China, was shot and killed by Nationalists on April 5, 1944.

Col. Demetrios Psarros, the leader of the Social Liberation Movement (EKKA), an anti–Communist Greek guerrilla army established to resist the German occupation, was murdered in April of 1944. Col. Psarros was killed by Aris Velouchiotis, a Communist guerrilla fighter. Velouchiotis was himself killed several years later during the Greek civil war.

On April 10, 1944, President Miguel Avila Camacho (1897–1955) of Mexico narrowly escaped assassination when a gunman fired a revolver into his chest. The president's life was saved by the bullet-proof vest he was wearing. The attempted assassin was identified as Sama Rojas, a pro–Nazi Mexican military officer. Rojas was shot by presidential guards at the scene and died of his injuries several days later.

On April 17, 1944, **Max Josef Metzger**, a Catholic priest and foe of the Hitler regime, was executed at Brandenburg. Father Metzger was born on February 3, 1887. He was ordained a priest in 1911, becoming the curate at Mannheim and Karlsruhe. He was the founder of the Peace League of German Catholics in 1917. In 1942 Father Metzger sent a letter to the Protestant archbishop of Uppsala calling for the removal of the Nazi regime in Germany. He was arrested by the Gestapo and condemned for treason by the People's Court.

Christian Wirth, the S.S. major who had served as head of the Polish death camp operations, was killed in street fighting with Yugoslav partisans on May 26, 1944. Wirth was born in Wurttenberg in 1885 and served with distinction in the German army during World War I. In the early 1930s he served with the police in his hometown, and was known for his brutal investigative methods. He rose in rank in the criminal police (KRIPO) and was, in 1939, placed in charge of liquidating the mentally ill by means of lethal injections and poison gas. In 1941 Wirth was sent to Poland to administer the elimination of over two million Jews in death camps at Chelmno, Belzec, Sobidor, and Treblinka. He performed his duties with an inhuman vigor and, in 1943 he was sent by Himmler to Yugoslavia. It was there that he perished during a skirmish in the streets of Trieste, possibly the intentional victim of Jewish revenge squads.

On June 6, 1944, **Prof. Marc Bloch**, a French historian at the University of Paris, was arrested, tortured, and shot by the Gestapo in France. Bloch had been a leading member of the French Resistance, and his execution came two weeks prior to the liberation of France.

Philippe Henriot, the French Vichy minister of propaganda, was killed by members of the French Resistance while in his bedchamber, in Paris, on June 28, 1944.

On July 8, 1944, Dr. Jose Antonio Arze, a leading Bolivian leftist, was shot twice in the back and seriously wounded. Arze's injuries forced his resignation from the seat in the Bolivian congress which he had won earlier in the year.

On July 20, 1944, the German anti–Nazi conspiracy made an attempt on the life of Adolf Hitler. A bomb was planted under a conference table in Rastenburg, East Prussia, during a meeting which Hitler was attending. Count Claus von Stauffenberg, who planted the bomb, believed that Hitler had been killed in the attempt, and directed that the planned coup against the Nazi regime proceed. Hitler had instead suffered only minor injuries, and quickly regained control of Germany. Most of the conspirators were rounded up, and many other Resistance leaders not involved in this particular plot were also arrested and tried. Over 150 alleged conspirators were executed as a direct result of the bomb attempt, including thirteen generals and two ambassadors. Fifteen other leading figures in the conspiracy committed suicide.

Though Hitler was not killed during the attack, several others in attendance at the meeting died from their injuries, including **Col. Heinz Brandt**, the chief of staff to Gen. Heusinger, deputy chief of staff of the army; **Gen. Gunther Korten**, the air force chief of staff; **Gen. Rudolf Schmundt**, an adjutant to Hitler; and **Berger**, the official stenographer.

Gen. Korten, who was born in 1898, was Luftwaffe chief of staff from August 25 until his death. He was close to resigning his position due to differences with Hermann Goering when he was critically injured in the bomb blast, dying two days later.

Gen. Schmundt, who was born on August 13, 1896, was chief of the Wehrmacht Personnel Office and Adolf Hitler's Wehrmacht adjutant at the time of his death. He had previously served as chief of army personnel. He died on October 1, 1944, from wounds suffered in the explosion.

The first reprisals against the conspirators took place on July 20, 1944, the same day of the plot. After the bomb explosion, **Count Claus Schenk von Stauffenberg** returned to the War Office in Berlin, where he was joined by **Col. Gen. Friedrich Olbricht**, the chief of staff and deputy commander of the Reserve Army; **Gen. Ludwig Beck**, the chief of staff of the German Armed Forces from 1935 to 1938; **Lt. Werner von Haeften**; and **Col. Mertz von Quirnheim**. As it became clear that the attempt on Hitler's life was unsuccessful, they were ordered arrested by the Reserve Army commander, Gen. Friedrich Fromm (q.v.). They were given a summary court-martial, and executed, with the exception of Gen. Beck, who was given the opportunity to take his own life.

Count Claus Schenk von Stauffenberg was born on November 15, 1907, in Upper Franconia. He was strongly influenced by his aristocratic and

Roman Catholic upbringing. In 1926 he joined the Germany army and, in 1930, was commissioned a second lieutenant. In 1936 he entered the General Staff College in Berlin and later served under Gen. Hoepner as a staff officer in Poland and France. Stauffenberg served at the Russian front after Hitler's invasion of the Soviet Union and, through his contact with Russian prisoners of war, became interested in Socialism. He was an early member of the German resistance movement, becoming one of the leading conspirators in the attempt to overthrow the Nazi regime. In 1943 Stauffenberg was gravely injured while serving with the Tenth Panzer Division in North Africa, losing his left eye and his right hand. Following his recovery and return to duty, Stauffenberg was named chief of staff to Gen. Friedrich Olbricht, the deputy commander of the Reserve Army, in Berlin. He was promoted to chief of staff to the commander of the Reserve Army, Gen. Friedrich Fromm, in June of 1944. At this post he was in a position to attend meetings at Hitler's headquarters, and was chosen by the conspirators to carry out the assassination of the Fuhrer. Two earlier plans to kill Hitler, on July 2, 1944, and July 15, 1944, were postponed, as the conspirators were hoping to also eliminate Hermann Goering and Heinrich Himmler. Stauffenberg, as a seriously wounded war hero, was not subjected to the usual vigorous searches conducted by Hitler's security forces, and was able to deliver a bomb in his briefcase on July 20. He arranged to be called away to the telephone prior to the detonation of the bomb, and returned to Berlin following the blast, convinced that Hitler had been killed. After his arrival in Berlin, Stauffenberg learned that the other conspirators had not taken control of the key installations as planned, but had been awaiting his return. When it was learned later in the night that Hitler had survived the assassination attempt, troops loyal to the Führer arrested Stauffenberg and other key conspirators at the War Ministry on the Bendlerstrasse. Stauffenberg was hastily court-martialed by General Fromm, and executed for treason in the War Ministry courtyard.

Col. Gen. Friedrich Olbricht was born in Leisnig on October 4, 1888. He served in the German army during World War I. In 1926 Olbricht served as a general staff officer and, in March of 1940, he was promoted to the post of second in command to the commander of the Replacement Army. He was an early member of the anti–Nazi conspiracy to remove Hitler and, with Claus von Stauffenberg, was instrumental in planning "Operation Valkyrie," which was to have allowed the Resistance to take power in Berlin following the elimination of Hitler. After Stauffenberg's attempt on Hitler's life, Olbricht was to have begun "Valkyrie," but delayed its implementation until Stauffenberg returned to Berlin. This delay cost the Resistance valuable time and resulted in the failure of the scheme once news reached the capital that Hitler was not dead. Olbricht was swiftly ordered arrested by Gen. Fromm. He was summarily court-martialed and executed with the other conspirators present at the War Ministry.

Gen. Ludwig Beck was born in the Rhineland on June 19, 1880. He served on the German general staff from 1911 and saw active duty during World War I. He rapidly rose in rank and power in the army and, in 1935, was named chief of the army general staff. Beck was a bitter critic of Hitler's adventurous military and foreign policies and frequently clashed with the Führer over these matters. On August 27, 1938, Beck resigned his position in the hopes that his fellow officers would do likewise. He was bitterly disappointed that little attention was given his departure, and that Hitler was now free to pursue his policies without a restraining hand at the head of the general staff. Beck became an active conspirator in the plot to remove Hitler, and was to have replaced Hitler as Germany's head of state had the July 20 conspiracy proved successful. Following the failure of the coup, Beck, who had joined with other conspirators at the War Ministry, was allowed to commit suicide with his pistol. When his first two attempts to end his life failed, an attending sergeant assisted him on a third successful attempt.

Lt. Werner von Haeften was born in Berlin on October 9, 1908. He served in the army during World War II and, in 1942, was sent to the Quartermaster's Office of the German high command. There he became adjutant to Count von Stauffenberg and became an active member of the conspiracy against Hitler. Lt. von Haeften had accompanied Stauffenberg to Hitler's conference in Rastenburg, and was arrested and executed with him following their return to Berlin and the failure of the plot.

On August 8, 1944, more leading anti–Nazi conspirators were executed following their conviction for treason by the People's Court. The Resistance leaders, who had been involved in the July 20 plot against Hitler, included **Field Marshal Erwin von Witzleben**, the highest ranking army officer involved in the conspiracy; **Col. Gen. Erich Hoepner**, a leading tank commander; **Count Peter Yorck von Wartenburg** (1903–44), a founder of the anti–Nazi Kreisau Circle; **Maj. Gen. Helmut Stieff** (1901–44), who prepared the bomb used in the assassination attempt; and **Capt. Friedrich Karl Klausing** (1920–44), **Lt. Gen. Paul von Hase, Reserve Lt. Dr. Albecht von Hagen**, and **General Staff Lt. Col. Robert Bernardis**.

Erwin von Witzleben was born in Breslau on December 4, 1881. He served in the German army and was appointed a field marshal on July 19, 1940, following the fall of France. Von Witzleben had long been involved in the conspiracy to remove Hitler, and was to have been named as commander-in-chief of the German Wehrmacht had the conspiracy succeeded. He was arrested on the day after the unsuccessful attempt on Hitler's life, and subjected to torture and humiliation prior to his execution.

Erich Hoepner was born on September 14, 1886, in Frankfurt. He was a veteran German tank commander who had been humiliated and dismissed by Hitler while serving as commander of the Fourth Armored Corps during the invasion of the Soviet Union. He was to have been the German minister of war in the post–Nazi government.

Throughout the year more trials took place in the Nazi People's Court and more conspirators were executed. The more prominent included **Wolf Heinrich Graf von Helldorf**, chief of police in Berlin; **Adam von Trott Zu Solz**, a German Abwehr official; **Otto Karl Kiep**, a member of the German Foreign Office; **Karl Heinrich von Stulpnagel**, the German military governor of France from 1942 to 1944; **Gen. Erich Felligiebel** (1888–1944), the German Army's chief signal officer; **Ulrich-Wilhelm Schwerin Schwanenfeld** (1902–44), assistant adjutant to Gen. von Witzleben; **Ulrich von Hassell**, the former German ambassador to Italy; **Joseph Wirmer** (1901–44), a leading Centre party politician; **Wilhelm Leuschner**, a leading trade union member; **Adolf Reichwein**, a leading Social Democratic politician; **Elizabeth von Thadden**, a leading educator; **Jens Peter Jessen**, an economics professor at the University of Berlin; **Count Friedrich Werner von Schulenberg**, the former German ambassador to the Soviet Union; **Bernhard Letterhaus**, a Catholic labor leader; and **Lt. Col. Caesar von Hofacker**, a member of Gen. von Stulpnagel's staff.

Wolf Heinrich Graf von Helldorf was born on October 14, 1896, in Merseburg. He served during World War I and was involved in the Kapp Putsch in 1920. He joined the Nazi party in 1926 and, in 1933 was elected to the Reichstag. Von Helldorf was named Berlin's chief of police in July of 1935. During the war von Helldorf became involved in the conspiracy against Hitler, and was arrested following the July 20 coup attempt. He was tried and, on August 15, 1944, executed.

Adam von Trott Zu Solz was born on August 9, 1909 in Potsdam. A leading anti–Nazi, he used his position in the German foreign office and the Abwehr to establish a link between the German Resistance and Allied and American leaders. He was arrested for his role in the July 20 plot, and tried before the People's Court. He was hung in Plotzensee Prison on August 26, 1944.

Otto Karl Kiep was born on July 7, 1886, the son of a German diplomat. He joined the German Foreign Office and was named counselor to the German Embassy in Washington in 1927. In 1930 he was appointed consul general in New York. He was recalled to Germany in 1933 following his attendance at a banquet honoring Albert Einstein. During the war Kiep was reinstated in the foreign office and became active in the German resistance movement. He was implicated by the Gestapo for treason after attending a tea party at the home of Elizabeth von Thadden (q.v.), another Resistance leader. He was tried by the People's Court and executed at Plotzensee Prison on August 26, 1944.

Karl Heinrich von Stulpnagel was born January 2, 1886, in Darmstadt.

He was quartermaster general on the German army's general staff from 1938 to 1940. He then served until October 1941 as commander of the German Seventeenth Army following the invasion of Russia. On March 3, 1942, he was named military governor of Paris. Stulpnagel had long been an opponent of the Nazi regime and was active in the conspiracy to overthrow Hitler. Following the July 20 attempt on Hitler's life, Stulpnagel successfully ordered the arrest of the senior S.S. and Gestapo officers in France, before it became apparent the coup attempt had failed. He was ordered back to Berlin and unsuccessfully attempted to take his own life en route. Though seriously injured, Stulpnagel was tried by the People's Court and, on August 30, 1944, hanged in the Plotzensee Prison courtyard.

Ulrich von Hassell was born in Pomerania in 1881. He joined the German Foreign Office in 1908, and later served in various diplomatic posts throughout Europe. He was the German ambassador to Denmark from 1926 to 1930, and ambassador to Yugoslavia from 1930 to 1932. In 1932 he was sent to the German embassy in Rome as ambassador to Italy. His dislike for the Nazis resulted in his removal from the diplomatic corps in 1938. He supported a military coup against Hitler, and was involved in several conspiracies against the Nazis' rule. Hassell was long suspected of disloyalty by the Gestapo, and was arrested shortly after the July 20 attempt on Hitler's life. He was tried by the People's Court and, on September 8, 1944, was hanged at Plotzensee Prison.

Elizabeth von Thadden was born on July 29, 1890, in East Prussia. She was the founder and administrator of Schloss Wieblingen, a Protestant boarding school near Heidelberg. During the war she became involved with the German resistance movement. She was implicated by the Gestapo for her activities following a meeting of anti–Nazis at her home, during a tea party organized by Frau Anna Solf. She was tried by the People's Court and, on September 8, 1944, executed.

Wilhelm Leuschner was born on June 15, 1888, in Bayreuth. He was an early member of the Social Democratic party and a leading figure in the German trade union movement. He was arrested by the Nazis in May of 1933 and imprisoned in a concentration camp for nearly a year. Upon his release he became active in the German Resistance, serving as a liaison between the outlawed trade unions and the leaders of the conspiracy. He was arrested shortly after the failure of the July 20 attempt on Hitler's life and was executed on September 29, 1944.

Adolf Reichwein was born on October 3, 1898, in Bad Ems. He joined the Social Democratic party prior to World War I, and served as a professor at Halle Teachers' College. In 1933, as a leading Socialist, his resignation was forced by the new Nazi regime. He was active in the German Resistance, and was arrested with Julius Leber (q.v.) on July 4, 1944, following a meeting with members of the underground Communist movement. He was tried and executed on October 20, 1944.

Jens Peter Jessen, an economics professor at the University of Berlin, was a member of the Nazi party during the early 1930s, but became disillusioned with them following the rise to power in 1933. He became involved with the Kriesau Circle and other resistance groups, and was arrested following the July 20 plot against Hitler. He was tried and sentenced to death, being executed in November of 1944.

Count Friedrich Werner von Schulenburg (1875–1944) was a leading member of the German diplomatic corps and an architect of the 1939 Non-Aggression Pact between Germany and the Soviet Union. He served as Germany's ambassador to the Soviet Union from 1934 until the German attack in 1941. Schulenburg, a lifelong friend of Gen. Ludwig Beck (q.v.), soon became involved with the conspiracy to remove Hitler. He was arrested following the failure of the July 20 plot, and executed on November 10, 1944.

Bernhard Letterhaus was born on July 10, 1894, in the Rhineland. He became involved in the organization and administration of Catholic labor unions following service in World War I. In 1928 he was elected union secretary of the Catholic Worker's Association. Letterhaus was an early advocate of resistance to the Nazi regime. During the war he served in the Abwehr and became directly involved in the conspiracy to overthrow Hitler. He was arrested with other conspirators following the July 20 attempt on Hitler's life, and was tried by the People's Court. Letterhaus was executed on November 14, 1944.

Caesar von Hofacker was born on March 2, 1896. He was the cousin of Count von Stauffenberg (q.v.) and shared his convictions that Germany would be better served by the elimination of Adolf Hitler. Serving as a staff officer for Field Marshal von Kluge in France, von Hofacker acted as a liaison between Gen. von Stulpnagel (q.v.), the German military governor of France, and the conspirators in Berlin. He was arrested and tried with Gen. Stulpnagel by the People's Court on August 29. Von Hofacker was sentenced to death for his part in the conspiracy, and executed on December 20, 1944.

Other Resistance leaders who died at the hands of the Gestapo and S.S. following this period included **Gen. Fritz Lindemann, Col. Frh. von Boeselager, Col. Georg Hansen** of the Abwehr, **Dr. Carl Langbehn, Hans Bernd von Haeften**, the brother of Werner von Haeften, **Gen. Hans Count von Sponeck, Major Ludwig von Leonrod, Count Heinrich von Lehndorff, Dr. Carl Sack, Count Berthold von Stauffenberg**, brother of Klaus von Stauffenberg, **Gen. Fritz Thiel**, chief of signals, OKH, and **Gen. Freiharr von Thuengen**, who had been appointed by Gen. Beck to succeed Gen. von Kortzfleisch on the day of the attempt on Hitler's life.

Another leading member of the conspiracy to replace Hitler, **Field Marshal Erwin Rommel**, was given the option of taking poison or being tried by the People's Court, once his part in the conspiracy became known. Erwin Rommel was born on November 15, 1891, in Heidenheim. He served with distinction in the German Third Army during World War I. His military talents caught the attention of Adolf Hitler and, in February 1941, he was appointed German commander in Libya, leading the "Afrika Corps." He became known as the "Desert Fox," and won the respect of the enemy, as well as his superiors, for his strategic abilities. Following the German defeat during the second battle of El Alamein, Rommel was promoted to field marshal and sent to command Army Group B in France, in anticipation of the Allied invasion. He was injured near St. Lo on July 17, 1944, during an air raid, and sent back to Germany to recover. During the course of the war, Rommel had become increasingly opposed to the Nazi regime and Hitler's war policy. He was approached by the German Resistance and indicated he would support their attempt to overthrow Hitler. Had the July 20 plot succeeded, Rommel, as an extremely popular figure with both the military and general public, was to be named chief of state. His injuries prevented him from taking a direct part in the coup attempt and its aftermath. Following evidence of the field marshal's complicity in the conspiracy, Rommel was arrested by the S.S. On October 14, 1944, Rommel swallowed poison, sparing his family the disgrace of his being executed for treason. The German government announced that he had died from the injuries he had suffered in France, and he was given a hero's burial.

On July 7, 1944, **George Mandel**, a leading French politician, was executed by order of the French Vichy police. Mandel was born on June 5, 1885, near Paris. Mandel became a close advisor to Georges Clemenceau, serving on his personal staff and assisting in the compilation of his journals. In 1919 Mandel was elected to the chamber of deputies, serving until 1924. He was elected once again, in 1928, and served until 1940. He served in several cabinet positions during the 1930s. In 1938 he was named minister of colonies, serving until 1940, when he was appointed minister of the interior. Mandel was greatly opposed to collaboration with Germany following the fall of France. He was ordered arrested by the collaborationist government of Marshal Petain, but was subsequently released. Mandel traveled to North Africa in the hopes of continuing France's war effort from the colonies, but was arrested in Morocco. He was tried for treason in 1941, and handed over to the Germans in November of 1942. After spending several years in German concentration camps, Mandel was returned to Paris in early July, where he was executed by order of Joseph Darnand (q.v.), the head of the Vichy French police.

Princess Mafalda, the daughter of the king and queen of Italy, and the wife of Prince Philip of Hesse, died during 1944 at Buchenwald, following the desertion of her father, King Victor Emmanuel II, from Hitler.

Ernst Thaelmann, the leader of the German Communist party, was shot to death in Buchenwald concentration camp on August 28, 1944, after more than a decade in captivity. Thaelmann was born in Hamburg on April 16, 1886. He joined the German Communist movement in 1903, and was active in the organization of trade unions in Hamburg. He served as a Communist deputy in the German Reichstag from 1924 until 1933, also serving on the executive committee of the Comintern, the Soviet-dominated government body of international Communism. Thaelmann, like most leaders of the German far left, failed to recognize the threat of Hitler's brand of fascism, assuming the Nazi party was little worse than the traditional brand of German conservatism. Thaelmann ran for the presidency of the Reich in 1925, gaining few votes. In the 1932 election, won by Paul von Hindenburg, Thaelmann placed third, behind Adolf Hitler, and received over ten percent of the vote. Thaelmann was arrested soon after the Nazis came to power in 1933, and was sent to Moabit Prison in Berlin. Having spent over a decade in various prisons and concentration camps, Thaelmann was murdered in Buchenwald on August 28, 1944.

Gen. Alfredo Noguera Gomez, an exiled Nicaraguan army officer, was killed in a skirmish with Costa Rican troops on October 9, 1944, while preparing to lead a revolt into Nicaragua from the Costa Rican border. Gen. Gomez, an admirer of Juan Peron of Argentina, wanted to set up a Fascist government in Nicaragua.

On November 7, 1944, **Richard Sorge**, who had served as a spy for the Soviet Union, was executed in Japan. Sorge, who had been on close terms with the German Embassy in Tokyo, had been privy to many German and Japanese military secrets while working for the Soviet Union. Sorge was born in Russia in 1895. His father was a German, and Sorge spent much of his youth in Germany. He became a member of the Communist party in 1918, and acted as an agent for the Comintern throughout Europe and Asia. As a respected journalist for the *Frankfurter Zeitung*, Sorge settled in Tokyo in the early 1930s. He established high-level contacts with the Japanese and the German Embassy there. Sorge served as Russia's leading espionage agent in Asia and was able to relay much valuable and strategic information to Joseph Stalin. Through Sorge's efforts the Soviets were able to learn the exact date of the German invasion of the Soviet Union. Sorge was arrested on October 16, 1941, by the Japanese authorities and, on November 7, 1944, he was executed.

Walter Edmund Guiness, First Baron Moyne, was assassinated by two Israeli terrorists at his home in Cairo, Egypt, on November 16, 1944. Baron Moyne, who was born in 1880, had served as a member of the British parliament from 1907 to 1931. He served in the cabinet as minister for agriculture from 1925 to 1929 and from 1940 to 1941. He served as colonial secretary and the leader of the House of Lords in 1941 and 1942. In 1942 he was appointed the deputy minister of state in Cairo, a position he held at the time of his death. His assassins were identified as Eliahu Bet-Tsouri (1921–45) and Eliahu Hakim (1924–45). They were tried and convicted of the murder on January 10, 1945, and executed on March 22 of that year.

1945

Until virtually the end of World War II many leaders of the anti–Nazi Resistance were executed by the Nazis. These included **Karl Friedrich Goerdeler**, the former lord mayor of Leipzig and the chief civilian leader of the German Resistance movement; **Dietrich Bonhoeffer**, a German Lutheran pastor; **Adm. Wilhelm Canaris**, the chief of the German Abwehr; **Maj. Gen. Hans Oster**, Canaris' chief of staff at the Abwehr; **Count Helmuth von Moltke** and **Hans von Dohnanyi**, members of the Abwehr staff; **Julius Leber**, a leading Social Democratic politician; **Nikolaus Gross**, a trade union leader; **Alfred Delp**, a Jesuit priest; **Fritz Goerdeler**, the brother of Karl Goerdeler; **Wolf von Harnack**, a leading Social Democrat; **Gen. Arthur Nebe**, the head of the German criminal police; **Albrecht Haushofer**, a professor of political geography; **Klaus Bonhoeffer** (1901–45), a lawyer and the brother of Dietrich Bonhoeffer; and **Count Albrecht von Bernstorff**.

Julius Leber was born on November 16, 1891, in Alsace. He was an early member of the Social Democratic party and served in the German army during World War I. During the early 1920s he served as editor of the left-wing newspaper *Volksbote* in Lubeck, and was elected to the Reichstag in 1924. He was a leading opponent of Hitler, and was the target of an unsuccessful assassination attempt following the Nazis' rise to power in 1933. He was imprisoned by the Nazis following the Reichstag fire later in the year, and spent the next four years in concentration camps. Upon his release he became an active conspirator against Hitler's regime and a close political ally of Count Claus von Stauffenberg (q.v.). He was arrested by the Gestapo prior to the attempt on Hitler's life on July 20, 1944, when he was denounced by a Gestapo spy while attending a meeting with members of the outlawed Communist party. He was sentenced to death on October 20, 1944, by the People's Court and, on January 5, 1945, hanged at Plotzensee Prison in Berlin.

Count Helmuth Graf von Moltke was born in Silesia on March 2, 1907. He was an early opponent of National Socialism and a founder of the Kreisau Circle, whose meetings he hosted at his Silesian estate. During the war, von Moltke served as a legal advisor to the Abwehr. He was arrested by the Gestapo in January of 1944, and, though he had not participated in the July 20 plot against Hitler, he was tried and convicted by the People's Court. He was hanged on January 23, 1945, in the Plotzensee Prison courtyard.

Nikolaus Gross, a German trade union leader, was born on September 30, 1898, in the Ruhr. During the 1930s he served as editor of the *Westdeutschen Arbeiterzeitung*, a German worker's newspaper. He was an early opponent of the Nazis and was arrested by the Gestapo on August 12, 1944, for complicity in the July 20 plot. Following a trial before the People's Court, Gross was executed on January 23, 1945.

Karl Friedrich Goerdeler was born on July 31, 1884, in Schneidemuhl. Following service in World War I, Goerdeler was appointed second burgomeister of Königsberg in 1922. He served in this post until May 22, 1930, when he became lord mayor of Leipzig. He was an early opponent of Hitler and National Socialism and, on March 31, 1937, was forced by the Nazis to resign his position. He soon became the leading civilian member of the German Resistance, and used his personal prestige to encourage a military coup. Following the defeat of the German army at Stalingrad, Goerdeler was able to convince some major figures in the German military to plan for Hitler's overthrow. Goerdeler went into hiding following the failure of the July 20 attempt on Hitler's life, which, had the plot succeeded, would have made him the chancellor of Germany. On August 12 he was arrested by the Gestapo in Marienwerder, and tried by the People's Court. He was sentenced to death on September 8, 1944, and hanged in Berlin on February 2, 1945.

Johannes von Popitz was born on December 2, 1884, in Leipzig. He served in the finance ministry during the 1920s, and was minister of finance in Prussia following the 1933 victory of the Nazi party. Von Popitz, a conservative and a monarchist, became involved in the conspiracy against Hitler in 1938. He was instrumental in attempting to persuade Heinrich Himmler to join the conspiracy against Hitler, an act which brought him under the surveillance of the Gestapo. Von Popitz was arrested the day of the unsuccessful attempt on Hitler's life on July 20, 1944. He was tried and condemned to death by the People's Court on October 3, 1944, but was not executed until February 2, 1945.

Alfred Delp was born on September 15, 1907, in Mannheim. He was ordained a Jesuit priest in 1937. For the next four years Delp served as an editor of *Stimmen der Zeit*, a Jesuit journal. He became active in the German Resistance in 1942, and was arrested by the Gestapo shortly after the failure of the July 20 coup attempt. He was tried by the People's Court and sentenced to be executed. He was hanged in the Plotzensee Prison on February 2, 1945.

Wolf Alexander Oskar Ernst von Harnack was born in Marburg on July 15, 1888. A Social Democrat, von Harnack served in various positions in the Prussian civil service prior to the Nazi victory of 1933. A member of the

German Resistance, he was arrested immediately after the failure of the July 20, 1944, attempt on Hitler's life. He was tried before the People's Court, and hanged on March 3, 1945.

Arthur Nebe was born on November 13, 1894, and served in the German army during World War I. Nebe joined the German criminal police (KRIPO) in 1924 and, in 1931, joined the S.S. After Hitler came to power in 1933, Nebe was appointed chief of the state police. In 1941 he was placed in charge of "Action Group B," an extermination unit active at the Russian front. During this period Nebe was instrumental in developing new methods of mass execution. Nebe was reportedly repelled by the inhumanity of the system he observed, and joined the German Resistance. He went into hiding following the failure of the plot against Hitler, but was subsequently arrested and tried for treason. It was reported that he was executed on March 21, 1945, but various reports during the 1950s and 1960s allege he survived the war, using his supposed execution to avoid prosecution for war crimes.

Hans von Dohnanyi was born on January 1, 1902, in Vienna. He served on the staff of the Reich Justice Ministry from 1929 until 1938, when he was named to the Leipzig Supreme Court. The following year he was appointed to the Abwehr, serving under Maj. Gen. Hans Oster (q.v.). He used his position to gather evidence of the illegal activities of the Nazis, to be used to justify the overthrow of Hitler. Von Dohnanyi's involvement with the Resistance was suspected by the Gestapo, and he was first arrested in April of 1943. He was released at that time due to lack of evidence, but was arrested again shortly before the July 20 attempt on Hitler's life. He was sent to the Sachsenhausen concentration camp and, following the discovery of his private papers detailing Nazi atrocities, he was tried for treason. Von Dohnanyi was sentenced to be executed, and was put to death on April 8, 1945.

Dietrich Bonhoeffer was born on February 4, 1906, in Breslau. A theologian and lecturer, he left Germany for London following the Nazis' rise to power in 1933. He returned to Germany in 1935 and founded the anti–Nazi German Confessing Church. He joined the German Resistance against Hitler near the start of World War II, and acted as a liaison between the conspirators and the Allies. He was arrested by the Gestapo for subversion on April 5, 1943, and imprisoned. He was sent to Buchenwald following the July 20 attempt on Hitler's life, and was later transferred to Flossenburg concentration camp where, on April 9, 1945, he was executed.

Wilhelm Canaris was born on January 1, 1889, in Westphalia. He served with naval intelligence in Spain and Italy during World War I, and took part in the Kapp Putsch following the war. On January 1, 1935, he was appointed chief of the Abwehr, the German military intelligence agency. Canaris supported some of the views of the Nazis, particularly their opposition to Communism, but did not favor many of their activities. He, along with his deputy, Hans Oster (q.v.), became involved with the conspiracy against Hitler in the late 1930s. In February of 1944 he was dismissed as Abwehr head and appointed to the Office for Commercial and Economic Warfare. He was an active participant in the July 20 attempt on Hitler's life, and was arrested shortly after the plot's failure. He was imprisoned at Flossenburg concentration camp, and executed for treason on April 9, 1945.

Maj. Gen. Hans Oster was born in Dresden on August 9, 1888. He served as a general staff officer during World War I and, in 1933, was named to the Abwehr as head of the Financial and Administrative Department. Oster was an active foe of the Nazis, and used his position in military intelligence to pass on German military plans to the Allies and assist Jews in fleeing from Nazi occupation. He was relieved of duties in April of 1943 and was arrested shortly after the July 20, 1944, plot against Hitler. He was sent to Flossenburg concentration camp, and was executed with his former commanding officer, Wilhelm Canaris (q.v.), on April 9, 1945.

Albrecht Haushofer was born on January 7, 1903, in Munich. He was the son of Prof. Karl Haushofer, the founder of Geopoltik. Haushofer was named to the faculty of the University of Berlin as professor of political geography in 1939. He was a close friend of Rudolf Hess, the deputy führer of the German Reich, and was possibly instrumental in planning Hess' flight to England in May of 1941, on a quest for a separate peace with Great Britain. Haushofer was involved in numerous anti–Hitler conspiracies and, in December of 1944, he was arrested by the Gestapo. He was imprisoned in Moabit Prison, in Berlin, and shot by members of the S.S. during the Battle of Berlin, on April 23, 1945.

During 1945 the Communist Vietminh executed a number of prominent Vietnamese politicians whom they considered potential rivals, including moderate leaders **Bui Quang Chieu** and **Pham Quynh**, and **Ta Thu Thau**, the leader of the Trotskyite faction of the Vietnamese Communists.

Bui Quang Chieu (1873–1945), a founder of the Constitutionalist party in French Indo-China, was arrested and killed by the Communists. Bui Quang Chieu was a moderate Vietnamese nationalist and the founder of the Constitutionalist party in 1917. His party gained control of the Cochin-Chinese Colonial Council following the elections of 1926, and Bui Quang Chieu used his influence to advocate constitutional rights for the Vietnamese. He served in the Council of France Overseas from 1932 to 1941, and was a strong contender to head the first independent Vietnamese government. He was executed by the Communist Vietminh in 1945 for his moderate views.

Pham Quynh (1892–1945), a Vietnamese writer and politician, was executed by the Communists as a French collaborator. He served as a founder and editor of the *France-Indochine* newspaper and, in 1933, he succeeded Ngo Dinh Diem (q.v.) as chief minister in the government of Bao Dai. His pro–French views resulted in his execution by the Communist Vietminh nationalists in 1945.

Col. Karl Koch, the S.S. commandant of the Buchenwald concentration camp, was executed by the S.S. on charges of theft and poor discipline. Koch had served as Buchenwald's commandant from its founding in 1937. He and his wife, Ilse (1906–67), known as the "Red Witch of Buchenwald," were notorious for their brutal treatment of the camp prisoners. In 1943 the Kochs were investigated by the S.S. on charges of mismanagement and theft. Following a two-year investigation, Karl Koch was convicted of stealing from the Nazi party and was executed by the order of the S.S. district leader, Gen. Josias von Waldeck-Pyrmont (1896–1967). Though Ilse Koch was acquitted by the Nazis, she was arrested and tried by the Allies as a war criminal following the end of the war. After several trials, she was convicted in 1950 and sentenced to life imprisonment. She committed suicide on September 1, 1967.

Sigmund Rascher (1909–45), a Nazi doctor who had carried out secret experiments at the Dachau concentration camp, was arrested and executed for child abduction. Rascher was one of the more notorious Nazi concentration camp doctors who conducted inhuman experimentation on prisoners at Dachau from 1941 to 1942. His experiments, which dealt with the ability of humans to withstand extreme temperature, caught the attention of Heinrich Himmler, who served as Rascher's patron for his barbarous acts. Rascher escaped being tried for war crimes, as he was executed by the Gestapo at Dachau in 1945, after it was learned that the children he claimed were his own had been abducted from other German families.

On February 1, 1945, war crimes trials in Bulgaria, which had begun in December of 1944, culminated in the execution of the three regents; **Prince Cyril**, brother of the late King Boris III (q.v.); **Bogdan Filov** (1883–1945), who served as premier of Bulgaria from 1940 to 1943; and **Lt. Gen. Nikola Mikhov**. **Dobri Boshilov** (1884–1945), who was Bulgaria's premier 1943–44, and **Ivan Bagrianov** (1892–1945), who was premier in 1944, were also executed. Other executions included 22 ministers, 68 members of parliament and eight of King Boris' advisors.

Jacques Larsac, the former police chief of Dijon, France, was hanged by a mob on February 15, 1945. Larsac, who was imprisoned on charges of ruthless treatment of French Resistance members, was dragged from his jail cell and killed before he could be tried.

Ahmed Maher Pasha, the premier of Egypt from 1944, was shot and killed on February 24, 1945. His assassination took place in the Egyptian parliament in Cairo after announcing Egypt's declaration of war against the Axis powers. Maher, a Saadist, was assassinated by Mahmoud Essawy, a pro–German lawyer. Essawy was hanged on September 18, 1945.

Col. Gen. Friedrich Fromm (1888–1945), who as chief of the German Replacement Army had ordered the arrest and execution of the leading participants in the plot against Hitler on July 20, 1944, was tried by the People's Court and executed by firing squad on March 19, 1945.

Johann Georg Elser (1903–45), a Swabian cabinet maker who had attempted to assassinate Adolf Hitler on November 8, 1939, was murdered by the Gestapo on April 9, 1945, while in Dachau concentration camp. Elser, who opposed Hitler's war policy, had placed a bomb beneath a podium Hitler was scheduled to use while addressing a group of "Old Fighters" in Munich. Hitler left the meeting shortly before the bomb exploded, which killed seven people and wounded many others. Elser was arrested by the Gestapo the same evening and sent to Sachsenhausen concentration camp. He was transferred to Dachau in 1944, where he was killed by the Gestapo the following year under the cover of an Allied air raid.

Benito Mussolini, the founder of Fascism and the dictator of Italy from 1922, was executed by Italian partisans near Dongo, on the shores of Lake Como, on April 28, 1945. Executed with Mussolini were his twenty-five-year-old mistress, **Clara Petacci**, and **Achille Starace** (1889–1945), the secretary general of the Italian Fascist party from 1932 until 1939. Also captured and executed at that time were fifteen other Fascist leaders, many of whom were members of Mussolini's government. They included **Alessandro Pavolini, Francesco Maria Barraci, Dr. Paolo Zerbini, Ruggero Romano, Fernando Mezzasoma, Augusto Liverani, Carlo Scorza, Guido Gasti, Goffredo Coppola, Ernesto Daquanno, Mario Luigi, Vitto Casalnuovo, Pietro Salustri, Marcello De Facci**, and **Nicolo Bombacci**.

Benito Mussolini was born at Dovia on July 29, 1883. In his youth, Mussolini became active in Socialist politics, but resigned from the Socialist party in 1915 when he could no longer reconcile his nationalism and support for Italy's entry in World War I with party doctrine. On March 23, 1919, Mussolini founded the Fasci di Combattimento in Milan. The political situation in Italy rapidly deteriorated in the early 1920s and, on October 28, 1922, Mussolini's Fascist supporters marched on Rome, forcing King Victor Emmanuel III to name Mussolini as prime minister. He was quickly able to consolidate his power, eliminating those who threatened to challenge his authority. He maintained a parliamentary government through the crisis presented by the murder of Italian Socialist leader Giacomo Matteotti (q.v.)

in 1924. Mussolini outlawed all other political parties in 1926, and fully established himself as Italy's dictator.

Despite the similarities of their political philosophies, Mussolini was originally opposed to Adolf Hitler's ambitions for Germany, particularly the Nazi leader's designs on Austria. After the Italian invasion of Ethiopia in the Abyssinian War of 1935, and the subsequent condemnation of his policies by England and France, Mussolini moved toward a closer alliance with Germany. In May of 1939 a military alliance was signed between the two countries. Mussolini delayed Italy's entry into World War II until June of 1940, when he thought that Germany had already established itself as the victor. A rapid series of military defeats for the Italian army in Greece and North Africa greatly reduced Mussolini's prestige, and resulted in his ouster by a vote of the Fascist Grand Council on July 25, 1943. The former dictator was ordered imprisoned by King Victor Emmanuel, but was freed on September 12, 1943, by a group of German commandos led by Otto Skorzeny. Mussolini, reduced to total dependency on the German army for his authority, was established as leader of a Fascist regime in German-occupied northern Italy. The Axis cause continued to deteriorate and, in April of 1945, Mussolini and other leading Fascists tried to escape into Switzerland in the wake of the Allied advance. Mussolini was captured by Italian Communist partisans led by Walter Audisio (1909–73), known as Colonel Valerio, and summarily executed.

Roberto Farinacci, another former secretary general of the Italian Fascist party, was also executed by Italian partisans on April 28, 1945, in Milan. Farinacci was born in Isernia on October 16, 1892. He was an early follower of Benito Mussolini (q.v.), and was the founder of the Fascist daily newspaper *Cremona Nuova*. He was appointed secretary general of the Italian Fascist party on February 12, 1925, but was replaced in March of the following year. He served as a member of the Fascist Grand Council from 1935, and was appointed minister of state in 1938. Farinacci escaped from Rome following the downfall of Mussolini in 1943. He was captured by partisans in April of 1945, and tried and executed for treason.

S.S. Gen. Richard Gluecks, who served as the Nazi inspector of concentration camps during World War II, was presumed murdered by a Jewish revenge group on May 10, 1945.

Odilo Globocnik, the S.S. officer who was in charge of the extermination of Jews in Poland during World War II, was also presumed killed by a Jewish revenge group on May 31, 1945. Globocnik was born on April 21, 1904, in Trieste. He joined the Nazi party in 1930 and became a member of the S.S. three years later. He was appointed the Nazi gauleiter of Vienna in 1938, but was dismissed the following year for misconduct. He was reassigned later in 1939 as S.S. leader in Lublin, Poland. In 1943 Globocnik was placed in charge of organizing extermination camps to liquidate Polish Jews. The following year he was placed in charge of the S.S. in the Adriatic region. Following the end of the war Globocnik was captured and murdered by Jewish partisans in Austria.

Andre Baillet, the director general of information in the French Vichy government, was executed at Fort De Chatillon on July 18, 1945. He had been convicted of treason and collaboration with the Germans during a trial that ended on June 20, 1945.

On August 14–15, 1945, rebel soldiers seized the Imperial Palace in an attempted coup d'etat to prevent the surrender of Japan. **Gen. Takshi Mori** was slain during the mutiny. Hidemasa Koga, the son-in-law of Gen. Hideki Tojo (q.v.) and a leader of the coup attempt, committed suicide following the coup's failure.

On August 25, 1945, **John Birch** (1918–1945), a Baptist missionary in China, was shot to death by Chinese Communists. Birch had assisted Lt. Col. James Doolittle and his crew when they parachuted into China following the air attack on Tokyo in 1942. He subsequently served as an intelligence officer and interpreter in China under Brig. Gen. Claire Chennault. He was transferred to the Office of Strategic Services in Northern China in May of 1945, and was responsible for leading Japanese occupation troops to the coast following the surrender of Japan. He was seized and killed by a band of Chinese Communists while performing this mission. Birch served as the inspiration and namesake for the extreme anti–Communist John Birch Society, founded by Robert Welch in 1954.

Dr. Joseph Pfitzner, the deputy mayor of Prague, Czechoslovakia, during the German occupation, was hanged in Prague as a traitor on September 6, 1945.

On September 11, 1945, Italian **Gen. Nicolo Bellomo** was executed by a firing squad for war crimes.

On October 1, 1945, **Archbishop Anba Theophilus**, the Coptic patriarch of Jerusalem, was shot to death while walking in an Upper Egyptian grain field.

Joseph Darnand, a leading French collaborator with the Nazis, and the head of the Milice, the S.S. French police force, was tried for treason. He was sentenced to be executed on October 3, 1945. Darnand had commanded a French S.S. unit on the Russian front in 1943, before returning to

France and becoming the secretary general for the maintenance of order. Darnand's Milice was responsible for many brutal acts against members of the French Resistance.

On October 11, 1945, **Jean-Harold Paquis**, a French propaganda broadcaster during the German occupation, was executed by a firing squad near Paris.

Pierre Laval, the French politician who served as premier of Vichy France during much of World War II, was executed as a traitor by a firing squad at the Prison of Fresnes on October 15, 1945. Laval was born in Chateldon on June 28, 1883. He was elected to the Chamber of Deputies in 1914 and became a senator in 1926. In January of 1931 he was named premier of France, serving until 1932. He served in various cabinet positions until June of 1935, when he again was named premier and minister of foreign affairs, serving until January of 1936. In July of 1940, following the French armistice with Germany, Laval, who had held no government position when France had entered World War II, was named vice premier in the Vichy government under Marshal Petain. He served in this position until December of 1940, advocating French acceptance of the terms of the armistice with Germany. In April of 1942 he became premier of France, remaining in power through the final days of the German occupation. In August of 1945 he was forced to flee France as the Allies advanced. He went first to Switzerland, and then to Spain, before returning to France, in July, to stand trial for treason. He was convicted and shot.

French right-wing journalist **Robert Brasillach** (1909–45) was tried for treason and executed in 1945. Brasillach was a leading collaborationist with the Germans during the occupation of France.

Vidkun Quisling, the Norwegian Fascist leader who betrayed his country to Adolf Hitler and served as Norway's prime minister during the German occupation, was executed for treason on October 24, 1945. Quisling was born on July 18, 1887, at Fyredal, in Norway. He served as an officer on the Norwegian general staff from 1911, and was named military attache in Russia and Finland from 1918 until 1921. Following his retirement from the army, he served as minister of defense in the Agrarian party's government from 1931 to 1933. He resigned his position to found the Nasjonal Samling (National Union) party, a Fascist movement based on Adolf Hitler's Nazi party. In December of 1939 Quisling met with Hitler to discuss the overthrow of the Norwegian government. In April of the following year he revealed Norwegian defense plans to the German leader, and assisted in Germany's invasion of Norway. Following the German occupation, Quisling became the sole political leader of Norway. He was appointed minister president of Norway on February 1, 1942, by the Germans. His name became synonomous with "collaborationist" and after the liberation of Norway, in May of 1945, he was charged with high treason and shot as a traitor.

On November 28, 1945, **Col. Antonio Brito**, a former Cuban chief of police, was assassinated.

Gen. Anton Dostler, the Nazi general and commander of the Seventy-fifth Germany Army, was executed by a firing squad in Aversa, Italy on December 1, 1945. He was tried by the United States Military Tribunal in Rome on October 12, 1945, and convicted of war crimes.

Josef Kramer (1906–45), the S.S. commander of the Birkenau and Bergen-Belsen concentration camps, was executed for war crimes on December 13, 1945. Kramer had joined the S.S. in 1932 and served as deputy to Rudolf Hoess (q.v.) at Auschwitz from 1940 until 1944. He was named commandant at Birkenau in December of 1944. He served in that position, and at Bergen-Belsen, during the final periods of mass slaughter, as the Russian army advanced toward the concentration camp sites. He became known as the "Beast of Belsen" by the world press when the remains of his victims were discovered by the British army. He was tried by a British military court at Luneberg, and was sentenced to death on November 17, 1945. He was executed the following month.

On December 30, 1945, Nazi **Lt. Gens. Friedrich G. Bernhardt** and **Adolf Hamann** were hanged in Bryansk for war crimes.

1946

On January 3, 1946, **William Joyce**, the British propagandist known as "Lord Haw-Haw" during World War II, was convicted of treason and hanged in Wandworth Prison. Joyce was born in the United States in 1906. His mother was English and his father was an American citizen. The family moved to England in 1921, and Joyce became a member of the British Fascist movement. He went to Germany in 1939 and used his wit and talent as a tool for Joseph Goebbel's propaganda machine. During the war he broadcast misleading information about the British war effort and encouraged English soldiers to give up the fight. He was arrested in Germany at the end of the war, and returned to England to stand trial.

Sir Amin Osman Pasha, a former Egyptian finance minister, was assassinated on January 5, 1946.

Dr. Laszlo De Bardossy, the premier of Hungary from 1941 to 1942, was hanged in Budapest for treason on January 10, 1946. Bardossy, who was born in 1880, became premier of Hungary on April 5, 1941, following the suicide of Count Pal Teleki. Hungary declared war on the Soviet Union during his premiership. He was replaced on March 9, 1942, by Admiral Horthy, the regent, due to his involvement in a massacre in occupied Yugoslavia and his handling of a bill to make Istvan Horthy, the regent's son, deputy regent.

On January 13, 1946, **Tarrad Moulheim**, a Syrian deputy, was assassinated.

Lt. Gen. Herman Winkler, the former Nazi commander of Nikolayev, and six other German officers were hanged on January 17, 1946 for war crimes.

Gen. Otto Blaha and **Gen. Robert Richtermoc**, of the Prague gendarmerie, were hanged for war crimes in Prague on January 21, 1946.

On February 17, 1946, **Milio Bushati**, who had served as premier of Albania during the German occupation, and regents **Anton Arapi** and **Levi Nossi** were convicted of war crimes and shot in Tirana.

Jean Luchaire, the president of the pro–Nazi *Paris Press*, was executed in Paris on February 22, 1946, for treason and collaboration with the Germans.

On February 23, 1946, **Gen. Tomoyuki Yamashita**, the Japanese commander-in-chief in the Philippines, was executed for war crimes. **Lt. Col. Seichi Ohta**, head of the Japanese Kempei Tai (thought police) of the Philippines, and **Takuma Higashiga**, a civilian interpreter, were also executed.

Gen. Yamashita was born in Tokyo in 1885. He served in the Japanese army during the Russo-Japanese War, World War I, and the Sino-Japanese War. In 1940 he was named inspector general of Japanese aircraft and, in 1941, he was appointed commanding officer of the Twenty-fifth Army. In that capacity he led the forces that overran Malaya and captured Singapore. In 1942 he was stationed as commanding general of the Japanese army in northern Manchuria. He was appointed commander-in-chief of the Japanese-controlled Philippines in July of 1944, and put up a sturdy defense against the American advance. Yamashita's efforts at resistance proved in vain and, on September 2, 1945, he signed the articles of surrender. He was subsequently arrested on charges of allowing atrocities to take place under his command near the close of the war.

Bela Imredy, a former premier of Hungary, was executed for treason by a firing squad in Budapest on February 28, 1946. Imredy, who was born in 1891, had been convicted of war crimes and anti–Jewish activities in November of 1945. Imredy became premier of Hungary on May 13, 1938, and attempted to decrease the power of the extreme right. He was also active in trying to win the support of the Allied powers for Hungary. Pressure from Germany made his attempts futile, and he led his country toward a more pro–German policy, introducing authoritarian measures and anti–Jewish legislation. He resigned his office on February 16, 1939.

Count Fidal Palfy, the wartime minister of agriculture of Hungary, was hanged for treason in Budapest on March 2, 1946.

Ferenc Szalasy, a former pro–Nazi premier of Hungary, was executed in Budapest for treason on March 12, 1946. Four of his aides, **Joseph Gera**, **Karoly Bereczky**, **Gabor Vaina**, and **Ferenc Rajniss**, were also executed at this time. Szalasy, who was born in 1897, was the leader of the major Fascist movement in Hungary, the Arrow Cross. He was the leader of a collaborationist government under the Germans following the ouster and imprisonment of Adm. Horthy, the regent, on October 17, 1944. Szalasy was removed from office following the Soviet army's occupation of the capital on February 13, 1945.

Maximilien Blokzijl, a sixty-one-year-old Dutch Nazi broadcaster during the German occupation, was executed as a traitor in the Hague on March 16, 1946.

On March 20, 1946, former Hungarian ministers **Eugen Szoelloesi**, **Baron Gabriel Kemeny**, and **Sando Csia** were hanged for treason.

Marcel Bucard, the French blue-shirt Fascist leader, was executed for treason near Paris on March 20, 1946.

Marshal Doeme Sztojay, another former Hungarian premier, was condemned to death for treason on March 22, 1946. Sztojay, who was born in 1883, served as Hungary's premier from March 22 until August 24 in 1944.

Gen. Masaharu Homma, who had led the Japanese invasion of the Philippines in 1941, was executed by a firing squad at Los Banos, Luzon, the Philippines, on April 3, 1946. **Lt. Gen. Hikotaro Tajima** was executed with Gen. Homma. Gen. Homma was born in Nigata in 1888. A member of the Japanese army, Gen. Homma served as an observer with the British during World War I. Following a tour of duty as Japanese resident officer in India,

Homma was appointed military attache in London in 1930. Shortly after the Japanese attack on Pearl Harbor, Gen. Homma led the Japanese forces that invaded and captured the Philippines. After the defeat of Japan, the general surrendered to United States military authorities on September 14, 1945. He was brought to trial in Manila on January 3, 1946, on charges that he was responsible for the Bataan "death march" and other atrocities committed during the Japanese occupation. He was convicted on February 11, 1946, and executed two months later.

On April 11, 1946, **Andor Jaross**, a former Hungarian minister, was executed by firing squad in Budapest. He, his undersecretary **Dr. Vitz Laszlo Endre**, and **Laszlo Baky**, a former gendarme chief, had all been sentenced to death for war crimes on January 7, 1946.

Maj. Gen. Masataka Kaguragi, along with four other Japanese officers, was hanged by United States authorities for war crimes in Shanghai on April 22, 1946.

Dr. Franz Anton Basch, the German minority leader in Hungary, was executed for treason in Budapest on April 26, 1946.

Anton Mussert (1894–1946), the Dutch Nazi party leader, was executed for treason on May 7, 1946. Mussert founded the Dutch National Socialist Movement in 1931, patterning his party on Benito Mussolini's Fascism. Following the rise of the Nazi party in Germany, Mussert became an admirer of Adolf Hitler and adopted many of Hitler's ideals, including the persecution of the Dutch Jews. After the German occupation of the Netherlands, Mussert was appointed by Hitler as the "leader of the Netherlands people" in December of 1942. Mussert was arrested following Germany's defeat in 1945, and was convicted of treason and collaboration with the enemy on December 12, 1945. He was executed by a firing squad in a small village near the Hague five months later.

Karl-Hermann Frank, a leader of the Sudenten German party, was hanged for war crimes on May 22, 1946. Frank was born in Karlsbad on January 24, 1898. He became deputy to Konrad Henlein, the leader of the Sudenten German party, and was elected to the Czechoslovak parliament in 1937. After the Nazi occupation, Frank was appointed chief of police in Prague. On August 20, 1943, he was named Reich minister for the Protectorate of Bohemia and Moravia. He was arrested by the Allies at the end of the war, and handed over to the Czechoslovak government. Frank was charged with war crimes, and convicted and hanged near Prague.

William Hagelin, the minister of the interior in Vidkun Quisling's (q.v.) wartime government in Norway, was executed for treason in Oslo on May 22, 1946.

Ion Antonescu, the leader of the pro–German wartime government of Romania, was executed for war crimes on June 1, 1946, near Ft. Jilava. **Mihai Antonescu** (1904–46), who served as Ion Antonescu's deputy prime minister and foreign minister, and **George Alexeanu** and **Gen. Constantin Vasiliu**, two close aides to Antonescu, were also executed.

Antonescu was born on June 15, 1882, in Pitesti. He served in the Romanian army during World War I and, in December of 1937, he was named minister of defense. He was dismissed, because of his Fascist leanings, in February of 1938. Following a period of increasing civil disorders, Antonescu was appointed prime minister by King Carol II on September 4, 1940. He later forced the abdication of King Carol and governed Romania as a dictator. Romania became closely allied with Nazi Germany and joined in the war against the Soviet Union in June of 1941. Antonescu was ousted by a coup led by King Michael, the son of King Carol II, on August 23, 1944. He was imprisoned by the Soviet occupation forces and tried for war crimes.

Desider Laszlo, the chief of staff of the Hungarian army during the war, was convicted of war crimes and shot by a firing squad on June 1, 1946.

On June 3, 1946, **Chen Kung-Po**, who served as president of Nanking under the Japanese, was executed for treason in Soochow.

Ananda Mahidol, the king of Thailand, was shot to death in the royal palace on June 9, 1946. Ananda Mahidol was born in Germany on September 20, 1925. The king, titled Rama VIII, assumed the throne of Thailand under a regency in 1935, following the abdication of his uncle, King Prajahlipok. The circumstances of his death have remained a mystery, but in 1954 the Thai Supreme Court ruled that the king had been murdered. Three people, including Ananda Mahidol's private secretary, were sentenced to death for complicity in the assassination.

Prof. Wen I-To, a leading Chinese poet and scholar, and **Prof. Li Kung-Po** were murdered by agents of Chiang Kai-shek's Kuomintang government on July 11, 1946. The victims were both members of the liberal Democratic League, and had been outspoken critics of the government's intellectual repression in the 1940s.

Gen. Draja Mihajlovic, the Serbian army officer who served as leader of the Free Yugoslavian, or Chetnik, underground army during World War II, was executed for treason in Belgrade on July 17, 1946. The Yugoslavian government convicted Mihajlovic and twenty-three other defendants of treason and collaboration with the Nazis. **Milos Glisich**, a former Chetnik leader; **Radoslave-Rade Radich**, a former Chetnik unit commander; **Oskare**

Pavlovich, the former police chief of Zagreb; **Dragomir Yovanovich**, the former police chief of Belgrade; **Tanisiji Dinich**, the former minister of the interior; **Djuro Dokich**, the former minister of commerce; **Velibor Ionich**, the former minister of education; and **Kosta Musicki**, an aide to Yugoslavia's King Peter, were executed with Mihajlovic. The remaining defendants were tried in absentia.

Gen. Mihajlovic was born in Serbia on March 27, 1893. He was serving in the Serbian army at the time of the German attack on Yugoslavia in April of 1941. Mihajlovic organized and led a guerrilla army, called Chetniks, to fight the German occupation forces. The Chetniks originally fought alongside a rival Communist-led resistance army under the leadership of Josip Broz, called Marshal Tito. Mihajlovic was appointed minister of war of the Yugoslav government in exile in January of 1942. Shortly after his appointment, Gen. Mihajlovic was accused of assisting the German army in eliminating his Communist rivals. The Allies began to give increasing support for Marshal Tito's army as Mihajlovic's loyalty was further questioned. After the liberation of Yugoslavia, Gen. Mihajlovic went into hiding, but he was captured by partisans on March 13, 1946. His subsequent trial and condemnation generated much controversy throughout Europe and the United States, but Mijajlovic was executed despite pleas for mercy from the Western powers.

On July 20, 1946, **Arthur Greiser**, who served as the Nazi Reich governor of the annexed western regions of Poland during World War II, was hanged for war crimes in Poznan. Greiser was born in Posen on January 22, 1897. He became a member of the Nazi party in 1929, and joined the S.S. in 1930. Greiser was elected deputy president of the Danzig senate in 1933, and became senate president the following year. He held that position until 1939, when he was appointed gauleiter of the Warthegau region in western Poland. He supervised the mass deportation of Poles and Jews from the areas in his jurisdiction. Greiser was captured by the Americans at the end of the war, and handed over to the Polish authorities to stand trial. He was convicted of wartime atrocities and publicly executed.

Gualberto Villarroel, the president of Bolivia, was murdered during a revolt on July 21, 1946. Villarroel was born in 1908 and joined the Bolivian army. He fought against Paraguay in the Chaco War from 1932 until 1935, and became a leading figure in the Bolivian military. Villarroel became president of Brazil following a military coup in December of 1943. During his administration he implemented reforms that benefitted the tin miners and the Bolivian Indians. His labor and land reform programs met with bitter opposition from the tin industry and land owners, and resulted in a rebellion against his regime. The presidential palace in La Paz was attacked by a mob on July 21, 1946, and Villarroel was thrown from a balcony and lynched from a lamppost in the Plaza Murillo below.

In August of 1946 **Gen. Andrei A. Vlasov** (1900–46), **Gen. Sergei Bunyachenko**, and five other Soviet generals who had fought alongside the Germans during World War II were hanged for treason in Moscow.

Gen. Vlasov was a respected officer in the Soviet Red Army and commanded the Twentieth Army against the Germans in the Battle of Moscow. He was captured by the Germans in July of 1941 at the Volkhov front. He was soon convinced by the Germans to lead an anti–Stalinist Russian Army of Liberation, consisting of Russian prisoners of war. The German-sponsored army saw little active duty during World War II and surrendered to the Allies in 1945. Vlasov and the other officers were returned to the Soviet Union after the end of the war and condemned as traitors.

Vojtech Balu Tuka, the Slovakian Fascist leader who served as premier and foreign minister in the Nazi-backed regime of Josef Tiso (q.v.), was sentenced to death as a collaborator on August 11, 1946.

Robert Wagner, the Reich governor of Alsace-Baden during World War II, was executed for war crimes in Strasbourg on August 14, 1946. Wagner was born in Lindach on October 13, 1895. He was an early follower of National Socialism and served as the Nazi gauleiter in Baden from 1925. In 1940 he was appointed Reich governor of Alsace in occupied France. He was responsible for the mass deportation of Jews in that area, until it was recaptured by the Allies in 1945. Wagner was imprisoned and tried for war crimes by a French military court.

Theodor von Renteln, the Nazi commissioner general of Lithuania during World War II, was hanged by the Russians for war crimes in 1946. Von Renteln was born in Russia on September 14, 1897. He moved to Berlin in his youth and joined the Nazi party in 1928. He was appointed the leader of the Nazi Students' League and the Hitler Youth in 1931, serving until the following year. In August of 1941 von Renteln was appointed commissioner general of Lithuania, and was responsible for Nazi activities in that area. He was captured by the Russians at the conclusion of the war, and tried for atrocities committed during the war.

Following the conclusion of World War II, many of the leading figures in Nazi Germany were tried before the International Military Tribunal at Nuremberg. Over a period of several years, 199 men were tried by the Tribunal. Thirty-six defendants were sentenced to death, twenty-two received life sentences, 103 received prison terms, 38 were acquitted, and five committed suicide during their trials. On September 30, 1946, the first trial of the major Nazi leaders was concluded. Eleven of the twenty-one defendants were sentenced to death by hanging. The sentence was carried out on October 15, 1946, for ten of the defendants. They included **Joachim von Ribbentrop, Wilhelm Keitel, Ernst Kaltenbrunner, Alfred Rosenberg, Hans Frank, Wilhelm Frick, Julius Streicher, Fritz Saukel, Alfred Jodl**, and **Arthur Seyss-Inquart**. Hermann Goering (1893–1946), the leader of the German Luftwaffe and Adolf Hitler's second in command, cheated the hangman by taking poison several hours before his scheduled execution.

Joachim von Ribbentrop was born on April 30, 1893, in Wesel. He served in the German army during World War I, and later engaged in business as a wine merchant. He joined the Nazi party, shortly after meeting Adolf Hitler, in August of 1932. He served as the Führer's chief advisor on foreign affairs after Hitler's appointment as chancellor the following year, and, in 1935, was named Germany's ambassador-at-large. He was appointed ambassador to Great Britain in August of 1936, serving in that position until he was named minister of foreign affairs in February of 1938. He negotiated the German-Soviet Non-aggression Pact in 1939, and was instrumental in developing the German, Italian, and Japanese alliance the following year. Von Ribbentrop was captured by the British in Hamburg in June of 1945, and indicted for war crimes. He was convicted of being "responsible for war crimes and crimes against humanity because of his activities with respect to occupied countries and Axis satellites," and was hanged at Nuremberg Prison on October 16, 1946.

Gen. Wilhelm Keitel was born on September 22, 1882, in Helmscherode. He served in the German army and was promoted to major general in 1934. In February of 1938 he was named by Adolf Hitler as chief of the armed forces high command. Keitel dictated the terms of armistice to France in June of 1940, and continued to serve as a leading military advisor to Hitler throughout the duration of World War II. Keitel was present at Rastenburg during the bomb attempt on Hitler's life on July 20, 1944, but was uninjured in the explosion. He later served as a member of the court which sentenced many of the military conspirators against the Nazi regime to death. On May 9, 1945, Keitel signed the articles of Germany's unconditional surrender to the Allies, and was subsequently arrested for war crimes. He was tried at Nuremberg by the International Military Tribunal. The verdict convicting him stated that he "put pressure on Austria . . . signed the orders for the attack on Belgium and the Netherlands" and had otherwise planned and waged a war of aggression. He was hanged on October 16, 1946.

Ernst Kaltenbrunner was born in Austria on October 4, 1901. He served as a legal advisor to the Austrian Nazi party from 1932, and, after the German occupation in 1938, he was appointed chief of police for Austria. In 1943 Kaltenbrunner, by then a general in the S.S., was appointed chief of the Gestapo and the Nazi Security Police, succeeding Reinhard Heydrich (q.v.). In this position he was directly responsible for numerous atrocities committed by the Nazis. He was captured by an American patrol after Germany's defeat and tried for war crimes. He was found guilty of having "played a leading part in the extermination of the Jews" and hanged on October 16, 1946.

Alfred Rosenberg was born in Estonia on January 12, 1893. He was an early member of the Nazi party, and served as editor of the party newspaper, *Volkischer Beobachter*. He was a leading promoter of anti-Semitism. When Hitler was imprisoned following the unsuccessful Beer Hall Putsch in 1923, Rosenberg was named leader of the Nazi party. He was named to lead the Nazi party's foreign policy office in 1931 and, following Hitler's appointment as German chancellor in 1933, he continued to be a leading spokesman for Nazi philosophy. After the fall of France in 1940, Rosenberg was placed in charge of removing valuable artworks and transporting them to Germany. He was arrested by the Allies after Germany's defeat in World War II, and was tried for war crimes. He was convicted on all four charges and was judged "responsible for plunder throughout invaded countries." He was hanged at Nuremberg Prison on October 16, 1946.

Hans Frank was born in Baden on May 23, 1900. He joined the Nazi party in 1926 and subsequently became Adolf Hitler's legal advisor. In 1933 Frank was appointed state minister of justice for Bavaria, and soon after was named Reich commissioner of justice. From 1939 until August of 1944 he served as Nazi governor general of Poland and was directly involved in the extermination of Polish Jews. He was arrested after the conclusion of World War II, and was tried at Nuremberg. He was convicted of "willing participation in a program involving the murder of three million Jews," and was hanged on October 16, 1946.

Wilhelm Frick was born in the Palatinate on March 12, 1877. He was an early member of the Nazi party, and participated with Adolf Hitler in the Munich Beer Hall Putsch in 1923. Frick was elected to the German Reichstag in 1924 and was appointed to the position of minister of the interior in Thuringia in 1930. Following the formation of the Nazi government in Germany in 1933, Frick was named minister of the interior for Germany, serving until 1943. On August 24 of that year he was appointed Reich protector of Bohemia and Moravia, serving there until the end of the war. He was captured by the Allies in 1945 and tried for war crimes. He was found guilty at Nuremberg for having been "largely responsible for bringing the German nation under the complete control of the Nazi party . . . for the legislation which suppressed trade unions, the church and the Jews." He was hanged on October 16, 1946.

Julius Streicher was born in Upper Bavaria on February 12, 1885. He was the founder of the German Socialist party and, in 1921 he joined his groups with Adolf Hitler's Nazi party. The following year he began publication of *Der Sturmer*, a virulent anti–Semitic journal, which he edited until 1943. In 1925 Streicher was named the Nazi gauleiter of Franconia, a position he held until 1940, when his penchant for obscene conduct resulted in his dismissal. He was arrested following the end of the war, and tried on charges that his writings were used to incite the extermination of Jews. His verdict said, "his persecution of Jews was notorious" and that "as early as 1938 he began to call for the annihilation of the Jewish race." He was hanged at Nuremberg Prison on October 16, 1946.

Fritz Sauckel was born on October 27, 1894, in Hassurt am Main. He joined the Nazi party in 1923 and was appointed gauleiter of Thuringia in 1928. In 1932 he was named minister of the interior in Thuringia and, the following year, he was appointed governor. Sauckel was appointed by Hitler as German commissioner general of manpower in occupied territories in 1942. He was arrested by the Allies following the end of World War II and convicted of having had "overall responsibility for the slave labor program." It was further charged that he was "aware of the ruthless methods . . . used to obtain laborers and vigorouly supported" those methods. He was hanged at Nuremberg Prison on October 16, 1946.

Gen. Alfred Jodl was born on May 10, 1890, in Wurzburg. He served in the German army during World War I and was named to the German general staff in 1919. An early supporter of Adolf Hitler, he was promoted to major general in 1939 and was named chief of the German general staff. He remained in this position for the duration of the war. On May 7, 1945, he signed the articles of surrender for the German army. Gen. Jodl was arrested and charged with war crimes and tried by the International Military Tribunal. He was found guilty of having been "in the strict military sense the actual planner of the war . . . active in planning the attack on Czechoslovakia . . . in preparing the Norwegian attack . . . in planning against Greece and Yugoslavia." He was hanged at Nuremberg Prison on October 16, 1946.

Arthur Seyss-Inquart was born on July 22, 1892, in Moravia. He was a practicing lawyer in Vienna when, in 1931, he joined the Austrian Nazi party. He was a supporter of Anschluss, the Austrian union with Germany, and, under pressure from Germany, Seyss-Inquart was named Austrian minister of the interior on February 16, 1938. Following the resignation of Chancellor Kurt von Schuschnigg in March of 1938, Seyss-Inquart was appointed the Reich governor for Austria, a position he held until April 30, 1939. In October of that year he was named deputy to Hans Frank (q.v.), the Nazi governor of Poland, and the following May he was appointed Reich commissioner for German-occupied Holland. He was arrested by Canadian soldiers following the conclusion of World War II, and was tried for his role in the deportation of Dutch Jews and for the shooting of hostages. He was convicted at Nuremberg of "ruthless application of terrorism," and hanged on October 16, 1946.

Of the remaining defendants, Rudolf Hess (1894–1987), Walter Funk (1890–1960), and Eric Raeder (1876–1960) received life sentences. Baldurr von Schirach (1907–74) and Albert Speer (1905–81) were sentenced to twenty years' imprisonment. Constantin von Neurath (1873–1956) was sentenced to fifteen years imprisonment, and Karl Doenitz (1891–1980) was sentenced to ten years' imprisonment. Hjalmar H.G. Schacht (1877–1970), Hans Fritzsche (1900–53), and Franz von Papen (1879–1969) were acquitted. Robert Ley (1890–1945), the leader of the German Labor Front from 1933–45, was scheduled to have been tried with the other defendants, but committed suicide on October 24, 1945, before the trials commenced. Martin Bormann (1900–45), the Nazi party secretary from 1940–45, was tried and sentenced to death in absentia, but it was later believed that he had been killed on May 1, 1945, while trying to escape from the advancing Russian armies.

A number of other important Nazi figures took their own lives during and after the war, many of whom would have certainly been charged with war crimes. The most prominent suicide was that of Adolf Hitler (1889–1945), the founder and leader of the Nazi party and chancellor of the German Third Reich. He and his mistress, Eva Braun (1912–45), committed suicide in his bunker in Berlin on April 29, 1945. Joseph Goebbels (1897–1945), the leading Nazi propagandist and one of Hitler's closest advisors, killed himself, his wife, and their six children, on May 1, 1945. Heinrich Himmler (1900–45), the head of the Gestapo and the Waffen-S.S. and Hitler's minister of the interior from 1943–45, took poison on May 23, 1945, while in British custody. Bernhard Rust (1883–1945), the Reich minister of science, education and popular culture from 1934–45; Konrad Henlein (1898–1945), the Reich governor of the Sudetenland; Josef Terboven (1898–1945), the Reich commissar in Norway; Third Reich historian Walter Frank (1905–45); Philip Bouhler (1899–1945), the head of the Nazi euthanasia program; Adm. Hans von Friedeburg (1895–1945), the last supreme commander of the German Navy; and air force general Robert Ritter von Greim (1892–1945) all committed suicide in May of 1945. Josef Burckel (1894–1944), the Nazi governor of Austria, killed himself on September 28, 1944, and Leonardo Conti (1900–45), the Reich minister of health, committed suicide on October 6, 1945. Theodor Dannecker (1913–45), the S.S. captain in charge of the deportation of Jews from France, Bulgaria, and Italy, ended his own life on December 10, 1945. Field Marshal Walther Model (1891–1945) chose suicide rather than capture on April 18, 1945. Otto Thierack (1889–1946), the Reich minister of justice and one-time president of the People's Court, killed himself on October 26, 1946. Thierack's successor as president of the People's Court, Roland Freisler (1893–1945), was killed on February 3, 1945, by Allied bombing while he was sitting on the bench. Ludwig Muller (1883–1946), Reich bishop and leader of the German Faith Movement, killed himself in March of 1946.

Gen. Otto von Stuelpnagel (1878–1948), the military governor of France from 1940 to 1942, committed suicide on February 6, 1948, and Herbert Backe (1896–1947), the Reich minister of agriculture and food, killed himself on April 6, 1947. Walter Buch (1883–1949), the president of the Nazi party Supreme Court, committed suicide on November 12, 1949, following his conviction for war crimes.

Col. Gen. Kurt Daluege (1897–1946), of the German Nazi Police, was executed for war crimes in Czechoslovakia on October 23, 1946. Daluege had served as deputy protector of Bohemia and Moravia after the assassination of Reinhard Heydrich (q.v.) in 1942, and was responsible for the Nazi retaliation against the Czechs. He was responsible for giving the order to destroy the Czech village of Lidice shortly after Heydrich's death.

Gen. Ferenc Szombathely, the former Hungarian chief of staff, was executed with a number of aides on November 6, 1946, at Novi Sad. He was convicted of war crimes and of having organized the massacre of Serbo-Croatians in 1942.

Gen. August Meissner, head of the Gestapo's regional bureau in Belgrade, Yugoslavia, was hanged in December of 1946, with eight other senior S.S. officers.

Marshal Sladko Kvaternik, the Croatian separatist leader and wartime premier of Yugoslavia, was hanged in 1946 as a collaborator.

Otomar Kula, the Czech anti–Semite leader, was executed in 1946 for war crimes and treason.

1947

On February 10, 1947, **Brig. Gen. R.W.M. De Winten**, the commander of the British Thirteenth Infantry Brigade, was shot to death in Pola, Italy, by an Italian woman. The assailant was angered over Pola having been given to Yugoslavia following the war.

A.E. Conquest, the deputy superintendent of police in Haifa, Palestine, was assassinated by a Jewish gunman on February 26, 1947.

Col. Gen. Alexander Lohr (1885–1947), a German Luftwaffe officer who commanded troops in the Balkans during World War II, was hanged for war crimes on March 16, 1947, in Yugoslavia. Lohr served in the Austro-Hungarian army during World War I. He served in the army of the

Austrian Republic as an air officer following the end of the war, and was named commander of the Austrian air force in 1936. In 1938 Lohr became a general in the German Luftwaffe, taking part in the Polish, Balkans, and Russian campaigns. From 1942 he was stationed in the Balkans, and it was during this period that he was judged to have committed war crimes.

On March 27, 1947, **Col. Gen. Karol Swierczewski** (1897–1947), the Polish vice minister of national defense, was assassinated near Sanok, Poland, by members of the Ukrainian underground. Gen. Swierczewski had fought with the Russians during World War I and participated in the Russian Revolution. He later served as a professor in the Moscow Military School. In 1936, during the Spanish Civil War, he served as a military advisor to the republican forces.

Rudolf Hoess, a German S.S. officer who served as director of the Auschwitz concentration camp from 1940 to 1943, was hanged on April 15, 1947, at Auschwitz. Hoess was born on November 25, 1900, in Baden-Baden. He joined the Nazi party in 1922 and the S.S. in 1934. He was stationed at Dachau concentration camp later in the year. Following a tour of duty at Sachsenhausen, from 1938 until 1940, he was appointed commandant at Auschwitz on May 1, 1940. During his three years at Auschwitz he was responsible for the extermination of over two million prisoners. In 1943 he was named deputy inspector general of concentration camps under Richard Gluecks (q.v.). Hoess was captured on March 2, 1946, and given over to the Polish government. He was tried by a Polish military tribunal in March of 1947, and executed the following month.

Fernand De Brinon, a leading French collaborationist with the Germans, was executed by firing squad in Forte De Montrouge on April 15, 1947. De Brinon was born on August 16, 1887, in Libourne, Gironde. He was a leading supporter of Franco-German reconciliation between the wars, and was active in the establishment of the Vichy regime following the German occupation. De Brinon was appointed the Vichy government's ambassador to occupied Paris in November 1940. Following the collapse of the Vichy regime, in September 1944, he was involved in an attempt to form another pro–German government, but met with little success. He was captured by the Allies near the end of the war and tried for treason.

Josef Tiso, the pro–German president of Slovakia during World War II, was hanged for treason in Bratislava, Czechoslovakia, on April 18, 1947. Tiso was born at Velka Bytca in Hungary on October 13, 1887. He became a Catholic priest in 1909, and became a leading member of the nationalist Slovak People's party following World War I. He was elected chairman of the party when Andrej Hlinka died in August of 1938, and in October of that year, became premier of Slovakia. He was selected as president of independent Slovakia on October 26, 1939, and allied his country with the German war effort. He was ousted from office following the Soviet and Czechoslovak capture of the capital of Bratislava in April of 1945. Tiso was arrested by the American army on May 21, 1945, and handed over to the new Czechoslovak government. His trial began in Bratislava on December 2, 1946, and Tiso was convicted of "conspiring against the Czechoslovak republic, suppressing democratic freedom and establishing a Fascist dictatorship, warring against Poland and the Soviet Union and committing war crimes."

On July 12, 1947, United States Senator John W. Bricker (1893–1986) of Ohio was uninjured in a shooting incident in the Senate office building in Washington, D.C. The attempted assassin was identified as William Kaiser, a former police officer. Bricker, a former Ohio governor, had run unsuccessfully for the United States vice presidency on the Republican ticket in 1944.

Sir Shafa'at Ahmad Khan, a member of the Moslem League, was stabbed to death in Simla, India, on July 18, 1947. Khan was murdered shortly after having joined the interim Indian government.

On July 19, 1947, five armed men attacked the executive council chamber in Rangoon, Burma, assassinating the chairman of the council, **U Aung San**, and seven other members of the council. The council members killed included Aung San's elder brother, commerce and supplies member **U Ba Win**, education and planning member **Abdul Bazak**, industry and labor member **Mahn Ba Khaing**, Socialist party leader and finance member **Thakin Mya**, transport and communications deputy secretary **Ohn Maung**, frontier areas counselor **Sao Sam Htun**, the sawba of Mong Pawn, and information member **U Ba Choe**. Most of those killed were members of Aung San's political party, the Anti–Fascist Peoples Freedom League. Several leading opponents of the new government were arrested for complicity in the assassination. On May 8, 1948, six Burmese citizens, including former premier **U Saw**, were executed for their participation in the crime.

U Aung San was born in Burma in 1914. He attended Rangoon University and, as a student there, spent time in prison for subversive activities conducted as a member of a nationalist movement. He fled to Japan near the start of World War II and was trained by the military. Following the Japanese occupation of Burma, Aung San founded the Burmese Anti–Fascist People's Freedom League, joining together the various nationalist movements in Burma to fight with the Allies. After the defeat of the Japanese, Aung San pressured the British into granting autonomy for Burma. He served as defense and external affairs counselor in the first interim government. He succeeded in achieving an agreement with Britain regarding Burmese independence, and, in April of 1947 his party won an overwhelming majority in the election of a constituent assembly. Aung San was almost certain to become the first leader of independent Burma before his death at the hands of political opponents.

Lyuh Woon-Heung, the chairman of the People's party and a leading Korean anti–Communist, was assassinated on July 19, 1947, in Seoul, South Korea, while riding in a car.

Huynh Phu So, the founder and prophet of the Hoa Hao, a Vietnamese peasant movement, was executed by Communists in 1947.

On September 12, 1947, **Sami Taha**, the secretary general of the Arab Labor Federation, was shot and killed on a street in Haifa, Palestine. Taha was a leading political foe of Haj Amin el-Husseini, the exiled grand mufti of Jerusalem.

Nikola Dimitrov Petkov, a leading Bulgarian politician, was hanged in Sofia on September 23, 1947, following a trial which accused him of plotting a coup d'etat. Petkov, who was born in 1889, was an early member of the Bulgarian Agrarian National Union. He was imprisoned on numerous occasions for subversive activities during the 1920s and 1930s. During World War II he became a leader of the Bulgarian Resistance, and achieved victory for his party in September of 1944. His inability to work out a compromise with the Russian-backed Communist party resulted in his resignation the following year. Petkov continued to advocate an Agrarian-Communist coalition government for Bulgaria, and, in June of 1947, he was arrested on charges of planning a military coup. He was subsequently convicted and executed, despite the protests of Great Britain and the United States.

On October 10, 1947, **Dr. Truong Dinh Tri**, the head of the Hanoi municipal council, was seriously injured in a grenade attack. He died the following day.

Alberto Bellardi Ricci, the retiring Italian minister to Sweden, was stabbed to death by Giuseppe Capocci, an Italian Fascist and mental patient, on December 25, 1947. Ricci, who had been appointed as Italy's minister to Chile, was attending a farewell party in his honor at the time of his attack.

1948

Mohandas K. Gandhi, the leading Indian Hindu nationalist and spiritual leader, was assassinated by a Hindu extremist on January 30, 1948, while attending a prayer meeting at his residence at Birla House in New Delhi. Gandhi was born in Porbandar, India, on October 2, 1869. He studied law in London in the late 1880s, and, after several years of practicing law in India, he went to South Africa in 1893. It was there that he first instituted his non-violent "passive resistance" to what he considered unjust and discriminatory laws. In January of 1915 Gandhi returned to India and soon after began a campaign for the political independence of India from Great Britain. In 1919 he organized the Satyagraha, a movement advocating non-cooperation with the British authorities. His movement escalated during the 1920s, and riots and violence resulted from some of his overenthusiastic followers' confrontations with the British. He was arrested on charges of sedition in 1922 and sentenced to six years in prison, though he was released two years later for reasons of health. In 1925 he was elected president of the Indian National Congress, and was again imprisoned briefly in 1931 for advocating civil disobedience against the British salt tax. He resigned from leadership of the Congress party in 1934, but remained the leading spokesman for Indian independence. Gandhi was again arrested during World War II and remained in detention until 1944. In 1946 the British announced their intention to withdraw from India, and the following year they decided that Moslem Pakistan would be partitioned from Hindu-dominated India. Gandhi disapproved of this plan, advocating that Indian Hindus and Moslems should live and work together in harmony. Religious riots followed Independence Day on August 15, 1947, and Gandhi soon after announced his intention to fast until the killings ended. The violence rapidly abated due to the tremendous love and respect the Indian people felt for the Mahatma. In January of 1948 he began another fast which resulted in a pact by the Indian government guaranteeing the safety of the Moslem minority. Later in the month Gandhi was shot and killed by Nathuram V. Godse, a radical Hindu, who felt Gandhi had betrayed the Hindus by criticizing anti–Moslem riots. Godse and other Hindu radicals, including Narayan Dattatraya Apte, Vishnu Ramrishkhma Karkare, Madan Lal, Gopal Vinayak Godse, Dattalraya Sadashiv Parchure, Shankar Kistayya, and Kashmirilal Pahwa, were tried for the murder. Godse and Apte were convicted and hanged at Ambala Jail on November 15, 1949. The other members of the conspiracy were sentenced to prison.

Yahya Ben Mohammad Ben Hamid Ed Din, the imam of Yemen from 1904, was assassinated, along with his chief minister, on February 17, 1948. Imam Yahya was born in 1876 and, in 1904 succeeded his father as the head of the Zaidi sect of the Shi'ite Moslems, thus becoming the hereditary monarch of Yemen. Yahya was initially opposed to the Turkish occcupation of Yemen, but in 1911 he reached an accommodation with the Sultan which resulted in the independence of Yemen. After the collapse of the Turkish empire following World War I, Yahya became embroiled in several territorial disputes with Great Britain which were not settled until the signing of the Anglo-Yemini treaty in 1934. Later the same year Yahya engaged in a brief and unsuccessful war with Saudi Arabia. Yemen became more involved in regional and international affairs following World War II, joining the Arab League in 1945 and the League of Nations in 1947. There was a premature report of the imam's death by natural causes in January of 1947, and his announced successor was **Sayyid Abdullah Ibn Ahmed Al Wazir**. Yahya was indeed dead by the end of the following month, the victim of an assassination. Sayyid Abdullah proclaimed himself the new imam and a brief civil war broke out, with two of Yahya's sons being killed in street fighting. The murdered imam's eldest son, Ahmad (q.v.), the crown prince, raised an army of royalist supporters and deposed the usurper Sayyid Abdullah, who was tried and executed with many of his followers on April 8, 1948. Ahmad was himself then proclaimed imam of Yemen.

Dieter Wisliceny, a major in the S.S. who was responsible for the deportation and murder of Jews in Eastern Europe, was executed for war crimes in Bratislava, Czechoslovakia, on February 27, 1948. Wisliceny was born in Rugularken on January 13, 1911, and became a member of the Nazi party in 1931. He joined the S.S. in 1934, and in September of 1940 he was appointed an advisor to the Slovak government on handling the extermination of Jews. In 1943 he organized the deportation of Jews from Greece, and the following year he was appointed deputy to Adolf Eichmann (q.v.) in Budapest, Hungary. He was arrested by the Allies at the end of the war and was handed over to the Czechoslovak government to stand trial for wartime atrocities.

On April 20, 1948, Walter P. Reuther (1907–69), the president of the United Auto Workers labor union, was seriously injured by a shotgun blast fired through a window of his home. The labor leader's assailant was not identified, and Reuther recovered from his injuries and resumed his duties. Reuther's brother, Victor Reuther (b. 1912), who was also active in the labor movement, was injured in an assassination attempt the following year. Victor Reuther also recovered from his injuries.

Mustafa el-Nahas (1876–1965), a former premier of Egypt, was uninjured in an assassination attempt on April 25, 1948. An automobile filled with explosives blew up in front of Nahas' home in Cairo.

Jan Masaryk, a Czechoslovak statesman and diplomat, died on March 10, 1948, from a fall from the window of his room in the Foreign Office.

Masaryk was born on September 14, 1886, in Prague. His father was Thomas Masaryk, the first president of the Czechoslovak Republic. Jan Masaryk joined the Czechoslovak Foreign Office in 1919, and in 1925 was appointed minister to London. He served at that post until 1938, when he resigned in protest of the Munich Pact, which resulted in the dismemberment of Czechoslovakia. From 1941 until 1945 Masaryk served as foreign minister and deputy prime minister in the Czechoslovak government in exile in London. He remained foreign minister in the post-war government, and stayed in office following the Communist-led coup on February 25, 1948. His death was announced by the Czech government as a suicide, but speculation exists that it was likely that Masaryk was pushed or thrown from his third-story office in the Czernin Palace in Prague.

Jorge Eliecer Gaitan, a Colombian liberal politician, was shot to death in Bogota on April 9, 1948. Gaitan was born in Bogota on January 26, 1902. He studied law and entered Colombian politics in the late 1920s. He was elected mayor of Bogota in 1935 and served in the cabinet of President Eduardo Santos as minister of labor. Gaitan ran for the presidency of Colombia in 1946 as a Liberal party candidate, but was defeated by Mariano Ospina Perez. In 1947 he became leader of the Liberal party. The following year, while planning another campaign for the presidency, Gaitan was assassinated by Juan Roa Sierra, a chauffeur, in the streets of Bogota. The assassin was killed by an angry mob.

On May 1, 1948, **Christop Ladas**, the fifty-seven-year-old Greek minister of justice and Liberal party secretary, was killed in a grenade attack on his car in Athens. The assassin was identified as Eustratos Moutosyannis, a member of a Communist terrorist group.

Maj. Augustin Sram, a Czech Communist leader, was assassinated in Prague, Czechoslovakia, on May 27, 1948.

Seven S.S. and concentration camp officials who had been convicted by the United States military tribunal at Nuremberg of war crimes in the "Doctors' Trial" on August 20, 1947, were hanged on June 2, 1948, at Landsberg Prison. The seven included S.S. **Gen. Karl Brandt** (1904–48), Adolf Hitler's personal physician and the leading medical officer for Nazi Germany; **Viktor Brack** (1903–48), the chief S.S. administrative officer, who was personally responsible for the euthanasia program used against German "undesirables" and the construction of death camps in Poland and the Soviet Union; **Joachim Murgowsky** (1905–48), the chief S.S. hygienist; **Prof. Karl Gebhardt** (1897–1948), the head S.S. surgeon; **Wolfram Sievers**, an ex–Military Research Institute director; **Waldemar Hoven**, the chief medical officer at Buchenwald; and **Rudolf Brandt**, the chief of the S.S. Hygienic Institute.

On August 22, 1948, **Dr. Joseph F. Buehler**, the former state secretary of Poland during the Nazi occupation, was hanged for war crimes in Cracow, Poland.

On September 1, 1948, **Juan Arevalo y Veitia**, a fifty-six-year-old Cuban anti–Communist labor leader, was shot to death by assassins in Havana, Cuba.

Count Folke Bernadotte of Wisborg, a Swedish diplomat representing the United Nations in Palestine, was assassinated in Jerusalem by three Jewish terrorists on September 17, 1948. **Andre Serot**, a French colonel who was accompanying the count, was also killed in the attack.

Bernadotte was born in Sweden on January 2, 1895, the nephew of King Gustavus V. He became a leading international statesman through his work with the Swedish Red Cross and the International Boy Scouts. During World War II he was active in attempting to insure the proper treatment of captured soldiers from both sides of the conflict. Near the end of the war he became directly involved in negotiations instigated by leading Nazis, including Heinrich Himmler, to reach a peace settlement with the Allies, excluding the Soviet Union. Though this plan proved unacceptable, Bernadotte's reputation as a mediator remained untarnished. Following the outbreak of hostilities in the Middle East during 1948, Bernadotte was called upon by the United Nations Security Council to serve as their mediator in the conflict on May 20, 1948. He succeeded in negotiating a cease-fire, but was slain by members of the Stern Gang, a Jewish terrorist organization, before he could complete his mission.

On September 17, 1948, **U Tin Tun**, the former foreign minister of Burma and the leader of the Anti-Fascist People's Freedom League, was seriously injured in a car bombing in Rangoon. The fifty-three-year-old Burmese politician died the following day.

Amir Sjarifuddin, the Indonesian nationalist leader who had served as the second prime minister of the Republic of Indonesia, was executed in December of 1948 following his participation in a Communist uprising. Amir Sjarifuddin was a co-founder of the left-wing Gerino party (Indonesian People's Movement) in 1937. He was named prime minister of Indonesia under President Sukarno in 1947. He served in that position until January of 1948. He lent his support to the abortive Communist rebellion later in the year. Following the army's suppression of the coup attempt, Sjarifuddin was captured and subsequently executed.

R.M. Suripino, the former Indonesian Republican envoy to Central Europe, and **Hadjono**, the secretary of the Indonesian Communist party, were also executed in December of 1948 for their role in the rebellion.

Selim Zaki Pasha, the chief of the Cairo city police in Egypt, was assassinated on December 8, 1948, by a member of the Muslim Brotherhood, a nationalist organization.

The major Japanese war crimes trial was held during 1948 at the Tokyo International Military Tribunal. Twenty-seven Japanese war criminals were to be tried at that time. Of that number, seven received the death penalty and were executed on December 23, 1948. They included **Gen. Hideki Tojo**, Japan's wartime premier; **Gen. Kenji Doihara** (1883–1948), who was responsible for the Mukden incident in 1931 which led to Japan's attack on Manchuria and who served as commander of Japanese forces in Malaya, Sumatra, and Java during World War II; **Gen. Heitaro Kimura** (1888–1948), Japan's vice minister of war under Premier Tojo; **Gen. Iwane Matsui** (1878–1948), who commanded the Japanese forces during the destruction of Nanking; **Gen. Akira Muto** (1883–1948), who served as the Japanese army's chief of staff in the Philippine campaign; **Koki Hirota** (1878–1948), Japan's premier from 1936 to 1937; and **Seishiro Itagaki** (1885–1948), who served as Japan's minister of war during much of World War II. Gen. Sadao Araki (1877–1966), Gen. Kuniaki Koiso (1880–1950), Gen. Jiro Minami (1874–1955), Gen. Kenryo Sato, Gen. Teichi Suzuki, Gen. Yoshijro Umezu (1882–1949), Marshal Shunroku Hata, Col. Kingoro Hashimoto (1890–1957), Adm. Takasumi Oka, Adm. Shigetaro Shimada (1883–1976), Baron Kiichiro Hiranuma (1867–1952), Haoki Hoshino (1892–1978), Okinori Kaya (1889–1977), Loichi Kido (1889–1977), Hiroshi Oshima, and Toshio Shiratori (1887–1949) all received terms of life imprisonment. Foreign Minister Mamoru Shigemitsu (1887–1957) was sentenced to seven years' imprisonment. Yosuke Matsuoka (1880–1946) and Osami Nagano (1888–1947) both died before the trials began, and Shumei Okawa (1886–1957) was removed from the trial due to mental illness.

Hideki Tojo, who was born on December 30, 1884, was a graduate of the Tokyo Imperial Military Academy. After serving as military attache at the Japanese Embassy in Berlin, Tojo served in various positions in the Japanese War Office in Tokyo. In 1937 he was named chief of staff of the Kwantung army in Manchuria, and the following year he was named vice minister of war. He was appointed minister of war in July of 1940 and, on October 16, 1941, became Japan's premier as well. He remained as leader of Japan during much of the war period, also assuming the post of chief of the general staff. In July of 1944 Tojo was forced to resign following major setbacks by the Japanese forces, including the successful invasion of the Mariana Islands by the United States. Tojo made an unsuccessful suicide attempt following Japan's surrender on September 11, 1945, but recovered and was subsequently arrested as a war criminal.

Koki Hirota was a leading nationalist and a respected member of the Japanese diplomatic corps. He served as Japan's ambassador to the Soviet

Union from 1930 until 1932. In 1933 he was named foreign minister, a position he held until March of 1936, when he was named premier. He served as premier until June of 1937, when he again became foreign minister until 1938. Hirota was a supporter of Japanese expansion, and implemented the Anti-Comintern Pact, which linked Japanese policy with that of Germany and Italy, during his term of office.

Mahmoud Fahmy El-Nokrashy Pasha (1888–1948), the prime minister of Egypt, was assassinated by a member of the Moslem Brotherhood on December 28, 1948. Nokrashy Pasha, a former teacher, had joined the Egyptian government in 1920 and had served in various posts during the 1920s and 1930s. He was Egyptian minister of the interior, education, and finance from 1938 to 1940. In 1945 he was elected president of the Saadist party and became prime minister of Egypt on February 25, 1945, following the assassination of Ahmed Maher Pasha (q.v.). He was forced to resign on February 15, 1946, but was again appointed prime minister in December of 1946. Nokrashy Pasha was named Egypt's military governor following Egypt's invasion of Palestine on May 14, 1948. He was a supporter of Egypt's policy advocating the elimination of the state of Israel, and was a proponent of the withdrawal of English forces from the Anglo-Egyptian Sudan. Nokrashy Pasha's assassin, Abdel Hamid Ahmed Hassan (1927–48), was a member of the Moslem Brotherhood, an extremist organization the prime minister had outlawed earlier in the month. The Brotherhood was critical of Nokrashy Pasha's inability to produce a military victory against Israel.

1949

Mohammad Reza Pahlavi (1919–80), the shah of Iran, was shot and wounded in Teheran on February 4, 1949. The Shah recovered from his injuries and his attempted assassin, Fakhr Rai, a member of the leftist Tudeh party, was killed by an angry mob.

On February 13, 1949, **Sheikh Hasan Al-Banna**, the leader of the nationalist Egyptian Moslem Brotherhood, was murdered in the streets of Cairo.

Four Iraqi Communist leaders, **Yusuf Salman Yusuf** (known as Fahd), **Saki Muhammad Basim, Husayn Muhammad Ash-Shabibi,** and **Yahuda Ibrahim Siddiq** were arrested and charged with taking part in a Communist uprising in 1948. They were sentenced to death and publicly hanged on February 13, 1949.

Tan Malaka, a founder and leader of the Indonesian Communist party, was executed by the Indonesian army on April 16, 1949. Tan Malaka, who had led the Indonesian Communist party (PKI) in the 1920s, had been exiled by the Dutch colonial government in 1922. In 1927 he organized the Indonesian Republican party (PARI) while in exile in Siam. During his years in exile he helped organize Communist groups in the Philippines, Malaya, and Singapore. He returned to Indonesia in 1942 and collaborated with the Japanese during World War II. In 1946 he led an unsuccessful coup against the Indonesian government. The Indonesian army suppressed the attempted overthrow and captured Tan Malak and many of his supporters. Tan Malaka was released from prison in 1948, shortly before the start of an uprising led by Musso, the Russian-backed leader of the Indonesian Communist party. Tan Malaka, a nationalist Communist, took no part in this coup attempt, and Musso was subsequently killed in battle. Tan Malaka then formed the Parta Murba (Proletarian party). His ambition to govern Indonesia was cut short in April of 1949, when he was captured by the army and executed.

On June 11, 1949, **Gen. Koci Xoxe** (Kochi Rodze), the former leader of the Albanian Communist party, was shot following his trial and conviction for anti–Soviet tendencies. Xoxe was born in Korce on May 1, 1911. He became active in political opposition to King Zog I and was imprisoned on several occasions. In 1941, during the Italian occupation of Albania, Xoxe founded the Albanian Communist party and, in 1943, organized the Albanian Liberation party. In March of 1946 he also became minister of the interior and deputy prime minister. As the virtual leader of Albania from 1946 through 1948, Xoxe was active in planning the unification of Albania with Yugoslavia. The break by Marshal Tito of Yugoslavia with the Soviet Union, and Tito's subsequent expulsion from the Cominform, put an end to this plan and resulted in Xoxe's own fall from power. He was dismissed from his positions and arrested on October 6, 1948. He was tried by the Albanian Supreme Court in Tirane and executed following his conviction.

Gen. Heliodor Pika, a former Czech deputy chief of staff, was executed for treason on June 21, 1949.

On June 26, 1949, **Kim Koo**, the seventy-three-year-old Korean rightist revolutionary and the leader of the Korean Independence party, was assassinated at his home in Seoul, South Korea. Kim Koo was a former president of the Korean provisional government and had been head of the exiled Korean government in China before he split with President Sygnan Rhee. He was also a bitter opponent of the division of Korea. Kim Koo was shot to death by Lt. Ahn Do Hi, a Korean army officer, following a political quarrel at his home.

On July 18, 1949, **Col. Francisco Javier Arana**, the chief of the Guatemalan armed forces, was assassinated in Guatemala City. Arana was also a leading potential candidate to succeed president Juan Jose Arevlo of Guatemala. The Guardia de Honor army garrison briefly revolted in the wake of the assassination, but the rebellion was quickly quelled.

On August 14, 1949, a coup by army officers in Syria resulted in the deaths of **Husni Ez-Zaim**, the president, and **Mushin Barazi** (1893–1949), who had been named prime minister two months earlier.

Zaim, who was born in 1897, had served in the Turkish army before joining the French in Syria. He had taken part in Vichy French action during World War II against the Allies, and was imprisoned briefly following the war. Shortly thereafter he was appointed inspector general of police for the Syrian Republic. He became chief of staff of the Syrian army in May of 1948. He was the leader of the military coup d'etat of March 30, 1949, that resulted in the overthrow of Shukri el-Kuwatli, and was elected president of Syria on June 25, 1949. Zaim and Barazi were seized in Damascus by rebellious army officers led by Col. Sami Hinnawi, who were distressed by the government's aim of cutting down the size of the armed forces. They were tried and quickly executed.

Laszlo Rajk (1909–49), a leading Hungarian Communist politician, was hanged on October 15, 1949, after having been found guilty of charges of plotting against the state. Also tried and hanged with Rajk were **Tibor Szonyi** (1903–49), the former head of the Communist party's cadres section, and **Andras Szalai** (1917–49), a deputy to Szonyi.

Laszlo Rajk joined the Hungarian Communist party in 1930 and fought during the Spanish Civil War. He was arrested by the Germans on several occasions during World War II. Following the conclusion of the war Rajk was named minister of the interior in February of 1946. In December of 1948 he was appointed minister of foreign affairs, and the following year he became secretary general of the People's Independence party. On May 16, 1949, Rajk was arrested for treason. He was tried on September 16, 1949, and convicted of anti-state activities. He was executed the following month.

Abdul Hussein Hajir (1897–1949), a former prime minister of Iran, was shot and mortally wounded on November 4, 1949. Hajir served in the Iranian cabinet as minister of the interior, and of commerce and industry during the early 1940s. In 1946 he was appointed finance minister and, on June 13, 1948, he became Iran's prime minister. He served in that position until his resignation on November 9, 1948. He was shot in a Teheran mosque on November 4, 1949, and died of his wounds the following day. His assassin, identified as Hussein Immami, was executed for the murder on November 9, 1949.

Duncan George Stewart, the British colonial governor of Sarawak, was seriously wounded in an assassination attempt on December 3, 1949. He died of his wounds on December 10. Stewart was born on October 22, 1904, and joined the British colonial office in 1928. He was stationed in Nigeria until 1944, when he was named colonial secretary of the Bahamas. In 1947 he was named to the financial staff of the colonial office in Palestine, and two years later was appointed governor of Sarawak. Less than a month after his arrival at his post, Stewart was attacked by a young Malay, identified as Rosli Bin Dobie (1931–50), who was charged with the murder. More than a dozen other Malay nationalists were also charged with conspiracy in the assassination.

Bulgarian Communist leader **Traicho Kostov** was tried for treason and executed on December 16, 1949, in Sofia. Kostov was born on June 17, 1897, and joined the Communist party in his youth. He was involved in a workers' uprising in September of 1923 and, following a period of imprisonment, he went to Moscow for several years. He returned to Bulgaria in 1931 and was again active in the Communist party. He fought with the Resistance during World War II and, following the war, was named a member of the ruling Politburo. On March 31, 1946, Kostov was named deputy prime minister of Bulgaria. The following year he also served as the chairman of the economic and financial committee in the Bulgarian cabinet. On April 4, 1949, Kostov was removed from the Politburo, and two months later was expelled from the Communist party. He was arrested on June 25, 1949, as an anti–Soviet agent, and tried for treason and espionage on December 7, 1949. He was convicted and executed the following week.

1950

On March 4, 1950, **Roman Shukhevych**, known as Lt. Gen. Taras Chuprynka, the chief of the Ukrainian Military Organization (UVO) and founder of the Ukrainian Insurgent Army (UPA), was killed by Soviet security forces at Bilohorshca, near Lwow. Shukhevych had remained in the Polish Ukraine after the Soviet Union had occupied the area, and was active in the campaign for Ukrainian independence.

On November 1, 1950, two Puerto Rican Nationalists made an unsuccessful attempt to assassinate President Harry Truman in Washington, D.C. Griselio Torresola and Oscar Collazo, the would-be assassins, approached Blair House, where Truman was staying, and engaged White House guards Pvt. Joseph O. Davidson, Pvt. Leslie Coffelt, Pvt. Donald T. Birdzell, and Pvt. Joseph Downs, and Secret Service agent Floyd Boring in a gun battle. Pvt. Coffelt and Torresola were killed during the exchange, and Pvt.

Downs, Pvt. Birdzell and Collazo were injured. The president, who was awakened by the shooting, had rushed to an open window and was told to get back. He complied and was uninjured in the attempt on his life. Collazo, a member of the Nationalist party of Puerto Rico, was sentenced to life imprisonment. He was released from prison in September of 1979 by then president Jimmy Carter.

Lt. Col. C. Delgado Chalbaud, the president of Venezuela, was shot and beaten to death by a group of men on November 13, 1950, in Caracas. Chalbaud, who was born in 1909, had served as president of the three-man military junta that had ruled Venezuela since November 1948. Police arrested most of the group responsible for the killing. Rafael Simon Urbina, the alleged leader of the assassination, was killed during an attempt to escape from a prison guard on November 14. The military junta remained in control of the country following the assassination, with Lt. Col. Marcos Perez Jimenez assuming the presidency.

1951

Ali Razmara, who had served as prime minister of Iran from June 1950, was assassinated on March 7, 1951, outside the Maschede Soltaneh mosque in Teheran, by a member of the Moslem extremist group Fidaya-i Islam. Razmara had served in the Iranian army and was the director of the Teheran Military Cadet College in 1938. He was made a general and given charge of reorganization of the military in 1944. In 1946 he was named commander-in-chief of the Iranian army. He was appointed prime minister in 1950 by the shah. During his term he opposed nationalization of the oil industry. His assassin, Abdullah Rastigar, was executed in January of 1956.

On March 19, 1951, **Abdul Hami Zanganeh**, the former Iranian minister of education and an ally of the slain prime minister Ali Razmara (q.v.), was critically wounded in a shooting by a Teheran University student. He died on March 25.

On June 7, 1951, seven Nazis convicted in 1946 and 1947 of war crimes were hanged in Landsberg Prison, following the refusal of the United States Supreme Court to allow another stay of execution. These were the last war criminals sentenced to be executed by the International Military Tribunal at Nuremberg. They included S.S. **Gen. Oswald Pohl**, who destroyed the Warsaw ghetto and supervised extermination systems in occupied countries; S.S. **Gen. Otto Ohlendorf**, who organized mass murders in the southern Ukraine; **S.S. Gen. Erich Naumann**, who massacred Jews and gypsies in the Soviet Union; S.S. **Col. Werner Braune**, who was responsible for mass murder in the Crimea; S.S. **Col. Paul Blobel**, who was responsible for the Kiev massacre in 1941; S.S. **Lt. Hans Schmidt**, the adjutant at Buchenwald concentration camp; and S.S. **Sgt. Georg Schallermair**, the Muehlendorf concentration camp roll call leader who personally beat inmates to death.

Otto Ohlendorf was born on Hoheneggelsen on February 4, 1907. He studied law and, in 1926, joined the Nazi movement as a member of the S.S. He later joined Reinhard Heydrich's (q.v.) intelligence service. In 1941 Ohlendorf was made commander of the S.S. Action Group D. (Einsatzgruppe D), which was in charge of locating and exterminating Russian Jews in the Ukraine. In 1943 he was assigned to the Reich Economic Ministry and, in November of 1944, was promoted to lieutenant general of the S.S. After Germany's defeat in World War II Ohlendorf was arrested by the Allies and tried at Nuremberg in April of 1948 with other Action Group leaders. He was convicted of war crimes and sentenced to death, with his execution coming nearly three years later.

Oswald Pohl was born in Duisberg on June 30, 1892. He served in the army during World War I and joined the Nazi party in 1922. He rose in the ranks of the S.S. and, in February of 1934, he was appointed chief administrative officer in the Reich Security Office. His close association with Heinrich Himmler resulted in further promotions and, in June of 1939, he was named a director in the Reich Interior Ministry. Pohl's major duties included the acquisition for the S.S. of the wealth and valuables of liquidated concentration camp inmates. Following Germany's defeat in World War II, Pohl went into hiding, but was arrested by the Allies in May of 1946. He was tried at Nuremberg on November 3, 1947, by a military tribunal, and was sentenced to death for war crimes. His execution was carried out more than three years later.

Riad Es-Sohl, the Lebanese statesman and former prime minister, was assassinated in Amman, Jordan, on July 16, 1951. Es-Sohl, who was born in 1894, was an early leader in the Lebanese Nationalist movement. During World War I he was deported by the Turkish rulers of Lebanon for subversive activities. He was later imprisoned by the French for his opposition to the French mandate in Lebanon. After his return from exile, es-Sohl became prime minister of independent Lebanon on August 29, 1943, serving until January of 1945. Es-Sohl again served as prime minister from June 6, 1947, until February 14, 1951. He was an opponent of a proposed merger of Lebanon, Syria, and Jordan under the rule of Jordan's King Abdullah (q.v.). He was ambushed and assassinated by three members of the Syrian National Socialist party at the airport in Amman, Jordan, while on a state visit to the Jordanian monarch.

King Abdullah Ibn Hussein, the king of Jordan, was shot to death on July 20, 1951, as he visited the tomb of his father in the Mosque of Omar in the Old City of Jerusalem. His assassin, Mustafa Ashu, who was identified as a follower of the exiled Mufti of Jerusalem, was killed by the king's guards. Abdullah was born in Mecca in 1882, the son of King Hussein of the Hejaz. Abdullah was raised in Turkey and served in the Ottoman parliament in 1908. During World War I Abdullah joined with his older brother, Feisal, and Lawrence of Arabia, in the Arab rebellion against the Turks. After the war Abdullah joined with his father and brother in a war against King Ibn Saud of Saudi Arabia. After the defeat of his forces Abdullah was persuaded by British colonial secretary Winston Churchill to become emir of Trans-Jordan in 1921. Abdullah remained a close ally of Great Britain, and his army, known as the Arab Legion, was trained and commanded by British Brig. John Glubb Pasha. On May 25, 1946, Abdullah was crowned king of independent Trans-Jordan.

In May of 1948 Jordan, in unison with other Arab nations, declared war on Israel. The Arab armies met with greater resistance than expected from the Israeli army, and open hostilities ceased the following year. In April of 1950 Abdullah annexed Arab Palestine, changing the name of his enlarged nation to the Hashemite Kingdom of Jordan. Abdullah envisioned a union between Jordan, Syria, Iraq, and Lebanon under a Hashemite ruler. He was slain by his political enemies before his plans could be put into effect. Abdullah was succeeded by his son, Talal, who abdicated the following year due to illness. Talal was in turn succeeded by Abdullah's grandson, Hussein.

On July 31, 1951, **Brig. Gen. Charles M. Chamson** (1902–51), the French commissioner for South Vietnam, and **Gov. Lap Thanh** (1896–51) of South Vietnam, were killed in a suicide grenade attack in Sadec, near Saigon, by a Communist.

S.S. **Gen. Jurgen Stroop** (1901–51), the Nazi officer who suppressed the Warsaw ghetto uprising in 1943, was hanged in Warsaw, Poland, on September 8, 1951, as a war criminal. Stroop was captured by the Allies after Germany's defeat in 1945, and was sentenced to death by an American military tribunal on March 22, 1947, for ordering the execution of American pilots in Greece during the war. He was subsequently extradited to Poland to stand trial for war crimes committed there, and was again sentenced to death.

On October 6, 1951, **Henry Lovell Goldworth Gurney** (1898–1951), the British high commissioner of Malaya, was assassinated by Communist guerrillas near Kuala Lumpur, in Malaysia. Gurney had served as an official in the British Colonial Office for nearly thirty years and had accepted the position in Malaya on October 6, 1948. He was ambushed and killed in the midst of his campaign to eliminate Communist terrorist activities.

Liaquat Ali Khan, the first prime minister of Pakistan, was assassinated on October 16, 1951, while addressing a public meeting in Rawalpindi. His assassin, Said Akbar, was identified as a member of the Khaksar semi-military. Liaquat was born on October 1, 1895, in Karnal. He received a degree in law from Exeter College in Oxford, England, and returned to India to practice law. He entered politics in 1923, joining the All-India Moslem League led by Mohammed Ali Jinnah. Liaquat served in the United Provinces Legislative Council from 1926 until his election, in 1940, to the Central Legislative Assembly. In 1936 Liaquat was elected secretary general of the Moslem League and, shortly thereafter, became Jinnah's deputy leader of the party. Following the establishment of independent Pakistan in August of 1947 Liaquat was appointed the first prime minister. After Jinnah's death the following year Liaquat assumed complete responsibility for the governing of Pakistan. The territorial dispute with India over Kashmir was the major issue facing Liaquat's government. His negotiations with Prime Minister Nehru of India and his refusal to consider a war with India led to his assassination by a Moslem fanatic.

On October 29, 1951, **Jean De Raymond** (1907–51), the French commissioner for Cambodia, was stabbed to death by his Vietnamese servant. The assailant was identified as Pham Ngoc Lam, an alleged Communist terrorist.

On November 16, 1951, **Cyril Ousman**, the British vice consul, was assassinated in Jidda, Saudi Arabia.

1952

On December 3, 1952, eleven Communist politicians in Czechoslovakia were executed for treason. They were arrested in November of 1951, and following a trial before the People's Court in Prague, were found guilty and sentenced to be hanged. Those executed included **Rudolf Slansky**, the former vice premier; **Vladimir Clementis**, the former foreign minister; **Otto Fischl**, the former deputy finance minister; **Josef Frank**, the former Communist party acting secretary; **Ludvik Frejka**, the former chief of the economic section of the president's office; **Bedrich Geminder**, the former head of the Czech Communist party International Section; **Richard Margolius**, the former deputy foreign trade minister; **Bedrich Reicin**, the former deputy defense minister; **Karel Svab**, the former deputy security minister; **Otto Sling**, the former Brno district Communist party secretary; and **Andre Simon**, the former editor of *Rude Pravo*, the Czech Communist newspaper.

Rudolf Salzmann Slansky was born on July 31, 1901. He joined the

Czechoslovak Communist party and, in 1929, was elected to the Central Committee of the party. He served in the Czech national assembly from 1935 until 1936, and in 1945 he was elected secretary general of the Communist party. In 1951 Slansky was named to the position of vice premier of Czechoslovakia. Several months later he was arrested on charges of leading an attempt to overthrow the Communist government, resulting in his trial and execution.

Vladimir Clementis was born in Slovakia on September 20, 1902. He served in the Czechoslovak parliament as a Communist deputy during the 1930s, and served as a legal council to the Czech government in exile in London during World War II. He was appointed undersecretary of state for foreign affairs following his return to Czechoslovakia after the war and, in 1948, was appointed foreign minister. He served in this position until March of 1950, and the following year he was expelled from the Communist party and arrested for subversion. He was subsequently tried and executed.

On December 5, 1951, **Farhat Hached** (1913–52), the secretary general of the Tunisian Labor Federation, was shot to death with machine guns outside of Tunis. Nationalist leaders blamed the killing on members of a secret society of French colonial groups called the Red Hand. Rioting and violence ensued throughout French North Africa as a result of Hached's murder.

1953

On April 20, 1953, **Brig. Gen. Mohammed Afshartus** (1908–53), the Iranian National Police chief, was found strangled to death near Teheran. Afshartus was an ally of Premier Mohammed Mossadegh.

Shedli Kastalli, the vice president of the municipal council of Tunis, Tunisia, was shot and killed by terrorists on May 2, 1953.

On June 19, 1953, **Julius** (1918–53) and **Ethel** (1915–53) **Rosenberg** were executed at Sing Sing Prison in New York, following their conviction on charges of conspiracy to transmit atomic secrets to the Soviet Union. The Rosenbergs had been arrested in the summer of 1950 after the United States government learned that Julius Rosenberg had acquired information from his wife's brother, David Greenglass, concerning the atomic bomb project during World War II. The Rosenbergs were sentenced to death for treason by Judge Irving Kaufman in a trial which began in March of 1951 in New York. Greenglass, who served as the government's chief witness at the trial, was sentenced to fifteen years' imprisonment, and two other associates, Harry Gold (1910–72) and Morton Sobell, were sentenced to thirty years in prison.

On July 1, 1953, **Prince Ezzedine Bey** (1881–1953), the heir to the throne of Tunisia, was assassinated in his palace in Tunis. Prince Ezzedine, who was known for his pro–French views, was a cousin of the bey of Tunisia. He was killed by Hei Ben Brahim Ben Ejebala Djeridi, an ex-convict who claimed to have been hired to kill the prince.

Hedi Shaker, the leader of the autonomist Tunisian Neo-Destour party, was assassinated in Tunis on September 12, 1953.

Wilhelm Stuckart (1902–53), the Nazi jurist who drafted the Nuremberg anti–Jewish racial laws of 1935, died in a suspicious car crash near Hanover in December of 1953. It was likely that Stuckart had been killed by members of a Jewish revenge squad organized to hunt down Nazi war criminals. Stuckart had been tried as a war criminal at Nuremberg in 1949, and was sentenced to four years' imprisonment. He was released soon after and settled in West Berlin.

Lavrenti P. Beria, the former head of the Soviet secret police and a close associate of Joseph Stalin, was executed in Moscow as a traitor. During a secret trial presided over by Marshal Ivan S. Konev, Beria and six others were sentenced to be executed. On December 23, 1953, they were executed by a firing squad. The other defendants included **V.N. Merkulov**, the former state security and state control minister; **V.G. Dekanozov**, the former Georgian internal affairs minister; **P.V. Meshik**, the former Ukrainian internal affairs minister; and **S.A. Goglidze** and **L.E. Vlodimirsky**, two former high-ranking police officials.

Lavrenti Pavlovich Beria was born in Soviet Georgia on March 29, 1899. He became a member of the Communist party in 1917 and, in 1921, joined the Soviet secret police. He was elected first secretary of the Georgian Communist party in November of 1931, and was an active participant in the Stalin purges in Georgia, Azerbaijan, and Armenia. He succeeded Nikolai Yezhov (q.v.) as commissar for internal affairs on December 8, 1938, and, in February of 1941, he was named deputy prime minister of the Soviet Union. He served on the State Defense Committee during World War II and, in March of 1946, was named to the Politburo. After the death of Joseph Stalin in March of 1953, Beria became the first of four deputy prime ministers. He was well positioned to succeed Stalin as leader of the Soviet Communist party, but, on July 10, 1953, he was removed from his posts, expelled from the party, and arrested on charges of treason. He was subsequently tried and executed with several of his aides.

1954

Amin Didi (1912–54), the first president of the Maldive Island Republic, died on January 19, 1954, from injuries recieved from an angry crowd of demonstrators. Amin Didi had served as president from January of 1953 until September 3, 1953, when he had been deposed in a coup. Didi had been living in exile on Male Atoll at the time of his death.

On March 1, 1954, five members of the United States Congress were wounded when four Puerto Rican Nationalists fired indiscriminately at the floor of the House of Representatives from the spectator's gallery. Bullets struck the table of the majority leader and the surrounding chairs. Rep. Alvin M. Bentley (1918–69) of Michigan, hit in the lung, liver, and stomach, was the most seriously injured. Rep. Ben F. Jensen (1892–1970) from Iowa, was wounded in the back. Rep. Clifford Davis (1897–1970) from Tennessee, Rep. George H. Fallon (1902–80) from Maryland, and Rep. Kenneth A. Roberts (b. 1912) from Alabama all suffered leg wounds. All five recovered and continued serving in the Congress. Four Puerto Rican nationalists were charged, tried, and convicted of assault with intent to kill. They were Rafael Cancel-Miranda (b. 1929), Irving Flores Rodriguez (b. 1924), Andres Figueroa Cordero (1919–79), and Lolita Lebron (b. 1920). Figueroa Cordero was released in 1978 for health reasons and died the following year. The other three were released by President Jimmy Carter in September of 1979.

Lucretiu Patrascanu, the former Romanian minister of justice, and **Remus Koppler** were tried for treason as United States sympathizers. They were both executed in Romania on April 18, 1954.

Albert L. Patterson (1895–1954), the Democratic nominee for attorney general for the state of Alabama, was shot to death in Phenix City, Alabama, on June 18, 1954. Patterson, a leading crusader against vice, was presumed murdered by gambling interests in Phenix City. Albert Fuller (1918–69), a former chief deputy sheriff, was sentenced to life in prison for Patterson's murder.

On August 4, 1954, Brazilian air force major **Rubens Florentino Vaz** was shot and killed in a car at the home of Brazilian opposition leader and journalist Carlos Lacerda in Rua Toneleros, Copacabana, Brazil. Lacerda, who was believed to be the target of the assassination attempt, was only slightly injured. The government of President Getulio Vargas was implicated in the shooting, and Vargas was asked to resign. Vargas committed suicide three weeks later, on August 24, 1954.

Kou Voravong (1914–54), the defense minister of Laos, was shot and killed on September 18, 1954, by terrorists while attending a dinner party at the home of Deputy Premier Phouy Sananikone in Vientiane, Laos.

On October 5, 1954, **Ibrahim El-Shalhi**(1894–1954), the Libyan palace affairs minister, was assassinated by El-Sherif Mohieddin El-Sinussi (b.

1934), a nephew of Queen Fatima of Libya. The shooting resulted in the exile of several members of the imperial family.

On October 26, 1954, President Gamal Abdel Nasser of Egypt escaped injury when several shots were fired at him in an assassination attempt. Mahmoud Abdel Latif, a member of the outlawed Moslem Brotherhood, was charged with the attempt. Latif and other Moslem Brotherhood leaders, including Youssef Talaat, Sheik Mohammed Farghali, Ibrahim Tayeb, Hindawi Duweir, and Abdel Kader Oda, were executed by hanging on December 7, 1954.

Hossein Fatemi (1918–54), the former Iranian minister of foreign affairs, was executed by a firing squad on November 10, 1954. Fatemi, an ally of Mohammed Mossadegh, was the founder of the newspaper *Bakhtar-i-Inruz* in 1949, and was a leading proponent of the nationalization of the Iranian oil industry. When Mossadegh assumed power as premier on April 29, 1951, Fatemi became his personal assistant, and was appointed minister of foreign affairs on October 11, 1952. Following Gen. Fazlollah Zahedi's successful Royalist rebellion on August 19, 1953, Fatemi was forced into hiding. He was located in March of 1954 and arrested. He was tried for treason against the monarchy and sentenced to death.

1955

Jose Antonio Remon, the president of Panama, was shot and killed by machine gun fire on January 2, 1955, while at a Panama City racetrack. Remon, who was born in 1908, joined the Panamanian National Police in 1931, and in 1947 was elevated to the position of first commandant of the police. This position enabled him to wield much power in the affairs of state and enabled him to become president in 1952. Remon's administration was noted for its seeming lack of corruption and sound fiscal policies. Jose Ramon Guizado (1899–1964), the first vice president of Panama, assumed office after the slaying, but was removed from his position by the Panamanian national assembly two weeks later after having been implicated in the assassination of Remon. Ruben Miro (b. 1912) confessed to having shot Remon after plotting the killing with Guizado and several others. The plotters hoped that Guizado, as president, could help relieve the personal financial difficulties they were then experiencing.

On August 12, 1955, **John E. Peurifoy** (1907–55), the United States ambassador to Thailand, was killed in an automobile accident outside of the capital of Bangkok. One of Peurifoy's sons was also killed in the crash. Peurifoy, a former deputy undersecretary of state, was known as an anti–

Communist diplomatic trouble shooter for the State Department. He had served as ambassador to Greece during the Civil War of the late 1940s. He was also instrumental in the deposing of left-wing president Jacobo Arbenz Guzman (q.v.) of Guatemala while Peurifoy was serving as United States ambassador to that country in 1954. His reputation and somewhat mysterious demise fueled speculation that his death may have been caused by leftist sympathizers.

Caliph Mohammed Berdadi, a leading supporter of the deposed sultan of Morocco, Sidi Mohammed ben Moulay Arafa, was stoned to death by an angry mob in Rabat on November 19, 1955.

1956

Dedan Kimathi (1920–56), a leader of the Kenyan nationalist terrorists known as the "Mau Mau" during the 1950s, was captured and executed in 1956. Kimathi, a Kikuyu tribesman, was a member of the Kenya African Union. He was a leading figure in uniting the various nationalist and insurgent groups in the country. Before his arrest he and his followers waged a number of guerrilla campaigns against the British in an attempt to win independence for Kenya.

Jesus De Galindez (1915–56), a Dominican lawyer, writer, and leading foe of Dominican dictator Rafael L. Trujillo (q.v.), disappeared from New York on March 12, 1956. As he was never found, it was assumed the exiled Galindez had been abducted and flown to the Dominican Republic on Trujillo's orders, and murdered following his arrival.

Gen. Juan Jose Valle, a leading Argentine army officer during the administration of deposed president Juan Peron, was executed following an attempted revolt against the provisional government in June of 1956.

Anastasio Somoza Garcia, the longtime president of Nicaragua, was shot and seriously wounded in Leon on September 21, 1956. He died of his injuries on September 29, 1956. His assailant, identified as Rigoberto Lopez Perez (1929–56), was immediately shot to death by Somoza's guards. Somoza, who was born in 1896, had risen to prominence in Nicaragua as the leader of the Civil Guard in the 1920s. After the murder of insurgent leader Cesar Sandino (q.v.) in 1934 and Somoza's consolidation of power, he ousted President Juan Bautista Sacasa in 1936 and assumed the presidency. He remained in office until 1947, and retained ultimate authority even after handpicking his successor. He again became president in 1950, serving until his death. During Somoza's reign the economic situation of

Nicaragua greatly improved due to the president's rigid control over the country. Somoza's personal wealth and that of his family also greatly increased. The Somoza dynasty did not die with Anastasio Somoza. Two of his sons, Luis Somoza Debayle and Anastasio Somoza Debayle (q.v.), later served as presidents of the country.

1957

On July 26, 1957, Guatemalan president **Carlos Castillo Armas** (1914–57) was shot to death in the Presidential Palace in Guatemala City. His assailant, Romero Vasquez Sanchez (1937–57), killed himself immediately following the murder of the president. Castillo Armas was a Guatemalan army officer when, in June of 1954, he led a military uprising against the leftist government of Jacobo Arbenz Guzman (q.v.), forcing his resignation. Castillo Armas became provisional president and was elected to a full term the following year. He was a vehement anti–Communist and purged the government and unions of those suspected of leftist sympathies. He also redesigned the agrarian reform programs of his predecessor, returning much of the land to the original owners. His assassin had been discharged from the army for Communist sympathies the previous year, and presumably killed Castillo Armas for his rightist policies.

1958

On April 28, 1958, **Ducasse Jumelle** (1899–1958), the Haitian minister of interior under President Magloire, and **Charles Jumelle**, both brothers of Clement Jumelle, presidential candidate against Francois Duvalier in 1957, were killed in their home on the orders of President Duvalier. Clement Jumelle died in hiding later in the year.

Otto Abetz, the German ambassador to Vichy France during World War II, died in an automobile accident on May 5, 1958, when his steering mechanism failed. It was speculated that his car may have been sabotaged in revenge for his role in persecuting French Jews during the war. Abetz was born on May 26, 1903, and entered the German Foreign Service in 1935. He served as Germany's ambassador to France during the occupation from 1940 until 1944. Following the war he was arrested as a war criminal and, in 1949, sentenced to twenty years' imprisonment. He was released in the early 1950s and died shortly afterward when his car malfunctioned on the Cologne-Ruhr autobahn in Dusseldorf, Germany.

Imre Nagy (1896–1958), the prime minister of Hungary from 1953 until 1955, was executed on June 17, 1958, following a trial conducted by the

Soviet government. Nagy, a Hungarian soldier during World War I, was captured by the Russians and joined the Communist party during his imprisonment. After his release he returned home and became instrumental in the development of the Hungarian Communist party. Nagy returned to the Soviet Union in 1930, and remained there until the end of World War II. He served as minister of agriculture in Hungary's first republican government from 1945 to 1946. He briefly served as minister of interior, and succeeded Matyas Rakosi as prime minister in July of 1953. Nagy was a protege of Georgi M. Malenkov, prime minister of the Soviet Union, and when Malenkov was forced out of office in February of 1955, Nagy soon followed. At the start of the Hungarian National Rising in October of 1956 Nagy was again named prime minister. One of the first acts of his new government was to announce the withdrawal of Hungary from the Warsaw Pact, and the establishment of Hungary as a neutral nation. The Soviet Union responded by sending in the Soviet army and forcing Nagy's removal from office. Nagy fled to the Yugoslav embassy in November of 1956, but was captured two weeks later when he emerged after being promised safe conduct by the Soviets. He was secretly taken to the Soviet Union, where he was tried and executed.

Maj. Gen. Pal Maleter, a supporter of Nagy and a leader in the 1956 Hungarian revolt against the Soviet Union, and **Miklos Gimes** and **Jozsef Szilagy**, two Hungarian journalists, were also tried by the Soviets and executed with Nagy on June 17, 1958.

On July 14, 1958, much of the Iraqi royal family was murdered during an army revolt. **King Feisal II**, along with **Abdul-Ilah**, the former regent, and many other members of the king's family, were slaughtered and their butchered bodies dragged through the streets of Baghdad after the king had surrendered the palace on a promise of safe conduct for his family within. **Nuri As-Said**, the premier of Iraq, was captured and killed the following day. The coup, led by Brigadier Abdul Karim Kassem (q.v.), was provoked by nationalist sentiments against the pro–Western Hashemite monarchy, and inspired by the success of the Nasser revolution in Egypt. Brigadier Kassem assumed leadership of the country following the revolt.

Faisal II was born in 1935 and succeeded his father, Ghazi, as king of Iraq when Ghazi was killed in an automobile accident on April 4, 1939. He ruled through the regency of his uncle, Abdul-Ilah, until he came of age in 1953. He attended school in England and was a classmate of his cousin, Hussein, who was to become king of Jordan. The two cousins remained close friends and planned to federate their nations in response to the militant nationalist policies of Gamal Nasser's newly formed United Arab Republic. This proposed federation died with Faisal.

Abdul-Ilah was born in Taif in 1913. He was the son of Ali ibn Husain, who had ruled as king of the Hejaz from 1924 until his defeat and ouster by

King Saud of Saudi Arabia in 1925. In 1939 Abdul-Ilah was named regent of Iraq for Feisal II, his nephew, on the death of King Ghazi. As regent, his moderate pro–Western policies brought him into conflict with some of the more militant Arab nationalists in the region. After Feisal came of age, Abdul-Ilah continued to served as the king's close advisor until their deaths.

Nuri as-Said was born in 1888 in Baghdad. He was an early Arab nationalist and a close advisor to King Feisal II's grandfather, Emir Feisal, serving as his chief of staff during the Arab Revolt led by Lawrence of Arabia during World War I. Nuri remained with Emir Feisal during his rule in Syria in 1920 and accompanied him the following year when he was named the first king of Iraq. Nuri was first named prime minister of Iraq in 1930 and served until 1932. During the next twenty-five years he remained a major political figure in Iraq, serving as prime minister 1930–40, 1941–44, 1946–47, 1949, 1950–52, 1954–57, and 1958. He was a leading proponent of Arab unity, and a founder of the Arab League in 1945. His opposition to Egypt's President Nasser along with his moderate pro–Western policies, which echoed those of the regent Abdul-Ilah and King Feisal II, met with opposition from the militant nationalists. Following the ouster of Feisal II, Nuri was captured and brutally killed, when he tried to escape from Baghdad dressed as a woman.

Also killed during the revolt was **Ibrahim Hashem** (1878–1958), who served as premier of Jordan from 1946 to 1947, 1955 to 1956, and 1957 until early in 1958. Hashem, who was Jordan's deputy prime minister at the time of the Iraqi revolt, was in Iraq to help administer the union between the two countries. Others killed included **Suleiman Toukan** (1892–1958), the Jordanian defense minister, and **Col. Graham**, the ambassadorial controller at the British Embassy in Baghdad. Two United States citizens, **Eugene Burns**, a newsman, and **George Colley**, the executive vice president of the Pacific Bechtel Corporation, were also murdered by a mob.

Following the Kassim revolt, numerous officials in the deposed government were tried by a People's Court. Among those convicted and sentenced to death were former Iraqi prime ministers Ahmed Mukhtar Baban, Fadhil al-Jamali, and Rashid Ali el-Gailani; ex-foreign minister Burhanuddin Bashayan; Gen. Mohammed Rafiq Aref, the former chief of staff of the Iraqi army; and Gen. Ghazi el-Daghistani, the former deputy chief of staff. While most were sentenced to be executed, it appears that the sentences of many were later commuted and the prisoners were eventually released.

1959

In January of 1959 Cuban rebel leader Fidel Castro overthrew the government of Fulgencio Batista. While Batista was able to flee the country, many of his aides and advisors were not so fortunate. Many of the deposed president's followers were tried and executed for "war crimes" during the year. On January 12 **Gen. Joaquin Castilla Lumpuy**, the commander of Las Villas Province, was executed by a firing squad in Santa Clara. **Capt. Pedro Morejon Caldes** (1921–59) was executed on January 31, and **Maj. Jesus Sosa Blanco** (1908–59), the leader of the Batista government's operations against the rebels in Oriente Province, was executed on February 18. On February 23 **Lt. Col. Ricardo Luis Grao** was executed. During the remainder of the year nearly 600 more former officials met the same fate.

Kamil Qazanchi, an Iraqi Communist leader, was shot and killed in Mosul on March 8, 1959, during a rebellion by soldiers under the command of **Col. Abdel Wahab Shawaf**. The rebellion proved unsuccessful and Col. Shawaf was reported killed the following day. **Brig. Nadhem Tabakchali**, the former commander of the Iraqi army, and four other officers were arrested for complicity and executed on September 20, 1959. Ex-interior minister **Said Qazzaz**, ex-security chief **Mahjat Attiyah**, ex–Iraqi police chief **Abdul Jabbar Ayyour**, and ex-governor **Abdul Jabbar Fehmi** of Baghdad were also executed at that time.

Abdel Aziz Ben Dris, a leading figure in the ruling Moroccan Independence party and a member of the National Assembly, was murdered on April 24, 1959.

Naim Moghabghab, a member of the Lebanese parliament and a former minister of public works, was attacked and beaten to death on July 28, 1959, near Beirut. Moghabghab was a prominent supporter of former Lebanese president Camille Chamoun.

Cho Bong Am (1899–1959), who twice ran for the presidency of South Korea as the Progressive party's candidate, was hanged for treason in Seoul on July 31, 1959.

On September 25, 1959, **Solomon W.R.D. Bandaranaike**, the prime minister of Ceylon, was shot by Talduwe Somarama Thero, a Buddhist monk. Bandaranaike died of his injuries the following day. Bandaranaike was born on January 8, 1899, in Colombo, Ceylon. He entered politics in the late 1920s and joined the United National party. He served as Ceylon's minister of health following independence in 1948 until 1951. He was a leading spokesman for the Buddhist Sinhalese in Ceylon and, in 1951, he founded the socialist Sri Lanka Freedom party. Following the unification of several of Ceylon's leftist parties with his own, Bandaranaike was elected prime minister in April of 1956. His pro–Sinhalese policies alienated the

Indian Tamils in Ceylon and caused widespread rioting and violence, culminating in the prime minister's assassination. The assassin was convicted of the murder and hanged on July 6, 1962. Bandaranaike's widow, Sirimavo, became Ceylon's prime minister the following year, serving until 1965 and again from 1970 until 1972.

Stefan Bandera (1909–59), a Ukrainian nationalist leader, died in exile in Germany in 1959 of poisoning. The death was officially ruled a suicide, but there was much speculation that Soviet agents had murdered him. Bandera fought against both the Germans and the Soviets during World War II in an attempt to secure independence for the Ukraine.

1960

In Caracas, Venezuela, on June 24, 1960, a bomb exploded in a car containing Venezuelan president Romulo Betancourt (1908–81). The president and the defense minister, Gen. Josue Lopez Henriquez, were slightly injured in the explosion. **Col. Ramon Armas Perez,**the chief aide-de-camp to the president, was killed.

On July 14, 1960, Nobosuke Kishi (1896–1987), the prime minister of Japan, was stabbed in the leg by an ultra-nationalist who was opposed to the prime minister's support for a new mutual security pact between the United States and Japan. Kishi recovered from his wounds but resigned his office four days later.

Hazza Majali (1916–60), the premier of Jordan from 1959, was killed in a bomb explosion in his office in Amman on August 29, 1960. Majali, a close advisor of King Hussein, and ten others, including **Suha Iddin Hammoud**, foreign affairs undersecretary, and **Assem Taijo**, the tourism department director, were killed in the explosion.

On October 12, 1960, **Inejiro Asanuma** (1899–1960), the chairman of Japan's Socialist party, was stabbed to death by Otoya Yamaguchi, a seventeen-year-old nationalist student. Asanuma, who was a leading supporter of the United States–Japanese Security Pact, was addressing a political rally in Tokyo at the time of the attack.

Yvon Emmanuel Moreau (1922–60), a Haitian senator and Episcopalian minister, was arrested on charges of plotting against President Francois Duvalier. He disappeared in November of 1960 and was presumed killed.

Felix-Roland Moumie (1924–60), the leader of the anti–French Union of Cameroons Populations in the Cameroon Republic, died of thalium poisoning on November 3, 1960, in Geneva. Moumie had entered a hospital two weeks earlier, claiming to have been poisoned by political opponents.

1961

On January 17, 1961, **Patrice Lumumba** (1926–61), who served as the first prime minister of the Congo Republic for eleven weeks, was murdered by Congolese soldiers loyal to the government of Joseph Mobutu. Lumumba was the founder of the Congolese National Movement (M.N.C.) in 1957 and a leader of left-wing anti-colonialism. He became Congo's prime minister following that nation's independence in July of 1960. One of the first problems of his administration was the secession of the Katanga province under Moise Tshombe (q.v.). Lumumba's inability to control the separatists, and his unpopularity with the army in Leopoldville, resulted in a military coup led by Col. Joseph Mobutu in September of 1960. Lumumba was fleeing to his hometown in Stanleyville when he was captured by Mobutu's troops. **Maurice Mpolo**, the former youth minister, and **Joseph Okito**, the vice president of the Senate, were also taken prisoner, and were killed with Lumumba.

On February 19, 1961, a group of Congolese politicians who had been allies of Patrice Lumumba were executed in Bakwanga, the Congo. **Jean-Pierre Finant**, the president of Oriental Province; **Maj. Jacques Fataki**, the former chief of the Stanleyville Military Police; **Gilbert Nzuzi**, Congolese National Movement youth leader; and **Pierre Elengesa**, a leader of the Leopoldville Liberal Circle, had been held captive for several months prior to their execution.

Gen. Mengestu Newaye, the former commander of the Ethiopian imperial guard, was hanged for treason on March 31, 1961. Gen. Mengestu was the leader of an unsuccessful rebellion against the emperor in December of 1960.

On April 22, 1961, **Jacques Alexis** (1922–61), a Haitian poet and author, and the founder of the Party of Popular Accord in 1959 in opposition to Francois Duvalier, was killed. He had returned from exile in April of 1961 and was captured near Mole Saint Nicolason on April 22, where he was bound and stoned to death by a crowd.

Rafael Leonidas Trujillo y Molina (1891–1961), the dictator of the Dominican Republic for over thirty years, was assassinated on May 30, 1961, by machine gun fire while he was driving outside the capital. Trujillo gained the presidency following a revolt against President Horacio Vazquez in February of 1930. His administration was known for its blatant corruption and violations of human rights. Trujillo's terms as president were from 1930 to 1938 and from 1942 to 1951, but he remained the ultimate authority in the Dominican Republic during the intervening years and up until the time of his death. Several of his alleged assassins, including Gen. J.T. Diaz, were captured and executed, but many involved in the conspiracy remained active in Dominican politics.

On August 14, 1961, **Salah Ben Youssef** (1910–61), the secretary general of the Neo-Destour party during Tunisia's bid for independence, was assassinated while in exile. Ben Youssef was a militant Arab nationalist and an opponent of Tunisian President Habib Bourguiba. He had been living in Frankfurt, West Germany, since his exile from Tunisia in 1955.

Dr. Inkongliba Ao (1903–61), the leader of the Naga State in India, was shot on August 24, 1961. He died of his injuries the following day. His assassin was a fanatic nationalist who objected to Nagaland becoming an Indian state.

Adnan Menderes (1899–1961), the premier of Turkey from 1950 to 1960, was executed on September 17, 1961, on Imrali Island in Turkey. Menderes had been ousted from office the previous year and was charged with treason. Two of his former aides, **Fatin Rustu Zorlu** (1910–61), the former foreign minister, and **Hassan Polatkan** (1915–61), the former finance minister, were hanged the previous day.

Menderes was born near Smyrna, Turkey, in 1899. He was elected to the National Assembly in 1930 and founded the Turkish Democratic party in 1946. His party won an overwhelming victory in the general elections on May 14, 1950, and Menderes was subsequently named prime minister. Menderes was an outspoken critic of Communism and directed Turkey's foreign policies on course with those of the United States.

On September 18, 1961, **Dag Hammarskjöld**, the secretary general of the United Nations, perished in an airplane crash while en route to a peace mission in the Congo Republic. Hammarskjöld was born on July 29, 1905, in Jonkoping, Sweden. He entered the Swedish civil service in his youth, serving in the Ministry of Finance as an undersecretary. In 1947 he was named to the Foreign Ministry and, four years later, was appointed to the Swedish cabinet as minister of state and deputy foreign minister. In 1951 Hammarskjöld also was named to Sweden's delegation to the United Nations, becoming chairman of the delegation the following year. He was elected secretary general of the United Nations in April of 1953, succeeding Trygvie Lie. He was an internationally respected statesman who performed his duties at the United Nations fairly and without political bias. He was reelected to a second term in 1957. During his terms of office he was active in attempting to settle the many disputes in the Middle East, particularly the Suez Canal crisis. In 1960 the United Nations became involved in the civil war in the Belgian Congo, which had recently gained independence. Hammarskjöld authorized the use of United Nations troops in an attempt to restore order in the area, an action which met with the disapproval of the Soviet bloc nations. It was during this conflict that Hammarskjöld was killed, while making a personal mission of peace to the Congo. The plane in which he was travelling crashed in Northern Rhodesia while en route to a meeting with the warring factions. The circumstances behind the crash remain uncertain, but much speculation exists that sabotage was involved. Hammarskjöld became the first, and only, posthumous recipient of a Nobel Peace prize when he was awarded it several months after his death.

Prince Louis Rwagasore (1929–61), the prime minister of Burundi, was shot and killed in a local restaurant on October 13, 1961. Prince Rwagasore had been the leader of the Urundi Union and Progress National party and was named Burundi's premier on September 29, 1961. Jean Kageorgis was arrested for the assassination. He was convicted and executed by a firing squad on June 30, 1962.

1962

Indonesian President Sukarno (1901–70) was uninjured in an assassination attempt on January 8, 1962. A bomb exploded in the path of the president's car while he was travelling in a motorcade in Macassar.

On May 31, 1962, **Adolf Eichmann** (1906–62), who was in charge of the deportation of Jews to extermination centers during World War II, was executed in Ramleh Prison in Israel. Eichmann, who had disappeared following the end of the war, was tracked down in Argentina by Israeli agents in May of 1960 and secretly captured and brought to Israel. He was tried between April 2 and August 14 of 1961 and was sentenced to death for crimes against humanity. Eichmann was born on March 19, 1906, and joined the Austrian Nazi Party in 1932. He joined Himmler's Security Service (S.D.) in 1934 and, in 1938, was put in charge of the Office of Jewish Emigration. He was personally in charge of the killing of millions of Jews throughout Europe before and during World War II. Following the end of the war Eichmann escaped trial as a war criminal and fled to Argentina. He was not located and brought to justice until fifteen years later.

President Kwame Nkrumah (1909–72) of Ghana was the target of an assassination attempt on August 1, 1962. Nkrumah was uninjured by a bomb tossed at his car while he was riding through Kulungugu, Ghana.

On August 22, 1962, French president Charles de Gaulle (1890–1970) was the target of an assassination attempt. The car in which he and his wife were riding near Petit-Clamart was barraged with gunfire, but de Gaulle and the other occupants were uninjured. The Organisation de l'Arme Secrete (OAS), a rebel military organization that blamed de Gaulle for the loss of Algeria, was responsible for the attempt on his life. Several conspirators were tried and, on March 11, 1963, Lt. Col. Jean-Marie Bastien-Thiry (1926–63) was executed by a firing squad in Paris for his role in the assassination attempt.

De Gaulle had survived a previous attempt on his life on September 9, 1961, when a bomb was set in the path of his car on a road leading from Paris. De Gaulle was uninjured in that attempt as well, when the bomb failed to detonate properly. It was believed the OAS was also responsible for that attack.

On September 18, 1962, **Sayf al-Islam Ahmed ibn Yahya**, the imam of Yemen, was reported to have died of natural causes. The imam, who had succeeded to the throne of his father, Mohammed ibn Yahya Hamid al-Din (q.v.) in 1948, had been shot and seriously wounded on March 27, 1961. Ahmed was succeeded by his son, Sayf al-Islam Mohammed al-Badr. On September 26, 1962, Imam Mohammed was deposed during a revolution. He was originally reported slain, but this proved untrue. **Hasan Bin Abrahin**, the Yemini foreign minister, and ten other officers were summarily executed on September 28, 1962, following the revolution.

1963

Sylvanus Olympio, the first president of Togo, was shot and killed near the United States embassy in the capital city of Lome on January 13, 1963. Olympio was born in 1902 in Agoue, Dahomey. He was a prominent businessman before entering politics. He served as prime minister, minister of finance, and minister of justice in the government of Togo before that nation's independence from France on April 27, 1960. Olympio was elected Togo's first president on April 9, 1961. Olympio's administration was marked by tension with Kwame Nkrumah's government of neighboring Ghana. Olympio was killed during a coup by former Togolese army soldiers. The president died while trying to escape into the United States Embassy following an attempt by the rebels to arrest him.

On February 8, 1963, **Abdul Karim Kassem** (1914–63), the premier of Iraq from 1958, was executed following a military coup against his government in Baghdad. Kassem had led the army in a revolt against King Feisal II (q.v.) in 1958 and had ordered the butchering of the king and his family.

He became the first leader of the new republican government. His inability to control the diverse forces in Iraq led to his downfall and death. Several days after the coup the new regime announced that some of Kassem's close advisors were also executed, including **Brig. Mahawdi**, the president of the former people's court, **Brig. Abdul Majid Jamil**, **Brig. Daoud Jannasi**, **Col. Ibrahm Kazim Moussawi**, and **Col. Hosni Dhidr Douri**.

On March 6, 1963, **Henri Lafond** (1895–1963), the president of the Banque de l'Union Parisienne and a member of the French Atomic Energy Commission, was assassinated while driving his automobile in Neuilly.

Quinim Pholsena (1915–63), the foreign minister of Laos, was shot and killed on April 1, 1963, by a soldier guarding his home in Vientiane. Quinim Pholsena was an associate of the Pathet Lao, a left-wing, pro–Communist party. He had been active in the Laotian Civil War in 1960, serving as an advisor to Capt. Kon Le in his fight against the pro–Western government. Quinim Pholsena had joined the coalition government after the conclusion of the Civil War.

Mohammed Khemisti (1930–63), the foreign minister of Algeria, was shot by a Moslem fanatic on April 11, 1963. He died several days later. Khemisti was a close political associate of Premier Ahmed Ben Bella and had served as his foreign minister since Algeria had gained its independence from France in 1962.

Grigoris Lambrakis, a Greek left-wing deputy, was murdered on May 22, 1963, when he was hit by a van driven by members of an extreme right-wing organization while attending a rally in Salonika. It was later determined that the murder had occurred with the knowledge and sanction of the local police. Lambrakis' murder was the basis for Costa-Gavras' 1969 film *Z*.

Medgar W. Evers (1926–63), the Mississippi field secretary of the National Association for the Advancement of Colored People for nine years, was shot to death on June 12, 1963. Evers was en route to an integration rally at a Jackson, Mississippi, church when he was killed. Byron De la Beckwith was accused of the murder, but two subsequent trials resulted in no conviction.

Clement Barbot, the chief of Haitian president Francois Duvalier's secret police, the Tontons Macoutes, until his arrest in July of 1960, was killed with his brother, **Harry Barbot**, by Haitian troops in a sugar cane field on July 14, 1963. Barbot had led an unsuccessful insurrection against Duvalier earlier in the year.

Ngo Dinh Diem (1901–63), the first president of South Vietnam, was killed following a military coup in Saigon on November 2, 1963. **Ngo Dinh Nhu** (1910–63), the head of South Vietnam's secret police and Ngo Dinh Diem's brother, was also killed.

Ngo Dinh Diem was born in Hue in 1901. He served as provincial governor in Emperor Bao Dai's government in French Indo-China in the early 1930s, but subsequently gained anti–French views and abandoned politics. He reentered politics in 1947 and formed the National Union Front, an anti–Communist, pro-independence party. In October of 1955 Ngo Dinh Diem, under the patronage of French and American interests in the area, was elected the first president of the Republic of South Vietnam. His rule was endangered by increasing Communist rebel activity sponsored by North Vietnam. Ngo Dinh Diem, a devout Catholic, was also beset by the opposition of Vietnamese Buddhists. Ngo Dinh Diem was ousted and killed by members of the Vietnamese army led by Gen. Duong Van Minh, with the apparent support of the United States government.

Ngo Dinh Dhu, the president's brother, was also an extremely powerful figure in South Vietnam. He was officially the supreme adviser to the president, but also controlled the secret police and the ruling national revolutionary movement. His wife, Madame Nhu, was the official "first lady" of South Vietnam, as the president was a bachelor.

A third brother, **Ngo Dinh Canh**, was the despotic governor of the northern part of South Vietnam. He was arrested by the new military regime following the ouster of his brother. Ngo Dinh Canh was tried for extortion and murder and, on May 9, 1964, was executed.

John F. Kennedy, the thirty-fifth president of the United States, was assassinated while riding in a motorcade in Dallas, Texas, on November 22, 1963. John Fitzgerald Kennedy was born in Brookline, Massachusetts, on May 29, 1917. He was the son of Joseph P. Kennedy, a millionaire businessman who served as ambassador to Great Britain during the administration of President Franklin Roosevelt. John Kennedy served in the United States Navy as a P.T.–boat commander during World War II. He was decorated for heroism following the sinking by the Japanese of P.T.–boat 109 in August of 1943. Following his discharge from the navy in 1945, Kennedy began his political career. He was elected to the United States Congress in 1946, representing the eleventh congressional district in Massachusetts. In 1952 he defeated Republican incumbent Henry Cabot Lodge for a seat in the United States Senate, and shortly after his inauguration married Jacqueline Lee Bouvier. In 1956 he authored *Profiles in Courage*, a study of his personal political heroes, and was awarded the 1957 Pulitzer Prize for Biography for his efforts. Kennedy was narrowly defeated for the 1956 Democratic nomination for vice president, but was easily reelected to the Senate two years later. He received the Democratic nomination for the presidency in 1960 and went on to defeat Richard M. Nixon in the general election later in the year.

John Kennedy was sworn in as the thirty-fifth president of the United States on January 20, 1961. His administration was noted for its support for civil rights legislation and the establishment of the Peace Corps. Kennedy's term of office was also marked by difficulties with the Communist-led government of Fidel Castro in Cuba. In 1961 a C.I.A.–sponsored attempt by Cuban exiles to overthrow the Castro regime met with failure in the "Bay of Pigs" incident. The following year Cuba became the base of Soviet nuclear missiles. In a confrontation known as the Cuban Missile Crisis, Kennedy threatened to blockade the island nation unless the Soviet offensive weapons were removed. Soviet Premier Nikita Khruschev agreed to their removal following a period of international tension.

President Kennedy's first term of office was cut short on November 22, 1963, when he was shot and killed by a sniper while traveling in a motorcade in downtown Dallas, Texas. He was struck by two bullets and was pronounced dead shortly after his arrival at a Dallas hospital. Texas Governor John B. Connally (b. 1917), who was riding with the president, was seriously injured in the shooting, but subsequently recovered. Lee Harvey Oswald, a twenty-four-year-old drifter, was arrested for the murder. On November 24, 1963, Oswald was himself shot and killed by Jack Ruby (1911–67), a Dallas nightclub owner, while being transferred from the Dallas police department.

Kennedy was succeeded by his vice president, Lyndon B. Johnson. The new president appointed a commission, chaired by United States Chief Justice Earl Warren, to investigate the president's killing. The Warren Commission ruled in 1964 that Oswald had fired the fatal shots from a window in the sixth floor of the Texas School Book Depository. The commission also reported that Oswald had acted alone in the planning and execution of the assassination and that there was no evidence of a conspiracy in either the slaying of President Kennedy or of Oswald. Subsequent investigations of the assassination have attempted to show that a conspiracy did exist, but these allegations have yet to be substantiated.

1964

Edwin O. Reischauer (b. 1911), the United States ambassador to Japan, was stabbed in the thigh by a deranged Japanese youth on March 24, 1964. Reischauer was leaving the United States Embassy in Tokyo at the time of the attack. He recovered from his wounds and continued to represent the United States in Japan.

On July 27, 1964, several Congolese political leaders were murdered by Communist rebel followers of Pierre Mulele (q.v.) in Albertville, the capital of the North Katanga province. **Jason Sendwe**, the provisional president of the province; **Fortunat Kabange Numbi**, the former provisional vice president; and **Saloman Ilunga** and **Luther Kabila**, both former cabinet ministers, were among the politicians killed.

Jigme P. Dorji (1919–64), the premier of Bhutan, was shot and killed in Punchholing, near the Indian border, on April 5, 1964, by a Bhutanese soldier. It was believed that the assassination of Dorji, an anti–Communist, had been encouraged by the People's Republic of China. Naik Jambey, the alleged assassin, and Gen. Chapda Namgyal Bahadur and Lt. Col. Sangyal Dorji were executed on July 9, 1964, for complicity in the murder.

Abid Es-Shishakli (1909–64), the former president of Syria, was assassinated while in exile in Brazil on September 28, 1964. Shishakli had seized control of Syria in a military coup in 1949. He became president on July 11, 1953, surviving over twenty plots against him, before his ouster on February 25, 1954, during another military coup.

1965

On March 21, 1965, Lt. Gen. Rene Barrientos Ortuno, the president of Bolivia, was shot and injured in an assassination attempt as he was driving on a road near Cochbamba, Bolivia. Barrientos recovered from his injuries and remained president of Bolivia until his death in an airplane crash on April 27, 1969.

Pierre Ngendamdumwe (1930–65), the premier of Burundi, was assassinated in the capital city of Bujumbura on January 15, 1965. Ngendamdumwe had served as Burundi's premier from July 17, 1963, until April 1, 1964. He was reappointed to the position by King Mwambutsa IV ten days before his death. Several former Burundian officials, including ex-premier Abin Nyamoya, were arrested for possible complicity in the murder. Ngendamdumwe's moderate policies were thought to have been the motive behind the assassination.

Hassan Ali Mansour (1923–65), the premier of Iran, was shot in Teheran while entering a government building on January 21, 1965. He died on January 26. Mansour had been appointed premier by Shah Mohammed Reza Pahlavi on March 7, 1964. The assassin was identified as Mohammed Bakaril, a twenty-one-year-old Moslem fanatic. Bakaril and three other plotters were executed on June 16, 1965.

On February 6, 1965, **Pratap Singh Kairon** (1901-65), the former chief minister of the Punjab region of India, was assassinated while driving near

New Delhi. Kairon had served as chief minister from 1956, until his resignation in 1964.

Lt. Gen. Humberto Delgado (1906–65), a leading opposition politician to Portuguese dictator Antonio De Oliveira Salazar, and an unsuccessful candidate for the presidency of Portugal in 1958, was reported missing from his home in exile in Algiers on February 13, 1965. He had reportedly been on his way to meet with anti–Salazar conspirators in Spain. In April his body and that of his secretary, Arajarir Campos, were found in a shallow grave near the Spanish town of Badajoz on the Portuguese border. Both had been murdered by heavy blows to the skull, presumably by agents of Salazar's regime.

On February 17, 1965, the government of the Congo in Brazzaville announced the assassination of **Lazare Matsokota**, the attorney general; **Joseph Pouabou**, the president of the Supreme Court; and **Anselme Massouemi**, the information agency director. Other sources indicated that the three men had been arrested by government troops shortly before their alleged assassination.

On February 21, 1965, **Malcolm X**, an American black nationalist leader, was shot to death while addressing a crowd at the Audubon Ballroom in New York City. Malcolm X, whose original name was Malcolm Little, was born in 1926. He joined Elijah Muhammad's Black Muslims in the early sixties, but split with the Muslim leader in March of 1964. Malcolm X subsequently founded his own rival group of Muslims, known as the Organization for Afro-American Unity. Talmadge Hayer (Thomas Hagan), Norman 3X (Norman Butler), and Thomas 15X (Thomas Johnson), all followers of Elijah Muhammad, were charged with the assassination.

Mohammed Al-Zubairy, the former deputy premier and minister of information and education in Yemen, was assassinated on April 1, 1965. Zubairy had been instrumental in arranging a cease-fire between the Royalist and and republican forces in Yemen in late 1964. He had resigned his offices after the cease-fire was broken.

On May 21, 1965, **Col. Ernesto Molina Arreaga** (1901–65), Guatemala's deputy defense minister, was shot to death in front of his home in Guatemala City. His assassins were believed to be left-wing terrorists.

Lt. Gen. Achmad Jani, the Indonesian army chief of staff, and five other army generals were found shot to death near the Halim air base on October 4, 1965. The generals had been kidnapped on September 30, 1965, following the start of a Communist uprising in Indonesia.

Mehdi Ben Barka, a leading Moroccan opposition politician and internationally known leftist figure, was abducted from his Paris home and presumed murdered in October of 1965. Ben Barka had been living in exile in France for several years. Ben Barka's disappearance was responsible for a major rift between the Moroccan and French governments. Several leading Moroccan politicians, including Interior Minister Gen. Mohammed Oufkir (q.v.) and Moroccan security chief Ahmed Dlimi (q.v.), were charged in absentia with the kidnapping by a French court. Dlimi arrived in France near the end of the trial and was arrested. After the trial was resumed Dlimi was acquitted of the charges against him, though Gen. Oufkir was convicted and sentenced to life imprisonment in absentia. Rene Thorp, Pierre Stibbe, and Michel Bruguier, who had served as counsels for the family of Ben Barka, all died several weeks apart between the first and second hearing of the case. Their deaths were presumably of natural causes.

On October 19, 1965, Leopold Biha, the premier of Burundi, was seriously injured when he was shot at his home in Bujumbura, the capital, during a coup attempt. The coup was unsuccessful and Biha recovered from his injuries the following year. He remained Burundi's premier until his ouster on July 8, 1966, following another coup.

Dipa Nusantara Aidit, the leader of the Communist party of Indonesia (PKI), was shot to death by the Indonesian army following a military coup in 1965. Aidit was born in North Sumatra in 1923 and served as the leader of the Indonesian Communist party from 1954 until his death. He was a nationalist as well as a Communist, and his party received some support from Sukarno, the Indonesian president. Aidit, **M.H. Lukman**, the deputy leader, and many other Communist politicians were captured and summarily executed following an abortive coup attempt by the communists followed by a military uprising in opposition.

1966

Alahaji Si Abubaker Tefawa Balewa (1912–66), who had served as Nigeria's prime minister since that nation's independence on October 1, 1960, was murdered during an army uprising on January 15, 1966. Northern Regional Premier **Sir Ahmadu Bello**, the sardauna of Sokoto, Western Regional Premier **Chief Samuel Akintola**, and Finance Minister **Okotie Eboh** were also killed during the revolt. The uprising was led by members of the military from Nigeria's Eastern region who were predominantly members of the Ibo tribe. The revolt was carried out by them in the hopes of breaking the hold that the Northern region's politicians had established in Nigeria, and in an attempt to eliminate the widespread corruption of the civilian government. Gen. Johnson Aguiyi-Ironsi (q.v.), the commander of the army, quickly moved to seize power in Nigeria, and successfully gained control of the country from the rebels.

On April 13, 1966, **Abdullah El-Airiny** (1919–66), the Yemeni administration minister, was shot and killed while in his office in Sana. Airiny had served as the acting president of Yemen since March of 1966. His assassin committed suicide shortly after the shooting.

Evariste Kimba (1926–66), the former prime minister of the Congo (Zaire), was hanged with three former cabinet members on June 2, 1966, after having been convicted on charges of conspiring to assassinate President Joseph Mobutu. Kimba had served as the Congo's prime minister from October to November of 1965. The other executed politicians who had all served in the cabinet of ex-premier Cyrille Adoula during the early 1960s were **Sen. Emmanuel Bamba**, the former finance minister; **Jerome Anany**, the former defense minister; and **Alexander Mahamba.**

Johnson T.U. Aguiyi-Ironsi (1924–66), the head of state of Nigeria, was kidnapped and murdered in Northern Nigeria by army officers on July 29, 1966. Aguiyi-Ironsi, who had come to power during a military revolt on January 15, 1966, was shot and killed with **Col. Adekunle Faguiyi**, the military governor of the Western Region of Nigeria, during another army revolt.

Ahmed Bassendawah, a member of the Supreme Council of Yemen, was assassinated in Aden in August of 1966.

Dr. Subandrio, Indonesia's former foreign minister, was sentenced to be executed in September of 1966. Dr. Subandrio, who had served as a close advisor to Indonesian president Sukarno, was also the former director of the Indonesian Central Intelligence Bureau. He was appointed foreign minister in the 1950s and had served in that position until his ouster in May of 1966. He had been tried for complicity in an unsuccessful Communist uprising the previous year. **Jusuf Muda Dalam**, the leftist former minister of central banking, and **Gen. Omar Dani**, the air force commander who had taken part in the rebellion, were also sentenced to death at this time.

Hendrik F. Verwoerd, the prime minister of South Africa, was stabbed to death during a session of Parliament in Capetown on September 6, 1966. Verwoerd was born in Amsterdam on September 8, 1901, and moved with his family to South Africa as an infant. He served as editor of the Johannesburg Nationalist daily newspaper *Die Transvaler* from 1937 until 1948, when he was elected to the Senate. In 1950 he was appointed minister of native affairs, becoming the leading administrator of apartheid in South Africa. On September 2, 1958, he was elected chairman of the Nationalist party and became prime minister of the nation. Verwoerd was shot and seriously injured on April 9, 1960, following the Sharpeville shootings. His assailant, David Pratt, was a white farmer who was sentenced to an asylum. Pratt committed suicide in 1961. Verwoerd was not as fortunate on the second attempt on his life. Dimitrios Tsafendas, a parliamentary messenger, stabbed the prime minister in the neck and chest while he was attending a session of Parliament. Verwoerd was pronounced dead when he arrived at a Capetown hospital. Tsafendas was declared mentally deranged and sentenced to a mental institution.

On December 7, 1966, **Tran Van Van**, a member of the South Vietnamese Constituent Assembly, was assassinated by Communist terrorists. Tran Van Van had been expected to be a candidate for the presidency of South Vietnam.

1967

Mohammed Khider (1914–67), the former secretary general of the Algerian National Liberation Front, was shot to death in front of his home in exile in Madrid on January 3, 1967. Khider had left Algeria in 1964 following a conflict with President Ahmed Ben Bella. He had remained active in Algerian exile circles and was a critic of Ben Bella and his successor, Houari Boumedienne. Associates of the slain exile leader blamed the regime of President Boumedienne for complicity in the assassination.

On April 17, 1967, **Gen. Emmanuel K. Kotoka** (1926–67), a close associate of Gen. J.A. Ankrah, the military ruler of Ghana who had ousted President Kwame Nkrumah the previous year, was slain during a military revolt. The coup attempt was unsuccessful and Gen. Akrah remained in power.

George Lincoln Rockwell (1918–67), the founder and leader of the American Nazi Party, was shot and killed in Arlington, Virginia, on August 24, 1967. Rockwell, who founded the American Nazi Party in 1958, was a great admirer of Adolf Hitler. John Patler, a twenty-nine-year-old member of Rockwell's organization who had been expelled earlier for extremism, was arrested for the murder.

Maj. Ernesto "Che" Guevara De la Serna, the Argentine-born Cuban revolutionary leader, was killed by government troops in Bolivia on October 9, 1967. Guevara was born in Rosario, Argentina, on June 14, 1928.

He joined the Communist party in Argentina and took part in revolutionary activities there. In the late 1950s Guevara joined the Cuban revolutionary movement and took part in the guerrilla war against the regime of Fulgencio Batista. He became a close aide to Fidel Castro and served as minister of industries after President Batista was ousted from power. In 1965 Guevara left Cuba and returned to revolutionary activities in South and Central America. At the time of his capture and death, Guevara was leading a band of guerrilla fighters in the mountains of Bolivia. While it was initially announced by the regime of President Rene Barriotos Ortuna that Guevara had been killed during a gun battle with members of the Fourth Bolivian Rangers Division, commanded by Gen. Joaquin Zenteno Anaya (q.v.), it appears likely that he was captured and summarily executed by the Bolivian army.

1968

In February of 1968 **Deendayal Upadhyaya**, the president of Jana Sangh, the second largest political party in India, was killed when he was shoved from a moving train while en route to New Delhi.

The Rev. Dr. Martin Luther King, Jr., the leading figure of the civil rights movement in the United States, was shot and killed in Memphis, Tennessee, on April 4, 1968. Dr. King was born on January 15, 1929, in Atlanta, Georgia. He was ordained a minister in 1947 and served as pastor of the Ebenezer Baptist Church in Atlanta. He became nationally identified with the civil rights movement in 1956 by leading a successful boycott of the Montgomery, Alabama, bus system in protest of their policy of racial segregation. King subsequently founded the Southern Christian Leadership Conference to assist him in his pursuit of racial desegregation. He was often imprisoned for his policy of civil disobedience to laws he considered discriminatory. On September 20, 1958, Dr. King was seriously injured by a knife-wielding deranged woman in New York. Following his recovery he organized and led a major civil rights march on Washington, D.C., in 1963 in support of the Civil Rights Act. The act was passed by Congress the following year. In 1964 Dr. King also received the Nobel Prize for Peace for his non-violent advocacy of equal rights for people of all races. Dr. King was shot and fatally wounded by a sniper in April of 1968 while standing on the balcony of the Lorraine Motel in Memphis. He was in the city in support of striking city sanitation department employees. His death brought forth a surge of racial violence in cities throughout the United States. His assassin was identified as James Earl Ray (b. 1928), who was captured in London, England, several months later. Ray pleaded guilty to the murder and was sentenced to life imprisonment.

On April 11, 1968, Rudi Dutschke (1940–79), a leader of the West German student revolutionary movement, was seriously injured in a shooting incident in West Berlin. Dutschke, who was shot three times by a pro–Nazi youth, survived his injuries, but never fully recovered.

Houari Boumedienne (1927–78), the president of Algeria, was unharmed when two men sprayed his limousine with machine gun fire on April 25, 1968. Boumedienne remained Algeria's leader until his death in 1978.

Camille Chamoun (1900–86), who served as president of Lebanon from 1952 until 1958, was the target of an assassination attempt on May 31, 1968. Chamoun, the leader of the National Liberal party, was shot at by a young Moslem, but was uninjured in the attempt on his life. Chamoun survived more than five other attacks on his life during his political career.

Robert F. Kennedy, a candidate for the Democratic nomination for the presidency of the United States, was assassinated in Los Angeles, California, on June 5, 1968. Kennedy, a Democratic senator from New York since 1965, was the brother of assassinated United States president John F. Kennedy (q.v.) and had served as attorney general during the Kennedy administration. Kennedy was born on November 20, 1925, in Brookline, Massachusetts. He worked in the United States Department of Justice during the early 1950s before managing the United States Senate campaign of his brother, John. Robert Kennedy subsequently served as the chief counsel for the select Senate committee on improper activities of labor from 1957 until 1960. In that year he managed his brother's campaign for the presidency of the United States. Following John Kennedy's election as president, Robert was appointed United States attorney general. Bobby Kennedy was a strong proponent of civil rights legislation. He also used his position to seek to eliminate labor union corruption. He remained as attorney general in the cabinet of President Lyndon Johnson following the assassination of President Kennedy in November of 1963. He resigned the following year to run for the United States Senate in New York, and defeated the Republican incumbent, Kenneth Keating, in the general election of that year. His support for social legislation and his outspoken criticism of President Johnson's Vietnam War policies established him as a leader of the Democratic party's liberal wing. Kennedy entered the campaign for the Democratic presidential nomination in March of 1968, and succeeded in winning several primaries during the spring. He was shot by Sirhan B. Sirhan (b. 1944), a Jordanian immigrant, in a Los Angeles hotel after winning the important California primary. Senator Kennedy died the following morning. Sirhan was tried and convicted of the murder and sentenced to life imprisonment.

On August 13, 1968, Georgios Papadopoulos (b. 1909), the prime minister of Greece who had seized power in a military coup the previous year, was uninjured when a bomb exploded in the path of his car. The government arrested numerous opposition leaders in the wake of this assassination attempt, charging over twenty people with complicity in the plot. The leader of the plot, Alexandros Panagoulis (q.v.) was sentenced to prison, where he remained until the ouster of the Papadopoulos government in 1973.

On August 28, 1968, **John Gordon Mein**, the United States ambassador to Guatemala since 1965, was shot to death by machine gun fire while riding in his car in Guatemala City. Mein was born on September 10, 1913. He joined the foreign service in 1947 and served in diplomatic positions in Italy, Norway, the Philippines, Indonesia, and Brazil. He was appointed United States ambassador to Guatemala in 1965. Mein was killed while fleeing from a group of urban guerrillas who were attempting to kidnap him. His assassins were believed to be members of the Revolutionary Armed Forces, a left-wing terrorist group. The same group was believed to be responsible for the murders of **Col. John Webber**, the chief of the United States military mission, and **Capt. Ernest Munro**, the chief of the United States Embassy naval section, in Guatemala earlier in the year.

On October 9, 1968, **Pierre Mulele** (1929–68), a Congolese rebel leader who had led a 1963 uprising in the Kwilu Province, was executed before a firing squad in Kinshasa. Mulele had returned to the Congo (Zaire) earlier in the year under a general amnesty proclaimed by President Joseph Mobutu. He was subsequently arrested and convicted of rebellion and terrorism by a military tribunal.

1969

On January 6, 1969, **Dr. Le Minh Tri** (1926–69), the South Vietnamese minister of education, was killed in Saigon when a grenade was thrown into a car he was riding in. His assassination was presumed to be the work of Communist guerrillas.

Eduardo Mondlane (1920–69), the leader of the Front for the Liberation of Mozambique (FRELIMO), was killed on February 3, 1969, when a bomb exploded in his mail in Dar es Salaam, Tanzania. Mondlane had served as a leader of the guerrilla organization seeking to free Mozambique from Portuguese rule since the mid–1960s.

On March 4, 1969, **Dr. Tranh Anh**, the acting dean of Saigon University's Medical College and an associate of Dr. Le Minh Tri (q.v.), was shot and killed by terrorists in Saigon.

Following an alleged attempted coup against President Francois Macias Nguema (q.v.) of Equatorial Guinea in 1969, several prominent members of the government were arrested and killed. They included **Bonifacio Ondo Edu**, who had served as Equatorial Guinea's premier during the nation's pre-independence days and had been defeated by Macias in the presidential election the previous year; **Saturnino Ibongo**, the country's ambassador to the United Nations; **Antanasio Ndongo**, the foreign minister; and **Armando Balboa**, the secretary of the National Assembly.

Alexandre Banza, a leading political figure in the Central African Republic, was tried and executed on April 12, 1969, following an unsuccessful coup attempt against President Jean Bedel Bokassa. Banza had served as the republic's minister of state for public health.

Gen. Ngalo, a leader of the 1964 rebellion in the Congolese region of Kisangani, was captured and executed in the Congo (Zaire) on June 10, 1969.

Moise Tshombe, the former premier of the Congo Republic (Zaire) who had led the successionist Katanga Province during the Congo's civil war in the early 1960s, died while in detention in Algeria on June 29, 1969. Tshombe had been imprisoned in Algeria for the previous two years after his private plane had been hijacked there while en route from his exile in Spain in June of 1965. The Algerian government detained Tshombe while deciding whether to free the ex-premier, or extradite him to the Congo, where he was under a sentence of death in absentia. Tshombe's death was reported to have been from natural causes, according to an autopsy signed by eleven Algerian doctors. While there is no strong evidence to support the likelihood that Tshombe was murdered, his controversial nature and sudden demise led to speculation that there may have been foul play.

Moise-Kapenda Tshombe was born in the Katanga region of the Congo on November 10, 1919. He was active in the political affairs of the pre-independent Congo, and was involved in the planning for Congolese independence from Belgium in 1960. Shortly after the Republic of the Congo was proclaimed on June 30, 1960, the country was beset by domestic turmoil. Tshombe then declared the southern province of Katanga independent from the rest of the country. He utilized European mercenary troops to repel the forces of Patrice Lumumba's (q.v.) central government. The following year Tshombe was held responsible for Lumumba's death when the recently deposed prime minister was captured and killed in Katanga by forces hostile to his government. The United Nations troops were twice repulsed by the Katangan forces and their mercenary allies, but in January of 1963, the United Nations was successful in crushing the Katanga successionists and driving Tshombe into exile in Spain. In July of 1964 Tshombe returned to the Congo's capital and was named prime minister in the government of Joseph Kasavubu. Tshombe was dismissed two years later, in October of 1965, and again went into exile in Spain. Tshombe, while in exile, was tried and condemned for treason and complicity in the death of Patrice Lumumba by the government of Joseph Mobutu, the Congolese army leader who had deposed Kasavubu shortly after Tshombe's ouster. After two years in exile Tshombe was kidnapped and taken to Algeria, where he remained until his death.

Augusto Vandor (1920–69), a leading Argentine labor organizer and president of the Argentine Metal Workers Union, was shot and killed by assassins on June 30, 1969, shortly after his refusal to participate in a general strike against the administration of Gen. Juan Ongania.

Thomas Mboya, a Kenyan nationalist leader and minister of economic planning, was shot to death in Nairobi on July 5, 1969. Mboya, a member of the Luo tribe, was born in Kenya in 1930. He joined Jomo Kenyatta's Kenya African Union in the early 1950s, becoming treasurer in 1953. He became active in the Kenyan Federation of Labor following the government's suppression of the political party, and became a leading advocate of independence for Kenya. In 1960 he was named general secretary of the Kenyan African Nation Union and served as Kenya's minister of labor from 1962 until 1963. In 1963 he was appointed minister of justice, and the following year he was named minister of economic development and planning. He was a leading presidential candidate when he was shot and killed in Nairobi by Isaac N. Njorage, a member of the Kikuyu tribe. Njorage was convicted of the murder and hanged on November 8, 1969.

In September of 1969 President Julius Nyerre of Tanzania returned several alleged plotters against the government of Sheikh Abeid Karume (q.v.) in Zanzibar to that island nation. **Kassim Nanga**, the former vice president of Zanzibar; **Othman Shariff**, Zanzibar's former ambassador to the United States; and **Ali Mwange Tambwe**, a former government minister, were arrested and executed on their arrival.

Somalian president **Abdi Rashid Ali Shermarke** (1919–69) was shot to death on October 15, 1969. Shermarke had served as his country's first prime minister from 1960 to 1964 and had been elected president in 1967. His regime had been marked largely by a domestic policy that invoked little unrest. Nevertheless, while visiting the rural city of Los Anod, north of the capital of Mogadiscio, Shermarke was shot and killed by Abulkadir Abdi Mohammed, a twenty-two-year-old policeman, who then surrendered to the authorities. The killing appeared to lack a political motive, and may have been the result of a tribal feud, as both the president and his killer were members of the same tribe. The Somalian army seized control of the country shortly after Shermarke's assassination. His assassin was convicted and sentenced to death the following year.

Carlos Marighela, the leader of the National Liberation Action, a Brazilian guerrilla organization, was killed on November 4, 1969, in a gun battle with Brazilian police in Sao Paulo.

Rt. Rev. Dillard H. Brown, U.S. Episcopal missionary bishop of Liberia, was murdered on November 19, 1969. His death resulted in a massive crackdown against opponents of Liberian president William Tolbert (q.v.).

On November 26, 1969, **Jorge Soliz Roman**, a Bolivian peasant leader who had served under President Rene Barrientos as minister of agriculture, was assassinated.

David Guerra Guzman, an anti–Communist Guatemalan congressman, was shot to death by left-wing terrorists in Guatemala City on December 17, 1969.

President Milton Obote (b. 1924) of Uganda was shot and seriously wounded following a political rally in Kampala on December 19, 1969. Obote recovered from his injuries and remained his country's president until his overthrow by Idi Amin in 1971. Obote again became head of state of Uganda in 1980, shortly after Amin's ouster, and served until 1985, when he was once again deposed in a coup.

1970

Labor leader **Joseph A. "Jock" Yablonski** was found murdered at his home in Clarksville, Pennsylvania, on January 5, 1970. Yablonski's wife, Margaret, and daughter, Charlotte Joanne, were also found shot to death. It was believed that the three had been killed on New Year's Eve. Yablonski had lost a campaign the previous month against W.A. "Tony" Boyle (1904–85) for the presidency of the United Mine Workers Union. The campaign had been a particularly brutal one, with Yablonski accusing the incumbent Boyle of corruption and mismanagement.

Yablonski, who was born on March 3, 1910, had long been involved in union activities. He had served as a member of the UMW's international executive board 1952–58, when he was elected president of the Washington, D.C. district. He was defeated for reelection to that position in 1966. Three men, believed to be hired killers, were arrested and convicted of the murder. In 1973 Boyle was himself indicted, convicted, and sentenced for life for having hired Yablonski's killers. He died while serving his sentence in June of 1985.

During 1970, terrorists assassinated many pominent political leaders in Guatemala. On January 13, 1970, **Justo Lopez Castanza**, head of Guatemala's intelligence service, was killed in Guatemala City by machine gun fire. **Isidoro Zarco**, associate editor of the pro-government newspaper *Prensa Libre*, was shot to death in Guatemala City on January 28, 1970. On January 30, 1970, **Col. Oscar Giron Perrone**, who had participated in the coup overthrowing President Jacob Arbenz Guzman (q.v.) in 1954, was found shot to death outside of Guatemala City. Giron Perrone was a supporter of Col. Carlos Arana Osoroio, the presidential candidate supported by the National Liberation Movement and the Institutional Democratic party. **Jose Bernabe Linares**, a former Guatemalan secret police chief, was shot to death in Guatemala City on March 11, 1970. He had headed the secret police from 1931 to 1944 and from 1954 to 1956.

On March 8, 1970, Archbishop Makarios III (1913–77), the president of Cyprus, survived an attempt on his life by right-wing Greek Cypriots. Makarios was not harmed in the attempt and remained the leader of Cyprus until his death in 1977.

Polycarpos Georghiades (1930–70), a former Cypriot minister of interior and defense, was found shot to death in his car on a road near Nicosia, Cyprus, on March 15, 1970. Georghiades, a hero in the Cypriot fight for independence, had served under Archbishop Makarios from 1960 to 1968. He had become an opponent of the president in recent years. Georghiades, with Glafkos Clerides, was a co-founder of the Unified Nationalist party, which was formed to contest future elections promised by Makarios. There was some speculation that Georghiades had been involved in a planned coup against the Makarios government at the time of his death.

Iman El Hadi El Mahdi, a Sudanese rebel leader, was killed while trying to escape to Ethiopia after an unsuccessful revolt against President Gaafar al-Nimeiry of the Sudan. Mahdi was killed on March 31, 1970, in an exchange of gunfire while he and his supporters were attempting to cross the Sudanese border in two jeeps.

Faisal Abdul Latif Al-Shaabi, the premier of South Yemen from April to June, 1969, was shot and killed on April 3, 1970, while trying to escape from a detention camp near Aden. Latif, who had also served as South Yemen's foreign minister, had been under house arrest since his ouster.

Count Karl von Spreti (1907–70), the West German ambassador to Guatemala, was kidnapped and killed by terrorists in Guatemala City. Von Spreti had been kidnapped from his home on March 31, 1970, by a Marxist group in Guatemala called the Rebel Armed Forces (FAR). Following the Guatemalan government's refusal to give in to their demands, the guerrillas killed von Spreti with a single bullet to the left side of his head. His body was found on April 4, 1970, in a mud hut outside of Guatemala City.

Right-wing terrorists killed several prominent Guatemalan politicians in reprisal for the killing of von Spreti. On April 8, 1970, **Cesar Montenegro Paniagua**, a Guatemalan labor leader and congressman during the 1950s, was strangled in Guatemala City. Another left-wing labor leader, **Francisco Barreno**, forty, was shot to death on a highway outside of Guatemala City after having been kidnapped on April 25, 1970. On April 28, 1970, **Julio Cesar De la Roca**, thirty-eight, a journalist, was shot and killed outside the capital. On May 6, 1970, **Marco Antonio Marroqui**, the mayor of Jocotan, Chiquimula, Guatemala, was ambushed and killed. **Rafael Horacio Sanchez**, a leading supporter of Carlos Arana Osorio, Guatemala's president-elect, was shot to death by machine gun fire in Guatemala City on May 11, 1970. **Victor Rodriguez**, another supporter of Arana, was assassinated in Chiquimula on July 8, 1970, and **Aldana Sanchez**, the mayor of Zacapa, Guatemala, was shot to death by leftists on July 12, 1970.

Chiang Ching-kuo (1910–88), the deputy premier of Taiwan, was uninjured during a shooting attempt on his life on April 24, 1970. Chiang, the son of Nationalist Chinese president Chiang Kai-shek, was attacked by a Taiwanese gunman while on a visit to New York City. Chiang remained a leading political figure in the Nationalist Chinese government in Taiwan, and succeeded his father as head of state in 1975.

In May of 1970 **Brig. Gen. Supardjo**, the highest-ranking army officer to take part in the 1965 Communist coup attempt in Indonesia, was executed by a firing squad.

Marco Antonio Yon Sosa, a Guatemalan guerrilla leader, and two of his followers were killed May 16, 1970, in a gun battle with Mexican soldiers on the Mexican side of the Guatemalan border. Yon Sosa, a lieutenant in the Guatemalan army until 1960, when he joined the rebellion against President Miguel Ydigoras Fuentes, was head of the Maoist MR-13 guerrilla revolutionary movement in Guatemala.

Hector Moran Charquero, the head of Uruguay's police intelligence, was machine-gunned to death on April 12, 1970, by Tupamaro guerrillas in Montevideo. He had headed a special anti-guerrilla police unit which had been charged with the torturing of political prisoners.

On June 10, 1970, **Maj. Robert P. Perry**, the United States Army attache to the United States embassy staff in Jordan, was shot and killed by Palestinian guerrillas at his home in Amman. Perry was born in Chicago on February 1, 1936, and had served as a foreign area specialist in the army.

He had served in Jordan from March of 1967, previously having been stationed at the U.S. Embassy in Beirut, Lebanon, from 1963 until 1966.

Former Argentine president **Pedro Eugenio Aramburo** was kidnapped by members of the Juan Jose Valle (q.v.) Command, a leftist guerrilla group, on May 29, 1970. The kidnappers announced his execution on July 1, 1970, and the ex-president's body was found near Buenos Aires on July 16. Aramburo was born on May 21, 1903, in Cordoba province, Argentina. He joined the Argentine army in 1922 and was promoted to brigadier general in 1951. He was appointed director of the national war college in 1954 and was active in the coup that deposed President Juan D. Peron in 1955. Aramburo served as provisional president of Argentina from November 13, 1955, until elections were held in 1958. He later made an unsuccessful bid for the presidency in 1963. Roman Catholic Rev. Alberto Carbone, forty-six, television script writer Carlos Maguid, twenty-seven, and Ignacio Velez, a twenty-seven-year-old student leader, were tried and found guilty on December 16, 1970, on charges in connection with the kidnap-murder. They all were sentenced to prison.

On August 8, 1970, **Gen. Teymour Bakhtiar**, an Iranian army officer and opponent of Shah Mohammed Reza Pahlavi, was assassinated in Iraq, near the Iranian border, by an aide accompanying him on a hunting trip.

Daniel A. Mitrione (1920–70), a U.S. police advisor to the government of Uruguay, was killed by Tupamaro guerrillas in Montevideo following a kidnapping by the left-wing terrorists on July 31, 1970. He was executed following the Uruguayan government's refusal to accede to the guerrillas' demand to release political prisoners. The kidnapping and murder of Mitrione was the basis for *State of Siege*, a 1973 film directed by Costa-Gavras.

On August 27, 1970, **Jose Varela Alonso** (1913–70), an Argentine labor leader, was shot and killed while driving to his office in Buenos Aires. Alonso, a moderate Peronist leader, was the head of the Argentine Textile Worker's Union. The Montoneros Command of the National Liberation Army, a left-wing terrorist group, claimed responsibility for the killing.

Pedro N. Taruc (1907–70), the leader of the Communist Hukbalahap agrarian rebel movement in the Philippines, was shot and killed by government soldiers in Angeles City on October 16, 1970. Taruc, who had led the Huks since 1964, was the secretary general of the Philippine Communist party.

On October 18, 1970, **Floro Crisologo**, a Philippine congressman from Ilocos Sur Province and an advisor to President Ferdinand Marcos, was shot and killed in Viga, the Philippines, while attending mass.

Pierre LaPorte, the minister of labor in Quebec, Canada, was killed by strangulation by French separatists in Quebec after having been kidnapped on October 10, 1970. LaPorte's body was found in a car near the Canadian military base at Saint-Hubert on October 18, 1970. The kidnappers, members of Le Front de Liberation du Quebec (FLQ), had previously abducted James R. Cross, the British trade commissioner, on October 5. They had demanded the release of twenty-three "political prisoners" and a ransom of $500,000 in gold for the release of LaPorte and Cross. The government refused to accept the demands and proclaimed a state of emergency. LaPorte was killed shortly after this proclamation. Cross was rescued unharmed several months later.

Belkacem Krim (1922–70), one of the leaders of the Algerian Front for National Liberation (FLN) during Algeria's struggle against France for independence, was found strangled in his Frankfurt, West Germany, hotel room on October 20, 1970. Krim had become active in the Algerian nationalist movement in 1947. He served as vice president and minister of the armed forces in the provisional revolutionary government in 1958 and was minister of foreign affairs for the rebels at the signing of the 1962 agreement with France allowing Algerian independence. He subsequently became involved in a dispute with Ahmed ben Bella, who became Algeria's first president after independence, and Krim retired from active politics. He opposed the regime of ben Bella's successor, Houari Boumedienne, and founded the Democratic Movement for Algerian Renewal, a Paris-based exile group, in 1967. His death was believed to have been caused by agents of the Algerian government.

Gen. Rene Schneider Chereau (1918–70), the commander-in-chief of the Chilean army from 1969, was shot on October 22, 1970, by right-wing terrorists as he was being driven to work in Santiago. He died on October 25, 1970. Schneider had encouraged the army to avoid political involvement during the administration of President Salvador Allende (q.v.).

Larry N. Kuriyama (1921–70), a Hawaiian state senator, was shot to death in the garage of his home on October 12, 1970. Kuriyama, a Democrat, had served in the Hawaiian state legislature since 1959. He was the chairman of the Senate Committee on Higher Education, and was unopposed for reelection in his Oahu Senate district.

On November 1, 1970, **Zygfryd Wolniak** (1922–70), the Polish deputy foreign minister; **Chaudhri Mohammed Nazi**, Pakistan's deputy intelligence chief; and **Mohammed Ashraf** and **Mohammed Yasin**, both Pakistani journalists, were killed during an airport reception for Polish president Marian Spychalski in Karachi, Pakistan. The deaths occurred when a truck driven by Feroze Abdulah drove through the crowd at the reception area.

Julio Caney Herrera, a Guatemalan law professor and leftist politician, was murdered on November 16, 1970, while driving to work in Guatemala City. On December 18, 1970, **Arnaldo Otten Prado**, a Guatemalan National Liberation Movement deputy, was also shot to death while driving in Guatemala City. **Jaime Monge Donis**, the secretary general of the Guatemalan Labor Federation, was shot and killed near his home in Guatemala City on December 23, 1970.

Maj. Gen. Teshome Erghietu (1918–70), the commander of the Ethiopian Second Army Division, was killed by rebel guerrillas on November 21, 1970. Erghietu was on an inspection tour in Northern Ethiopia at the time of the attack.

On November 27, 1970, Pope Paul VI (1897–1978) escaped serious injury while he was attacked by a man wielding a knife. The pope was on a visit to the Philippines at the time of the assassination attempt. Paul VI remained the leader of the Roman Catholic church until his death in 1978.

1971

On January 13, 1971, **Adolfo Mijangos Lopez** (1929–71), a leader of the Guatemalan opposition coalition, was killed by machine gun fire in Guatemala City while his driver was helping him from his wheelchair into his car.

On January 15, 1971, three Cameroonian opposition leaders convicted of treason and of plotting the assassination of President Ahmadou Ahidjo were executed. They included **Ernest Ouandie**, an early anti–French nationalist leader and the president of the banned Union of Cameroonian Peoples; **Gabriel Tabeu**, the head of the Holy Cross for the Liberation of Cameroon; and **Raphael Fotsing**, a member of Ouandie's group.

Jacobo Arbenz Guzman, who was president of a Communist-leaning government in Guatemala in the early 1950s, drowned in the bathtub of his home in Mexico City on January 27, 1971. Col. Arbenz served as Guatemala's minister of defense in the government of President Juan Jose Arevalo in the late 1940s. After the assassination of Arbenz's leading rival, Francisco Arana (q.v.), a right-wing Guatemalan politician, Arbenz was elected to the presidency. He began his term of office on March 15, 1951.

During his administration he continued the agrarian reform programs of his predecessor and encouraged relations with Communist countries. Guatemala's relationship with the United States deteriorated due to the Arbenz government's appropriation of the United Fruit Company's interests in the country. Arbenz became known as the "Red Colonel," and in June of 1954, he was ousted in a military coup led by right-wing Col. Carlos Castillo Armas (q.v.). The coup was supported by the United States government and the Central Intelligence Agency. John Peurifoy (q.v.), the United States ambassador to Guatemala, was believed to have been a principal architect of the revolt. Arbenz fled the country and spent the rest of his life in exile. His death in 1971 was attributed to drowning under a stream of scalding tap water after a fall in his bathtub. It was reported that Arbenz was horribly burned from the hot water. Arbenz's death was ruled an accident, but the unusual nature of his demise, coupled with his controversial past, led some to question the true cause of his death.

Hardan Takriti, the former vice president of Iraq, was shot to death in a hospital courtyard in Kuwait on March 30, 1971. Takriti, who had also served as Iraq's air marshal, had been living in exile in Kuwait since October of 1970, following his ouster as vice president.

Col. Roberto Quintanilla Pereira (1928–71), the Bolivian consul general to Hamburg, was shot and killed in his office in Hamburg on April 1, 1971. Quintanilla was the head of intelligence in Bolivia under former president Rene Barrientos.

In April of 1971 **Kyin Pe**, the general secretary of the Burmese Karen National Union Front, a Communist insurgent organization, was killed by government troops at his headquarters in Burma.

On April 7, 1971, **Vladimir Rolovic**, the Yugoslavian ambassador to Sweden, was shot by a Croatian separatist. He died on April 15, 1971.

Gen. Ziadin Farsiou (1919–71), the chief of the Iranian military court, was shot by terrorists as he was leaving his home in Teheran on April 7, 1971. He died of his wounds on April 11, 1971.

Alberto Larrea Humerez, the Bolivian minister of economics under former president Rene Barrientos, was assassinated on April 19, 1971.

On May 5, 1971, **Pietro Scaglione**, the chief public prosecutor of Palermo, Italy, was shot and killed. His assassins were believed to have been members of the Mafia.

Ephraim Elrom (1912–71), the Israeli consul general to Turkey, was murdered in Istanbul on May 22, 1971, by left-wing terrorists who had kidnapped him a week earlier. Elrom, a former Israeli Criminal Investigation Department chief, had interrogated Nazi war criminal Adolf Eichmann (q.v.) before Eichmann's trial and execution in 1962. Elrom had been with the Israeli Foreign Service since 1969.

Maximiliano Gomez (1943–71), the exiled secretary general of the Dominican Popular Movement (MPD), a leftist opposition movement, was murdered in Brussels, Belgium, on May 23, 1971.

On June 8, 1971, **Edmundo Perez Zukovic** (1912–71), the former minister of the interior in Chile and a leader of the Christian Democratic party, was shot and killed by left-wing terrorists in Santiago.

In June of 1971 leftist army officers launched a coup attempt against Sudanese president Gaafar al-Nimeiry. The revolt was suppressed by forces loyal to President Nimeiry, and most of the coup leaders were seized. Fourteen participants in the rebellion were tried and executed during the month. The dead included **Maj. Hashem Atta** (1935–71), the leader of the coup; **Lt. Col. Babakr Al-Nur Osman**, who had been named president of the revolutionary council; **Maj. Farouk Osman Hamadallah**, an aide to Lt. Col. Nur; **Abdul Khalek Mahjoub**, the leader of the Sudanese Communist party and alleged mastermind of the coup; **Joseph Garang**, a former Communist minister for Sudanese southern affairs; **Shafie Ahmed El-Sheikh**, the leader of the Communist-led Trade Union Federation; **Col. Abdul Moneim Mohammed Ahmed**, the commander of the Third Armored Division; **Lt. Col. Osman Hussein**, commander of the Presidential Guard; and **Maj. Mohammed Ahmad Al-Zein, Lt. Ahmad Osman Abdel Rahman Al Hardale**, and **Capt. Muawiya Abdul Hay**, members of the rebel junta.

On July 6, 1971, **Jose Luis Arriaga Arriola** (1935–71), a Guatemalan congressman and member of the opposition Revolutionary party, was shot to death near his home in Guatemala City.

On July 10, 1971, during an unsuccessful military coup against King Hassan II of Morocco, several guests at a birthday reception for the king were killed at Sikrit Palace outside of Rabat. They included **Marcel Dupret**, the Belgian ambassador to Morroco; **Ahmed Bahnini**, the president of the Moroccan Supreme Court; and several Moroccan generals. **Gen. Ahmed Medbouh** and **Col. Mohammed Ababou**, the leaders of the coup, were accidentally shot and killed by their own men. **Gen. Bougrine, Gen. Hamou, Gen. Mustapha, Gen. Habibi**, and six colonels were executed on July 12, 1971, for complicity in the coup.

Mohammed Mustafa Shreim, known as **Abu Ali Ayad**, a Palestinian guerrilla leader and military aide to Yasir Arafat, was shot to death by Jordanian soldiers near Amman, Jordan, on July 22, 1971.

Mahmud Mustafa, the vice president of Nesame Islam, a rightist party in East Pakistan, was shot and killed while addressing a crowd near Dacca on August 11, 1971.

Germain M'Ba, a leading opponent of Gabon's president Albert Bongo, was assassinated in Libreville, Gabon, in September of 1971.

On September 12, 1971, **Lin Piao**, the Chinese Communist leader who had been selected to succeed Chairman Mao Tse-tung, was reported to have been killed in a plane crash following an alleged coup against Mao. Lin's wife, **Yeh Chun**, a member of the Chinese Communist Politburo, and seven other supporters of Lin were also reported killed in the crash. The plane, which was possibly shot down, was said to have been over Mongolia en route to the Soviet Union when it crashed. It was also reported from the Soviet Union that the bodies of the passengers were riddled with bullet wounds.

Lin Piao was born in 1908 in the Hupeh Province of China. He had served as a general in Mao's Long March in 1934, and had fought with the Communist insurgents during the Civil War in 1946. He was appointed deputy premier in 1954, and served as a member of the Politburo from 1955. Lin, who had become minister of defense in 1959, was instrumental in organizing the Chinese Cultural revolution of the mid–1960s. He had been named as heir apparent to Chairman Mao as Communist party leader in 1969.

On September 17, 1971, **Carlos Lamarca** (1938–71), a leading Brazilian terrorist, was shot and killed by military police. Lamarca, a former captain in the Brazilian army, had been wanted by the government for acts of political terrorism for the previous three years.

Abdul Konem Khan, the governor of East Pakistan from 1962 to 1969, was assassinated in his home in Dacca on October 14, 1971.

Nguyen Van Bong (1929–71), a founder and leader of the Progressive Nationalist party, a non–Communist opposition group to Vietnamese president Nguyen Van Thieu, was killed in Saigon when a bomb planted in his car exploded on November 10, 1971.

On November 25, 1971, **Yukio Mishima**, an internationally acclaimed Japanese author, led a group of four followers to the headquarters of the Japanese Eastern Regional Command. Once there, Mishima seized Lt. Gen. Kanetoshi Mashita, the regional commander, and demanded that the troops assemble in the courtyard beneath the balcony of Mashita's office.

Mishima then delivered a speech criticizing the lack of militarism and discipline in Japanese society. Following his address and a cry of "Long live the Emperor," Mishima returned to Mashita's office, where he committed *seppuku*, a ceremonial ritual disembowelment suicide of ancient Japan. Mishima stabbed himself in the abdomen with a dagger, after which an aide, Masakatsu Morita, decapitated the author. Morita then committed *seppuku* himself. Mishima's three surviving followers were then taken into custody by Japanese police.

Mishima, who was born in Tokyo in 1925, was considered a leading contender for the Nobel Prize in literature. His first novel, *Confessions of the Mask*, an autobiographical work written when he was nineteen years old, gained him an international reputation. His works, which numbered over 100 novels, short stories, and plays, included *Temple of the Golden Pavilion*, *Patriotism*, *The Sailor Who Fell from Grace with the Sea*, and *The Sea of Fertility*. Mishima's political philosophy was dominated by militaristic ideals and samurai ethics. In 1968 he founded a right-wing paramilitary organization known as "Tafeno-Kai," or Shield Society, which he hoped to use to return Japan to a militarist state. The four men who accompanied him in his capture of the Eastern Regional Command were members of this organization. Mishima's followers claimed that the author was hoping to inspire a rebellion in the Japanese armed forces with his balcony address, and when that seemed to have failed, he hoped his suicide would encourage a return to militarism.

On November 28, 1971, Jordanian prime minister **Wasfi At-Tal** (1920–71) joined the many Middle Eastern victims of political assassination when he was shot to death by gunmen in the lobby of the Sheraton Hotel in Cairo after returning from a meeting of the Arab League being held in Egypt. Jordanian foreign minister Abdullah Salah was slightly wounded in the assault. Two of the assailants were captured near the hotel, and two others were captured later in the day. The assassins claimed to be members of the Black Ilul, or Black September, movement, formed to avenge the deaths of Palestinians during clashes between the Jordanian army and the Palestinians in September of 1970. Tal had been prime minister of Jordan at the time and was held directly responsible for the killing of the radical Palestinians. Tal had served as Jordan's prime minister on four occasions during the 1960s before being selected to lead King Hussein's government in the fall of 1970. Tal, a hard-line supporter of the moderate Jordanian monarch, was regarded as one of the Palestinian militants' deadliest foes.

On December 12, 1971, **John Barnhill** (1906–71), a militant Protestant member of Northern Ireland's ruling Unionist party, was murdered by members of the Irish Republican Army, who then blew up his mansion in Strabane, near the Irish Republic border.

Prince Sisowath Rattasa, an uncle of former Cambodian chief of state Prince Norodom Sihanouk, was killed by a grenade thrown by a terrorist on a street near the palace in Phnom Penh on December 21, 1971.

1972

On January 24, 1972, **Sheik Khaled bin Mohammed Al Qasimi** (1926–72), the ruler of Sharjah, was killed during an unsuccessful coup attempt led by Sheikh Saqir ben Sultan, the former ruler. Nine members of the sheik's family were also killed. Sheik Sultan, who had been ousted from power six years earlier, was arrested following the coup attempt. Sheik Saqr bin Mohammed al-Qasimi, the youngest brother of the slain ruler, succeeded to the throne.

Maj. Gen. Mohammed Omran (1922–72), the former Syrian minister of defense and deputy premier, was shot and killed while in exile in Tripoli, Lebanon, on March 4, 1972. Omran had been active in the 1963 Baathist coup in Syria and served in his posts until 1964, when he went into exile in Lebanon.

Sheik Abeid Karume (1905–72), who had seized power in Zanzibar during a bloody coup in January of 1964, met his own end in a violent fashion on April 7, 1972. Karume became vice president of Tanzania when Zanzibar merged with the mainland African nation of Tanganyika in April of 1964, but he still maintained an iron hand in his rule of Zanzibar. The island strongman died of gunshot wounds when four gunmen burst into a meeting of his ruling Afro-Shirazi party. Sheikh Tabit Kombo, the secretary general of the party, was critically wounded. Two of the gunmen were killed during the assault, and a third was later found dead, a presumed suicide.

On April 10, 1972, **Gen. Juan Carlos Sanchez** (1919–72), an Argentine army officer with the Second Army Corps, was shot and killed by terrorists while en route to his headquarters in Buenos Aires.

Aberdan Sallustro (1915–72), an executive with the Argentine Fiat auto company, was murdered by terrorists on April 10, 1972. He had been kidnapped three weeks earlier on March 21, 1972, in Buenos Aires. Sallustro was killed when police raided the terrorist hideout where he was being held.

In early April of 1972 **Charles Ndizeye**, who had ruled the tiny East African nation of Burundi as **Ntare V** for four months in 1966, was invited to return to his country by Michel Micombero, the man who had deposed him in November of 1966. Burundi had a long history of political violence even before its independence in 1962. Ntare's brother, Prince Louis Rwagosore (q.v.), had been assassinated in 1961, and two of the country's first three premiers had also died at the hands of assassins. Ntare himself had led the coup which deposed his father, Mwambutsa IV, in 1966. A former resident described the nation as "a country in which *Macbeth* is constantly being reenacted." Ntare, who had been living in exile in West Germany, accepted Micombero's invitation to return after being granted a presidential guarantee of safe conduct. Upon arriving in Bujumbura, the capital, he was seized by government troops and placed under "protective custody." This protection was short lived, as in less than a month Ntare V was dead, slain by Burundian troops in Gitega, sixty miles east of the capital, on April 29, 1972. The government claimed the killing came as a result of supporters attempting to free the twenty-five-year-old ex-king during an abortive coup.

On May 15, 1972, Governor George C. Wallace (b. 1919) of Alabama, a candidate for the Democratic nomination for president, was shot and seriously wounded in a Laurel, Maryland, shopping center parking lot during a campaign speech prior to the Maryland primary. His assailant, identified as Arthur Bremer, was arrested and convicted of the crime. Governor Wallace survived his injuries, though he was partially paralyzed and confined to a wheelchair. He was unsuccessful in his bid for the presidential nomination in that year and again in 1976, although he continued to serve as Alabama's governor until 1979 and again from 1983 until 1987.

On June 25, 1972, **Olivero Castaneda Paiz**, a leader of the National Liberation Movement (MLN) and first vice president of the Guatemalan congress, was shot and killed.

Ghassan Kanafani (1936–72), a leader of the Popular Front for the Liberation of Palestine, died in an explosion in his car in Beirut, Lebanon, on July 8, 1972. Kanafani had served as a leading spokesman for the Palestinian organization and was the editor of *Al Hadaf*, its weekly journal. Palestinian sources claimed that the Israeli intelligence service was responsible for the slaying.

On July 17, 1972, **Kjell Richard Haeggloef** (1942–72), the first secretary of the Swedish Embassy in Bogota, Colombia, was shot and killed while riding in his car in Bogota. Haeggloef had earlier been asked to leave Colombia following reports that he had contacts with guerrilla groups operating in the area. His assassin was identified as Karl Iver Reinhold, a Swedish newsman.

Col. Artigas Alvarez, the chief of Uruguay's civil defense, was shot and killed by Tupamaro guerrillas in Montevideo on July 25, 1972.

On August 16, 1972, King Hassan of Morocco survived a coup attempt when the plane in which he was flying was attacked by fighters of the Royal Moroccan Air Force. The alleged leader of the rebellion, **Gen. Muhammad Oufkir** (1920–72), the Moroccan minister of defense, was reported to have committed suicide in the capital following the coup's failure. Oufkir had previously served as Hassan's minister of the interior and had been convicted in absentia in a French court of masterminding the abduction and murder of Moroccan opposition leader Mehdi Ben Barka (q.v.) in 1965. Seven air force officers were subsequently arrested for complicity in the coup attempt and were excecuted the following year.

On August 26, 1972, **Phan My Truc**, the publisher of a pro-government newspaper in Saigon, South Vietnam, was shot to death in a Saigon restaurant.

On September 5, 1972, eight terrorists belonging to the Arab Black September guerrilla movement attacked the compound housing Israeli athletes at the Olympic Village in Munich, West Germany. Weight lifter **Yossef Romano** and wrestling coach **Moshe Weinberger** were killed during the initial assault. The terrorists, with their nine remaining hostages, were transported by helicopter to Munich's Furstenfeldbruck airport, where they intended to proceed to Cairo, Egypt, and ransom the captured athletes for the release of fellow terrorists held in Israel and West Germany. The West German authorities opened fire on the guerrillas before they could board the plane designated to carry them to Egypt. During the subsequent gun battle six of the terrorists were slain, and the remaining two were wounded and captured, but not before the nine Israelis were murdered. A terrorist threw a hand grenade into the helicopter containing track coach **Amitzur Shapira**, weight lifter **David Marc Berger**, fencing master **Andrei Spitzer**, wrestler **Mark Slavin**, and rifle coach **Kehat Shorr**, killing all of them in the explosion. The four hostages in the remaining helicopter were then shot to death by two of their captors. They included weight lifter **Zeev Friedman**, weight lifting judge **Yacov Springer**, wrestler **Eliezer Halfin**, and wrestling referee **Yossef Gutfreund**. It was believed that Palestinian leader Ali Hassan Salameh (q.v.) had been the mastermind behind the assault.

George Duckett, Bermuda's commissioner of police, was murdered by unknown assailants at his home in Hamilton, Bermuda, on September 9, 1972.

Benedicto Kiwanuka (1922–72), the chief justice of the Ugandan Supreme Court, who had served as that nation's first prime minister from October 9, 1961, until May 1, 1963, was seized and murdered by agents of Ugandan president Idi Amin on September 21, 1972.

Amin, who had seized power in Uganda in 1971 and remained president until his own ouster in 1979, orchestrated the political murder of over 100,000 of his countrymen during his eight years in power. Henry Kyemba, who served as a minister in Amin's government until 1977, recorded some of the more prominent victims of Amin's reign. They included Anglican archbishop Janani Luwum (q.v.); **Lt. Col. Michael Ondoga**, the Ugandan ambassador to the Soviet Union from 1971 to 1973 and foreign minister from 1973 until 1974; **Yekosfati Engur**, minister of culture and community development; **Haji Shaban Knuto**, minister of works under Milton Obote, Amin's predecessor; **William Kalema**, former minister of commerce; **Basil Bataringaya**, former minister of internal affairs; **John Kakonge**, former minister of agriculture; **Joshua Wakholi**, former minister of public service; **Alex Ojera**, former minister of information; **Haji Ali Kisekka**, former deputy minister for the East African Community; **James Ochyola**, former minister of local government; **Frank Kalimuzo**, vice chancellor of Makerere University; **Joseph Mubiru**, governor of the Central Bank; and **Brig. Charles Arube**, chief of staff of the Ugandan army.

Hachem Jawad, the United Nations Development Program's representative in the Middle East, was killed in his office near Beirut, Lebanon, on October 11, 1972. Jawad, a former Iraqi foreign minister, was shot by Ahmed Mahmoud Jaafry, his former driver, who subsequently committed suicide.

On October 16, 1972, **Abdel Wael Zuaiter**, a clerk at the Libyan Embassy in Rome, was shot and killed in the lobby of his Rome apartment. Zuaiter, a Jordanian, was reportedly the top agent in Italy of the Palestinian organization Al Fatah. His assassins were believed to have been members of the Israeli Secret Service.

Imelda Marcos (b. 1931), the wife of President Ferdinand Marcos of the Philippines, survived an assassination attempt on December 7, 1972. Mrs. Marcos was injured when she was attacked by a knife-wielding man while addressing a crowd in Manila. The assassin was slain by Mrs. Marcos' guards, and she recovered from her injuries. Mrs. Marcos remained the first lady of the Philippines until the ouster of her husband in early 1986.

On December 8, 1972, **Mahmoud Hamshari**, a leading Palestinian diplomat in Paris, was fatally injured by a bomb planted in his apartment telephone. He died on January 9, 1973. Hamshari, who was reputed to be a member of the Black September guerrilla movement, was believed to have been assassinated by members of the Israeli Secret Service.

1973

Amilcar Cabral (1926–73), the secretary general of the African Party for the Independence of Guinea and Cape Verde (PAIGC), was shot to death near his home in Conakry, Guinea, on January 20, 1973. His assailants were believed to be rival members of Cabral's independence movement. Cabral had founded the independence party in 1956, and had led a guerrilla campaign to free Guinea-Bissau from Portugal's colonial empire. He had conducted his campaign against the Portuguese from the neighboring Republic of Guinea. He was widely respected throughout Africa as a leading nationalist statesman, and his death cost the Guinean independence movement its most able leader. Guinea-Bissau achieved independence from Portugal the following year, with Amilcar Cabral's brother, Luis, serving as the nation's first president.

Palestinian leader **Hussein Abad Al-Chir** was killed in an explosion in his hotel room in Nicosia, Cyprus, on January 24, 1973. Al-Chir, reportedly a liaison between the Palestinians and the Soviets, was believed to have been a victim of Israel's Secret Service.

In February of 1973 **Col. Francisco Alberto Caamano Deno**, who was a leader of the anti-government troops during the Dominican Republic's 1965 Civil War, was shot and killed in the central mountains area. Caamano Deno, a leftist who had been living in exile in Cuba, had reportedly led a small group of guerrillas in an attempt to overthrow the government of President Joaquin Belaquer.

On March 1, 1973, an armed band of Palestinian guerrillas stormed the Saudi Arabian Embassy in the Sudan during a party given in honor of the departing United States charge d'affaires **George Curtis Moore** (1926–73). Several diplomats in attendance were wounded during the attack. Following the failure of the Sudanese government to negotiate with the guerrillas, members of the Black September movement, the attackers killed Moore, United States ambassador **Cleo A. Noel, Jr.** (1919–73), and Belgian charge d'affaires **Guy Eid**.

Cleo Noel had served in the State Department from 1949 and was a veteran specialist in Middle Eastern affairs. He had served in diplomatic positions in Lebanon and Saudi Arabia, and had been stationed in Khartoum twice previously, in 1961 as vice consul and in 1966 as deputy chief of mission. He was appointed United States ambassador several months earlier, following the restoration of diplomatic relations between the United States and the Sudan.

George Curtis Moore had joined the Foreign Service in 1950, serving as a resident officer in Frankfurt, Germany. In 1953 he was stationed in Cairo and subsequently served in other embassies in the Middle East. In 1969 Moore was sent to Khartoum as counselor and charge d'affaires, serving as the head of the Embassy there in the absence of an ambassador. He was scheduled to leave the Sudan the following week.

Sir Richard Christopher Sharples (1916–73), the British governor of Bermuda, was murdered on the grounds of the Government House in the capital of Hamilton on March 10, 1973. Sharples had served in the British army during World War II and was Field Marshal Montgomery's military assistant in the early 1950s. He was elected to Parliament in 1954. A member of the Conservative party, he served as minister of state for home affairs in the government of Edward Heath from 1970 until 1972. He was appointed governor of Bermuda in October of 1972. Sharples' chief aide, **Capt. Hugh Sayers**, was killed with the governor. The murder remained unsolved but seemed related to the killing six months earlier of George Duckett (q.v.), the Bermudan police commissioner.

Col. Hector J. Irabarren, the chief of military intelligence for the Argentine Third Army in Cordoba province, was assassinated on April 3, 1973, by leftist terrorists.

Basil Al-Kubaisi, a Palestinian law professor affiliated with the Popular Front for the Liberation of Palestine, was shot and killed in the streets of Paris on April 6, 1973. His assassination was believed to have been arranged by members of the Israeli Secret Service.

Mohammed Yussef Najjar ("**Abu Yussef**"), a leader and one of the founders of Al Fatah; **Kamal Adwan**, a Palestinian guerrilla who was reportedly in command of guerrilla operations in Israeli occupied territories in the 1967 war; and **Kamal Nasser** (1928–1973), a leading Arab poet and spokesman for the Palestine Liberation Organization, were shot to death by Israeli soldiers on April 10, 1973, when their guerrilla headquarters in Beirut, Lebanon, were raided in a surprise attack.

On April 12, 1973, **Zaid Muchassi**, a Palestinian leader, was killed in an explosion in his hotel room in Athens, Greece.

Ange Diawara, a Congolese leftist leader, was killed by government troops on April 23, 1973, after having been accused of leading a rebellion against President Marien Ngouabi (q.v.) of the Congo. Diawara had been a member of the Politburo of the Congolese Worker's party.

On May 29, 1973, **Sheik Mohammed Ali Othman** (1910–73), a member of the three-man ruling council of North Yemen, was ambushed and killed by bazooka fire near his home. Othman was the leader of the ruling faction in Ta'izz, the second largest city in North Yemen.

United States Lt. Col. Lewis L. Hawkins (1931–73), an army colonel stationed in Teheran as an advisor to the Iranian armed forces, was shot to death on June 1, 1973, by two gunmen.

On June 28, 1973, **Mohammed Boudia**, an Algerian who was reportedly active in the Palestinian terrorist network, was killed when a bomb exploded in his car in Paris, France. Boudia was believed to have been the victim of the Israeli Secret Service.

Gen. Hammad Chehab (1922–73), the defense minister of Iraq, was assassinated during an abortive coup attempt on June 30, 1973. Chehab and Lt. Gen. Saadoun Gheidan, the interior minister, were kidnapped from a state banquet by **Nazim Kazzar** (1938–73), the Iraqi security chief and leader of the coup attempt. Chehab was killed and Gheidan wounded after Iraqi troops attempted to apprehend the plotters. Kazzar and thirty-five others were captured and, on July 6, 1973, executed.

Col. Yosef Alon (1927–73), the deputy military attache of the Israeli Embassy in Washington, D. C., was murdered at his home in Chevy Chase, Maryland, on July 1, 1973.

Capt. Arturo Araya (1928–73), a naval aide to Chilean president Salvador Allende (q.v.), was killed on July 27, 1973, by machine gun fire while standing on the balcony of his home in Santiago, Chile.

On August 20, 1973, right-wing Laotian air force **Gen. Thoa Ma** (1930–73), was killed while leading an unsuccessful coup attempt against the Laotian coalition government. Thoa Ma died when his plane was shot down at the Vientiane airport. He had been living in exile in Thailand since 1966, when he had fled Laos after leading another unsuccessful coup attempt.

On August 26, 1973, **Outel Bono**, an exiled opponent of President Francois Tombalbaye (q.v.) of Chad, was assassinated in Paris, France. Bono, a former director of health services, had been in the process of creating a Chadian opposition party at the time of his murder.

James Shebazz, a leader of the Black Muslims, was shot and killed in front of his home in Newark, New Jersey, on September 5, 1973. Shebazz, fifty-two, was a close associate of Malcolm X (q.v.) and had become the leader of his New York mosque following Malcolm X's assassination in 1965.

Mohammad Hashim Maiwandwal, who had served as prime minister of Afghanistan from 1965 until 1967, was reported to have hanged himself in prison. Maiwandwal had been arrested earlier in the month and charged with involvement in a coup attempt against the government of President Mohammed Daud Khan (q.v.)

Salvador Allende Gossens, the Marxist president of Chile, was killed during a military coup on September 11, 1973. Allende was born in Valparaiso, Chile, on July 26, 1908. He was a founder of the Chilean Socialist party in 1933 and served as a deputy in the Chilean Congress. He was named minister of health in 1939 and helped organize relief efforts following a massive earthquake later that year. Allende was elected to the Senate in 1945 and, in 1952, made his first race for the presidency of Chile. He was defeated in that campaign as well as in two subsequent races in 1958 and 1964. Allende again ran for president in 1970 and received a plurality in the general elections held on September 4 of that year. The following month he was officially elected president by a vote of a joint session of Congress and, on November 4, 1970, he was sworn in to head the first freely elected Marxist government in South America. Allende's term of office was marked by civil disorders and a failing economy. The Chilean government was near collapse when a military uprising, presumably with the assistance of the United States Central Intelligence Agency, launched an attack on the Presidential Palace. Allende was killed during the assault. He was replaced by a military junta led by Gen. Augusto Pinochet.

On September 15, 1973, **Tommy Herron**, an Irish Protestant leader, was shot and killed by assassins near Lisburn, Northern Ireland. Herron, thirty-six, had been the deputy leader of the militant Ulster Defense Association.

Jose Rucci, a leader of the Argentine labor movement, was assassinated by machine gun fire at his home in Buenos Aires on September 24, 1973. Rucci, a moderate ally of Juan Peron, served as secretary general of the Confederacion General de Trabajo, the leading Argentine labor union. His assassination was believed to have been the work of the leftist Marxist People's Revolutionary Army. Several days later, leftist guerrillas were responsible for the slaying of **Enrique Grinberg**, another moderate labor leader.

German Castros Rojas, the former governor of Talca, Chile, was executed in Quillota on September 25, 1973, on charges of killing a policeman while trying to blow up a dam. Castros Rojas was a leading leftist in the area and had been a supporter of deposed Chilean president Salvador Allende (q.v.)

Marcus A. Foster (1923–73), the superintendent of the Oakland, California, city school system, was shot and killed on November 6, 1973, while walking to his car at his office parking lot following a school board meeting. Robert Blackburn, Foster's assistant superintendent, was also shot and critically injured at that time. Foster had formerly served as associate superintendent of community affairs for the Philadelphia School District before his appointment by the Oakland Board of Education in 1970.

Russell Little (b. 1949) and Joseph Remiro (b. 1946) were subsequently arrested and charged with Foster's murder. They were tried and convicted of the killing, but the convictions were later overturned. Remiro and Little were members of the Symbionese Liberation Army (SLA), a terrorist organization that also kidnapped newspaper heiress Patricia Hearst on February 4, 1974. Six members of the SLA, including Donald "Field Marshal Cinque" DeFreeze (1944–74), the leader of the group, were killed in a shootout with Los Angeles police on May 17, 1974. The other SLA members killed at that time were Nancy Ling Perry (1948–74), the group's spokesperson, who had written a letter claiming the SLA's responsibility for Marcus Foster's assassination; Patricia "Mizmoon" Soltysik (1950–74); Camilla "Gabi" Hall (1945–74); William "Cujo" Wolfe (1951–74) and Angela "Gelina" Atwood (1949–74).

Patty Hearst, who was believed to have been indoctrinated by the SLA following her abduction, was subsequently charged with armed robbery, kidnapping, and other felonies. She was arrested on September 18, 1974, along with William and Emily Harris, two other surviving members of the SLA. Ms. Hearst and the Harrises were tried the following year and convicted on most charges.

On November 22, 1973, **John A. Swint** (1917–73), the general manager of Transax, a Ford Motor Company–owned manufacturing plant, was assassinated by leftist guerrillas while en route to Cordoba, Argentina.

Abdus Samad Khan Achakzai (1907–73), the leader of the Pathan Khawa National Awami party and a member of the Legislative Assembly in Baluchistan, Pakistan, was murdered on December 2, 1973, during a grenade attack on his home in Quetta, Pakistan.

Adm. Luis Carrero Blanco, the premier of Spain, was killed on December 20, 1973, when a bomb planted underneath his car exploded in front of a church in Madrid. Carrero Blanco was born on March 4, 1903, in Santona, Spain. He was an officer in the Spanish navy and was appointed by Gen. Francisco Franco, the Spanish head of state, to the position of chief of naval operations in 1939. In 1946 he was named undersecretary to the presidency, and he served as a minister in Franco's government from 1951. In October of 1967 Carrero Blanco was named vice premier and, in June of 1973, he was elevated to the post of premier. His assassination six months later was believed to have been the work of the Basque separatist movement.

1974

On March 12, 1974, **Billy Fox**, a thirty-six-year-old senator from the Republic of Ireland, was ambushed and slain by a gang of assassins in County Monaghan. Fox, a Protestant member of the Fine Gael party, was an outspoken critic of British military actions in Northern Ireland.

Jose De la Torriente (1904–74), a former Cuban agriculture minister, was shot and killed by a sniper at his home in Coral Gables, Florida, on April 13, 1974. De la Torriente had served as a leader of exiled Cubans hoping to overthrow Fidel Castro.

Judge James Lawless of the Washington (state) Superior Court was killed when a mail bomb delivered to the county courthouse in southeastern Washington exploded on June 3, 1974. Lawless, fifty, had served on the superior court for the previous sixteen years.

Walter Hildebrand, the president of the Supreme Court of Liechtenstein, was shot to death on June 20, 1974, during a court session. His assassin was identified as Reinhold Glatt, a Swiss national.

Mohammed Ahmed Noman, the former foreign minister of North Yemen, was shot and killed on June 28, 1974, in Beirut, Lebanon. Noman had served as foreign minister prior to his ouster during a military coup two weeks before his assassination.

Arturo Mor Roig (1915–74), the former Argentine interior minister, was shot and killed in Buenos Aires on July 15, 1974. Mor Roig served as the president of the Argentine chamber of deputies from 1963 until 1966. In March of 1971 he was named minister of the interior by the military government of Gen. Lanusse. While serving in that office Mor Roig was responsible for implementing the election procedures which were to return Argentina to civilian rule. He was widely praised for his role in insuring that the Argentine elections in March of 1973 were conducted in a fair and honest manner. Mor Roig retired from political activities following the establishment of the new government. He was ambushed and murdered by four unidentified assailants while having lunch near the metallurgical company at which he was employed.

On August 15, 1974, **Madame Park Chung Hee**, the wife of the president of South Korea, was struck and killed by a bullet aimed at her husband while attending a speech given by President Chung Hee Park (q.v.) at the National Theater in Seoul. The president was uninjured in the assault. Madame Park, who was born Yook Young Soo in 1926, was a popular figure in South Korea and was known for her charitable activities. The assassin, identified as Mun Se Kwang, was tried and, on December 20, executed for the murder.

Rodger P. Davies, the United States ambassador to Cyprus, was fatally injured in Nicosia when a Greek Cypriot sniper fired bullets into the American Embassy there on August 19, 1974. Davies was born in 1921 and joined the Foreign Service in 1946. He served in various diplomatic positions throughout the Middle East and, in 1962, was named deputy director of the Office of Near Eastern Affairs. In 1965 he was named deputy assistant secretary of state. Davies was appointed ambassador to Cyprus in May of 1974.

On September 30, 1974, **Gen. Carlos Prats** (1915–74), the former leader of the Chilean army during the administration of President Salvador Allende (q.v.), died with his wife when a bomb exploded in the car in which they were riding. Prats was living in Buenos Aires, Argentina, at the time, having fled Chile after the overthrow of Allende in 1973.

Alberto Villar (1923–74), the federal police chief of Argentina, died in a bomb explosion aboard his cabin cruiser in Buenos Aires on October 31, 1974.

On November 9, 1974, **Guenter Drenkman**, the president of the West German Supreme Court, was shot and killed by members of the Baader-Meinhof guerrilla movement while at his home in Bonn.

Sixty former officials of the Ethiopian government, including eighteen generals and fourteen other military officers, as well as leading aristocrats, former cabinet ministers, and provincial governors, were executed in Addis Adaba on November 23, 1974. The dead included **Lt. Gen. Aman Michael Andom** (1924–74), chairman of the ruling military council of Ethiopia, who was killed at his home when he resisted arrest following his ouster. Others executed include **Akililu Habte-Wold** (1908–74), the prime minister of Ethiopia from 1961 until 1974; **Endalkachew Makonnen** (1926–74), an

Ethiopian diplomat who served as prime minister in 1974; **Rear Admiral Alexander Desta**, grandson of Emperor Haile Selassie; **Adm. Eskinder Desta**, a former navy commander; **Prince Ras Asrate Kassa**, the former head of the Crown Council; **Ras Mesfin Sileshi**, the former governor of Shoa Province; **Col. Solomon Kedir**, the former chief of security; **Lt. Gen Abiye Abebe**, the former defense minister; **Lt. Gen. Yilma Shibeshi**, the former police commissioner; **Lt. Gen. Haile Baikedagne**, the former deputy armed forces chief of staff; and **Assefa Ayene**, the former communications minister and armed forces chief of staff.

1975

On January 2, 1975, **Lalit Narayan Mishra**, the Indian minister of railways, was killed in a bomb explosion in Samastipur Bihar, India. His assassins were believed to be Anand Marg terrorists.

Hayat Mohammad Khan Sherpao, the senior minister of Pakistan's Northwest Frontier province, was killed in a bomb explosion at Peshaward University on February 7, 1975. Sherpao was a close ally of Pakistan's prime minister Zulfikar Ali Bhutto (q.v.).

On February 5, 1975, **Col. Richard Ratsimandrava** (1931–75) was selected as president of the Malagasy Republic by the ruling military government. Six days later, on February 11, he was dead, the victim of an assassin's bullets. Ratsimandrava was shot and killed while en route from the presidential palace to his residence in Tananrive. Two of the president's bodyguards were also killed, and it was reported that two of the assassins perished in the subsequent gunfight. The military leadership remained in power, selecting Gen. Gilles Andrinmazo as the new head of state.

John P. Egan (1913–75), the United States honorary consul in Cordoba, Argentina, was murdered by Montoneros guerrillas, and his body was dumped on a roadside near Cordoba on February 27, 1975. Egan had been kidnapped by the leftist terrorists two days earlier.

On March 10, 1975, **J.M. Kariuki**, a leading critic of the Kenyan government, was found shot to death near Nairobi. Kariuki was reported missing on March 1.

Herbert W.T. Chitepo, a Rhodesian black nationalist leader and outspoken critic of the white Rhodesian government, died in a car bomb explosion in Lusaka, Zambia, on March 18, 1975. Chitepo was born on June 5, 1923, and was the first black lawyer to practice in Rhodesia. In the early

1960s Chitepo went into exile in Tanganyika and was elected chairman of the Zimbabwe African Nation Union. He later moved to Zambia, where he retained his leadership of the black nationalist organization until his death.

Faisal Ibn Abd Al-Aziz (1905–75), the king of Saudi Arabia, was assassinated on March 25, 1975, in Riyadh, the capital, during an audience with the oil minister of Kuwait. Faisal became Saudi Arabia's third king in March of 1964, following the removal of his brother, King Saud, from the throne. Faisal and Saud were both sons of Ibn Saud, who conquered the Arabian peninsula in 1926 and became the first king. Faisal served as his father's foreign minister and, in November of 1953, was named Saudi Arabia's first prime minister and crown prince under his brother, Saud. As king, Faisal was the first Arabian monarch to use his oil-rich country's leading export as a weapon against Western countries in an attempt to sway their Middle Eastern policies. He was shot to death by Prince Faisal Ibn Musad Ibn Abdel Aziz, a nephew, who was beheaded for the killing three months later. The king was succeeded by Crown Prince Khalid, his brother.

On April 13, 1975, luck ran out for **N'Garte Tombalbaye**, the first president of the landlocked and poverty stricken African nation of Chad. Tombalbaye, who had ruled Chad since its independence from France in 1960, had survived eight previous assassination attempts. Earlier in the year, Mrs. Kattouma Guembang, the former head of the Progressive party's women's wing, was tried for attempting to kill Tombalbaye with witchcraft, in which she had hired several wizards to pierce the eyes of a black sheep, representing the president, and bury it alive. Tombalbaye's demise came in a less esoteric manner. He was mortally wounded by machine gun and mortar fire directed at his official residence during an army revolt against his despotic administration. The fifty-six-year-old dictator died of his wounds later in the day. The coup was led by Gen. Mbaila Odingar and resulted in the freeing of Gen. Felix Malloum, who had been imprisoned since 1973 for allegedly conspiring to overthrow the government during a previous coup attempt. Malloum was himself named Chad's head of state as Tombalbaye's successor.

Mujibur Rahman, the founder and president of Bangladesh, was killed during an army coup on April 15, 1975. Sheikh Mujib was born on March 17, 1920. He was the founder of the East Pakistan Muslim Students' League in the 1950s. In 1959 he was the co-founder of the Awami League, a political organization advocating autonomy for East Pakistan. He was imprisoned on several occasions during the administration of Gen. Mohammed Ayub

Khan. In the 1970 general election the Awami League received an over-whelming majority of votes in East Pakistan. Sheikh Mujib was arrested the following year after he initiated a campaign of non-cooperation with West Pakistan. Violence erupted in East Pakistan when government troops tried to enforce martial law. At the end of the year, East Pakistan, with the assistance of India, emerged victorious in what had become a civil war. The independent nation of Bangladesh was proclaimed, and, on January 12, 1972, Mujib became the first prime minister. He had great difficulty restoring order and economic stability in the war-torn country. In January of 1975 Mujib took the office of president and began governing by executive degree. Four months later he and several members of his family were killed in a military coup. Khondkar Mushtaque Ahmed, a former close associate of the slain president, was chosen by the leaders of the coup as Sheikh Mujib's successor.

On April 25, 1975, **Lt. Col. Andreas Baron von Mirbach**, the military attache at the West Germany Embassy in Stockholm, Sweden, was killed by terrorists during an assault on the Embassy. During a subsequent shootout with the police, much of the Embassy was destroyed and seven of the terrorists were captured.

Col. Paul R. Shafer, Jr., and **Lt. Col. John H. Turner**, military officers stationed at the United States Embassy in Teheran, Iran, were shot to death by three Iranian terrorists on May 21, 1975.

On July 30, 1975, **James R. Hoffa** (1913–75), the former president of the International Brotherhood of Teamsters, was reported missing. Hoffa was elected to the presidency of the Teamsters union in 1957. He remained in office through his 1967 conviction on charges of fraud, conspiracy, and jury tampering. He resigned the presidency in June of 1971 and was subsequently released from prison when his twelve-year sentence was commuted by President Richard Nixon. A condition of his release was that he not take part in any union activities until 1980. Hoffa was challenging that stipulation in court at the time of his disappearance. Hoffa was last seen on the evening of July 30, 1975, at a restaurant in Bloomfield Township, Michigan. It was suspected that Hoffa had been killed by organized crime figures or rival union associates. His body was never recovered.

On September 5, 1975, United States president Gerald R. Ford (b. 1913) was assaulted by a young woman with a pistol in Sacramento, California. The weapon was wrestled away from the woman by a Secret Service agent before a shot could be fired. The assailant was identified as Lynette "Squeaky" Fromme, a twenty-six-year-old follower of mass murderer Charles Manson. She was tried and convicted of the attempt on the president's life and sentenced to prison.

Several weeks later, on September 22, 1975, another attempt was made on the life of President Ford, when a woman fired a pistol shot at the president as he left his hotel in San Francisco. The bullet missed its target, and the president was again uninjured in the assassination attempt. The second would-be assassin was identified as Sara Jane Moore, a forty-five-year-old civil rights activist.

Bernardo Leighton, the vice president of Chile's Christian Democratic party in exile, was shot and killed in Rome, Italy, on October 6, 1975.

On October 6, 1975, **Gen. Ramon Arthur Rincon Quinones**, the inspector general of the Colombian army, was shot to death while driving to the Ministry of Defense in Bogota. Rincon Quinones had been active in suppressing leftist terrorists in Colombia, and was believed to have been a victim of them.

Danis Tunaligil (1915–75), the Turkish ambassador to Austria, was shot and killed in his office at the Turkish embassy in Vienna on October 22, 1975. The Armenian Liberation Organization claimed responsibility for the assassination. **Ismail Erez** (1919–75), the Turkish ambassador to France, was shot and killed two days later, on October 24, 1975, by Armenian terrorists while riding in his car through the streets of Paris.

Prof. Gordon Hamilton Fairley (1930–75), a leading British cancer researcher who was responsible for the tumor research unit at St. Bartholomew's Hospital in London, was killed in a bomb explosion. The bomb was planted under the car of Hugh Fraser (1937–87), a Conservative party member of Parliament. Caroline Kennedy, the daughter of slain United States president John F. Kennedy (q.v.), was Fraser's house guest at the time of the attempt on his life and had been planning to use the automobile when the bomb went off. Fraser and Ms. Kennedy were uninjured in the blast that killed Prof. Fairley, who was walking past the car when the explosion occurred.

On October 27, 1975, **Guillermo De Vega** (1932–75), an aide to Philippine president Ferdinand Marcos, was shot and killed in his office near the Presidential Palace in Manila.

On November 6, 1975, **Mohammed Mansoor Ali** and **Tajuddin Ahmed**, two former prime ministers of Bangladesh, were executed in Dacca, after having been imprisoned for three months following the army coup that deposed and killed President Mujibur Rahman (q.v.). **Syed Nasrul Islam**, the former vice president, and **A.H.M. Kamuruzzaman**, the former commerce minister, were also slain at that time.

Brig. Khaled Mosharraf, a leader of the army dissidents who had overthrown President Mujibur Rahman (q.v.) of Bangladesh earlier in the year, was assassinated in November of 1975, in Dacca.

Ross McWhirter (1925–75), the co-editor of the *Guinness Book of World Records*, was shot to death in front of his home in London on November 27, 1975. Ross McWhirter and his twin brother, Norris, were British sportswriters and television personalities before they began editing the best-selling trivia books. The McWhirters were also strong proponents of civil liberties and outspoken critics of terrorist activities. Ross McWhirter had recently offered a cash reward for information that could be used to track down terrorists. It was believed his assassination was the work of agents of the Irish Republican Army.

Sheikh Kassem Imad (1922–75), the Moslem governor of North Lebanon, was killed in a barrage of machine gun fire near his home in Tripoli on December 20, 1975.

Richard S. Welch (1929–75), the chief of the United States Central Intelligence Agency in Greece, was shot and killed in front of his Athens residence on December 23, 1975. Welch had previously been stationed in Greece in the 1950s and had also served in the intelligence field in Cyprus and Central America. His death was believed to have been caused by left-wing terrorists who were aware that his official listing as special assistant to the ambassador was a cover for his CIA affiliation.

1976

Murtala Ramat Mohammed, the leader of the Nigerian military government, was killed during an unsuccessful coup attempt on February 13, 1976. Mohammed had served in the Nigerian army during the Civil War in Biafra during the late 1960s. He had become Nigeria's head of state following the overthrow of Gen. Yakubu Gowon on July 29, 1975. Mohammed was shot and killed by dissident army officers during the early stages of the coup. The rebel officers, led by **Lt. Col. Bukar S. Dimka**, were subsequently arrested by government troops. Thirty-seven participants in the planned overthrow, including Dimka, were executed on March 11 and 15. Mohammed was succeeded as Nigeria's head of state by Olusegun Obasanjo.

Boonsanong Punyodyana, the secretary general of the Thailand Socialist party, was shot to death in Bangkok on February 28, 1976.

On April 13, 1976, Brig. Gen. Felix Malloum (b. 1932), the president of Chad, was uninjured in an assassination attempt. Shots were fired at President Malloum during a parade marking the first anniversary of the coup that deposed former President Francois Tombalbaye (q.v.) and installed Malloum in power.

On May 1, 1976, **Alexandros Panagoulis**, a deputy in the Greek Parliament, was killed in an automobile accident which was suspected of having been a planned political assassination. Panagoulis, who was born on July 2, 1939, had made an unsuccessful attempt to assassinate Georgios Papadopoulos, the former head of state of Greece, on August 13, 1968. He was imprisoned until 1973 and returned to Greece following the overthrow of the Papadopoulos government in 1974.

Gen. Joaquin Zenteno Anaya (1923–76), the Bolivian ambassador to France, was shot to death in Paris on May 11, 1976. Gen. Zenteno had served as Bolivia's foreign minister from 1964 until 1966. He had also led the army's campaign against the guerilla forces of Che Guevara (q.v.), which culminated in Guevara's death in 1967. Gen. Zenteno was named army chief of staff in 1971. He remained in that position until 1973, when he was appointed to the French diplomatic post. His assassins claimed to be members of the "International Che Guevara Brigade," and said the murder was in retaliation for the killing of Guevara nine years earlier.

On May 16, 1976, **Zelmar Michelini** and **Hector Gutierre Ruiz**, two former members of the Uruguayan Senate, were kidnapped and murdered by right-wing terrorists in Buenos Aires, Argentina. Michelini and Gutierre Ruiz had been living in exile in Argentina for several years.

Juan Jose Torres Gonzales (1921–76), a former president of Bolivia, was reported kidnapped from his home in exile in Buenos Aires, Argentina, on June 1, 1976. Torres had served as Bolivia's president for ten months between 1970 and 1971 before being deposed by a right-wing military coup. He fled to Peru following the coup, then moved to Argentina in 1973. Two days after Torres' kidnapping, police reported finding his body, blindfolded and shot three times in the head, beside a bridge sixty miles from Buenos Aires. Thus, a Bolivian refugee became the most prominent exiled leftist to meet death at the hands of right-wing extremists in Argentina, joining over 300 others at the time of his death.

Carlos Abdala, the Uruguayan ambassador to Paraguay, was mortally wounded in Asuncion, Paraguay, on June 7, 1976. His assassin, Danziv Danjanovic, was intending to murder the Yugoslav ambassador and shot Abdala by mistake. Abdala died of his wounds the following day.

On June 16, 1976, **Francis E. Meloy, Jr.**, the United States ambassador to Lebanon, and **Robert O. Waring**, the United States economic counselor, were shot and killed in Beirut. The two men were en route to a meeting with warring Moslem and Christian factions in Beirut in the hopes of establishing a truce.

Francis Meloy was born in Washington on March 28, 1917. He had joined the diplomatic corps and, in 1946, was stationed in Saudi Arabia as a vice consul. During the Truman administration Meloy served as Secretary of State Dean Acheson's personal assistant. From 1962 until 1964 he served as director of the Office of Western European Affairs. In 1964 he was appointed the deputy chief of missions in Rome, and in 1969 was named United States ambassador to the Dominican Republic. In April of 1976 he arrived in Lebanon as United States ambassador.

Robert O. Waring was born in New York in 1920. He joined the State Department in 1944 and became a leading economic advisor at various United States embassies. He served as economic counselor at the embassies in Austria and West Germany from 1961 until 1966. He was sent to Beirut in June of 1972 and became the senior member of the Embassy staff there.

Gen. Cesareo Cardozo (1926–76), the federal police chief of Argentina, was killed when a bomb exploded under his bed on June 18, 1976, in Buenos Aires.

Christopher Ewart-Biggs, the British ambassador to Ireland, was killed in an explosion of a land mine in the Dublin Mountains on July 21, 1976. Ewart-Biggs was born on August 5, 1921. He served in the British Foreign Service from 1949 and had held diplomatic positions in the Middle East, the Philippines, Belgium, and France. He was appointed ambassador to Ireland on July 8, 1976. His death three weeks later was believed to have been the work of Irish Republican Army members.

On July 25, 1976, Ethiopian army officers **Lt. Col. Berhanu Haile** and **Lt. Haile Marian Hassan** were executed at Assab on the Red Sea by the ruling military government of Ethiopia. **Lt. Bewookatu Kassa** and **Lt. Seleshi Beyene**, former members of the Ethiopian Dergue, were executed on August 10, 1976.

Orlando Letelier (1932–76), the foreign minister of Chile during the presidency of Salvador Allende (q.v.), was killed in Washington, D.C., when a bomb exploded in his car on September 21, 1976. **Ronnie Karen Moffit** (1951–76), who assisted Letelier at the Institute for Policy Studies in Washington, was also killed in the explosion. Letelier had also served as

Chile's ambassador to the United States from 1971 until May of 1973. Following the overthrow of President Allende, Letelier had been an outspoken critic of the regime of Gen. Pinochet. The Chilean secret police (DINA) was believed responsible for the murders.

On October 1, 1976, **Fikre Merid**, an Ethiopian politician and a leading advisor to the Dergue, was shot and killed while driving his car in Addis Adaba.

Juan Maria De Araluce y Villar (1917–76), an advisor to King Juan Carlos of Spain, was assassinated by machine gun fire on October 4, 1976, at his home in San Sebastian. His assailants were believed to have been members of a Basque separatist group.

Marie Drumm (1920–76), a leading political organizer of the Irish Republican Army, was assassinated in her hospital bed on October 28, 1976. Mrs. Drumm had served as vice president for the Provisional Sinn Fein, the legal political wing of the I.R.A., until her resignation several weeks earlier for reasons of health.

On November 9, 1976, **Guetenet Zewed**, the Ethiopian permanent secretary in the Ministry of Labor and Social Affairs, was shot and killed in Addis Adaba.

Prince Jean De Broglie (1921–76), a former French deputy foreign minister, was shot and killed on the streets of Paris on December 24, 1977. De Broglie had been a Conservative member of the French National Assembly since 1958. As the French state secretary for the French Sahara in 1961, he was instrumental in negotiating the treaty for Algerian independence. De Broglie's murder appeared to lack a political motive and was more likely due to his private business dealings.

1977

Diallo Telli, the former national minister of Guinea and secretary general of the Organization of African Unity from 1964 until 1972, died in a Guinean prison. Telli had been imprisoned by the government of President Sekou Toure on charges of attempting to overthrow the Guinean government. His death was not announced until November of 1978.

Ato Tsegaye Debalke, a leading figure in the Ethiopian Ministry of Culture, was shot to death at his home in Addis Adaba on February 2, 1977.

Brig. Gen. Teferi Benti (1921–77), who had served as head of state and chairman of the provisional military administrative council of Ethiopia since 1974, was killed during a gun battle at the headquarters of the governing council on February 3, 1977. The gun battle was a result of a clash between supporters of Brig. Gen. Benti and those members loyal to Lt. Col. Mengistu Haile Mariam. Six of Benti's followers were either slain during the battle or executed shortly afterwards. They included **Capt. Alemayehu Haile, Capt. Mogus Wolde-Michael, Lt. Col. Asrat Desta, Lt. Col. Hiruy Haile Selassie, Capt. Tefera Deneke**, and **Corporal Halu Belay. Lt. Col. Daniel Asfaw**, a council member loyal to Lt. Col. Mengistu, was also slain during the fighting. Benti had joined the Ethiopian army in the mid–1950s. He has served as Ethiopia's military attache in Washington and had taken part in the military coup that ousted Emperor Haile Selassie in 1974. Benti was named chairman of the council on November 28, 1974, following the murder of Lt. Gen. Aman Michael Andom (q.v.) several days earlier. Benti was succeeded by Lt. Col. Mengistu.

On February 16, 1977, **Janani Luwum** (1925-77), the Anglican archbishop of Uganda and a leading critic of President Idi Amin, was killed after having been arrested by Ugandan police. **Lt. Col. Erinaya Oryema**, the minister of land and water resources, and **Charles Oboth-Ofumbi**, the minister of internal affairs, were also killed. The Ugandan government officially announced the deaths as being the result of an automobile accident, but it was far more likely that they were murdered on orders from President Amin.

On February 18, 1977, Gen. Jorge Rafael Videla (b. 1925), the president of Argentina, was uninjured in an assassination attempt in Buenos Aires. This incident marked the third unsuccessful attempt on Gen. Videla's life within a year.

Dr. Muhammed Al-Fadel (1919–77), the president of Damascus University, was shot and killed near his office in Damascus, Syria, on February 22, 1977. Dr. Fadel had previously served as Syria's minister of justice in 1966.

Kamal Jumblatt, a Lebanese Moslem leftist leader, was shot to death by machine gun–wielding terrorists on a mountain road near Beirut on March 16, 1977. Jumblatt was born on December 6, 1917, in Mukhtara, a village near Beirut. He was the hereditary chieftain of the Jumblatist Druse clan and, in 1940, he assumed leadership. He was elected to the Lebanese Parliament in 1947 and, two years later, founded the Progressive Socialist party. He remained an important figure in Lebanese political circles and was responsible for the rise and fall of several Lebanese presidents.

Although he was a Socialist and greatly admired in the Soviet Union, having received the Lenin Peace Prize in 1973, he was opposed to Communism. Political violence was not unusual to the Jumblatt family. Kamal Jumblatt's father was murdered in the 1920s and his sister, Linda Atrash, was assassinated in Beirut on May 27, 1975. The killing of Kamal Jumblatt was a serious blow to the stability of Lebanon and a major factor in reopening the ongoing Civil War there.

Marien Ngouabi (1938–77), the president of the Democratic Republic of the Congo, was shot and killed in his living quarters at his general staff headquarters in Brazzaville on March 18, 1977, during an unsuccessful coup attempt. During the 1960s Ngouabi had served on the Central Committee of the National Movement for the Revolution, the only legal political party in the Congo. He was a leader of the military coup that deposed President Alphonse Massamba-Debat (q.v.) on September 5, 1968. Ngouabi himself became president of the Congo on January 1, 1969. Ngouabi, a Marxist, changed the nation's name to the Democratic Republic of the Congo and established closer ties with other Communist countries. He was killed during a coup attempt led by Capt. Barthelemy Kikadidi and reportedly organized by former President Massamba-Debat. Ngouabi was succeeded by Joachim Yhombi-Opango as leader of the military government.

Emile Cardinal Biayenda (1927–77), the Roman Catholic archbishop of Brazzaville, was kidnapped and murdered on March 22, 1977, four days after the murder of the Congo's president, Marien Ngouabi (q.v.). Biayenda was reportedly slain by members of the assassinated president's family. Biayenda was ordained a priest in 1950 and was named archbishop of Garba, the Congo, in 1970. The following year he was named archbishop of Brazzaville, and in 1973, he became the Congo's first cardinal.

Alphonse Massamba-Debat (1921–77), the former president of the Congo, was executed on March 25, 1977, for complicity in the murder of Congolese president Marien Ngouabi (q.v.) the previous week. Massamba-Debat had become the president of the Congo on August 16, 1963, following the forced resignation of President Fulbert Youlou. Massamba-Debat was himself deposed by a coup in September of 1968 and eventually succeeded by Ngouabi.

Chalard Hiranyasiri, a former Thai general, was executed in April of 1977 for complicity in an attempted coup the previous month. Chalard had been ousted from the army in October of the previous year following a military coup. He subsequently became a Buddhist monk, but left the monastery to help organize a coup against the regime that had ousted him.

On April 7, 1977, **Siefried Buback** (1920–77), a federal attorney general in West Germany, was shot and killed while riding in an automobile in Karlsruhe, West Germany. Buback had been involved in the 1975 trial of members of the Baader-Meinhof gang, and his assassination was thought to be a revenge killing by surviving members of that organization.

Abdulla Ahmed Hajari (1912–77), a former premier of the Yemen Arab Republic, was shot and killed near his hotel in London, England, on April 10, 1977. Hajari's wife, Fatimah, and **Abdulla Ali Al-Hammami** (1932–77), minister and plenipotentiary of the Yemen Arab Republic Embassy, were also killed in the attack. Hajari had served as North Yemen's premier from December 30, 1972, until March 3, 1974. He was deputy chief of the Yemeni Supreme Court at the time of his murder.

Mauricio Borgonovo Pohl (1940–77), the foreign minister of El Salvador, was kidnapped on April 19, 1977, by leftist terrorists. He was murdered on May 10, 1977, after the government refused to meet the kidnappers' demands to release imprisoned political prisoners.

On June 9, 1977, **Taha Carim**, the Turkish ambassador to the Vatican, was shot and killed near his residence in Rome. Carim was believed to have been the victim of an Armenian terrorist organization.

Brig. Gen. Abdul Hami Razouk, the commander of the Syrian army's missile corps, was killed by assassins at his home in Damascus, Syria, on June 18, 1977.

Dr. Mohammed Hussein Al-Zahabi (1913–77), the former Egyptian minister of religious endowments and Al Azhar affairs, was kidnapped on July 3, 1977, by members of a Moslem cult of fanatics called the "Jamaat al-Tafkeer wal-Hirja" ("Society for Atonement and Flight"). Dr. Zahabi had attempted to eliminate the cult during his term as minister from May of 1975 until November of 1976. His body was found on July 6, 1977, near the Giza pyramids. The cult's leader, Shukri Ahmed Mustafa, and many other members were arrested for the murder.

Osmin Aguirre Salinas (1889–1977), the former president of El Salvador, was shot to death near his home in San Salvador on July 12, 1977. The eighty-eight-year-old former politician had served as El Salvador's president from October 21, 1944, until February 28, 1945. His assassins were presumed to be members of a leftist terrorist organization.

On July 13, 1977, **Delorme Mehu**, Haiti's ambassador to Brazil, was shot to death in Salvador, Brazil, by a hired assassin.

Abdullahi Yousuf, a leading Ethiopian politician in the Harar Province, was assassinated on July 30, 1977. The head of the Ethiopian Security Police, **Lt. Col. Mulugetta Alemu**, was shot and killed on August 3, 1977.

On September 16, 1977, **Carlos Alfaro Castillo** (1925–77), the rector of the University of El Salvador, was shot and killed by a band of assassins in San Salvador.

Steven B. Biko (1947–77), a South African black student leader, died of head wounds on September 12, 1977, while being held in police custody. Biko was the founder of the Black Consciousness Movement, the South African Students' Organization, and other groups whose purpose was to bring non-violent pressure on the South African authorities to eliminate the apartheid system. He was arrested by South African police for violating apartheid rules. An inquest into Biko's death acquitted the authorities involved of responsibility, but world opinion placed the blame on the South African government.

Seamus Costello (1939–77), a leader of the Marxist Irish Republican Socialist party, was shot and killed in Dublin on October 5, 1977.

On October 8, 1977, **Augusto Unceta Barrenechea**, the president of the provincial council of Vizcaya, in the Basque province of Spain, was shot and killed by militant Basque separatists.

Col. Ibrahim Al-Hamidi (1943–77), the head of the state of the Yemen Arab Republic, was assassinated at the home of his brother on October 11, 1977. Hamidi's brother, **Lt. Col. Abdullah Mohammed Al-Hamidi**, and **Col. Ali Kannas Zahra**, the commander of the North Yemeni armed forces, were also killed in the attack. Hamidi, who had served as president of North Yemen from June 13, 1974, was scheduled to make a state visit to Marxist South Yemen later in the week. His assassination was suspected of having been carried out to prevent discussions of a union between the two Yemens. Hamidi was succeeded by Ahmed al-Ghashmi (q.v.).

Hans-Martin Schleyer, a West German industrialist and a leader of the West German employers' association, was kidnapped by leftist terrorists in Cologne on September 5, 1977. Schleyer was born on May 1, 1915, and was active in the Nazi party during World War II. He had become a major figure in the reemergence of the West German automobile industry during the post-war period and served as the director of the Daimler-Benz Automobile Company. His body was found on October 19, 1977, in the eastern section of France.

Schleyer's kidnapping and murder were carried out by members of the Red Army Faction, an off-shoot of the anarchist terrorist group the Baader-Meinhof Gang. Schleyer was killed the day after the Baader-Meinhof co-founder, Andreas Baader, and Jan-Carl Raspe, a member of the gang, had shot and killed themselves with guns that had been smuggled into their cells in a maximum security prison in Stuttgart, West Germany. Gudrun Ensslin, another imprisoned terrorist, hanged herself in the same prison, and Irmgard Moller stabbed herself with a butter knife, but survived. Those four had been among the eleven imprisoned terrorists whose release was demanded by four hijackers of a Lufthansa airliner. The suicides followed a successful West German commando raid at Mogadishu, Somalia, in which three of the four hijackers were killed and the passengers freed. Ingrid Schubert, another of the eleven terrorists the hijackers were hoping to release, hanged herself in Munich's Stadelheim Prison on November 11, 1977. Baader, Raspe and Ensslin had all been imprisoned since 1972 and Schubert had been arrested in 1970. The other Baader-Meinhof co-founder, Ulrike Meinhof, had hanged herself the previous year, on May 9, 1976, in Stammheim Prison in Stuttgart, while being tried for terrorist activities. Gang member Holger Meins had died in November of 1974 following a hunger strike. The anarchist Baader-Meinhof Gang had been responsible for numerous terrorist activities since it was founded in the late 1960s. They were also believed responsible for the murders of Siefried Buback (q.v.), a West German federal prosecutor, and Jurgen Ponto, a prominent banker, earlier in the year. Terrorists Christoph Wackernage, who was believed involved in Schleyer's kidnapping, and Gerd Richart Schneider, were wounded and captured by Dutch police on November 11, 1977. Willy Peter Stoll, who was believed to have organized the kidnapping of Schleyer, was shot and killed by German police in Dusseldorf on September 6, 1978.

Saif Ibn Said Al-Ghubash (1937–77), the state minister for foreign affairs for the United Arab Emirates since 1973, was shot to death on October 25, 1977. Ghubash was killed during an unsuccessful assassination attempt on Syrian foreign minister Abdel Halim Khaddam.

Lt. Gizew Temesgen, the information minister of the Ethiopian Dergue, was assassinated on November 2, 1977. In a separate incident on the same day, **Guta Sernesa**, a member of the governing assembly in Addis Adaba, Ethiopia, was shot and killed. **Lt. Solomon Gesesse**, another member of the Ethiopian Dergue, was assassinated on November 13, 1977.

On November 12, 1977, **Lt. Col. Atnafu Abate** (1937–77), the vice chairman of the ruling revolutionary council of Ethiopia, was executed by the military regime. **Haile Frida**, the principal Marxist theoretician of Ethiopia, was also executed at that time.

Dr. Avi Ahmad Khoram, the minister of planning of Afghanistan from 1974, was shot and killed near his office in Kabul on November 16, 1977.

Robert Smit (1933–77), a leading South African economist and a former director of the International Monetary Fund, was found murdered with his wife at their home in Johannesburg, South Africa, on November 23, 1977. Smit, who was a National party candidate for Parliament, was considered a leading candidate to become South Africa's next minister of finance.

1978

Innocent Belmar, a member of the Grenadan cabinet, was shot and killed on January 4, 1978.

Said Hammami (1941–78), the London representative of the Palestine Liberation Organization, was shot to death by assassins on January 4, 1978, in London. Hammami was a moderate Palestinian nationalist and a critic of terrorist activities. He had served in his position in London since 1972. His assassin was believed to be a member of an extremist Palestinian organization.

Pedro Joaquin Chamorro Cardenal, the editor of the leading Nicaraguan opposition newspaper to the Somoza regime, was shot and killed in Managua on January 10, 1978. Chamorro was the editor and publisher of *La Prensa* and the founder of the Democratic Union of Liberation, a coalition of opposition political parties. Chamorro had been arrested in the early 1940s during the administration of President Anastasio Somoza Garcia (q.v.). He had remained an outspoken critic of the Somoza family during the administrations of the elder Somoza's two sons, Luis and Anastasio Somoza Debayle (q.v.). His death was attributed to supporters of the Somoza regime, and widespread civil unrest followed his funeral.

On January 25, 1978, **Joaquin Viola Sauret**, a former mayor of Barcelona, Spain, died in his home when a bomb strapped to his chest by left-wing terrorists exploded. Sauret had served as Barcelona's mayor from 1975 until 1977. It was believed that Sauret's assassins, members of the International Communist party, had intended to kidnap the former mayor when the bomb detonated accidentally.

In February of 1978 **Toivo Shiyanga**, the South African minister of health for South West Africa (Namibia) and the leader of the Ovambo tribe, was shot to death by Namibian nationalists.

Youssef El-Sebai (1918–78), the editor of the Egyptian newspaper *Al Ahram*, was shot and killed in a hotel lobby in Nicosia, Cyprus, by Palestinian radicals on February 18, 1978. Sebai was a close adviser to Egyptian president Anwar Sadat (q.v.) and had previously served as information minister in the Egyptian government.

Gen. Reynaldo Perez Vega (1925–78), a leading military adviser to Nicaraguan president Anastasio Somoza Debayle (q.v.), was killed by Sandinista guerrillas during a kidnapping attempt on March 8, 1978. Gen. Perez Vega was a former director of the Nicaraguan Immigration Department and had served as a member of the ruling military junta from 1967 until 1974.

On March 22, 1978, **Jesus Haddad Blanco**, the director general of the Spanish prison system, was shot and killed by machine gun fire as he entered his car in Madrid. Haddad Blanco, thirty-nine, had been appointed prison director three months prior to his assassination. His assailants were believed to be members of the leftist First of October Groups of Anti-Fascist Resistance.

Clemens Kapuuo (1923–78), a leading South-West African tribal chief, was assassinated in the black township of Katatura on March 27, 1978. Kapuuo, the chief of the Hereros tribe since 1970, was the leader of the Democratic Turnhalle Alliance, a pro–South African organization in South-West Africa. He was considered a leading candidate to become the first president of the South-West African territory.

Miguel Tobias Padilla (1943–78), the undersecretary for economic coordination in Argentina, was shot to death in Buenos Aires on April 11, 1978. Tobias Padilla was also a leading government advisor on labor affairs.

Amir Aqbar Khabir, the leader of the leftist Parcham (Flag) party of Afghanistan, was assassinated on April 17, 1978, in Kabul. His murder led to widespread civil disorders in Afghanistan against the regime of Mohammad Daud Khan (q.v.).

On April 28, 1978, **Sardar Mohammad Daud Khan** (1909–78), the president of Afghanistan, was killed following a leftist coup on April 28, 1978. Several thousand other Afghanistani politicians, including President Daud's brother, **Mohammed Naeem**, the vice president, and the air force chief of staff, were also killed during the coup. Daud had served as Afghanistan's premier under King Muhammad Zahir Shah from 1953 until 1963. In July of 1973 he had overthrown the king and became Afghanistan's president. Nur Mohammad Taraki (q.v.), a leader of the coup, assumed the role of chief of state following President Daud's ouster and murder.

Henri Curiel (1914–78), a founder of the Egyptian Communist party, was shot and killed in Paris, France, on May 4, 1978. Curiel, a suspected leader of international terrorism, was believed killed by Organization Delta, a right-wing terrorist organization.

Aldo Moro, a former Italian premier who had been kidnapped by leftist Red Brigade terrorists on March 16, 1978, was murdered by his captors on May 9, 1978. Moro was born in Maglie, Italy, on September 23, 1916. He served as president of the Federation of Italian University Catholics from 1939 until 1942, and in 1948 was elected to represent Apulia in the Italian Chamber of Deputies. He served as Italy's minister of justice from 1955 until 1957 and was minister of education from 1957 until 1959. In 1959 he was selected as secretary of the Christian Democratic party. Moro first became Italy's premier on December 5, 1963, as the leader of a center-left coalition. He remained premier until June 5, 1968, and was subsequently appointed foreign secretary. He again was selected as premier on November 23, 1974, serving until July 30, 1976. In October of 1976 Moro was elected president of the Christian Democratic party and remained a leading figure in Italian politics and a likely candidate for the Italian presidency. His kidnappers demanded the release of thirteen of their fellow Red Brigade terrorists held in prison, and murdered Moro when the Italian government refused to accede to their demands. Moro's body was found in a parked car near the center of Rome.

Bruce McKenzie, a former Kenyan minister of agriculture, was killed on May 24, 1978, when a bomb exploded as the airplane in which he was flying took off from Uganda's Entebbe Airport.

Ali Soilih (1937–78), the deposed president of the Comoro Islands, was shot and killed, allegedly while trying to escape captivity, on May 29, 1978. Ali Soilih had been overthrown during a coup led by Robert Denard, a former French mercenary, on May 13, 1978. Ali Soilih had served as president of the Comoro Economic Development Society in 1964 and was elected to the territorial assembly in 1968. He served as the minister of public works from 1970 until 1972 in the colonial government of Prince Said Ibrahim. He had overthrown the government of President Ahmed Abdallah and had become president of the former French colony on August 3, 1975, one month after the Comoros had gained their independence. Ali Soilih was succeeded as president by Ahmed Abdallah.

Lt. Gen. Ari Nazar Geidarov (1926–78), the interior minister of the Soviet Republic of Azerbaijan; **Saladin Kyazimov**, the deputy interior minister; and **Lt. Col. Aziz Saikhanov** were shot and killed in June of 1978. Geidarov, who had served in his position since 1970, and the others were killed by Muratov, an Azerbaijani prison official, who subsequently committed suicide.

On June 13, 1978, **Tony Franjieh**, the son of Christian militia leader and former Lebanese president Suleiman Franjieh, was killed with his family by shellfire directed at his home by rival Falangists. The death of Franjieh came after weeks of fighting between the rival factions and precipitated violent acts of retaliation by the Franjieh clan.

Ali Yassin, a moderate Palestine Liberation Organization official in Kuwait, was shot and killed at his home on June 15, 1979.

Ahmad Al-Ghashmi (1941–78), the head of state of the Yemen Arab Republic, was killed when a bomb exploded in his office in the capital of Sana'a. The bomb was in a briefcase carried by an envoy from President Salem Ali Rubayyi (q.v.), the president of South Yemen. The Rubayyi government denied any knowledge of the assassination plot. President Ghashmi had come to power in North Yemen following the assassination of his predecessor, Lt. Col. Ibrahim Al-Hamdi (q.v.), in October of 1977.

Salem Ali Rubayyi, the head of state of the People's Democratic Republic of Yemen, was ousted in a leftist coup and summarily executed by a firing squad in Aden on June 26, 1978. Rubayyi had become leader of the Southern Yemen Presidency Council on June 22, 1969. The coup was led by Abdel Fattah Ismail (q.v.), an extreme pro–Soviet member of the Presidency Council. President Rubayyi had attempted to have Ismail arrested for complicity in the assassination of North Yemen's president Ahmad Al-Ghashmi (q.v.) several days earlier. Ismail's militia defeated troops loyal to Rubayyi after a day of heavy fighting. Executed with Rubayyi were **Jassem Saleh** and **Salem Al-Aouar**, two of the deposed president's leading advisers.

Abdul Razzak An-Naif (1933–78), a former premier of Iraq, was shot and mortally wounded on July 9, 1978, in London, England. He died the following day. Gen. Naif, a former deputy director of the Iraqi military intelligence system, became premier of Iraq on July 17, 1968, following a military coup. He was deposed and arrested two weeks later on July 30. Gen. Naif subsequently went into exile in England. He was the target of an unsuccessful assassination attempt in 1972.

On July 21, 1978, **Brig. Gen. Juan Sanchez Ramos** (1914–78), a Spanish artillery officer in charge of military supplies, and **Lt. Col. Juan Perez Rodriguez**, his aide, were shot and killed by left-wing terrorists in Madrid.

Ezzedine Kalak (1948–78), the chief representative of the Palestine Liberation Organization in Paris, was assassinated with his aide, **Hammad Adnan**, in their Paris office on August 3, 1978. Kalak, a leading supporter of P.L.O. chief Yassir Arafat, was thought to have been the victim of Palestinian extremists backed by Iraq.

Georgi Markov (1929–78), a Bulgarian writer who had defected in June of 1969, died on September 11, 1978, after having a poison contained in an alloy ball injected into his leg by the point of an umbrella. Markov was a successful author and playwright in Bulgaria. He defected to Italy in 1969 and, in 1971, moved to London. He joined the British Broadcasting Corporation's Bulgarian Service, and became a broadcaster for Radio Free Europe. Markov, who had reported receiving death threats, was jabbed in the thigh by an umbrella while walking past a London bus stop on September 7, 1978. Four days later Markov died. A small ball, thought to have contained a poison, was found in Markov's leg following an autopsy. Markov's mysterious death was presumed to have been the work of Bulgarian agents.

Rafael Pardo Buelvas (1928–78), a former Colombian minister of the interior, was shot and killed in Bogota on September 12, 1978, by a member of the leftist M-19 terrorist group.

On October 3, 1978, **Capt. Francisco De Asis Liesa** (1922–78), who was second in command of the Spanish naval base at Boilboa, was shot to death by terrorists during a kidnapping attempt near his home.

Fedele Calvosa, the public prosecutor of Frosinone, Italy, was shot and killed by terrorists on November 8, 1978.

Jose Francisco Mateu Canovas (1920–78), a Spanish jurist who had headed Gen. Francisco Franco's Court of Public Order from 1968 until 1975, was assassinated by gunmen near his home in Madrid on November 16, 1978. Mateu had been a substitute of the Spanish supreme court following the dissolution of the Court of Public Order in 1975.

On November 18, 1978, United States Representative **Leo Ryan** (1925–78) was killed with four members of his party while departing from a meeting with leaders of the People's Temple commune in Guyana. Ryan had served as a Democratic congressman from California since 1973. He had been in Guyana to investigate allegations that the Reverend Jim Jones (1931–78) was holding members of his cult against their will at the People's Temple headquarters in Jonestown, Guyana. As Ryan was preparing to depart from the Port Kaituma airstrip, he and his party were attacked by armed members of the commune. Ryan, three newsmen, and another passenger were shot and killed in the assault.

Jones, who had moved his commune from San Francisco earlier in the year, ordered his followers to take cyanide-laced drinks following the attack on the visiting party. When Guyanan troops arrived at Jonestown on November 19, 1978, they found the dead bodies of Jones and over 900 of his followers.

George Moscone (1929–78), the mayor of San Francisco, and **Harvey Milk** (1930–78), a member of the San Francisco board of supervisors, were shot and killed in their offices by Dan White, a former supervisor, on November 27, 1978.

George Moscone, a Democrat, was elected to the San Francisco board of supervisors in 1963. In 1966 he was elected to the California state senate and served as floor leader from 1967 until 1976. In December of 1975 he was elected mayor of San Francisco and was sworn in the following January.

Harvey Milk had been elected to the board of supervisors in November of 1977. He was an avowed homosexual and an outspoken leader in the fight for homosexual rights.

Dan White was elected to the board of supervisors at the same time as Harvey Milk. He was a conservative and often at odds with Milk and Mayor Moscone. White had resigned his office for personal reasons earlier in the month. He changed his mind and requested that Mayor Moscone reappoint him to the position he had vacated. When the mayor rejected his appeal, White fired four bullets into him. He then found Supervisor Milk and shot him five times. White was arrested and charged with the murders, but was found guilty of voluntary manslaughter. His defense claimed that he was not responsible for his actions due to a temporary deranged condition caused by overindulging in junk food. White was sentenced to seven years and eight months in prison, and was paroled in 1984. He committed suicide the following year.

1979

On January 3, 1979, **Maj. Gen. Constantine Ortin Gil**, sixty-three, was shot to death outside his apartment in Madrid, Spain. Ortin was the military governor of Madrid and a veteran of the Spanish Civil War from 1936 to 1939. His assassination was believed to have been carried out by Basque separatists.

Ali Hassan Salameh (1943–79), a Palestinian guerrilla leader known as **Abu Hassan**, was killed in a bomb blast in front of his home in Beirut,

Lebanon, on January 22, 1979. Abu Hassan was believed to have been the mastermind behind the massacre of Israeli athletes at the 1972 Munich Olympics (q.v.). He had survived several previous attempts on his life. At the time of his death he was serving as chief bodyguard to Palestinian leader Yasir Arafat.

Alberto Fuentes Mohr (1928–79), a former Guatemalan minister of finance and foreign affairs, was shot to death by submachine gun fire on January 25, 1979. Mohr had been kidnapped by leftist guerrillas in 1970 while serving as foreign minister. He was subsequently exchanged for the release of a jailed guerrilla. As an opposition member of Congress, Fuentes Mohr was a leading critic of extremism on both the left and the right.

Magistrate **Emilio Alessandrini**, the public prosecutor of Milan, was shot and killed on January 29, 1979, by an unknown assassin.

On February 14, 1979, **Adolph Dubs**, the United States ambassador to Afghanistan, was shot to death after being abducted by Moslem terrorists en route to the United States Embassy. Dubs was born in Chicago on August 4, 1920. A thirty-year veteran of the diplomatic corps, he had served as a foreign service officer in West Germany, Liberia, Canada, the Soviet Union, and Yugoslavia. He was acting chief of the United States mission to the Soviet Union from 1972 until 1974, and in 1975 was named deputy assistant secretary of state for Near Eastern and South Asian affairs. In 1978 he was appointed ambassador to Afghanistan.

On March 5, 1979, **Brig. Gen. Agustin Munoz Vazquez** (1913–79), a retired Spanish general, was shot to death en route to his daughter's home in northern Madrid. His alleged killers were the First of October Anti-Fascist Revolutionary Group. Gen. Munoz Vazquez was a quartermaster officer who had last served in the Spanish enclave of Ceuta in North Africa. He had been semi-retired since 1977.

On March 21, 1979, **Andre Michaux**, a Belgian national bank official, was shot to death by two men in front of his Brussels home as he was parking his car. Michaux, forty-seven, was believed to have been shot by mistake, as his residence was near that of a British diplomat.

Manuel Colon Argueta, forty-seven, a former mayor of Guatemala City (1970–74) and leader of the United Front of the Revolution, was killed by machine-gun fire while driving to work in Guatemala City on March 22, 1979. Mr. Colon had gained popularity as a strong critic of the military regimes that have ruled Guatemala, and was one of the most popular leftist leaders in that country.

Muazzam Zaki, a high-ranking Palestine Liberation Organization official in Pakistan, was shot and killed at his home in Islamabad by an unknown assassin on March 22, 1979.

Sir Richard Sykes, fifty-eight, the British ambassador to the Netherlands, was killed by two gunmen outside his home in the Hague as he was leaving for the Embassy on March 22, 1979. The provisional wing of the Irish Republican Army was thought to have gunned down the British ambassador. Sykes had joined the Foreign Office in 1947 and served in Peking, Brussels, Santiago, Athens, and London before being appointed as ambassador to Cuba in 1970. He served there for two years. Sir Richard was then sent to Washington as deputy chief of mission to Ambassador Sir Peter Ramsbotham. He gained a reputation for his keen grasp of military and defense issues. He was knighted in 1977. Before being sent to his post at the Hague, in June of 1977, he had been the chief investigator of the bomb murder of Christopher Ewart-Biggs (q.v.), Britain's ambassador to Ireland, in July 1976. Sir Richard, who was deputy undersecretary of state at the British Foreign Office at that time, recommended tighter security at all British diplomatic missions.

On March 30, 1979, **Airey Middleton Sheffield Neave**, a leading British Conservative politician, was killed when a bomb placed in his car exploded outside of the House of Commons garage. Neave was born in London on January 23, 1916. He served in the army during World War II and was a member of the British prosecution team at the Nuremberg trials. He was first elected to the House of Commons in 1953. He was an early supporter of Margaret Thatcher and was instrumental in her selection as Conservative party leader, and later prime minister. In 1975 Neave became the Conservative party's parliamentary spokesman on Northern Ireland, which made him an important target for Irish Republican Army terrorists.

Zulfikar Ali Bhutto, the former prime minister of Pakistan, was hanged on April 4, 1979. Bhutto was born in Larkana, Sind, in what is now Pakistan, on January 5, 1928. He was trained as a lawyer and, in 1958, he was appointed Pakistani minister of commerce. He was named foreign minister in 1963, and used his position to encourage an improved relationship with Communist China. He resigned his office in 1966 and founded the Pakistan People's party (PPP). Bhutto was elected president of Pakistan in 1971, serving until August of 1973, when he assumed the position of prime minister. Bhutto's reign became increasingly unpopular following allegations of election fraud during general elections held in March of 1977. Four months later Bhutto was ousted by Gen. Mohammad Zia-ul-Haq, the army chief of staff. Bhutto was subsequently arrested and charged with the murder of Nawab Mohammad Ahmad Khan, the father of a political opponent. Bhutto was convicted of the murder and sentenced to death on March 18, 1978. Despite pleas for clemency, the Pakistani government proceeded with the execution, and Bhutto was hanged, on April 4, 1978, at Rawalpindi Jail.

Amir Abbas Hoveida, a former prime minister of Iran, was executed by the Iranian revolutionary government on April 7, 1979. Hoveida was born in Teheran on February 18, 1919. He served in the Iranian Foreign Ministry prior to his appointment as prime minister by the shah in January of 1965. During the later years of his term of office Iran was increasingly beset by revolutionary activity. Hoveida's inability to eliminate the political opponents of the shah resulted in his ouster as prime minister on August 7, 1977. Hoveida was briefly imprisoned the following year by the military government of the shah, and he was again imprisoned following the shah's ouster by the Islamic fundamentalist followers of the Ayatollah Khomeini in February of 1979. Hoveida was tried by the Islamic Revolutionary Court for his role in the shah's government, and was convicted and shot on April 7, 1979, in Teheran.

On April 11, 1979, **Adel Mini**, the attorney general of the Syrian State Security Court, was assassinated. Mini was an aide to Syrian president Hafez Assad. Mini's death came amid rising violence between the Alawite Moslem sect, of which Mini was a member, and the majority Sunni Moslems of Syria.

Gen. Vali Ullah Gharani, a leading Iranian army officer, was shot and killed by three gunmen in the back yard of his Teheran home on April 23, 1979. Gharani had served as the first chief of staff of the Iranian army following the Revolution that deposed the shah of Iran in February of 1979. He has resigned his position on March 27, 1979, after he had ordered the army to put down a rebellion in Kurdistan. Gharani had served as head of the Army Intelligence Service in the 1950s until his dismissal by the shah in 1957. He had remained in retirement until his appointment as army leader on February 15, 1979.

Ayatollah Morteza Motahari (1919–79), a leading member of the ruling Iranian Revolutionary Council, was shot and killed while leaving a meeting with Prime Minister Mehdi Bazargan in Teheran on May 1, 1979. Motahari's assassins were reported to be members of the Forghan Fighters, an underground revolutionary group who also claimed responsibility for the assassination of Gen. Vali Ullah Gharani (q.v.) the previous month.

Carlos Antonio Herrera Rebollo, the minister of education in El Salvador, was shot and killed while driving to his office in San Salvador on May 23, 1979. Herrera Rebollo had previously served as mayor of San

Salvador, and was a member of the Christian Democratic party. His assassins were believed to be members of the Popular Liberation Group, a left-wing terrorist organization.

On May 25, 1979, Ayatollah Hashemi Rafsanjani, a leading Iranian political and religious figure, was injured in an assassination attempt. Rafsanjani recovered from his wounds.

Lt. Gen. Luis Gomez Hortiguela (1910–79), the leader of the Spanish army's personnel department, was assassinated by machine gun fire on May 25, 1979, while driving in Madrid. **Col. Agustin Laso**, an aide; **Col. Juan Avalos Gomariz**, the general's secretary; and **Luis Gomez Borrego**, the general's chauffeur, were also killed in the attack. The killings were believed to have been work of a Basque separatist group.

On May 30, 1979, **Hugo Wey** (1930–79), the Swiss charge d'affaires in San Salvador, was killed during a kidnapping attempt by leftist terrorists.

The chief of staff of the Guatemalan army, **Gen. Jose Cansino** (1927–79), was assassinated by terrorists on June 10, 1979, while riding through Guatemala City. Gen. Cansino was the third-ranking member of the ruling Guatemalan military government.

Lt. Gen. Fred W. K. Akuffo, the military head of the state of Ghana, was overthrown during a coup led by Flight Lt. Jerry Rawlings (b. 1947) on June 4, 1979. The new government accused Akuffo and other high-ranking officials of corruption. On June 16, 1979, **Gen. Ignatius Kutu Achaempong** and **Lt. Gen. Akwasi Afrifa** (1913–79), Akuffo's predecessors as head of state of Ghana's military government, were executed. Lt. Gen. Akuffo was himself executed on June 26, 1979.

Lt. Gen. Akwasi Afrifa was commissioner of finance when he replaced Lt. Gen. Joseph Ankrah as Ghana's head of state on April 2, 1969. He served in that position until September 30, 1969, when he became chairman of a three-man presidential commission under a civilian administration. In August of 1970, Afrifa was replaced by Edward Akufo-Addo.

Gen. Ignatius Achaempong was born on September 23, 1931. He was an officer in the Ghanian army when he led the military coup which overthrew the civilian government of Kofi Busia on January 13, 1972. Ghana's economic and political situation rapidly deteriorated under Achaempong's arbitrary rule. Gen. Achaempong was himself overthrown on July 5, 1978, under charges of mismanagement and corruption.

Lt. Gen. Fred Akuffo, who led the military coup against Gen. Achaempong, was born on March 21, 1937. He had served on the ruling military council from 1975. Akuffo proceeded too slowly in his attempts to stabilize Ghana's economy and reestablish a constitutional government. Less than a year after he had seized power, Akuffo was himself removed from office.

On June 25, 1979, United States Gen. Alexander Haig (b. 1924), the supreme commander of the Allied forces in NATO, was uninjured when a land mine exploded in his car's path in Belgium. It was believed that the attempt on Gen. Haig's life was organized by West German Red Brigade terrorists.

On July 13, 1979, Police **Col. Antonio Varisco** was murdered by terrorists in Rome, Italy. Col. Varisco was the director of security of the central courts in Rome.

Zuheir Mohsen (1936–79), the leader of the Saiqa, a pro–Syrian Palestinian guerrilla organization, was assassinated in Nice, France, on July 24, 1979. Mohsen, who was also the leader of the Palestine Liberation Organization's military department, had led the Saiqa since 1971. His murder was believed to have been orchestrated by Israeli agents.

Louis Mountbatten, Earl of Burma, was killed in a bomb blast aboard his fishing boat off the coast of County Sligo, Ireland, on August 27, 1979. Also killed in the explosion were Nicholas Knatchbull, Mountbatten's fourteen-year-old grandson, and Paul Maxwell, a local crew member.

Lord Mountbatten was born on June 25, 1900, in Windsor, England. He served in the Royal Navy during World War I. Mountbatten was the commander of a destroyer in the early days of World War II and took part in the Battle of Crete. He later served on the British Chiefs of Staff Committee and was a major planner for the invasion of Normandy in 1944. He was appointed by the Allies as supreme commander for Southeast Asia, and led his forces to victory over the Japanese, recapturing Burma. After the conclusion of the war, Mountbatten was appointed the last British viceroy of India in 1946 and oversaw the British withdrawal from colonial rule in that country. Following India's independence on August 14, 1947, Mountbatten was named India's first governor general, and remained in that position until June of 1948. He subsequently returned to the Royal Navy and, in 1955, was appointed first sea lord of the Royal Navy. From 1959 until his retirement in 1965 Mountbatten served as the first chief of the British Defense Staff and reorganized Britian's defense forces. His assassination fourteen years later was attributed to the Provisional Irish Republican Army. Thomas McMahon, an explosives expert in the I.R.A., was tried for the killings. He was convicted and sentenced to imprisonment for life.

Jose Javier Romero Mena, an educator and the brother of President Carlos Romero of El Salvador, was killed by leftist guerrillas near his home in Apopo, El Salvador, on September 6, 1979.

Nur Mohammad Taraki, the head of state of Afghanistan, was ousted and killed in a coup on September 16, 1979. Taraki had become Afghanistan's leader following a coup in April of 1978, in which President Mohammad Daud Khan (q.v.) was overthrown. Taraki had served in the Afghanistani Foreign Office during the reign of King Mohammad Zahir Shah and, in 1963, was the founder of the leftist Khalq ("Masses") party. Taraki opposed the rule of Daud Khan, who had overthrown the king in 1973. Taraki, with Soviet support, led the bloody coup against President Daud Khan in 1978. Taraki was in turn overthrown by Hafizullah Amin (q.v.), his prime minister. His death was announced on October 9, 1979, as having been the result of a severe illness, though it is believed that Taraki was killed in a gun battle with Amin's forces on the day of the coup.

Carlo Ghiglieno, an executive of the Fiat Automobile Company, was shot and killed by Red Brigade terrorists in Turin, Italy, on September 21, 1979.

On September 23, 1979, **Gen. Lorenzo Gonzalez-Valles Sanchez** (1920–79), the military governor of the Guipuzcoa province in Spain, was assassinated by Basque separatists while he was walking along a seaside boardwalk in San Sebastian.

Cesare Terranova, a Sicilian judge, was assassinated by terrorists in Palermo, Italy, on September 25, 1979.

Francisco Macias Nguema (1922–79), the dictatorial ruler of Equatorial Guinea until his ouster on August 3, 1979, was executed by the new government on September 29, 1979. Macias became the first president of the former Spanish colony in October of 1968. Three years later he proclaimed himself president for life. His rule was marked by a campaign of terror which forced nearly a quarter of Equatorial Guinea's population into exile. It is estimated that during his eleven-year reign over 50,000 people were executed, including two-thirds of the legislators and virtually all cabinet ministers and senior civil servants. Macias was ousted by Todoro Obiang Nguema Mbasogo, a relative who had served as his deputy defense minister. Macias was tried and convicted on numerous charges, including treason and genocide, and was executed with six of his followers on September 29, 1979.

Vincent Teekah (1941–79), who had served as minister of education in Guyana from 1977, was shot and killed while driving in Georgetown, Guyana, on October 25, 1979.

Chung Hee Park, the president of South Korea, was assassinated while dining in a Seoul restaurant on October 26, 1979. Park was born in the Son Son Province of Korea on September 30, 1917, and served in the Japanese army during World War II. Following Korea's independence after the war, Park became an officer in the Korean army. In 1953 he was promoted to the rank of brigadier general. In 1961, Park led a military revolt against the civilian government. He served as leader of the ruling military junta until 1963, when he was elected president of South Korea. His autocratic rule received the support of the United States primarily due to his anti–Communist policies. Park also initiated a series of reforms which benefitted the South Korean economy. Madame Park (q.v.), the president's wife, was killed in an assassination attempt against President Park in 1974. The president was himself killed during a coup attempt led by Kim Jae Kyu, the head of the Korean Central Intelligence Agency. **Cha Choi Chol**, a leading advisor and chief bodyguard of the president, and four other aides were also slain in the attack.

On December 17, 1979, **Mohammed Mofatteh**, a close aide to Iranian leader Ayatollah Khomeini, was shot and killed near the Islamic College in Teheran. Mofatteh was a leader of the anti-shah movement before Khomeini's return from exile, and was the director of the leading Islamic religious school in Teheran.

Hafizullah Amin, who had become president of Afghanistan during a coup three months earlier, was overthrown and killed on December 27, 1979. Amin, who was born on August 1, 1929, in Paghman, Afghanistan, had been a member of Nur Mohammad Taraki's (q.v.) Khlaq party in the 1960s. He was instrumental in organizing the 1978 coup which overthrew President Mohammad Daud Khan (q.v.) and installed Taraki as president. Amin served in the Taraki government as minister of foreign affairs and, from March 27, 1979, as prime minister. On September 16, 1979, Amin overthrew Taraki and assumed the presidency for himself. Amin's anti–Islamic policies increased opposition to the Soviet-sponsored regime, and Amin was killed following direct Soviet military intervention in Afghanistan. He was succeeded by Babrak Karmal.

Viktor S. Paputin (1926–79), the Soviet deputy interior minister, was also reported killed during the Afghanistani coup which deposed Amin. Paputin was allegedly the architect of the Soviet-backed coup.

1980

On January 31, 1980, thirty-nine people were killed in a fire at the Spanish Embassy in Guatemala City. The Embassy building had been seized by Guatemalan Indian peasants during the week, and most of the people inside died in the flames. The dead included **Eduardo Caceras Lehnhoff**, a former vice president of Guatemala and **Adolfo Molina Orantes**, Guatemala's former foreign minister.

Mario Zamora Rivas, the attorney general of El Salvador, was shot and killed by right-wing gunmen in San Salvador on February 23, 1980. He was a prominent moderate leader and a member of the Christian Democratic party.

Former United States representative **Allard K. Lowenstein** of New York was shot and killed on March 14, 1980, in his New York law office. Dennis Sweeney, a former associate of Lowenstein, was charged with the murder. Lowenstein was born in Newark, New Jersey, on January 16, 1929, and was a teacher at Stanford University. He was an early supporter of the civil rights movement of the 1960s and an opponent of American involvement in the war in Vietnam. In 1968 Lowenstein was a leader of the "Dump Johnson" movement, and succeeded in persuading Sen. Eugene McCarthy of Minnesota to run for the Democratic nomination for the presidency that year. McCarthy's early primary showings as a peace candidate eventually resulted in the withdrawal of President Lyndon Johnson from the race. In 1968 Lowenstein was elected to Congress from the Fifth Congressional District in New York, representing Long Island. He served only one term, being defeated in six later bids for the office. In 1977 he was appointed as the United States representative to the United Nations Commission on Human Rights.

Russell G. Lloyd (1932–80), the former mayor of Evansville, Indiana, died on March 21, 1980, of gunshot wounds he received in a shooting incident earlier in the week. Lloyd, who had stepped down as mayor three months earlier, was shot by Julie Van Orden, who had claimed that city inspectors were harassing her about the condition of her home. It was believed that Lloyd's assailant was not aware that he was no longer Evansville's mayor.

On March 24, 1980, Salvadoran Roman Catholic archbishop **Oscar Arnulfo Romero y Galdames** was shot and killed by an unknown gunman in San Salvador. Archbishop Romero was born in El Salvador on August 15, 1917. He was appointed the Roman Catholic archbishop of El Salvador in 1977. While he was previously considered a conservative, he became a leading critic of the regime of Gen. Carlos Humberto Romero and of human rights violations in El Salvador. In 1979 he was nominated for the Nobel Peace Prize for his attempts to better the life of the poor people of his nation. He had received numerous threats from right-wing factions in El Salvador before his death.

On April 12, 1980, President **William R. Tolbert, Jr.**, of Liberia was shot and killed during a coup led by Master Sgt. Samuel Doe. More than twenty-five other prominent Liberian political figures died during the coup or were executed shortly afterward. On April 22 the new military government put to death by firing squad President Tolbert's brother **Frank Tolbert**, the president of the Senate; **Reginald Townsend**, the leader of the ruling True Whig party; **Cecil Dennis**, the foreign minister; **James Phillips**, the finance minister; **Cyril Bright**, the agriculture minister; **John Sherman**, the commerce minister; **James Pierre**, the chief justice of the Liberian supreme court; **Joseph Chesson**, a jurist; **Frank Stewart**, the budget director; **Richard Heneries**, the speaker of the House of Representatives; Congressman **Charles King**; and **Clarence Parker**, the treasurer of the True Whig party.

President Tolbert was born on March 13, 1913, and entered Liberian politics in the early 1940s. He was elected to the House of Representatives in 1943. In 1951 he became vice president under President William Tubman and succeeded to the presidency on Tubman's death on July 23, 1971. Tolbert, who had also served as president of the Baptist World Alliance from 1965 to 1970, became increasingly unpopular as Liberia's economy declined and corruption increased. These factors eventually resulted in his ouster and death.

Gurbachan Singh, an Indian religious leader who was regarded by the several hundred thousand followers of the Nirankari Sect as a living saint, was shot and killed near his New Delhi home by two assassins on April 24, 1980.

Farrokhrou Parsa, the minister of education in the government of the deposed shah of Iran, was executed by a firing squad on May 8, 1980. Mrs. Parsa had also served as the first female member of the Iranian parliament. She had been arrested following the overthrow of the shah and was tried and condemned by a revolutionary court.

On June 2, 1980, Bassam al-Shaka, the Palestinian mayor of the West Bank city of Nablus, and Karim Khalef, the mayor of Ramallah, were seriously injured in separate car bombings. Shaka lost both legs in the explosion. An attempt was made on the life of another West Bank mayor on the same day. A Jewish terrorist organization claimed responsibility for the bombings.

Guyanan historian **Walter Rodney** was killed in June of 1980 in an explosion in Guyana. Rodney was also a member of the opposition party Working People's Alliance (WPA).

Gun Tazak (1931–80), the deputy chairman of the Turkish right-wing National Action party, was shot to death at his home in Ankara in June of 1980.

On July 15, 1980, **Lt. Col. Roger Vergara Campos** (1937–80), the director of Chile's army intelligence school, was assassinated by four leftist gunmen in Santiago.

Nihat Erim, a former prime minister of Turkey, was assassinated in Istanbul by left-wing gunmen on July 18, 1980. Erim was born in Kandira, Turkey, in 1912. A lawyer and a teacher at the University of Ankara, Erim became the legal adviser to the Ministry of Foreign Affairs in 1942, and was elected as a Republican People's party member to Parliament in 1945. From 1948 to 1950 he was vice premier and minister of public works. On April 15, 1973, he became prime minister of Turkey, leading a coalition government. He served in this office until April 17, 1972. Erim was known as a strong proponent of law and order and a supporter of the right-wing policies of the Turkish government.

Also on June 18, 1980, former Iranian premier Shahpur Bakhtiar (b. 1916), was attacked by three gunmen at his home in Paris. Bakhtiar, who had served as the last prime minister of the deposed shah of Iran, was uninjured in the shooting, which claimed the lives of two people. Bakhtiar was a leading exiled opponent of the regime of the Ayatollah Khomeini.

On July 21, 1980, **Salah Ad-Din Bitar**, a former Syrian premier, was shot and killed while in exile in Paris. Bitar was born in Damascus, Syria, in 1912. He was a founder of the Ba'ath (Renaissance) party in 1943 and served as foreign minister in the 1950s. Bitar was an architect of the United Arab Republic, the short-lived union of Egypt and Syria, in 1958, and served as minister of state during that period. He served as premier of Syria for the first time from March to November of 1963 and again from May to October of 1964. His last term of office was from December, 1965, until his ouster by a military coup in February of 1966. Bitar went into exile in Paris and served as the editor-in-chief of the *Al Ahaa al-Arabi* (*Arab Renaissance*) journal. He was also regarded as a leading opponent of the regime of President Hafez al-Assad.

Ali Akbar Tabatabai (1931–80), the former spokesman and press attache for the Iranian Embassy in Washington, was shot and killed at his home in Washington on July 22, 1980. Before coming to the United States, Tabatabai had served as the director general of foreign information at the Iranian Information Ministry in Teheran under the shah. He was also the founder of the Iranian Freedom Foundation and a leading critic of the regime of the Ayatollah Khomeini.

Riyad Taha (1926–80), the president of the Lebanese publisher's syndicate since 1967, was shot to death on July 23, 1980, while en route to his office in Moslem West Beirut.

On July 28, 1980, **Musa Shaib**, the forty-two-year-old secretary of the Ba'ath party in Lebanon, was shot to death by machine gun fire near the Beirut International Airport.

On July 30, 1980, **Galip Ozmel**, the Turkish attache in Athens since 1977, was shot and killed in the Athens suburb of Pangrati.

Gen. Enrique Briz Armengol (1916–80), a Spanish logistics officer, was shot and killed on September 2, 1980, by gunmen in Barcelona, Spain. His assassins were thought to be members of the October First Revolutionary Antifascist Group (GRAPO), a left-wing terrorist organization.

Felix Garcia Rodriguez, a Cuban attache at the United Nations, was shot and killed in New York City while driving in his car on September 11, 1980. An anti–Castro terrorist group was believed responsible for the murder.

On September 17, 1980, **Anastasio Somoza Debayle**, the deposed ruler of Nicaragua, was killed by bazooka and machine gun fire while in exile in Asuncion, Paraguay. Somoza was born on December 5, 1925, in Leon, Nicaragua. Somoza's father, Anastasio Somoza Garcia (q.v.), had ruled Nicaragua from 1937 until his assassination in 1956, and his older brother, Luis, had served as Nicaragua's president from 1956 until 1963. Anastasio Somoza himself became president on May 1, 1967, and ruled the country in fact, if not in name, until his ouster by the Sandinista National Liberation Front on July 17, 1979. Somoza was widely criticized during his reign for human rights abuses and corruption. The years of his rule were marked by a bloody civil war that eventually resulted in his exile. He settled in Paraguay, the scene of his assassination.

Political violence from the left and the right resulted in the death of many prominent El Salvadorans during 1980. **Maria Magdalena Henriquez**, the El Salvadoran Human Rights Commission's spokeswoman, was found murdered near San Salvador on October 7. She had been kidnapped in downtown San Salvador on October 3 by right-wing gunmen.

On October 9, 1980, leftist terrorists executed **Archibald Gardner Dunn**, the South African ambassador to El Salvador. Dunn had been kidnapped on November 28, 1979, by members of the Popular Liberation Forces guerrilla group, and was killed following the El Salvadoran government's refusal to negotiate with the kidnappers.

Melvin Rigoberto Orellana, the El Salvadoran Christian Democratic party's chief spokesman, was shot and killed by the leftist Popular Liberation Forces on October 10, 1980, near his home in the capital. Right-wing gunmen shot and killed **Ramon Valladares**, the administrator of El Salvador's Human Rights Commission, on October 26, in San Salvador, and **Felix Antonio Ulloa**, the rector of the University of El Salvador, was shot and killed on October 29. **Manuel De Jesus Rivas Rodriguez**, El Salvadoran business leader and director of El Salvador's International Trade Fair, was assassinated on November 3.

On November 27, 1980, the bodies of six prominent El Salvadoran leftists were found near the capital following their kidnapping during a meeting. The dead included **Enrique Alvarez Cordoba**, the leader of the Democratic Revolutionary Front (FDR); **Juan Chacon**, leader of the Popular Revolutionary Bloc; **Manuel Franco** of the Communist National Democratic Union; **Enrique Barrera**, a member of the National Revolutionary Movement; **Humberto Mendoza**, a member of the Popular Liberation Movement; and **Donoteo Hernandez**, a labor union leader. The Maximilian Hernandez Brigade, a right-wing terrorist organization, claimed responsibility for the killings.

On December 4, 1980, the bodies of three American nuns and one lay worker were found outside of San Salvador. The dead included **Sister Dorothy Kazel**, forty; **Sister Ita Ford**, forty; **Sister Maura Clarke**, forty-six; and **Jean Donovan**, twenty-seven. The four had been shot and strangled. The murderers were thought to be right-wing extremist members of the El Salvadoran army.

On November 16, 1980, **Eduardo Garcia**, the Dominican Republic's ambassador to Colombia, was shot to death in Bogota by Rafael Sanchez, the Dominican consul. The Colombian police indicated the killing was not politically motivated.

Sultan Ibraimov (1927–80), the premier of the Khirgiz Soviet Socialist Republic in the Soviet Union, was killed while sleeping at a sanitorium near the capital city of Frunz on December 4, 1980.

On December 8, 1980, **John Lennon**, a British composer, musician and a founding member of the Beatles, was shot to death in front of his New York apartment by Mark David Chapman. Lennon was born in Liverpool, England, on October 9, 1940. When he was seventeen he organzied the Quarrymen, his first rock group. In the late 1950s he joined with Paul McCartney, George Harrison, and eventually Ringo Starr to form the Beatles. In the early 1960s these four musicians became one of the most popular musical phenomena of all time. Lennon was lead singer, lyricist and composer for the group and was known as a social and political activist during the late 1960s. He was also an outspoken proponent of the peace movement. In 1970 the Beatles disbanded but Lennon continued to write and record music until 1975. He then spent five years in retirement to be with his wife, Japanese artist and musician Yoko Ono, and their son, Sean. In 1980 he began recording again, only to have his career cut short by his murder.

Sarik Ariyak, the Turkish consul general in Sydney, Australia, was shot to death in his car on December 17, 1980. The shooting was believed to be the work of Armenian terrorists.

On December 27, 1980, **Darwich El-Zouni**, an associate of Syrian President Hafez al-Assad, was assassinated in Damascus. El-Zouni, fifty-six, was a leading member of the Unionist Socialist party of Syria.

Gen. Enrico Calvaligi, the deputy commander of northern Italy's Carabinieri anti-terrorist force, was shot to death in Rome on December 31, 1980. Calvaligi, sixty-one, was also the security director of the maximum security prison where most convicted terrorists were being held.

1981

On January 3, 1981, two Americans involved in El Salvador's land redistribution program and the head of the country's agrarian program were shot to death by gunmen in a hotel coffee shop in San Salvador. **Michael P. Hammer**, forty-two, of Potomac, Md.; **Mark David Pearlman**, thirty-six, of Seattle; and **Jose Rodolfo Viera**, thirty-five, the president of El Salvador's Institute for Agrarian Transformation, were the victims. Hammer and Pearlman were affiliated with the American Institute for Free Labor Development in Washington, D.C. Hammer had been involved with the institute for seventeen years and was regarded as an expert on agrarian affairs in South and Central America. Pearlman had spent the previous seven months in El Salvador in an attempt to design a workable land redistribution program. The assassinations were thought to be the work of right-wing death squads who were in violent opposition to land redistribution.

On January 12, 1981, **Hammad Abu Rabia** (1929–81), a Bedouin member of the Israeli Knesset, was assassinated in Jerusalem. Rabia had been a member of the Knesset since 1974.

Artemio Camargo, a leader of the Bolivian Tin Miners Union; **Jose Reyes Carvajal** and **Arcil Menacho**, both former Bolivian national deputies;

and four university professors were found dead on January 15, 1981, after having been arrested by Bolivian police in La Paz. The slain leftist leaders were thought to have been executed by the Bolivian police under the command of Col. Luis Arce Gomez, the interior minister.

Bernadette Devlin McAliskey (b. 1947), a militant Irish political activist, was seriously wounded in an assassination attempt on January 16, 1981. Mrs. McAliskey and her husband, Michael, were shot by militant Protestant terrorists at their home in County Tyrone, Ireland.

On January 21, 1981, **Sir Norman Stronge** (1895–1981), a leading Protestant and former speaker of the Stormont, Northern Ireland's parliament, was shot to death with his son, **James Stronge**, at his home in Tynan Abbey castle in South Armagh. The killings were thought to be the work of the Irish Republican Army, who destroyed the castle with explosives. Stronge had been speaker of the Stormont from 1945 to 1969.

President Ahmed Sekou Toure (1922–84) of Guinea was the target of an unsuccessful assassination attempt at the Conakry airport on February 20, 1981.

On March 2, 1981, **Tariq Rahim**, a Pakistani diplomat, was shot and killed while aboard a Pakistan International Airlines plane that was hijacked by a terrorist group led by the son of Zulfikar Ali Bhutto (q.v.), Pakistan's executed former president. The plane was taken to Kabul, Afghanistan, where the remaining passengers were released following negotiations with the Pakistani government.

Two Turkish diplomats, **Tecelli Ari** and **Resat Morali**, were shot by Armenian terrorists in Paris on March 4, 1981, as they were leaving the Turkish Embassy there. Ari was killed instantly in the attack, and Morali died a short time later.

On March 7, 1981, **Chester Bitterman**, a United States Bible translator working with the Summer Institute of Linguistics, was murdered by leftist guerrillas in Bogota, Colombia. Bitterman, who had been kidnapped in January, was accused of being a United States Central Intelligence Agency agent.

President Ronald Reagan (b. 1911) of the United States was shot in the chest on March 30, 1981, outside of the Washington Hilton Hotel after giving an address to a labor group. He was immediately rushed to a hospital and, after undergoing surgery, recovered from his injuries. The attempted assassin was identified as John W. Hinckley, Jr., twenty-five. Presidential press secretary James S. Brady was critically injured in the attack, and Secret Service agent Timothy J. McCarthy and District of Columbia police officer Thomas Delahanty were also seriously wounded. All the of the victims survived the assault. Hinckley was tried for the assassination attempt but found not guilty due to insanity. The court ordered him committed to a mental institution.

Heinz Nittel (1931–81), a leader of the Austrian Socialist party and the president of the Austrian-Israeli Friendship League, was shot to death on May 1, 1981, outside his Vienna home. Nittel was the transportation minister for the regional government in Vienna.

On May 4, 1981, **Brig. Gen. Andres Gonzalez De Suso** was shot to death outside of his apartment in Madrid. The assassins were thought to be members of GRAPO, a Maoist terrorist group.

Heinz Herbert Karry (1920–81), the minister of economic affairs in Hesse, West Germany, and the state deputy prime minister, was shot to death while sleeping at his home in Frankfurt on May 11, 1981. Karry was a member of the Free Democratic party and had recently been involved in supporting the construction of new atomic power plants.

Pope John Paul II (b. 1920) was shot and seriously wounded on May 13, 1981, in Rome. The pope was struck by two bullets which were fired at him as he was being driven through a crowd in St. Peters' Square. He was immediately rushed to the hospital, where he underwent surgery for the partial removal of his intestines. Following a long hospital stay the pope eventually recovered. The assassin was identified as Mehmet Ali Agca, twenty-three, a Turk, who was convicted of the crime and sentenced to life imprisonment. Ali Agca had previously been convicted of the murder of a moderate Turkish newspaper editor, Abdi Ipekci, on February 1, 1979. There was speculation that a wider conspiracy involving the Bulgarian Secret Service existed. Several Bulgarians were indicted in that regard, and tried for complicity in the shooting.

Ziaur Rahman (1936–81), the president of Bangladesh, was murdered on May 30, 1981, during an unsuccessful coup attempt. President Zia, two aides, and several bodyguards were shot to death while sleeping in a guest house in Chittagong. Zia had assumed power in Bangladesh in 1975 and was elected president in 1977. Though Bangladesh remained one of the world's poorest nations, Zia was given credit for having brought about some reforms and stability to his nation. Vice President Abdus Sattar took office as president shortly after the assassination and succeeded in putting down the revolt. On June 2, 1981, it was reported that **Maj. Gen. Manzur Ahmed**, the leader of the coup, and two other high-ranking officers were killed by enraged guards following their arrest.

On June 1, 1981, **Naim Khader**, an official of the Palestine Liberation Organization, was shot to death in Brussels, Belgium, while on his way to work. Khader had been working in the PLO's Brussels office since 1976 as a lobbyist for the PLO in the Common Market. Khader, a moderate, was killed by a lone gunman who shot him at close range. The assassination was speculated to be the work of either the Israeli Secret Service or Arab extremists.

On June 22, 1981, following the ouster of Abolhassan Bani-Sadr as president of Iran, a number of his supporters were executed as "counter-revolutionaries." Among the thirty-two people shot by a firing squad were **Saeed Soltanpur**, a poet and playwright; **Ali-Ashghar Amirani**, editor and publisher of a biweekly news magazine critical of the government; and **Borzu Abbasi Shirin-Abadai**, who was said to have been the head of Savak, the deposed shah's secret police. Shirin-Abadai was also thought to have participated in the 1954 coup that had returned the shah to the throne. Between June and October over 2,000 more executions took place in Iran.

Hojatolislam Mohammed Ali Khameini, a leading Iranian defense adviser to the Ayatollah Khomeini, was seriously injured in a bomb blast while he was addressing a crowd in a Teheran mosque on June 27, 1981. Khameini recovered from his injuries.

Other Iranian leaders were less fortunate on the following day as an explosion on June 28, 1981, ripped the offices of the Islamic Republican party in Teheran, resulting in the deaths of over thirty people. Included among the dead were chief justice **Ayatollah Mohammed Beheshti**, environmental minister **Dr. Mohammed Ali Fayazbaksh**, deputy commerce minister **Assadolah Zadeh**, transport minister **Musa Kalantari**, and **Hojatoleslam Mohammed Montazeri**, a Teheran prayer leader and member of the Iranian parliament. Other victims included two other members of the Iranian cabinet, eight deputy ministers and nearly two dozen members of the Majlis (parliament). More than seventy other party members were injured in the bomb blast that occurred while Beheshti, the party leader, was addressing the assembly. The explosive device was placed near the speaker's podium during a meeting called to select a new Iranian president following the ouster of Abolhassan Bani-Sadr.

Ayatollah Mohammad Hossein Beheshti was born in 1929 in Isfahan, Iran. Beheshti had served as a member of Iran's ruling Islamic Revolutionary Council since February 3, 1979, and became the first secretary of the Council shortly thereafter. Beheshti was a close advisor to Ayatollah Ruhollah Khomeini and had played a leading role during the seizure of the

American Embassy in Teheran and the subsequent hostage crisis. Shortly before his death Beheshti had orchestrated the ouster of Iranian president Abolhassan Bani-Sadr. He was in the process of selecting Bani-Sadr's replacement at the time of his death.

Political violence continued in Iran throughout the remainder of the year. During the period of July 8–15, 1981, over forty leftists and supporters of deposed president Bani-Sadr were executed. The slain included **Karim Dastmalchi** and **Ahmad Javameriyan**, both prominent Teheran businessmen and members of the Teheran Bazaar, a group of merchants who had helped finance the ouster of the shah in 1979.

On July 23, 1981, **Hojatolislam Seyyed Hassan Beheshti**, the nephew of the assassinated Ayatollah Beheshti (q.v.), was himself killed at his home in Isfahan. The younger Beheshti was a candidate for the Majlis at the time of his death. **Hassan Ayat**, a member of the ruling Islamic Republic party and one of its leading theoreticians, was shot and killed in Teheran on August 5, 1981. **Saleh Khosravi**, a mullah from Sanandaj, Iran, was assassinated with his son while leaving a mosque on August 16, 1981.

The rash of assassinations and political killings culminated on August 30, 1981, when a bomb exploded in the office of Iranian premier **Mohammed Jad Bahonar**. Bahonar, President **Mohammed Ali Raja'i**, Col. **Houshang Dastgerdi** of the national police, and five others died as a result of the explosion. The Mujahedeen-i-Khaq, a leftist guerrilla group and the leading opposition front to the Ayatollah Khomeini's regime, was considered to be responsible for this and other attacks on the Iranian leadership. It was later announced by Teheran radio that **Massoud Kashmiri**, a secretary to Prime Minister Bahonar, was directly involved in the placing of the bomb. Kashmiri had also died in the explosion.

President Raja'i was born in 1933 in Kazvin, Iran. Raja'i, a former bricklayer and teacher, became actively involved in opposition to the rule of the shah during the 1970s. He had served time in the shah's prisons and had reportedly been subjected to torture by the shah's secret police. Following the fall of the shah in the 1979 Revolution, Raja'i became minister of education. The following year he was appointed prime minister by President Bani Sadr. Raja'i became a leading spokesman for the fundamental Moslem extremists against the leadership of President Bani-Sadr, and following the ouster of the latter in June of 1981 Raja'i assumed the office of the presidency himself.

Premier Bahonar was born in 1933 in Kerman, Iran. Bahonar, who had been imprisoned during the reign of the shah, was instrumental in the writing of Iran's constitution following the shah's ouster in 1979. He succeeded Mohammad Ali Raja'i as minister of education in 1981 and succeeded Ayatollah Mohammad Hossein Beheshti (q.v.) as leader of the Islamic Republic party when Beheshti died in an explosion in June of 1981. Bahonar also succeeded Raja'i as Iran's prime minister following the removal of President Bani-Sadr and the assumption of that position by Raja'i.

On August 31, 1981, **Hojatolislam Nasser Jamali**, a court officer in Teheran, and clergyman **Hojatolislam Mortraza Ayatollahi Tabataba Yazdi** were assassinated in Teheran. On September 5, another bomb explosion killed **Hojatolislam Ali Qoddousi**, the Iranian revolutionary prosecutor general. On September 11 **Ayatollah Assadollah Madani**, a leading advisor to Ayatollah Khomeini, was assassinated during a grenade attack in Tabriz, the capital of the Iranian East Azerbaijan province. Seven others were killed during the attack, including the assassin, who had rushed Madani while holding a hand grenade. **Hojatolislam Abdulkarim Hashemi Nejad**, an Iranian parliament member, was also killed in a suicide grenade attack on September 29. Nejad was the Islamic Republic party's secretary general in Meshed, Iran.

On December 11, 1981, **Ayatollah Abdol-Hossein Dastgheib** (1912–81), the Ayatollah Khomeini's representative in Shiraz, was killed with seven others during a bomb attack at his home. Two other supporters of the Ayatollah Khomeini, **Mojtaba Ozbaki**, a member of the Iranian parliament from Shahr-I-Kourd in central Iran, and **Gholamali Jaaffarzzadeh**, the governor of Meshed, were slain by grenades in Meshed on December 22. The two were traveling in a motorcade toward a Shiite Moslem holy shrine when they were attacked by two grenade-wielding men on a motorcycle.

In other parts of the world political violence also continued during the year. On July 3, 1981, **Chen Wen-Cheng**, a professor at Carnegie-Mellon University in Pittsburgh, was found dead on the campus of the National Taiwan University. Chen's death occurred following an interrogation by Taiwan security forces regarding his association with a Taiwan independence movement in the United States. The United States State Department requested a full investigation of Chen's death.

On July 6, 1981, the body of **Giuseppe Taliercio**, an Italian executive of the Montredison petrochemical works, was found in the trunk of an automobile near his business. Taliercio had been kidnapped by Red Brigade terrorists in May of 1981.

Thomas Weh Syen, Liberia's deputy head of state, and four other members of the ruling People's Redemption Council were executed on August 14, 1981, following an unsuccessful coup attempt against Samuel Doe, the nation's leader. The executed men had all been supporters of Doe when he seized power in the 1980 coup that deposed President William Tolbert (q.v.).

On September 4, 1981, **Louis Delamare** (1922–81), the French ambassador to Lebanon, was shot and killed while driving in West Beirut. Delamare had served in Lebanon since 1979, and had previously held diplomatic positions in Romania, Turkey and Tunisia. He had served as France's ambassador to Dahomey (Benim) from 1969 to 1975, and was the French Foreign Ministry's director of press information from 1975 until assuming his post in Lebanon.

On September 15, 1981, Gen. Frederick Kroesen, the commander-in-chief of United States forces in Europe, was slightly injured when an anti-tank grenade struck the car he was riding in near his Heidelberg, West Germany, headquarters.

Anwar As-Sadat, the president of Egypt, was assassinated during a military parade on October 6, 1981, by a group of commandos who charged the reviewing stand with grenades and machine guns. At least eight other members of Sadat's party were killed, including the president's private secretary, chief chamberlain, and official photographer. A delegate from Oman was also slain. The Belgian and Irish ambassadors to Egypt, leading Coptic clergyman Bishop Samuel and three American military observers were among the dozens injured. The attack was led by Lt. Khaled Ahmed al-Istambouly. Istambouly and four others were indicted and convicted of direct participation in the attack. Twenty other Egyptians were also indicted for conspiracy, including Aboud el-Zoumar, who was considered the leader of the conspiracy, and Sheik Omar Abdel Rahman, a mufti from Asyut, Egypt. The assassination was intended to install a Moslem religious government with Sheik Rahman as head of state. Sadat was succeeded by his vice president, Hosni Mubarak, who vowed to continue Sadat's domestic and foreign policies.

Anwar Sadat was born in the Nile Delta of Egypt on December 25, 1918. He graduated from the Cairo Royal Military Academy in 1938 and was active during World War II in the movement to liberate Egypt from British rule. In 1942 he was arrested by the British on charges of being a spy for Germany, but escaped shortly thereafter. In 1945 Sadat was again arrested and charged with complicity in an attempt to assassinate Nahas Pasha, then prime minister of Egypt. Sadat joined Gamal Abdel Nasser's Free Officers in 1950 and was active in the ouster of King Farouk in 1952. During Nasser's rule Sadat served in numerous governmental positions including minister of state from 1955 to 1956, chairman of the national assembly from 1961 to 1969, and speaker of the national assembly from 1961 to 1969. Sadat also served two terms as Egypt's vice president, the first from 1964 to 1966 and the second from 1969 until Nasser's death in 1970. At that time Sadat succeeded Nasser to the presidency as interim president and was subsequently elected to the position in October of 1970.

Early in his presidency Sadat began a policy ending Egypt's military assistance by the Soviet Union and began seeking closer ties with the United States. In October of 1973 Sadat resumed armed conflict with Israel, and succeeded in crossing the Suez Canal with Egyptian troops. In November of 1977 Sadat took a major step toward peace in the Middle East by accepting the invitation of Israeli prime minister Menachem Begin to address the Knesset (parliament) of Israel. During the next several years Sadat and Begin began a series of negotiations which, with the assistance of United States president Jimmy Carter, culminated in March 1979 at Camp David, Maryland, with the signing of the Israeli-Egyptian peace treaty. Sadat and Begin were joint recipients of the 1978 Nobel Peace Prize for their achievements toward ending the strife in the Middle East. Sadat's actions were viewed with much hostility throughout most of the Arab world. Civil unrest at home also plagued the later years of his rule, as Moslem fundamentalists began actively to seek his removal from office. This was accomplished when President Sadat was slain in an armed attack on his reviewing stand as he watched a military parade pass by.

Majed Abu Shrar, a leading member of the Palestine Liberation Organization, died in a bomb explosion in his hotel room in Rome, Italy, on October 9, 1981.

Mohinder Paul, leader of the opposition Janata party in India, was assassinated by Sikh assassins in Punjab on October 23, 1981.

The Rev. Robert John Bradford (1941–81), a Northern Ireland politician and Methodist clergyman, was shot and killed by Irish Republican Army gunmen in Belfast on November 14, 1981. He became the first member of the United Kingdom Parliament from Northern Ireland to be assassinated. The Rev. Bradford was a leading Protestant politician in Northern Ireland. He was first elected to the Northern Ireland Assembly in 1973 and served as a member of the Official Unionist party from South Belfast in the United Kingdom Parliament from 1975. He was a leading opponent of the Irish Republican Army and an advocate of the death sentence for convicted terrorists.

On December 18, 1981, **Mehmet Shehu**, the premier of Albania, who was considered to be a potential successor to Albanian Communist party chairman Enver Hoxha, was reported to have committed suicide. Speculation indicated that Shehu may have been executed instead. Shehu was born in Corush, Albania, on January 10, 1913. He was expelled from the Naples (Italy) Military Academy in the late 1930s for his Communist sympathies, and later fought in the Spanish Civil War. Shehu fought with an Albanian partisan unit during World War II, and became chief of staff of the Albanian army following the war. He became a close associate of Albanian Communist party leader Enver Hoxha, and served as a member of the party's Politburo from 1948, also serving as minister of the interior until 1954, when he became premier. The absence of a state funeral indicated that Shehu's cause of death may have been the result of an execution following his fall from power rather than suicide, as had been officially announced.

1982

Lt. Col. Charles Robert Ray, a forty-three-year-old United States military attache to the American Embassy in Paris, was shot dead outside his home on January 18, 1982, by a lone gunman. A Beirut terrorist organization called the Lebanese Armed Revolutionary Faction claimed responsibility for the assassination.

On January 28, 1982, **Kemal Arikan** (1928–82), the Turkish consul general in Los Angeles, was assassinated by two gunmen while he sat in his car at a busy intersection. An Armenian terrorist group, the Justice Commandos of the Armenian Genocide, claimed responsibility for the killing. Arikan was the twentieth Turkish diplomat slain by Armenian terrorists in the past ten years.

On May 4, 1982, **Orham Gunduzi**, the honorary Turkish consul general in New England, was shot to death in Somerville, Massachusetts. His assailant was also believed to be an Armenian.

On March 12, 1982, **Sgt. Maj. Willem Hawker**, the leader of an unsuccessful rebellion in Suriname in 1981, was executed by the ruling national military council.

Ali Hajem Sultan, the third secretary of the Iraqi Embassy in Beirut, Lebanon, was assassinated by three gunmen in the Lebanese Christian-dominated suburb of Hazmiye on March 22, 1982.

Benedicto Santos, the chief of the Guatemalan National Police Command Six, was shot and killed by leftist rebels while driving near the capital of Guatemala on March 28, 1982.

Datuk Mohammad Taha Abdul Talib, the speaker of the Negri Sembilan State Assembly in Malaysia, was assassinated on April 14, 1982. Talib was a United Malays National Organization candidate for the National Assembly at the time of his murder. **Datuk Mokhtar Bin Haji Hashim**, the Malaysian federal minister of culture, youth, and sports, was charged with the killing and executed in April of 1983.

On April 26, 1982, **Sheik Ahmed Assaf**, a Lebanese Moslem religious leader, was shot to death in Moslem West Beirut.

Muhammad Seddik Ben Yahia (1932–82), the foreign minister of Algeria, died in a mysterious plane crash on May 3, 1982. Ben Yahia, who had been instrumental in negotiating the release of American hostages from Iran in 1981, was on a diplomatic mission to seek a solution to the war between Iraq and Iran. It was speculated that Ben Yahia's plane may have been deliberately shot down by a faction in Iran which did not want Ben Yahia's peace initiatives to take place.

Angel Pascual Mugica, the director of Spain's Lemoniz Nuclear Power Plant, was shot to death by Basque terrorists while driving to work on May 5, 1982.

On June 3, 1982, Shlomo Argov, Israel's ambassador to Great Britain, was seriously injured in an assassination attempt in London. Black June, a militant Palestinian terrorist group led by Abu Nidal, claimed responsibility for the attack.

Erkut Akbay, an attache at the Turkish embassy in Portugal, was shot and killed by Armenian terrorists on June 7, 1982, outside his home in Lisbon.

On June 17, 1982, **Kamal Hussein**, a Palestine Liberation Organization official in Rome, Italy, was killed in a car bomb explosion near his office. It was believed that Hussein's killers were members of a Jewish terrorist organization.

Koenyame Chakela, the secretary general of the outlawed Basotho Congress party of Lesotho, was shot and killed in July of 1982.

On July 23, 1982, the deputy director of the Palestine Liberation Organization's office in Paris, **Fadel El-Dani** (1944–82), was killed by a bomb blast outside his Paris home.

On August 4, 1982, **Romiro Ponce**, the mayor of San Lorenzo, El Salvador, was killed by leftist guerrillas.

Ruth First (1925–82), a South African political activist and writer, was killed on August 17, 1982, by a letter bomb sent to her office at the Centre for African Studies in Maputo, Mozambique. First had been a leading opponent of South Africa's apartheid system, and was a member of the banned Revolutionary Council of the African National Congress. She had been imprisoned by the South African government in the early 1960s, and had lived in exile in Mozambique since 1978.

Col. Atilla Altikat, a Turkish military attache in Ottawa, Canada, was shot and killed by Armenian terrorists while driving to work on August 27, 1982.

Gen. Carlos Alberto Dalla Chiesa, one of Italy's highest ranking police officers, was shot and killed in Palermo, Sicily, on September 3, 1982. Dalla Chiesa, as prefect of police for Palermo, was a leading figure in the fight against the Mafia in Italy.

Zahoorul Hasan Bhopali, a member of the Pakistani Federal Council, was slain by gunmen at his office on September 13, 1982.

On September 14, 1982, President-elect **Bashir Gemayel** of Lebanon was killed in a bomb blast which leveled the headquarters of his Lebanese Christian Phalangist party in Beirut. Bashir Gemayel was born on November 10, 1947, in Beirut. He was the sixth son of Pierre Gemayel, the leader and founder of the Phalangist party. He studied law in the United States and became active in politics on his return to Lebanon. During the Lebanese Civil War of 1975–76, Gemayel became known as a fierce and ruthless leader of the Christian militias in their fight against Palestinians and Moslems. In the following years Gemayel continued conducting an armed struggle against his foes, as well as against fellow Christian militia rivals. He had twice before been the target of assassination attempts. The second attempt, on February 23, 1980, resulted in the death of his eighteen-month-old daughter, Maya, in a car bombing. When Lebanese president Elias Sarkis announced his retirement in mid–1982, Gemayel became a candidate for the presidency. With the tacit support of Israel, Gemayel was elected by the Lebanese parliament on August 23, 1982. At 34 he would have become Lebanon's youngest president had he survived until his inauguration later in the month. Amid the continuing deterioration of the political situation in Lebanon the parliament selected Gemayel's older brother, Amin, as the new president.

Brig. Saad Sayel (1929–82), known as **Abu Walid**, was killed by gunmen near Beirut, Lebanon, on September 28, 1982. Walid was a leading military strategist for the PLO and had organized resistance to the Israeli siege of Lebanon.

On October 15, 1982, **Ayatollah Ashrafi Isfahani** (1899–1982), was killed by a grenade blast in Bahtaran, Iran. Isfahani was the Ayatollah Khomeini's special representative in the Bahtaran Province. The attacker, who was also killed in the blast, was thought to be a member of the underground People's Mujahedeen guerillas.

Gen. Victor Lago Roman, sixty-three-year-old Spanish commander of the elite Brunete First Armored Division in Madrid, was shot to death by machine gun fire on November 4, 1982.

1983

Ahmed Dlimi (1931–83), a leading military advisor to King Hassan II of Morocco, was killed in a car crash on January 25, 1983, in Marrakesh. Dlimi was in charge of the Moroccan army's operations against the Polisario Front in the Western Sahara at the time of his death. While serving as Morocco's security chief in the 1960s, Dlimi had been tried and acquitted by a French court for the abduction of Moroccan exile leader Mehdi Ben Bella (q.v.) in Paris in 1965. It was speculated that Dlimi may have been involved in the conspiracy against King Hassan, and that he may have been assassinated.

In March of 1983, **Attati Mpakati**, an opponent of Malawi president Hastings Banda, was assassinated in Zimbabwe.

Issam Sartawi, a moderate leader of the Palestine Liberation Organization, was shot to death in his hotel lobby on April 10, 1983, while attending a meeting of the Socialist International in Portugal. Sartawi was born in Palestine in 1935. He was a heart surgeon working in the United States in 1967, but following the Arab-Israeli War, he returned to the Middle East to join the Palestine Liberation Organization's guerrilla wing, Al-Fatah. His militancy toward Israel declined over the years, and Sartawi became one of the leading voices of moderation in the PLO. A close adviser to PLO chairman Yasir Arafat, Sartawi was one of the few Palestinian leaders to openly advocate Palestinian co-existence with Israel. The Revolutionary Council of the Fatah (or Black June group), led by terrorist leader Abu Nidal, claimed responsibility for the killing.

Dick Matenje, the secretary general of the Malawi Congress party, was killed with three other political leaders in an automobile accident on May 22, 1983. **Aaron Gadama**, the minister of the central region; **John Sangala**, a former minister of health; and **David Chiwanga**, a former member of Parliament, were also killed. Matenje was thought to be a potential rival to President Hastings K. Banda, and some claimed that Matenje and the others had been killed following an unsuccessful coup attempt.

On August 21, 1983, **Benigno Simeon Aquino, Jr.**, a leading opponent of President Ferdinand Marcos of the Philippines, was shot and killed as he was deboarding an airplane at the Manila airport. Aquino was born in Tarlac, the Philippines, on November 27, 1932. In 1955, following a career as a journalist, Aquino was elected mayor of Concepcion. He became governor of Tarlac Province in 1961, following two years as vice governor. In 1966 he became the secretary general of the Liberal party, and the following year he became the only member of his party to win a seat in the Senate. Aquino was viewed as a potential rival to the presidency of Ferdinand Marcos, but was imprisoned following Marcos' declaration of martial law on September 23, 1972. Aquino was sentenced to death and served eight years in prison. In 1980 he was allowed to travel to the United States for open-heart surgery. He remained in the United States for the next three years, until deciding to return to the Philippines in the summer of 1983. Aquino, who had received death threats prior to his arrival, was shot and killed on the heavily guarded tarmac as he left the plane at Manila Airport. His alleged assassin, Rolando Galman, was immediately killed by security guards. A number of high-ranking army officers were subsequently implicated for complicity in the assassination of Aquino, including armed forces chief of staff Gen. Fabian Ver and airport security chief Brig. Gen. Luther Custodio, but charges were never substantiated. The killing of Aquino led to increased pressure on the government of Ferdinand Marcos, culminiating in his defeat as president by Aquino's widow, Corazon, in early 1985.

A bomb attack in Burma on October 9, 1983, killed nineteen people, including six top aides to South Korean president Chun Doo Hwan. The bomb exploded when South Korean officials, on a state visit to Burma, were lined up at Rangoon's national cemetery. Chun escaped death in the blast due to his motorcade's delay in traffic. Among those killed were **Lee Bum-Suk** (1925–83), South Korean foreign minister and a former ambassador to Tunisia and India; **Kim Jae-Ik** (1938–83), a senior presidential economic adviser who was the architect of South Korea's economic liberalism; **Kim Dong-Whie** (1932–83), South Korean minister of commerce and industry and former ambassador to Iran; **Suh Sang Chul** (1935–83), the minister of energy and resources; **Suh Suk-Joon** (1938–83), deputy premier and economic planning minister; and **Hahm Pyong-Choon** (1932–83), chief secretary. The South Korean ambassador to Burma was also among the dead. The seriously injured included Lee Kee-Baek, chairman of the joint chiefs of staff, and Lee Ki-uk, the vice finance minister. The South Korean government blamed the attack on North Korean terrorists.

Political violence in El Salvador escalated on October 10, 1983, with the murder of **Victor Manuel Quintanilla**, a leftist politician in El Salvador and mayor of Usulutan from 1979 to 1980. Also killed at this time were **Jose**

Antonio Garcia Vasquez, a member of the Democratic Revolutionary Front; **Santiago Hernandez**, secretary general of the Unified Labor Federation; and **Prof. Doira Munoz Castillo**, a chemistry professor at the National University. Fifteen other labor activists and three other professors had been kidnapped or killed during the previous six weeks. The Maximiliano Hernandez Martinez Anti-Communist Brigade, a rightist death squad, claimed it carried out the killings. The bodies were dumped along a highway north of San Salvador.

Another victim of right-wing violence was **Marianella Garcia Villas**, a founder of the Salvadoran Commission for Human Rights, who was murdered on March 14, 1983.

Maurice Bishop, prime minister of Grenada since 1979, was executed on October 19, 1983, after his removal from office in a coup. Others shot following the coup were foreign affairs minister **Unison Whiteman**, education minister **Jacqueline Creft**, housing minister **Norris Bain**, **Cecil Maitland**, and **Keith Hayling**. An estimated sixty other people also died during and after the coup.

Bishop was born in Grenada on May 29, 1944. While practicing law in Great Britain, Bishop became interested in the black militancy movement and returned to Grenada in 1970. He was a founder of the left-wing New Jewel Movement in 1972 along with his law partner, Bernard Coard. Bishop's group was a leading voice of opposition to Prime Minister Eric Gairy and was thus a prime target of the political violence unleased by Gairy's secret police, called the Mongoose Gang. Bishop was beaten on several occasions, and in 1974, his father, Rupert, was murdered. In 1976 Bishop was elected to the Grenada parliament, and in March of 1979, he seized power while Gairy was out of the country. Bishop was an avowed Marxist and gained financial assistance for his country from Cuba and the Soviet Union. Following an attempt by Bishop to improve relations with the United States, the more radical members of his government, including Coard and Gen. Hudson Austin, seized power and arrested Bishop and several of his aides. It was reported that Bishop was freed from house arrest by a mob of supporters, but was subsequently recaptured by the army and executed within Fort Rupert. Following the overthrow of the new government by direct American military intervention, the coup leaders were arrested. In February of 1984 eleven people were accused in Magistrates Court of conspiracy to commit an act of terrorism and causing the deaths of Bishop and the others. The accused included Bernard Coard, the Marxist deputy prime minister who led the coup attempt; his wife, Phyllis; Gen. Hudson Austin, head of the military junta; Selwyn Strachan, Bishop's minister of national mobilization; and Leon Cornwall, Grenada's ambassador to Cuba under Bishop.

Sheik Halim Takieddine (1923–83), a moderate Druze religious judge in West Beirut, Lebanon, was shot to death on December 1, 1983, by a lone assassin.

1984

Malcolm H. Kerr (1932–84), the president of the American University of Beirut, Lebanon, was shot and killed by two gunmen on January 18, 1984. Dr. Kerr, a scholar in Middle Eastern affairs, was ambushed as he stepped from an elevator leading to his office at the university.

On January 21, 1984, **Amar Tagazy**, the Libyan ambassador to Italy, was shot and mortally wounded by two gunmen near his home in Rome. Tagazy died of his injuries on February 10.

Giuseppe Fava (1925–84), an Italian novelist and journalist who was a prominent critic of organized crime, was found murdered in his car in Catania, Sicily, on January 5, 1984.

On January 27, 1984, **Ricardo Arnoldo Pohl**, a member of El Salvador's Constituent Assembly, was shot to death. Pohl, a rightist, was ambushed by two gunmen while driving in San Salvador.

Spanish **Lt. Gen. Guillermo Quintana Lacaci** (1917–84), the retired military commander of Madrid, was shot and killed by two Basque terrorists near his home in Madrid on January 29, 1984.

Ravindra Mhatre, the assistant Indian high commissioner in Birmingham, England, was kidnapped on February 3, 1984, by members of the Kashmir Liberation Army. Mhatre's abductors demanded the release of condemned Kasahmiri separatist leader **Maqbool Butt**. When the demands were not met, Mhatre was murdered by his kidnappers on February 5. Butt, who was under a sentence of death in New Delhi, was subsequently hanged on February 11.

Gen. Gholam Ali Oveisi, an exiled Iranian army officer, was shot to death on a Paris street on February 7, 1984, by an unidentified gunman. Oveisi, who had served as a leading military adviser to the deposed shah of Iran, was the head of an exile organization hostile to the government of the Ayatollah Khomeini.

Khalifa Ahmed Abdel Aziz Al-Mubarak (1944–84), the United Arab Emirates ambassador to France since 1980, was shot and killed near his apartment in Paris on February 8, 1984. The Arab Revolutionary Brigade claimed responsibility for the assassination.

On February 23, 1984, **Enrique Casas Vila**, a Basque Socialist party senator in Spain, was murdered. The killing was thought to be the work of an extreme faction of Basque terrorists.

Kenneth Whitty (1939–84), the British consul's assistant cultural representative in Athens, Greece, was shot to death on March 28, 1984, while driving in downtown Athens. His lone assailant was thought to be an Arab.

Joaquim Alfaredo Zapata Romero (1925–84), the highest ranking Salvadoran employee at the United States Embassy in El Salvador, was shot and killed by leftist rebels near San Salvador on April 16, 1984. The rebel group FPB claimed that Zapata was the chieftan of right-wing death squads which acted in conjunction with the United States Embassy.

Colombian Minister of Justice **Rodrigo Lara Bonilla** was shot and killed on April 30, 1984, in northern Bogota. His assassination was believed to be the result of his efforts to eradicate the drug traffic in Colombia.

On May 3, 1984, **Hanna Moqbell**, the forty-two-year-old secretary general of the Arab Journalists Union, was shot and killed in Nicosia, Cyprus. Moqbell was a prominent opponent of PLO leader Yasir Arafat.

Manuel Buendia Tellez Giron, a prominent Mexican journalist, was shot to death on May 30, 1981, in Mexico City on the way home from his office. Buendia, fifty-eight, was the author of "Red Privada" ("Private Network") in the Mexican daily *Excelsior*. He had frequently been responsible for exposure of corruption in politics, labor and business during his thirty-five-year career. At the time of his assassination he was engaged in writing a series of articles on Mexico's oil industry.

On June 18, 1984, radio talk show host **Alan Berg** was shot and killed outside his home in Denver, Colorado. Berg, fifty, was a former criminal lawyer who had gained a large following as a controversial host of a radio call-in program. Berg's murder was perpetrated by a member of an extremist anti-Semitic group.

Jarnail Singh Bhindranwale, a Sikh extremist leader, was killed during an Indian army attack on the Golden Temple, the holiest of Sikh shrines, in Amritsar, Punjab, on June 6, 1984. Jarnail Singh Bhindranwale was born in the Faridkot District of Punjab, India, in 1946, and began his religious education at an early age. He was adopted by Kartar Singh Bhindranwale, a Sikh leader, and assumed his name and title when he died in 1977. Bhindranwale became actively involved in Sikh extremism in 1980 and was charged in connection with the murder of moderate Sikhs. After his surrender to Indian authorities, and subsequent release three weeks later, Bhindranwale challenged the Indian government to grant autonomy to the Punjab region. On May 31, 1984, he openly rebelled against the government by threatening to withhold food and power produced in the Punjab from the rest of India. The Indian army was sent by Prime Minister Indira Gandhi (q.v.) to crush the uprising. Bhindranwale was killed with hundreds of his followers when the army entered the Golden Temple at Amritsar.

Brig. R.S. Puri, a leading Indian army commander, was shot and killed in the northeastern state of Bihar on June 9, 1984. Suspected Sikh extremists assassinated **Hardyal Singh**, acting president of Indira Gandhi's Congress party in the Punjab's Jullundur district, on June 16, 1984.

The violence in India culminated on October 31, 1984, with the assassination of Prime Minister **Indira Gandhi**. She was shot and killed near her New Delhi office by her Sikh bodyguards. Indira Priyadarshini Gandhi was born in Allahabad, India, on November 19, 1917. She was the only child of Jawaharlal Nehru, India's first prime minister. In 1942, after studying in England, Mrs. Gandhi married Feroze Gandhi, against her father's wishes. This marriage later ended in divorce. In 1959 she first became prominent in political affairs with her election as president of the ruling Congress party. Following the death of her father in 1964, Mrs. Gandhi served as minister of information in the government of his successor, Lal Bahadur Shastri. When Shastri died in 1966, she became prime minister.

Mrs. Gandhi proved to be a capable and forceful politician at home and abroad. In 1971 she joined India in a successful war for independence of Bangladesh (formerly East Pakistan) from West Pakistan and, in 1971, incorporated the kingdom of Sikkim into India proper. Following a period of economic and political reversals in 1975, Mrs. Gandhi declared a state of emergency and ruled by decree. During this period she instituted a number of unpopular measures, including sterilization in over-populated areas, and arrested political opponents. In 1977 she was defeated for election and replaced by the opposition Janata party. Following her defeat she was arrested on two occasions on charges of abuse of authority. In 1980 Mrs. Gandhi again became prime minister as her Congress (I) party defeated the Janata party. That same year saw the death of her elder son and potential successor, Sanjay Gandhi, in an aircraft accident.

Her greatest threat during her later years in office came from the Punjab region, where militant Sikhs agitated for an autonomous state. The unrest culminated in an attack by the Indian army on the Golden Temple, the Sikhs' holiest shrine, in Amritsar, resulting in the death of Sikh extremist leader Sant Jarnail Singh Bhindranwale (q.v.) and many of his followers. Several months later, Mrs. Gandhi was assassinated by her two Sikh bodyguards while walking to her office in New Delhi. The assassins were identified as Beant Singh and Satwant Singh. Beant Singh was killed during a subsequent shoot-out with palace guards and, in January of 1986, Satwant Singh was sentenced to death. Two other Sikhs, Kehar Singh and Balbir Singh, were convicted of conspiracy and also received a death sentence. Mrs. Gandhi was succeeded by her second son, Rajiv, as prime minister.

On October 12, 1984, a bomb exploded in the Grand Hotel in Brighton, England, where the Conservative party was holding its annual meeting. British Prime Minister Margaret Thatcher, who was staying in the hotel at the time, was uninjured in the blast, which claimed the lives of **Sir Anthony Berry**, a member of parliament; **Roberta Wakeman**, the wife of Conservative party whip John Wakeman; **Jeanne Shattock**, the wife of the West England Conservative leader; and **Eric Taylor**, a Brighton party official. Over thirty other people at the hotel were injured, including John Wakeman and Norman Tebbit, the trade and industry secretary. The Irish Republican Army claimed responsibility for the attack, citing Mrs. Thatcher's policy on Northern Ireland as the reason.

Santos Hernandez (1928–84), who had served as a member of Guatemala's Constituent Assembly since July as a member of the right-wing Movement of National Liberation party, was shot to death by gunmen as he walked along a street in southern Guatemala City in October of 1984.

On October 29, 1984, the body of Polish **Rev. Jerzy Popieluszko** (1947–84) was found in the waters of a reservoir, eleven days after he had been kidnapped by secret police officers. Popieluszko had been an active anti–Communist Roman Catholic clergyman in Poland and a strong supporter of the Polish Solidarity labor movement. He was the parish priest at St. Stanislaw Kostka Church in Warsaw, and had gained much attention for his "Masses for the Homeland," which he began in January of 1982. During these services Popieluszko had used his sermon as a forum to denounce the Polish Communist authorities for their imposition of martial law or banning of trade unions. In October of 1984 Popieluszko was abducted near the town of Torun, near Warsaw. Eleven days later his brutally beaten body was found in the Wloclawek reservoir. Three secret police officers, Capt. Grzegorz Piotrowski, Lt. Waldemar Chmielewski and Lt. Leszek Pekala, were charged with the abduction and murder.

Jim Ntuta, a Zimbabwe African People's Union (ZAPU) member of Parliament in Zimbabwe, was shot and killed on his Matabeleland farm in November of 1984. Ntuta was a supporter of Joshua Nkomo.

Moven Ndlovu (1934–84), a senator and member of the Zimbabwe African National Union (ZANU), was assassinated in Beitbridge, Zimbabwe, on November 9, 1984.

Evner Ergun (1932–84), the Turkish deputy director of the United Nations Center for Social Development and Humanitarian Affairs in Vienna, Austria, was assassinated on November 18, 1984, while driving through downtown Vienna. The Armenian Revolutionary Army claimed responsibility for the killing.

Fouad Kawashmeh, the forty-eight-year-old former mayor of the Israeli-occupied West Bank town of Hebron, was shot to death in front of his home in Amman, Jordan, on December 29, 1984. Kawashmeh was an Executive Committee member for the Palestine Liberation Organization and a supporter of chairman Yasir Arafat.

1985

In January of 1985 violence broke out in the French colony of New Caledonia, an island group in the Pacific Ocean. Radical separatist Caledonians, or Kanaks, conducted a series of violent acts to drive the French into granting independence to New Caledonia. **Eloi Machoro**, a Kanak separatist leader, was killed in a shoot-out with police, and over a dozen other people died during the upheaval.

On January 11, 1985, **Domingo Aviles**, the fifty-five-year-old rightist mayor of Santa Elena, El Salvador, was assassinated by four unidentified gunmen while in his office. Aviles was a member of the National Conciliation party in El Salvador. A second rightist El Salvadorean politician was assassinated on Jaunary 18, 1985: **Graciela Monico Palma** (1960–85), mayor of San Jorge in eastern El Salvador and a member of the right-wing Nationalist Republican Alliance party, was shot to death in her office. On January 23, 1985, **Medardo Avelar Bonille**, a National Republican Alliance candidate for the National Assembly in El Salvador, was shot to death in San Salvador.

On January 25, 1985, **Rene Audran** (1930–85), a French Ministry of Defense official, was shot to death near his Paris suburb home. Audran was in charge of international arms sales. Direct Action, a left-wing guerrilla group allied with the German Red Army Faction, claimed responsibility for the assassination.

Ernst Zimmerman (1930–85), a West German armaments manufacturer, was shot and killed at his home near Munich on February 1, 1985. Zimmerman was the chief executive of the Motoren und Turbinen Union G.m.b.H., a company which supplied engines for combat planes and tanks used by NATO and the West German military. The Red Army Faction, a left-wing guerrilla organization, claimed responsibility.

On February 14, 1985, **Leamon Hunt**, the American director general of the multinational peace-keeping force in Egypt's Sinai Peninsula, was shot and killed near his apartment in Rome, which was the headquarters of the group designed to monitor observance of the Israeli-Egyptian peace treaty. The fifty-six-year-old Hunt had served in the Foreign Service for thirty-two years and was formerly assigned as charge d'affaires in Beirut, Lebanon.

Lt. Col. Ricardo Aristides Cienfuegos, the El Salvadoran army's chief spokesman, was shot to death by unidentified gunmen at a private club near San Salvador on March 7, 1985. The assassins were believed to be members of the left-wing Farabundo Marti National Liberation Front, or FMLN. This group claimed responsibility for a second high-ranking assassination on March 23, 1985, with the killing of retired **Gen. Jose Alberto Medrano**. Gen. Medrano was a former commander of the National Guard and the founder of the National Intelligence Agency and the National Democratic Organization, or Orden, which had been responsible for the killing of Salvadoran leftists in the 1970s. Medrano, a hero of the border war with Honduras in 1969, had been an unsuccessful presidential candidate in 1972.

On March 21, 1985, **Valentin Khitrichenko** (1937–85), a Soviet economic attache stationed in New Delhi, India, was assassinated by a gunman near the Soviet Embassy.

Gerardo Veracruz Berrocal, the Peruvian mayor of Pampa Cangallo in the Ayacucho department, was assassinated by left-wing Shining Path guerrillas on March 26, 1985.

Prof. Ezio Tarantelli (1942–85), an Italian labor economist, was assassinated in Rome by Red Brigade terrorists on March 27, 1985. Tarantelli was an advisor to the Italian Federation of Unionized Workers and president of the Institute of Economic Studies at Rome University.

William Buckley (1928–85), who was reportedly the Beirut station chief for the United States Central Intelligence Agency, was kidnapped in Beirut, Lebanon, on March 16, 1984. Buckley, who had been in Lebanon for several months prior to his capture, was presumed to have been in charge of reorganizing the United States' intelligence gathering network in the area. His kidnappers were identified as members of an Iranian-backed extremist group called the Islamic Jihad. On October 14, 1985, the Islamic Jihad announced that Buckley had been executed in retaliation for an Israeli raid against the Palestine Liberation Organization's headquarters in Tunisia. Though Buckley's body was not found, it was later assumed that he had perished in June of 1985, as the result of torture and lack of medical care.

Haruo I. Remeliik (1934–85), the president of the western Pacific island republic of Palau, was shot and killed on June 29, 1985, at his home in the capital city of Koror. Remeliik had become Palau's first president in January of 1981. He had been reelected to a second term in the United States trusteeship in November of 1984. Four men were arrested and charged with the assassination in July. Among those charged were Melwert Tmetuchel, the son of Roman Tmetuchel, a political rival of Remeliik; Leslie Nisang; Anghelio Sadino; and Francisco Gibbon.

On July 24, 1985, **Ziad J. Sati**, the forty-year-old first secretary of the Jordanian Embassy in Turkey, was shot to death by Shiite Moslem assassins while driving a car in Ankara, Turkey.

Vice Adm. Fausto Escrigas Estrada of the Spanish defense ministry was assassinated on July 29, 1985, by suspected Basque guerrillas while driving in downtown Madrid. The fifty-nine-year-old Escrigas was the fiftieth Spanish military officer killed by Basque terrorists since the assassination of Prime Minister Luis Carrerro Blanco (q.v.), an admiral, in 1973. Later in the day, **Agustin Ruiz**, forty-three, the deputy police chief of Vitoria, the Basque capital, was shot and killed near police headquarters by a lone gunman.

On July 31, 1985, **Lalit Maken** (1951–85), a first-term Congress (I) member of the Indian parliament and a prominent labor union leader, was shot and killed near his home in New Delhi. His wife, Geetanjali, and a party worker were also slain in the attack.
On August 20, 1985, **Dev Dutt Khullar**, a sixty-two-year-old Congress party member and Hindu village leader, was killed in an attack on the home of Gurdial Saini, the Congress party president. Saini was seriously wounded in the attack, which was believed to have been carried out by Sikh militants.

Harchand Singh Longowal, president of Akali Dal, the leading Sikh moderate party, was shot and killed by militant Sikhs in Punjab, India, on

August 20, 1985. The assailants were reported to be Malvinder Singh and Gian Singh, both of whom were arrested and charged in the slaying. Sant Harchand Singh Longowal was born in Laungowal, Punjab, India, in 1928. Longowal had joined the Akali Dal party in 1944 and had been a disciple of Mahatma Gandhi's policy of non-violent civil disobedience. In 1964 he had become president of the local chapter of the party, and in 1980 became president of the party. Longowal had been a moderate voice in the face of Sikh extremism, which culminated in militants Sikhs, under the leadership of Jarnail Singh Bhindranwale (q.v.), barricading themselves in the Golden Temple at Amritsar, and the subsequent storming of that Sikh holy shrine by Indian troops. Longowal's assassination followed the signing of an agreement with Prime Minister Rajiv Gandhi allowing Sikh autonomy for the Punjab, a move supported by the majority of Sikhs, but vehemently opposed by the extremists, who then orchestrated Longowal's assassination.

Arjun Dass, another leading Indian political figure, was shot to death on September 4, 1985, in New Delhi. Dass, a Congress (I) party member of the New Delhi city council and a supporter of Prime Minister Rajiv Gandhi, was assassinated by Sikh militants in a raid on his council office.

On August 1, 1985, **Pierre Mizael Andrianarijoana**, the leader of a Madagascan anti-government kung fu sect, was killed with nineteen of his followers in an attack by a government security force on their Antananarivo headquarters.

Albert Atrakchi (1955–85), an administrative attache at the Israeli Embassy in Cairo, Egypt, was shot to death by machine gun fire near Cairo on August 20, 1985. Atrakchi was the first Israeli diplomat slain in Egypt since diplomatic recognition was established by Egypt in 1979.

Mustafa Kassem Khalife, a senior Palestinian guerrilla leader and supporter of Yassir Arafat, was killed at his home in the Ein el-Hilweh refugee camp in Sidon, Lebanon, on August 29, 1985. Four days earlier, **Mohammed Shikhaani**, another Palestinian leader loyal to Arafat, had also been assassinated.

Gregorio Murillo, the governor of the southern Philippines province of Surigao del Sur, was shot to death on October 23, 1985, in the capital of Tandag. He was thought to be a victim of Communist insurgents.

During a seventeen-hour siege on November 6 and 7, 1985, leftist guerrillas of the April 19 Movement took control of the Palace of Justice in

Bogota, Colombia, and seized numerous hostages. Colombian soldiers, under orders from President Belisario Betancur, successfully ended the siege on November 7, 1985, by blowing down the walls of the Palace of Justice. Over fifty bodies were found within, including those of ten Supreme Court justices and most of the guerrillas. The dead included Chief Justice **Alfonso Reyes Echandia**, magistrate **Manuel Gaona**, and auxiliary magistrate **Maria Ines Ramos**. Also killed were guerrilla leader Andres Almarales and other rebel leaders including Vera Grave, Afranio Para, Antonio Jacquim, Francisco Otero, and Guillermo Eluencio Ruiz.

Gen. Thomas Quiwomkpa, a leader of an unsuccessful coup attempt against President Samuel K. Doe of Liberia on November 12, 1985, was captured by loyalist troops and shot to death on November 15. Quiwomkpa was one of the officers who had aided Doe in seizing power for President William Tolbert (q.v.) in 1980, and had served as Liberia's armed forces commander from 1980 until 1983.

On November 29, 1985, **Gerard Hoarau**, exiled leader of the opposition to President France-Albert Rene of the Seychelles, was shot to death in front of his home in London.

1986

Ignacio Gonzalez Palacios, the director of the Guatemalan secret police, was shot and killed while driving in Guatemala City on January 2, 1986.

On January 13, 1986, **Abdul Fattah Ismail** (1939–86), a former president of South Yemen; **Ali Ahmed Nasser Antar**, the vice president and first deputy premier of South Yemen; and **Salih Muslih Qasim**, the defense minister, were killed following a coup attempt against President Ali Nasser Mohammed. Fighting between the factions of Ismail and Nasser developed into a civil war, with the forces loyal to Ismail emerging victorious several weeks later. It was announced in February that Ismail had died in an incinerated armored vehicle that tried to rescue him from Party Headquarters shortly after fighting broke out. Antar and Qasim were both killed during the initial fighting. Ismail, an extreme leftist Yemeni politician, had participated in the coup in June of 1978 that resulted in the ouster of President Salem Ali Rubayyi (q.v.). Ismail became president of South Yemen on December 27, 1978, and served until 1980.

Rear Adm. Cristobal Colon De Caravajal y Maroto (1925–86), the seventeenth duke of Veragua and director of the Naval Museum in Madrid, was assassinated in downtown Madrid on February 6, 1986. Caravajal, a direct descendant of Christopher Colombus, was believed to have been a victim of Basque separatist terrorists.

Evelio Javier, the director of Corazon Aquino's presidential campaign in the province of Antique, the Philippines, was ambushed and murdered on February 11, 1986. It was believed that Javier was assassinated by supporters of President Ferdinand Marcos.

Olaf Palme, the prime minister of Sweden, was shot and killed by an unknown assassin on February 28, 1986. Palme was killed as he was walking with his wife down a Stockholm street shortly after having left a movie theatre. Palme was born in Stockholm on January 30, 1927. He first gained international prominence in the late 1960s when, as Sweden's minister of education, he joined protestors in a march against America's involvement in Vietnam. Palme, as chairman of the Social Democratic party, was elected Sweden's prime minister on October 14, 1969. He served in that office until September 20, 1976. He remained a leading spokesman of the opposition until 1982, when he was again selected as prime minister.

Zafir Al-Masri, who had recently been appointed mayor of the occupied West Bank city of Nablus, was shot and killed on March 2, 1986, while walking to work. Al-Masri, a moderate Arab, had replaced the Israeli military administration when he was appointed mayor in December of 1985. His murder was believed to have been the work of Palestinian extremists.

Manuel Santan Chiri, the Peruvian governor of the southern province of Ica, was murdered by assassins near his home on March 24, 1986. Santan Chiri was a leading member of the APRA party in southern Peru.

On April 28, 1986, **Sant Sing Lidder**, a Congress (I) party member of the assembly in Punjab, was shot and killed in Likhar, India.

Rear Adm. Carlos Ponce De Leon Canessa, a Peruvian naval officer, was killed in a grenade attack launched by leftist guerrillas outside of his home in Lima, Peru, on May 5, 1986.

Gen. Arun S. Vaidya (1926–86), India's former army chief of staff, was shot to death in the western Indian city of Pune on August 10, 1986. Vaidya, who had retired in January of 1986, had been a prominent target of Sikh extremists for having supervised the Indian army's attack on the Sikh Golden Temple shrine at Amritsar in 1984.

On September 1, 1986, **R.P. Gaind**, an additional district and sessions judge in Chandigarh, India, was shot to death by Sikh assassins in the northern Indian state of Punjab.

Col. Fedor I. Gorenkov, the Soviet deputy military attache for air and naval matters in Pakistan, was shot and killed by a gunman in Islamabad on September 16, 1986. The assailant was identified as Zafar Ahmed, a Pakistani with a history of mental illness.

On September 18, 1986, **Col. Christian Goutierre** (1926–86), the French military attache in Beirut, Lebanon, was shot and killed near the French Embassy by a member of a radical Arab organization.

On October 10, 1986, **Gerold von Braunmuehl** (1935–86), an official in the West German Foreign Ministry, was shot and killed by leftist terrorists. Braunmuelh was an assistant to foreign minister Hans-Dietrich Genscher and served as head of the Foreign Ministry's political department.

Samora M. Machel (1933–86), the first president of Mozambique, was killed in an airplane crash near the border of South Africa. Machel was returning from a meeting in Zambia with other African leaders. While the South African government claimed the crash was an accident, attributable to weather conditions and human error, some African leaders speculated that the government was responsible for Machel's death. Mozambique was often used as a base for anti-apartheid guerrillas for attacks on South Africa. Samora Machel had led Mozambique's Marxist government since its independence from Portugal in 1975. His administration had often been at odds with the South African government and military action had been threatened by both countries.

A number of senior Mozambiquan officials were also killed in the crash, including **Luis Alcantara Santos**, the transport minister; **Jose Carlos**, the deputy foreign minister; and **Fernando Joao**, a senior official in the defense ministry.

Onkar Chandh, the leader of Indian prime minister Rajiv Gandhi's political party in Hajipur, India, was found dead on October 25, 1986. Chandh had been stabbed to death by Sikh terrorists.

Gen. Rafael Garrido Gil, the Spanish military governor of the Basque province of Guipuzcoa, was killed on October 25, 1986, when a bomb placed on top of his car exploded. The general's wife and son were also killed in the attack, which was believed to have been carried out by Basque separatist guerrillas.

On November 5, 1986, the body of **Ivan Menendez Macin** (1948–86), a prominent Mexican journalist, was found shot to death in the trunk of his car in Mexico City. Menendez, who had served as an economic consultant to the Mexican government from 1970 until 1976, was the director of the Spanish edition of *Le Monde Diplomatique*. He was the fifth Mexican journalist to be murdered in 1986. **Dr. Jorge Brenes** (1940–86), the publisher of *El Rio* in Rio Bravo and *Frontera* in Reynosa, was murdered at his home on June 17, 1986. **Ernesto Flores Torrijos**, the publisher of *El Popular* in Matamoros, and **Norma Moreno Figueroa**, the paper's assignments editor, were shot and killed in July. **Odilon Lopez Urias**, a political columnist for *La Voz del Agora* in Sinaloa, was abducted and murdered in October.

Rolando Olalia (1934–86), the leader of the left-wing People's party in the Philippines and a prominent supporter of President Corazon Aquino, was abducted following a union meeting on November 12, 1986. His bullet-riddled body was found near a Manila highway the following day. Olalia was also the leader of the May First Movement, a leftist trade union, and had threatened to lead a general strike if the Philippine military attempted the ouster of Mrs. Aquino.

David Puzon (1921–86), a former member of the Philippine parliament, was shot to death by gunmen near his factory in Manila on November 19, 1986. Puzon was a leading member of the right-wing business community and a close ally of defense minister Juan Ponce Enrile.

Ulbert Ulama Tugong (1939–86), a leading Moslem politician in the southern region of the Philippines, was shot and killed in downtown Manila on November 22, 1986. Tugong was also an influential supporter of President Aquino.

Georges Besse (1928–86), the president of the French Renault automobile company, was shot and killed near his home in Paris on November 17, 1986. Besse's assassination was the work of the left-wing French radical group Direct Action.

In December of 1986 Goukouni Oueddei, who served as president of the African nation of Chad from 1979 until 1982, was shot and wounded in the legs by Libyan soldiers in Tripoli. Oueddei, who was being assisted by Libyan president Moammar Gadhafi during a civil war in Chad, had recently began feuding with the Libyan leader. He was hospitalized following his injury, and subsequently placed under house arrest.

On December 10, 1986, **Edward King** (1933–86), the mayor of Mount Pleasant, Iowa, was shot and killed during a city council meeting. The assassin, Ralph Orin Davis, also critically injured two members of the council, Joann Shankey and Ronald Dupree. Davis, who claimed he shot Mayor

King because the city would not pay for repairs on his basement caused by a backup in the sewage system, was charged with murder.

Mosbah Mohammed Gharibi, the financial attache of the Libyan Embassy in Damascus, Syria, was ambushed and killed by machine gun fire on December 25, 1986, in Taanayel, a small city near Beirut, Lebanon.

Bibliography

Books

Alexandrov, Victor. *The End of the Romanovs*. Boston: Little, Brown, 1966.

Amirsadeghi, Hossein. *Twentieth Century Iran*. New York: Holmes and Meier, 1977.

Archer, Jules. *The Dictators*. New York: Bantam, 1968.

_____. *Legacy of the Desert*. Boston: Little, Brown, 1976.

Arvil, Pierre. *Politics in France*. Baltimore: Penguin, 1969.

Ayling, S.E. *Portraits of Power*. New York: Barnes and Noble, 1961.

Bar-Zohar, Michael. *The Avengers*. New York: Hawthorn, 1967.

Beevor, Antony. *The Spanish Civil War*. New York: Peter Bedrick, 1982.

Bergue, Jacques. *French North Africa: The Maghrib Between Two World Wars*. New York: Frederick A. Praeger, 1967.

Bishop, Jim. *The Day Lincoln Was Shot*. New York: Harper and Row, 1964.

_____. *The Day Kennedy Was Shot*. New York: Funk and Wagnalls, 1968.

Bizzarro, Salvatore. *Historical Dictionary of Chile*. Metuchen, N.J.: Scarecrow, 1972.

Bork, Albert W., and George Maier. *Historical Dictionary of Ecuador*. Metuchen, N.J.: Scarecrow, 1973.

Bornstein, Joseph. *The Politics of Murder*. New York: William Sloane, 1950.

Bulygin, Paul. *The Murder of the Romanovs*. New York: Robert M. McBride, 1935.

Byas, Hugh. *Government by Assassination*. New York: Alfred A. Knopf, 1942.

Caillou, Alan. *South from Khartoum*. New York: Hawthorn, 1974.

Can, Raymond. *Spain, 1908–1939*. Oxford, England: Clarendon, 1966.

Carrol, Raymond. *Anwar Sadat*. New York: Franklin Watts, 1982.

Coffey, Thomas M. *Agony at Easter: The 1916 Irish Uprising*. New York: Macmillan, 1969.

Columbia Encyclopedia. Morningside Heights, N.Y.: Columbia University Press, 1950.

Conot, Robert E. *Justice at Nuremberg*. New York: Harper and Row, 1983.

Creedman, Theodore S. *Historical Dictionary of Costa Rica*. Metuchen, N.J.: Scarecrow, 1977.

Crozier, Brian. *South-East Asia in Turmoil*. Baltimore: Penguin, 1978.

Daniels, Robert V. *Red October: The Bolshevik Revolution of 1917*. New York: Charles Scribner's Sons, 1967.

Davis, Robert H. *Historical Dictionary of Colombia*. Metuchen, N.J.: Scarecrow, 1977.

Deakin, F.W., and G.R. Storry. *The Case of Richard Sorge*. New York: Harper and Row, 1966.

Delpar, Helen, ed. *Encylcopedia of Latin America*. New York: McGraw-Hill, 1974.

Demaris, Ovid. *America the Violent*. Baltimore: Penguin: 1970.

Diederick, Bernard, and Al Burt. *Papa Doc: The Truth About Haiti Today*. New York: Avon, 1969.

Encyclopaedia Britannica. Chicago: Encyclopaedia Britannica, various editions.

Fitzgerald, Constantine. *Red Hand: The Ulster Colony*. Garden City, N.Y.: Doubleday, 1972.

Flemion, Philip F. *Historical Dictionary of El Salvador*. Metuchen, N.J.: Scarecrow, 1972.

Ford, Franklin L. *Political Murder*. Cambridge, Mass.: Harvard University Press, 1985.

Fox, Sylvan. *The Unanswered Questions About President Kennedy's Assassination*. New York: Award, 1965.

Galante, Pierre. *Operation Valkyrie*. New York: Dell, 1983.

Grant, Bruce. *Indonesia*. Australia: Penguin, 1967.

Gregorian, Vartan. *The Emergence of Modern Afghanistan*. Stanford, Calif.: Stanford University Press, 1972.

Heinl, Robert Debs, Jr., and Nancy Gordon Heinl. *Written in Blood: The Story of the Haitian People 1492–1971*. Boston: Houghton Mifflin, 1978.

Hennessy, Maurice N. *The Congo*. New York: Frederick A. Praeger, 1961.

Holden, David, and Richard Johns. *The House of Saud*. New York: Holt, Rinehart and Winston, 1981.

Hook, Donald D. *Madmen of History*. Middle Village, N.Y.: Jonathan David, 1976.

Howe, Irving. *Leon Trotsky*. New York: Viking, 1978.

Jonas, George. *Vengeance*. New York: Bantam, 1985.

Katkov, George. *Russia 1917: The February Revolution*. New York: Harper and Row, 1967.

Keddie, Nikki R. *Roots of Revolution: An Interspective History of Modern Iran*. New Haven, Conn.: Yale University Press, 1981.

Key, V.O., Jr. *Southern Politics*. New York: Vintage, 1949.

Khadduri, Majid. *Independent Iraq: A Study in Iraqi Politics from 1932 to 1958*. London: Oxford University Press, 1960.

Kinross, Lord. *Ataturk*. New York: William Morrow, 1965.

Kousoulas, D. George. *Modern Greece: Profile of a Nation*. New York: Charles Scribner's Sons, 1974.

Kyemba, Henry. *A State of Blood*. New York: Ace, 1977.

Langley, Lester D. *Central America: The Real Story*. New York: Crown, 1985.

Langville, Alan R. *Modern World Rulers: A Chronology*. Metuchen, N.J.: Scarecrow, 1979.

Lineberry, William P. *East Africa*. New York: Wilson, 1968.

Livermore, H.V. *A New History of Portugal*. Cambridge, Mass.: Harvard University Press, 1966.

Logan, Rayford W. *Haiti and the Dominican Republic*. London: Oxford University Press, 1968.

McCombs, Don, and Fred L. Worth. *World War II Super Facts*. New York: Warner, 1983.

McConnell, Brian. *The History of Assassination*. Nashville, Tenn.: Aurora, 1969.

Metraux, Guy S., and Francois Crouzet. *The New Asia*. New York: New American Library, 1965.

Meyer, Harvey K. *Historical Dictionary of Honduras*. Metuchen, N.J.: Scarecrow, 1976.

Moore, Richard E. *Historical Dictionary of Guatemala*. Metuchen, N.J.: Scarecrow, 1973.

Nash, Jay Robert. *Among the Missing.* New York: Simon and Schuster, 1978.
O'Connor, Richard. *The Cactus Throne.* New York: G.P. Putnam's Sons, 1971.
Palmer, Alan. *The Facts on File Dictionary of 20th Century History.* New York: Facts
  on File, 1979.
Pearlstein, Edward W., ed. *Revolution in Russia!* New York: Viking, 1967.
Perusse, Roland I. *Historical Dictionary of Haiti.* Metuchen, N.J.: Scarecrow,
  1977.
Prochnik, Leon. *Endings.* New York: Crown, 1980.
Richmond, J.C.B. *Egypt 1798–1952.* London: Methuen, 1977.
Rudolph, Donna K., and G.A. Rudolph. *Historical Dictionary of Venezuela.*
  Metuchen, N.J.: Scarecrow, 1971.
Shirer, William L. *The Rise and Fall of the Third Reich.* New York: Simon and
  Schuster, 1960.
————. *The Collapse of the Third Republic.* New York: Simon and Schuster,
  1969.
Smith, Bradley F. *The Road to Nuremberg.* New York: Basic, 1981.
Snyder, Louis L. *Encyclopedia of the Third Reich.* New York: McGraw-Hill,
  1976.
Sparrow, Judge Gerald. *The Great Assassins.* New York: Arco, 1968.
Speer, Albert. *Inside the Third Reich.* New York: Macmillan, 1970.
————. *Spandau: The Secret Diaries.* New York: Macmillan, 1976.
Steel, Ronald. *North Africa.* New York: Wilson, 1967.
Sterling, Claire. *The Terror Network.* New York: Berkley, 1982.
Storry, Richard. *A History of Modern Japan.* Baltimore: Penguin, 1968.
Swearingen, Ben E. *The Mystery of Hermann Goering's Suicide.* New York: Harcourt
  Brace Jovanovich, 1985.
Taylor, Lawrence. *A Trial of Generals—Homma, Yamashita, MacArthur.* South
  Bend, Ind.: Icarus, 1981.
Thomas, Hugh. *The Spanish Civil War.* New York: Harper and Row, 1961.
Toland, John. *The Last 100 Days.* New York: Bantam, 1967.
Tsoucalas, Constantine. *The Greek Tragedy.* Baltimore: Penguin, 1969.
Tuckman, Barbara. *The Guns of August.* New York: Dell, 1963.
Tunney, Christopher. *A Biographical Dictionary of World War II.* New York: St.
  Martin's, 1972.
Watt, Richard M. *The Kings Depart.* New York: Simon and Schuster, 1968.
Webster's Biographical Dictionary. Springfield, Mass.: Merriam, 1976.
Who's Who in America. Chicago: Marquis Who's Who, various editions.
Who's Who in the World. Chicago: Marquis Who's Who, various editions.
Wiedner, Donald L. *A History of Africa South of the Sahara.* New York: Vintage,
  1962.
Willis, Jean L. *Historical Dictionary of Uruguay.* Metuchen, N.J.: Scarecrow,
  1974.
Wilson, Colin, ed. *Men of Mystery.* London: Star, 1977.
Wise, L.F., and E.W. Egan. *Kings, Rulers and Statesmen.* New York: Sterling,
  1967.
Wistrich, Robert. *Who's Who in Nazi Germany.* New York: Bonanza, 1982.
Woddis, Jack. *Introduction to Neo-Colonialism.* New York: International, 1972.
World Book Encyclopedia. Chicago: World Book-Childcraft International, various
  editions.
Ziegler, Philip. *Mountbatten.* New York: Alfred A. Knopf, 1985.

Periodicals

Current Biography (New York), 1940–1986.
Encyclopaedia Britannica Book of the Year (Chicago), 1940–1986.
Facts on File (New York), 1940–1986.
Memphis Commercial Appeal (Memphis), 1935–1986.
Memphis Press Scimitar (Memphis), 1945–1983.
Newsweek (New York), 1950–1986.
New York Times (New York), 1895–1986.
Time (New York), 1920–1986.
Washington Post (Washington, D.C.), 1948–1986.
The World Almanac (New York), 1960–1986.

Index

Listed under the names of countries are assassination and execution victims from those countries (surnames only). These persons are also listed individually in separate entries.

A

Ababou, Col. Mohammed 167
Abate, Lt. Col. Atnafu 193
Abdala, Carlos 186
Abdulah, Feroze 165
Abdul-Aziz 8–9, 13
Abdul Aziz Ben Dris 141
Abdul-Ilah 139–140
Abdullah Ibn Hussein, King of Jordan 130–131
'Abdullahi Ibn Mohammed (the Khalifa) 22
Abe 33
Abebe, Lt. Gen. Abiyc 181
Abetz, Otto 138
Abu Ali Ayad *see* Shreim, Mohammed Mustafa
Abu Hassan *see* Salameh, Ali Hassan
Abu Walid *see* Sayel, Brig. Saad
Abu Yussef *see* Najjar, Mohammed Yussef
Achaempong, Gen. Ignatius K. 203
Achakzai, Abdus Samad Khan 178
Adler, Friedrich 36
Ádnan, Hammad 198
Adwan, Kamal 175
Afghani, Sayyed Jamal ad-Din Al- 19–20
Afghanistan: Amin 206; Assis Khan 58; Daud Khan 195; Habibullah Ghazi 55; Habibullah Khan 42; Khabir 195; Khoram 194; Maiwandwal 177; Mohammed Osman 55; Nadir Khan 58; Naeem 195; Taraki 205

Afrifa, Lt. Gen. Akwasi 203
Afshartus, Brig. Gen. Mohammed 133
Agabekov, G.A. 74
Aguirre Salinas, Osmin 191
Aguiyi-Ironsi, Gen. Johnson 153
Ahidjo, Ahmadou 165
Ahmad 121
Ahmad Khan, Nawab Mohammad 201
Ahmed, Col. Abdul Moneim Mohammed 167
Ahmed Ibn Yahya, Sayf Al-Islam 146
Ahn Do Hi, Lt. 126
Aidit, Dipa Nusantara 152
Airiny, Abdullan El- 153
Aizawa, Lt. Col. Sabura 64
Akbay, Erkut 221
Akintola, Chief Samuel 142
Akuffo, Gen. Fred W.K. 203–204
Alabama 135, 171
Albana y Sanz, Dr. Jose Maria 66
Albania 11; Arapi 106; Bushati 106; Essad 44; Nossi 106; Shehu 219–220; Xoxe 126
Aleksandrov, Todor 51
Alemu, Lt. Col. Mulugetta 192
Alessandrini, Emilio 200
Alexander 37
Alexander Obrenovich, King of Serbia 24–25
Alexander I, King of Yugoslavia 62–63
Alexander II, Czar of Russia 11, 26, 37
Alexandra, Czarina 36–37, 38–39
Alexeanu, George 109
Alexis, Czarevitch 36, 38–39
Alexis, Jacques 143

243

C

J

L

O

P

Z